*Life-Span Research
on the Prediction
of Psychopathology*

Life-Span Research
on the Prediction
of Psychopathology

Edited by

L. Erlenmeyer-Kimling
Nancy E. Miller

 LAWRENCE ERLBAUM ASSOCIATES, PUBLISHERS
1986   Hillsdale, New Jersey   London

Lawrence Erlbaum Associates, Inc., Publishers
365 Broadway
Hillsdale, New Jersey 07642

Library of Congress Cataloging in Publication Data
Main entry under title:

Life-span research on the prediction of psychopathology.

Bibliography: p.
Includes indexes.
1. Mental illness—Forecasting—Longitudinal studies
—Addresses, essays, lectures. 2. Developmental
psychology—Longitudinal studies—Addresses, essays,
lectures. I. Erlenmeyer-Kimling, L. II. Miller,
Nancy E.
RC455.2.F67L54   616.89   85–10310
ISBN 0–89859–587–8

Printed in the United States of America
10 9 8 7 6 5 4 3 2 1

This volume is dedicated to the memory of
Barbara Dohrenwend

Contents

Preface

The impetus for this volume devloped from a conference organized by Barbara Snell Dohrenwend and the editors on behalf of the Society for Life History Research in Psychopathology, the Society for the Study of Social Biology, and the Center for Studies of Mental Health of Aging at the National Institute of Mental Health. The theme of the conference was life span research on the prediction of psychopathology, and the goal was to bring together outstanding researchers who are engaged in longitudinal investigations and whose work, collectively, covers the entire life-span, from infancy to old age. The papers that were delivered at the conference have since been updated, so that the chapters that follow represent current, state-of-the-art considerations in some of the best ongoing studies concerned with the prediction of psychopathology.

L. Erlenmeyer-Kimling, Ph.D.

Introduction:
The Prediction of Psychopathology Across The Life-Span: The Value of Longitudinal Research

Nancy E. Miller

THE MARRIAGE OF SUBSTANTIVE SIGNIFICANCE WITH METHODOLOGICAL RIGOR IN CLINICAL LONGITUDINAL RESEARCH

This volume stands as a tribute to those investigators who are courageous enough, persistent enough, long-lived enough, and some might say misguided enough, to embark on the tantalizing, yet arduous—ever treacherous—search for clues to the origins and development of mental disorder, by virtue of systematically following the unfolding of individual lives over time.

The empirical studies included in this volume are concerned with psychopathology and its prediction across the total life-span. In their focus on development, the studies range in scope from emphases on prenatal determinants and early childhood predictors, to the consideration of biological, behavioral, and cognitive variables across the span of adolescence and adulthood, culminating in the farthest reaches of old age. Many varieties of functional and organic mental illness are encompassed, including, for example, the spectrum of schizophrenic disorders, the major and minor affective illnesses, disorders of sexual identity, as well as progressive and irreversible diseases of the brain, among others.

This book can also be viewed from another perspective. If read more closely for the nuances of its subtext, it provides a functional barometer of the strains, tensions, and challenges that represent the current growth and development of the field itself: These struggles reflect disparities between the demands of methodological rigor and the constraints of the practical research world. Whereas differences in viewpoint are not unique to longitudinal work, they have become increasingly apparent in recent years, as the study of psychopathology over time

1

has begun to grow more rapidly. These cogent differences in point of view reappear throughout the text of this book and especially in the chapters by our excellent discussants, as they highlight what should be, rather than what is.

Many of these issues are crystallized in the thoughtful chapter by Erich Labouvie on methodological issues, which presents an agenda for positively enhancing the validity and quality of longitudinal studies of mental disorder. Labouvie formulates a number of important points, reminding investigators that the presence or development of psychopathology emerges within a complex matrix of behavioral and ecological events, and that it is the relationship among such multiple variables that must be examined for a deepening of understanding.

Rather than focusing solely on the specification of a single causal antecedent relationship—as some researchers in this volume have done—Labouvie suggests expanding and enriching the developmental viewpoint to include a closer approximation to reality through an appreciation of the principle of "multiple causation." Such an approach, he suggests, will yield predictions and outcomes that will be significantly more robust and reliable than could be obtained through a focus on a single biological or behavioral antecedent.

Sheppard Kellam, in his discussion, joins Labouvie in suggesting that our research strategy in the study of pathology over time take advantage of complex causal modeling approaches. In addition to the outcome variables of interest, these should include multiple intermediate assessments of such measures as social adaptation, social structure, psychological variables, biological conditions, etc. Kellam cautions that, if such conditions are not included in the equation, they will probably attentuate the strength of the relationship between the early conditions of interest and later outcomes. The strategy should be to build models that predict to early outcomes and, then, to predict from early outcomes to longer term outcomes.

Labouvie takes up the question of the length of time intervals between initial assessment of base-line predictors and the later measurement of outcome criteria. He notes that, as far as predictive purposes are concerned, it is common to find that relationships decrease in strength as time lags increase. Accordingly, concurrent or short-term predictors are likely to yield greater accuracy than long-term predictors. In expanding this viewpoint further, and in urging even closer attention to a "true developmental perspective in longitudinal research," Denise Kandel notes that one of the major contributions of the life history investigation is the dynamic description of "sequential developmental patterns," leading into different psychopathological syndromes. Together with Lee Robins, Kandel suggests that it may be as important to specify these developmental phases in behavior, by decomposing samples into appropriate groups at risk for involvement in the next phase of the sequence, as it is to be able to predict later behaviors from the knowledge of earlier events.

Labouvie's third and final point concerns what he considers to be "the most basic issue" facing the study of psychopathology from a developmental viewpoint. This is "the problem of the functional equivalence of measures" in relation to underlying concepts: How do we know whether a given measure actually relates to the same concept in different (age, cohort, race, gender, etc.) groups, and how can we determine whether different measures are related to the same concept, either in the same or in different populations? Are the corresponding measures conceptually equivalent and do they have equal units of measurement and equal reliabilities across populations? Labouvie states that, unless the validity of assumptions concerning equivalence are tested empirically, interpretations of population differences in prediction-criterion relationships can lead to ambiguous or even erroneous conclusions. The solution, he suggests, is to test for validity empirically, using multiple sets of measures for *each* concept that is being considered, in order to establish systematic patterns of convergent and discriminant validity.

Labouvie's eloquent chapter setting forth the problems of equivalence, multiple causation, and time intervals in longitudinal research, as well as the thoughtful discussions by Kellam, Kandel, Robins, and others, points the way to elegant methodological approaches to research. Yet, they bring into bold relief the rift in the marriage between methodological rigor and the search for findings of substantive significance in longitudinal clinical research. Ideal methodology may not be possible to achieve in practice, given the resources available to most investigators.

Longitudinal studies started years ago are especially apt to be unable to meet the requirements of modern methodology. Nevertheless, the value of the data emerging from these studies is unquestioned. Further, as the chapters in this volume indicate, chance and serendipity have played important roles in much of longitudinal research, and it is essential that investigators continue to be able to capitalize on unexpected opportunities and on leads suggested by their data. Thus, longitudinal studies may rarely be capable of meeting the more exacting methodological standards. They are, nonetheless, incomparable resources, contributing to the construction of valid theory in psychopathology, clarifying the nature of the precursors of mental illness across the life-span, and pointing the way to viable approaches to treatment, intervention, and potentially, prevention.

The work reported on in this volume represents some of the best of ongoing longitudinal research. The investigators have embarked on long, and sometimes wearying, journies of discovery that can only result in the enrichment of our understanding of the life-span prediction of psychopathology.

PREDICTING PSYCHOPATHOLOGY IN CHILDHOOD AND ADOLESCENCE

The study of risk factors, or observable characteristics that manifest themselves prior to the onset of a definable clinical disorder, is especially important in that it often casts fresh light on the etiopathogenesis of disease. A major goal of the work of Cornblatt and Marcuse has been to identify predictive indicators of future schizophrenia in the offspring of schizophrenic parents, many years before the onset of disorder, with the hope that such data will ultimately lead to preventive intervention.

Their work is representative of much longitudinal developmental research, in which an individual's later outcome is predicted on the basis of earlier attributes. However, it also differs, in that it represents one of the most difficult of longitudinal studies to carry out, because of the rarity of the outcome of interest and the difficult process that enters into the selection of the appropriate sample. Yet both the investigators' studies included here are notable for the richness of their data, as they cover the spectrum from biological to psychological and social variables.

Their initial chapter considers the prediction of childhood characteristics in the offspring of schizophrenics from observations made during infancy. The authors concentrate on two specific types of indicators that have been noted in this high-risk population: The first, obstetrical and perinatal complications, has received considerable attention since Mednick and Shulsinger described a high incidence of pregnancy and birth complications in the disturbed offspring of schizophrenic parents. The second is the evaluation of the presence of neurological "soft signs," including a variety of motor dysfunctions, visual–motor deficits, right–left confusion, and other subtle, nonfocal neurological abnormalities, which have also been previously reported by Barbara Fish.

Although Cornblatt and Marcuse report no significant differences between high-risk and normal-control infants on obstetric and perinatal variables, their neurological findings on children at risk for schizophrenia are more promising. However, because positive neurological signs have been found in children of parents with other varieties of psychiatric disorders as well, it is therefore not possible to suggest that neurological signs represent a vulnerability indicator that is specific for schizophrenia. With the exception of work by Fish and the chapter by Shaffer et al. included in this volume, there has been minimal prospective work relating early neurological signs to later psychiatric outcome. In the study by Shaffer et al., soft neurological signs at age 7 were not found to be predictive of schizophrenia in young adulthood, although they did appear to be related to other forms of psychopathology, suggesting again the possibility of nonspecificity for schizophrenia.

In their subsequent chapter, Cornblatt and Marcuse focus on the question of whether there is any evidence for a link between early cognitive dysfunction in childhood and subsequent behavioral disturbance in adolescence, which possibly might reflect the first clinical manifestations of schizophrenia. In reviewing the major studies of children at risk for schizophrenia, the authors demonstrate that, when subgroups of the most deviant performers *within* the high-risk group are identified, findings across major risk studies are in good agreement in showing a considerably larger percentage of high-risk than normal-control subjects in a deviant performance subgroup.

Cornblatt and Marcuse conclude that the three major areas of cognitive function that appear most promising for continued research in the high-risk schizophrenia area are: (1) studies of sustained attention, (2) investigations of distractibility and the ability to process information under conditions of overload, and (3) research on attention span and short-term memory. They discourage reaction-time studies, however, because these deficits have not been reliably detected in children at risk.

In yet another study of risk factors in adolescence, Joseph Lowman and David Galinsky discovered an unusually high level of psychopathology on the MMPI in a subsample of adolescents who outwardly appeared quite normal, manifesting few unusual behavioral patterns or personality aberrations. In their study, the authors attempt to determine to what extent this striking MMPI profile elevation represents measurement error, arising from the use of the instrument with adolescents, and to what extent it represents the presence of underlying predispositions that, although not surfacing in observable distress at the time, are predictive of eventual dysfunction.

When the investigators rescored the MMPI data according to adolescent norms, which were unavailable at the time the data were initially collected, the correction resulted in a reduction by half of the estimation of the level of pathology present. This finding clearly highlights Labouvie's caution that the use of norms obtained from a specific age group may lead to systematic biases in the description and measurement of psychopathology when applied to other age groups. Elevated MMPI profiles collected during adolescence should, therefore, not be considered valid predictors of later psychopathology or of inadequate functioning based on the presence of scale elevations alone. On the basis of this study, the authors, in accord with Labouvie, suggest the strong need to adjust risk indicators of psychopathology for both the stage of the life cycle, as well as for the specific cultural, ethnic, and socioeconomic group from which they were collected.

The research reported by Meyer–Bahlburg et al. includes a sophisticated review of what is known of the effects of prenatal sex hormones over time on later gender identity, gender-role behavior, and sexual preference. Because experimental manipulation of prenatal hormones in human beings is ethically unacceptable, the investigators took advantage of serendipitously available data, by focusing on spontaneously occurring accidents of nature, on patients with abnormalities of prenatal hormone production or utilization, as well as on offspring from pregnancies in which hormone levels were manipulated for clinical reasons. Methodologically, this represents an exceedingly difficult area to study in humans, because the investigators are solely dependent on experiments of nature, so that the number of affected individuals available for study is small, unavoidably restricted, and samples are never randomly drawn.

In summarizing the literature on the impact of androgens, the major masculinizing hormones, on psychosexual differentiation in genetic females, the investigators found that prenatally androgenized females differed significally from controls in manifesting high-energy levels in outdoor play and sports, and low interest in parenting rehearsal, doll play, and infant care. The findings suggest that this characteristic pattern of gender-role behavior in prenatally androgenized girls continues beyond childhood, into adulthood. The investigators also found a tendency towards social withdrawal in approximately 50% of the sample, and, in addition, depressive symptoms were manifested in at least one-third of these women.

Also studied were offspring from pregnancies that were treated with progesterone, a hormone that protects the brain from the masculinizing effects of androgens. Systematic differences were found between hormone-exposed girls and controls in the expected direction of demasculinization, with hormone-exposed girls manifesting higher interest in stylish clothing, lower levels of aggression, and decreased frequency of tomboyism. Similarly, in their study of the impact of progestogen–estrogen combinations on girls, they also found increased femininity, with increased interest in children over career, increased closeness to mother, decreased athletic skills, increased interest in cosmetics, sex preference for female groups, etc. In these women, such behaviors were directly opposite those (noted previously) in the prenatally adrogenized girls, who were more often high-energy tomboys, with strong interests in athletics.

This form of careful longitudinal study has yielded important data suggesting that the prenatal endocrine milieu affects the developing brain, with prenatal sex hormones contributing to the development of behavioral differences between the sexes. Although sociocultural factors obviously play a critical role in human psychosexual differentiation, these studies suggest that the prenatal hormonal environment, early on, introduces particular neurophysiologic biases, which facilitate the impact of sex-typing pressures on temperment and behavior that are encountered by the individual in the average expectable social environment.

In another longitudinal project from the Collaborative Perinatal Project, Shaffer et al. examine the relationship between the presence of minor neurological signs in childhood and the development of psychiatric disorder in adolescence. Rather than beginning with a focus on signs of brain damage and then proceeding to search for their relationship to the neurologic substrate, the present study focuses on the identification of neurological markers and then sets out to uncover their *behavioral* correlates. The investigators focus upon the question of whether minor degrees of brain dysfunction in childhood significantly affect behavior past puberty. In measuring involuntary movements, motor abnormalities, and sensory integrative abnormalities, the investigators discovered that two motor signs (mirror movements and dysdiadchokinesis) persisted into adolescence, showing significant stability over time. Both of these soft neurological signs measured in 7-year-olds were also found to predict the psychiatric diagnosis of affective disorder in the children at age 17.

In a different kind of effort, Elsie Broussard has attempted to identify factors that place neonates at risk for subsequent psychosocial disorder. Broussard studied the relationship of the mothers' perception of her newborn to the child's subsequent psychosocial disorder. In noting that the way a mother relates to her child is influenced by her perception of her baby, and that the child's behavior is affected by her handling of him/her, Broussard formulated a Neonatal Perception Inventory (NPI), a projective measure of the mother's perception of her newborn as compared to her concept of the average infant. Using the NPI, the investigator evaluated infants at approximately 1 month of age, as being at high or low risk for possible development of psychosocial disorders. She discovered that those infants predicted to be at high risk at 1 month of age were more likely to have psychosocial disorder at age 4½, than those who were at low risk. At age 10, there was also a significant association between the NPI predictive risk at 1 month and the child's subsequent psychiatric rating. The mother's perception of her 1-month-old-firstborn continued to be predictive of a higher incidence of psychopathology, even at age 15.

One serious methodological problem with the study, however, was the degree of attrition over time; not only did the number of children followed up at each age differ, but sample attrition increased at each testing, so that by age 15, only 31% of the original children were reexamined. Despite continuing problems of attrition and the unavailability of objective diagnostic criteria at the outset of the study, Broussard still concludes that the association between maternal perception of the neonate and the subsequent psychosocial development of the child tends to persist over time and is predictive of the probability of mental disorder at age 15.

PREDICTING PSYCHOPATHOLOGY IN ADULTHOOD AND OLD AGE

In systematically following people over long spans of time, the question of evaluating those cultural shifts that color the character of an era, remains a special difficulty and challenge for longitudinal researchers interested in the study of aging. The question arises as to which changes in function we should attribute to age itself, and which to the powerful generational forces that also impact on cognitive and affective parameters. Warner Schaie and others in the aging community have repeatedly stressed the importance of cohort effects on function and performance.

It is in this context that the Midtown Manhattan Study needs to be evaluated. Whereas the results of this project cannot be considered definitive, the historical importance of the study cannot be overestimated. At the time it was conceived, this study represented a landmark effort to examine the severity of self-reported psychiatric symptoms at a single point in time in a randomly selected sample of the general population. The project was not designed with any long-term follow-up in mind. More than two decades later, however, the investigators determined that a follow-up study should be undertaken and would be feasible. Though they made valiant attempts to recover as many cases as possible, this effort was difficult, especially because identifiers were not collected at the outset. Moreover, whereas the identical symptom inventory used in 1954 was included in the 1974 study, thus yielding a measure of symptom severity and of social-role function, nevertheless, specific diagnoses were not formulated at Time 2.

Although some critics have viewed the study's reliance on a health–sickness gradient as imprecise, it is useful to remember that the field has made major advances in this respect only recently. Only in the past several years, for example, has a stringently operationalized diagnostic classification system been available and only recently have valid and reliable structured clinical interview questionnaires, formulated explicitly for research purposes, been available. Although it is now possible to both validly and reliably interview community-dwelling persons within the contexts of their homes, the capacity to achieve such a high degree of rigor and consistency in diagnostic assessment in a community sample was not possible for the investigators at the time the study was implemented.

In describing their findings, Srole et al. contrast persons of identical chronological age born into different birth cohorts. They found that later cohorts have an impairment rate that is significantly lower than that of the earlier generation and conclude therefore that general mental health has improved. They also found gender differences in improvement rates, with women in the later cohort showing the greatest decrease in impairment; that is, women now in their 40s and 50s manifest fewer symptoms than did women in these age ranges 20 years ago. The investigators attribute this to the change in women's status and role over the past 20 years, though they have no firm data as yet to support this hypothesis. Their conjecture, however, about the developmental effects of being in different parts of the life cycle in different historical epochs and their notions concerning the impact of the prevailing cultural milieu during the formative stages of a generation's development are intriguing. Srole discusses the possible effect of Victorian social mores on sexual repression and women's roles, which he believes may have been partially responsible for the high rates of impairment in the older cohort of women.

The study of depressive symptoms as a risk factor for mortality and for major depression by Weissman et al. highlights the great distance that psychiatric classification and diagnosis of mental disorder in the community has come since the Midtown Manhattan effort in 1954. It also underscores the recent significant developments in the rapidly expanding field of psychiatric epidemiology, yet, at the same time, is characterized by many of the same dilemmas that confront all longitudinal investigations. This study attempts to clarify the prognostic significance of depressive symptoms, which have been reported to be ubiquitous in the general community, by assessing "risk factors" both for the development of major affective disorder and for mortality.

Initiated in 1967 as a systematic study of a sample of the population of a community mental health center catchment area, the same population was reinterviewed again in 1969 and in 1975. The investigators found that there were significant differences in both the second and third waves of interviews between the original sample and those who were not reinterviewed. Problems with differential attrition in longitudinal research are often unavoidable, as is witnessed by the reports of Srole, Broussard, and Lowman and Galinsky, among others in this volume. An unfortunate fact of investigative life, the best that can be hoped for is that the biases introduced by differential drop-out rates will be taken fully into account by the investigators.

Building on the work of Srole and others in the Midtown Manhattan Project in the initial survey, the primary interest at that time was in the overall severity of psychiatric symptomatology, rather than a specific focus on depression, as a psychiatric syndrome. Whereas the instrument used initially was the Index of Mental Status, later, information for making diagnostic judgments was collected on the Schedule for Affective Disorders and Schizophrenia (SADS), and subjects were then classified using the Research Diagnostic Criteria. Labouvie's points about test equivalence can be appropriately raised here, in that the more precise SADS instrument was not yet developed or available for use when the earlier waves of the study were begun.

Weissman et al. discovered that depressive symptoms do significantly increase the risk of a future major depression. They also found a dose-response relationship between symptoms and syndrome, in that individuals with a high level of depressive symptoms tended to have a higher risk for major depression than did those with a mild symptom level. On the other hand, the investigators found no substantial association between depressive symtomatology and increased risk of mortality. In terms of potential clinical implications, the data suggest there is useful value in the routine assessment of depressive symptoms, even using relatively simple self-report measures. The impression, often reported in the clinical literature, suggesting that persons with many symptoms but no definable disorder are at increased risk for developing a clinical disorder is supported by these data—there is also some implication that the reduction of symptomatology may reduce the risk of subsequent depression, thus suggesting that preventive intervention for individuals with depressive symptoms might offset the full-blown clinical disorder. However, this suggestion must remain in the realm of conjecture, until such time as the appropriate empirical studies are undertaken, in order to estimate the efficacy of early therapeutic intervention.

It is well known that of all age groups reporting depressive symptoms, it is the elderly who clinically manifest the highest rates of complaint. In offering further illumination to this area, the work of Wilder et al. focuses upon the relationship between depressive symptoms, the clinical diagnosis of depression and the presence of chronic disability in a sample of elderly persons interviewed twice, within a 4–5-year interval between interviews. The investigators hypothesized that those elderly who suffered both from severe physical disability and who were also demoralized at the initial interview would manifest the highest rate of depressive symptoms at follow-up. Though they did find quite a high rate of demoralization in that group (50%), still, almost as high a rate was found among those with prior disability who had not been previously demoralized (44.2%). In other words, subsequent demoralization was high among the disabled elderly, regardless of whether there was prior demoralization. But most striking was the finding that by far, the highest rate of symptomatology (61.6%) was found among those individuals who were previously demoralized but not previously disabled. Thus, there was a strong significant relationship between prior and subsequent demoralization, tending to suggest that episodes of demoralization may be chronic, lasting for at least 5 years in late life.

Although there was a significant association between physical and mental distress, what is of special interest is the finding that chronic demoralization often occurs independently of chronic physical disability. It is clear that further work is needed to determine whether depression is typically preceded by demoralization in late life, or whether there are differences among depressions, depending on whether or not they are preceded by demoralization.

With reference to this chapter, we are once again reminded of Labouvie's principle of equivalence, in that whereas many of the instruments used in psychiatric epidemiology are effective in distinguishing between patients and nonpatients, they are often imperfectly related to diagnosed psychiatric disorder in the general population and were not initially derived or validated on such groups. As with other studies reported in this volume, with only two points in time, it is not possible to unravel differential cause and effect. Accordingly, whereas these findings are promising, teasing apart the relationship between chronic and recent demoralization and physical disability in the elderly will clearly demand a longer, more extensive follow-up, with assessments at more points in time.

John Clausen's follow-up of a cohort of patients first admitted to a mental hospital with diagnoses of schizophrenia and affective psychosis in the 1950s, represents yet another investigation that was not planned initially as a longitudinal study. It arose, as so many long-term studies do, out of the intensity of human curiosity, out of a desire to learn what eventually happened to these seriously ill individuals as the span of their lives unfolded, and as a result of the serendipitous opportunity, on the part of the investigator, to access the initial data sets and to collect more current information. As Lowman and Galinsky, Cornblatt and Marcuse, Srole, Weissman, and others included in this volume all tried to take into account new research developments, whether in assessment, diagnosis, or instrumentation, and to incorporate these into their ongoing studies, so too does Clausen take advantage of the fresh advances in classification, as he rediagnosed all the cases in his sample, using Research Diagnostic Criteria.

Clausen's findings regarding the outcome of schizophrenic illness, although similar to those of Bleuler, are more sanguine than many reports. He notes that studies of the course of illness over time often leads to a more accurate picture of function than do follow-up studies of cross sections of patients discharged from mental hospitals, without reference to the number of their previous admissions. Clausen found that whereas the majority of patients had received treatment subsequent to their initial hospitalization, most patients were functioning and living in the community 15 to 20 years following their initial hospitalization.

In general, women patients had significantly less favorable outcomes than men in this sample, both in terms of having had greater numbers of episodes of treatment, and having had greater severity of symptoms. Whereas many of the male patients had improved significantly, not a single woman classified at time 1 as schizophrenic was symptom free at follow-up. These findings suggest that in attempting to predict later psychopathology from early performance, it is probably useful that data be separately analyzed by gender. In a telling point underscored by Lee Robbins, however, it is suggested that perhaps the men in the study were more positively selected than the women: For example, it is known that male schizophrenics have an especially low rate of marriage and a high rate of marital dissolution. Therefore, currently married male schizophrenics are a particularly rare and unusual group, and it is possible that generalizations to all schizophrenics on the basis of these findings may not be warranted.

In addition to gender variables, the study also suggests a significant impact of age on course and outcome of illness. Rates of readmission to inpatient services, for example, declined with each 5-year period for all patients. In addition, age of onset of schizophrenic illness was also associated with outcome of illness: for example, male patients diagnosed schizophrenic, with initial hospitalization after the age of 35, were much less likely to be symptomatic in the 5 years prior to follow-up than patients who had been younger at initial hospitalization. Similarly, though females did less well, those admitted after 35 were less likely to be persistently impaired.

Despite the significant statistical power of the predictive markers Clausen delineates, he cautions against the serious problem of attempting to make reliable predictions in the individual case. In providing a number of rich and poignant clinical illustrations, Clausen eloquently highlights this point, by describing instances in which—though all prognostic signs and predictors of risk pointed to a strongly favorable outcome—the patient continued to progressively deteriorate. Clausen's chapter skillfully integrates sensitive clinical observation and insight together with a careful reading of scrupulously collected empirical data, to yield a well-balanced portrayal of the course of serious psychiatric illness over time.

In contrast to John Clausen's generally favorable findings about long-term outcome in schizophrenia, Ming Tsuang's study of patients diagnosed with schizophrenia are considerably less optimistic. In his study, Tsuang questions which features of the selection criteria are best used to predict outcome in schizophrenia. Drawing his data from the Iowa 500, an unusually well-studied clinical cohort that has been conscientiously followed for 30 to 40 years, Tsuang attempts to identify variables associated with underlying psychopathological factors that can enhance our understanding of good and poor outcomes in psychosis.

Subjects were selected according to strict operational diagnostic criteria and were followed up over the entire life-span, including recovered and deceased patients. The study's most serious limitation, however, stems from the effort to graph a lifetime course of illness with only two points in time on the graph. Because the outcome of chronic illness may vary enormously at different times in the life cycle, as John Clausen's clinical vignettes indicates, and because a generally good outcome patient may be in relapse at the time of the follow-up, it is difficult to truly estimate prognosis, unless one examines the effects of predictors at different points in time. In John Clausen's study of schizophrenia, it was found that in instances in which more than a single follow-up interview was undertaken marked shifts in the patient's condition and life circumstances were often found. There is no such thing as the "perfect" longitudinal study; rather, there evolves a slowly growing accumulation of evidence that, over time, carries with it the weight of empirical conviction.

Contrary to Clausen's findings, Tsuang reports that schizophrenia, as defined by research criteria, shows a poor overall outcome: Over 50% of the subjects in this study had incapacitating mental symptoms, even after 30 or 40 years. Of all the admissions variables examined, those predictive of poor outcome included memory deficit, visual hallucinations, and verbal blocking. Many of the schizophrenics with symptoms of memory deficit and disorientation at admission still complained of memory difficulties at follow-up after 30–40 years. This finding, regarding the presence of memory deficit at admission in predicting poor outcome, was more striking than any other. Tsuang's work suggests that memory deficit may be a highly stable variable over the span of three, or even four decades. Whether such memory deficits can be assumed to be manifestations of thought disorder or possibly of some subclinical organic pathology remains to be determined. A prospective neurometric study of the psychopathology of memory deficit in schizophrenia is clearly indicated.

The findings of Clausen and Tsuang agree, in suggesting that later onset of schizophrenic illness is associated with a significantly more benign outcome than is the case with early disease onset, which occurs far more commonly. As the disorder of schizophrenia can be characterized by a mean and modal age of onset, which typically peaks in late adolescence and early adulthood, similarly, so can those neuropsychiatric brain disorders be described that are developmental diseases—in the sense that they typically arise in early middle age and in later life, respectively. Huntington's Disease and Senile Dementia of the Alzheimer's type, for example, are two chronic, progressive, and irreversible dementias that are age specific in terms of time of onset, thereby resembling schizophrenia— only in the sense that the younger the patient at onset of illness, the more virulent the course of disease and the more severe and rapid the development of the symptomotology.

Falek et al. have collected detailed pedigrees for 98 extended Huntington's Disease (HD) families over the course of 12 years. Huntington's Disease, an autosomal dominant genetic neuropsychiatric disorder with onset typically in mid-life, provides longitudinal investigators with a unique opportunity to gain an understanding of the interaction of environmental and genetic variables, examined in the context of advancing chronological age.

The investigators analyzed their data from a developmental framework, with an eye towards relating a variety of factors to age of onset, including the consistency of age of onset within families, the influence of the sex of the transmitting parent, and the impact of a parent being close to his own Huntington's onset at the time of parenting a child (who subsequently inherits the HD gene) on the age of onset in that offspring. The data regarding consistency of age of onset within families revealed a significant correlation of parent and offspring onset ages, suggesting that the onset of HD may be influenced by either common environmental factors or by shared genetic factors. This finding of within-family consistency of onset has particular relevance for studies of aging, because within-family analyses of variables related to aging may reveal patterns that are not apparent in random samples. The nature and structure of such patterns can only be elucidated within the scope of a longitudinal framework.

In studying the influence of the sex of the transmitting parent, it was found that the majority of those patients with unusually early onset, who exhibited symptoms before the age of 21, inherited the HD gene from an affected father. Moreover, there was also a shift toward earlier onset for all offspring with paternal inheritance of HD. Whereas the basis for this difference remains unknown, Falek et al. suggest the possibility that paternal carriers also transmit, together with the HD, a factor that hastens the onset of disorder. Clearly, further studies are needed in order to better illuminate the gender-linked source of this discrepancy in onset ages.

As in other longitudinal high-risk research, a major focus of investigation in HD studies has been the effort to isolate and develop valid markers that could predict the onset of disease in carriers prior to the onset of HD symptoms, which usually occur in middle age, after the peak years of reproduction have come to a close. In reviewing the literature the investigators indicate that no one marker has proven valid or reliable for early detection in the individual case. One possible explanation for this difficulty may be that the different markers may identify certain subsamples of patients but may not be sufficiently sensitive to detect all gene carriers. As has been postulated for other psychiatric disorders discussed in this volume, including Schizophrenia, Major Affective Disorder, and Senile Dementia of the Alzheimer's type, it may well be that HD represents a spectrum of disorders with more than one etiological basis. There is also the possibility that because it is an age-linked disorder the gene for HD may become active only in mid-life, with tests prior to that time failing to detect those who will later be affected.

In addition to their search for behavioral and/or biologic markers, Falek et al. have gone one step further in attempting to delineate, in addition to the cognitive-motoric symptoms and precursors of disease, its affective concomitants, which are so frequently overlooked in developmental research. Because of the present inability to slow or divert the course of this illness, it has come to be considered a terminal disease in slow motion, lasting as long as 10 to 20 years. As such, it offers investigators the opportunity to evaluate the psychological impact in those affected individuals of overt exposure to one's own mortality on a longitudinal basis. Using a projective indice for measuring the subjective concept of time, the investigators attempted to determine whether individuals at risk of inheriting HD had integrated the knowledge that this disorder could significantly shorten their lives. They found that, whereas persons at risk for HD were cognizant of the threat on a conscious, verbal level, this information was not at all incorporated into the individual's self-concept on an affective level. This finding carries with it clinical implications for patient management, suggesting that the intrapsychic defensive mechanism of denial may protect the individual who is at risk of inheriting HD from believing that he could possibly be a carrier of the gene. As such, simply providing further factual material to such persons, without an affective exploration of the subjective meanings of such knowledge, may result in intellectualized verbal acceptance of the information, rather than in an integrated acceptance on an emotional level, with associated change in behavior.

Like Huntington's Disease, Senile Dementia of the Alzheimer's Type (SDAT) is a debilitating neuropsychiatric disease representing pathologic rather than normal physiologic aging, for which no treatment is currently available to halt or reverse the progressive deterioration of memory and cognitive ability. This disorder, however, can only be definatively diagnosed at autopsy with the identification of characteristic neurofibrillary tangles and neuritic plagues.

In the context of reviewing available evidence for genetic factors in the development of dementia, LaRue and Jarvik present data regarding their own attempts to define a behavioral phenotype for dementia-prone individuals, using material from a 20-year longitudinal study of aging twins. On the basis of family studies, the investigators present strong empirical evidence for the presence of genetic factors in the etiology of Senile Dementia of the Alzheimer's type. The work of Larsson, for example, suggests that the risk of Senile Dementia is four times greater for first-order relatives of probands with SD than for age-matched controls, and the findings of Heston have revealed significant familial relationships among Alzheimer's Disease, Down's Syndrome, and myeloproliferative disorders. The two possible models of genetic transmission proposed thus far include autosomal dominance with partial penetrance, with disease expression under the partial control of a single dominant gene, and a polygenic model, with manifestation of the disease controlled by many genes. The authors also review the findings regarding abnormal chromosomes, ultimately recommending that a combination of family-study and cytogenetic methodologies, combined with studies of cognition, should yield promising information regarding prediction of dementing illness.

Because progressive cognitive loss is the key diagnostic feature in the dementias of old age, it makes sense to longitudinally investigate the premorbid cognitive characteristics of those persons who subsequently develop dementia. Unfortunately, of the handful of longitudinal studies of older persons available, few have collected data that include both psychometric and psychiatric measures.

Based on data collected in the course of a 20-year longitudinal follow-up of aged twins, the authors present fresh data bearing on the issue of premorbid cognitive predictors. The subjects were the survivors of a group of 268 twins who had entered the New York State Psychiatric Institute Study of Aging Twins between 1947 and 1949, with a mean age of 70. The investigators discovered that, as a group, those individuals who later developed symptoms resulting in a psychiatric diagnosis of dementia had significantly lower scores on cognitive tests (especially on the Vocabularly. Similarities, and Digit Symbol Subtests of the Wechsler–Bellevue and the Stanford–Biret Intelligence Scales) as long as 20 years before the diagnosis of dementia was made.

Despite the fact that, like Wilder et al., Srole et al. and others, LaRue and Jarvik present information derived from only two points in time, nevertheless, they have made a significant contribution in presenting evidence of having identified a subgroup of individuals who fell into the lower ranges of the normal distribution on certain cognitive tests as early as 1947. Their analysis also reveals that those subjects who subsequently developed dementia declined more rapidly between 1947 and 1967 than those who did not (especially on the Vocabulary and Digit Symbol subtests); that is, not only did dementia-prone subjects score lower on these cognitive tests when initially examined, but they also experienced further loss of function at a more pronounced rate than did age-matched controls.

Whether the gestation of dementing illness of the Alzheimer's type takes place over a far longer time course than previously assumed, and whether those individuals whose initial scores were low, had already suffered some degree of subclinical cognitive impairment, even though they did not, as yet, manifest the full-blown signs of Alzheimer's Disease, remains to be seen. More extensive investigation is clearly called for, in order to determine whether or not there is a specific configuration of subtests that will be particularly useful in prospectively differentiating dementia-prone persons. LaRue and Jarvik remind us that the measures found (in the present study) to vary significantly with Dementia Status (e.g., Vocabulary, Similarities, and Digit Symbol) are identical to those previously labeled as "critical loss tests," in which declining performance in the aged is significantly correlated with nearness to death. These results auger well for research, in suggesting that reliable prognostic indices, based on premorbid behavioral, biological, and genetic parameters, may be formulated in order to successfully predict the onset of SDAT in years to come.

The presence of reliable research tools, appropriate to all the age ranges in the span of human development, from earliest infancy through the farthest reaches of old age, should aid substantially in illuminating the course and etiopathology of the spectrum of psychopathologic disease, hastening the day when preventive, protective, and ameliorative measures can be implemented with greater efficacy, humanity, and precision, in order to stem the tide of human suffering.

1 Long-Term Implications Of The Prenatal Endocrine Milieu For Sex-Dimorphic Behavior

Heino F. L. Meyer–Bahlburg
Anke A. Ehrhardt
Judith F. Feldman

The question of the role of prenatal sex hormones in human psychosexual differentiation originated in the clinical context of intersexuality and its management problems. What criteria does one rely on in deciding whether a newborn with ambiguous genitalia should be assigned to the male or female sex? Does the prenatal endocrine abnormality that caused the genital intersexuality also affect early brain development and later behavior, including the degree of behavioral masculinity or feminity and the gender identity of an intersex individual? The initial findings were negative (Money, Hampson, & Hampson, 1955a, 1955b): Gender identity, at least, seemed to depend on rearing rather than the prenatal endocrine milieu. However, sex-dimorphic behavior other than gender identity had not really been assessed in these studies. A few years later, animal research began accumulating overwhelming evidence of a decisive influence of the hormonal milieu on the early development of the brain and subsequent sex-dimorphic behavior such as mating, parenting, and aggressing (see, for instance, Beatty, 1979; Money & Ehrhardt, 1972, Chapter 5, pp. 65–94). Such effects were demonstrated in fish, amphibia, birds, and mammals up to the level of subhuman primates. These animal findings soon stimulated comparative studies on human psychosexual differentiation. Four behavioral areas were the focus of the human studies (Ehrhardt & Meyer–Bahlburg, 1981):

1. Gender identity: the primary identification with one sex or the other—for most people a permanent characteristic that develops early in postnatal life.
2. Gender-role behavior: all those aspects of behavior in which normal females and males differ from each other in our culture at this time in history.

3. Sexual orientation: erotic attraction to one sex or the other, i.e., homo-, bi-, and heterosexuality.

4. Cognitive sex differences: gender-typical strengths and weaknesses of mental abilities.

This chapter discusses only the first three categories. (For the fourth category, see Ehrhardt & Meyer–Bahlburg, 1979; Meyer–Bahlburg & Ehrhardt, 1980.) The hormones of interest are the three main types of sex hormones: androgens as the major masculinizing hormones, and estrogens and progestogens primarily in their role of androgen antagonizers (although their effects are likely to be more complex). Experimental manipulation of prenatal hormone levels is the approach typical of animal research in this area but is not justified in human research. Instead, the investigator of human behavior can rely on two nonexperimental sources of evidence of prenatal hormone effects. One source involves patients with prenatal endocrine syndromes, that is, spontaneously occurring abnormalities of prenatal hormone production or utilization in fetal life. The other source consists of offspring from pregnancies in which hormone levels were manipulated by the administration of estrogens and/or progestogens for clinical reasons, usually to maintain at-risk pregnancies.

ANDROGENS

The studies concerning androgens have largely been confined to clinical samples of patients with genetically caused abnormalities of androgen production or utilization in fetal life. In this context, patients with congenital adrenal hyperplasia (CAH) have been of particular interest. Individuals with this genetically based error in the function of their adrenal cortex are unable to produce cortisol and, instead, overproduce adrenal androgens (Lee, Plotnick, Kowarski, & Migeon, 1977). Due to their prenatal exposure to high androgen levels, genetic females with CAH are born with masculinized external genitalia. Optimal clinical management requires the suppression of excess androgen production by replacement treatment with corticosteroids so that the disturbed feedback system of pituitary and adrenal is corrected; thus, it is possible to limit the exposure to abnormally high levels of androgens to the prenatal phase. In the genetic female, early surgical correction of the masculinized external genitalia is also required so that she can grow up looking like a normal girl. Under these optimal circumstances, one can study the effects of prenatal androgens on behavioral development without major confounding postnatal factors.

Do abnormally high levels of prenatal androgens and virilized external genitalia in genetic females have long-lasting effects on their *gender identity?* Several studies (e.g., Ehrhardt, Epstein & Money, 1968a; Ehrhardt & Baker, 1974) have demonstrated that gender identification is consistent with the sex of assignment and rearing, provided the medical diagnosis as well as surgical and hormonal correction are initiated early and the child is not raised with major ambiguity in her or his parents' minds. This is true for those children who were correctly diagnosed as females and reared as such. It is also true for those genetic females who were incorrectly diagnosed as boys and subsequently consistently reared in the male sex. In the latter cases, male gender development occurs in contrast to the presence of female sex chromosomes, ovaries, and a uterus, but in agreement with the sex of rearing. If the correct medical diagnosis is established later in childhood, the decision to maintain or change the assigned sex has to be primarily based on the person's gender identity as it has developed by then, rather than on purely medical considerations.

Under what circumstances does a child develop gender-identity confusion? A disturbed gender identity is not an obligatory sequel of ambiguities in prenatal hormone levels or sex organs at birth, because one does not find gender-identity conflicts in those studies that have focused on optimally managed, early-diagnosed, and early-treated children. However, from long-term follow-up studies (e.g., Money & Ehrhardt, 1972) of individual cases, we know that gender-identity confusion may occur, if ambiguities persist in the rearing style of the parents, that is, if the parents themselves remain confused about the correct sex of their child.

The following case reported by Money (1968) demonstrates this type of situation:

> The patient was born with ambiguous genitalia. She was first thought to be a boy, then reassigned to the genetically correct sex of a female. The diagnosis made in the first few weeks of life was congenital adrenal hyperplasia in a genetic female. For some reason, surgical correction was not undertaken. After initial treatment with cortisone, follow-up was interrupted. The local physician told the parents that this child was born half boy/half girl and that nothing could be done about it. Physical virilization progressed until, at age 10, the child's problem was noted in school, leading to an appropriate referral. The resulting detailed psychological evaluation showed that the child had an ambiguous gender identity that was more male than female. Accordingly, the child underwent sex reassignment with surgical masculinization and began to live as a male. Several years of follow-up showed that he made a good adjustment in the male role.

The second area of investigation is *gender-role behavior*. It is here that human research has been stimulated most by the data from animal experiments. Briefly, the findings from studies of lower species can be summarized as follows: Regardless of the genetic sex of an individual animal, androgens present during the species-specific prenatal or perinatal time of differentiation will masculinize its behavior, and deprivation of androgens will feminize it (Beach, 1977). In addition to studies of observable behavior, the work on rodents has progressed to the point of identifying sex hormone-dependent structural alterations of the brain. Sex hormones affect the size of certain cell clusters, shapes of dendritic trees, and types of synapses; such sex-dimorphic structures have been localized in several areas of the brain, particularly in the hypothalamus and the preoptic area (e.g., Gorski, Gordon, Shryne & Southam, 1978; Raisman & Field, 1973; Toran–Allerand, 1984). It has been shown that the areas of the brain in question contain both androgen and estrogen receptors and that testosterone is partly converted into estradiol at the hormone-sensitive brain cell itself to interact with estrogen receptors (McEwen, 1983; McEwen, Lieberburg, MacLusky & Plapinger, 1976). Because the same areas can easily be identified in the human brain, analogous hormone influences on the brain and behavior of human beings seem likely.

Is there any evidence that prenatal androgens affect sex-dimorphic behavior in human beings? Female individuals with CAH serve as the human analogue to the animal experimental studies. Ehrhardt et al. (1968a) studied a sample of 15 early-treated girls with CAH at Hopkins, using a matched control group design. Subsequently, Ehrhardt and Baker (1974) studied a total clinic population at Buffalo Children's Hospital that included 17 females who were compared to their unaffected sisters. In both studies, the authors used detailed interviews with parents and children and a battery of psychometric tests. The results indicated that the prenatally androgenized females differed significantly and markedly from the controls in two clusters of childhood behavior: The patients showed high energy expenditure in outdoor play and sports and low interest in parenting rehearsal, doll play, and infant care. In both samples, the findings were highly consistent.

We believe that the findings reflect actual hormonal effects on behavior and not methodological artifacts. The interviews used were semistructured, tappping operationally defined behavior. Interviews were transcribed and rated by two independent raters; one rater was blind as to the patient-control status of the subjects in the earlier study. Interrater reliability was very high; agreement between mother and child interviews was high also (Ehrhardt, 1969). The clusters of behavior apparently affected by the prenatal hormonal abnormality certainly are in agreement with animal research. The enhancement of energetic play after early androgen exposure has also been found in rats (Olioff & Stewart, 1978) and rhesus monkeys (Goy & Phoenix, 1971), and decreased parenting behavior is a well-known characteristic of androgen-exposed rodents (e.g., Rosenblatt, Siegel & Mayer, 1979).

What are the long-term consequences of this pattern of childhood sex-dimorphic behavior? The kind of follow-up data one would like to have falls into three rather separate categories: (1) What happens to long-term tomboyism in adolescence and adulthood?; (2) how does general behavior adjustment proceed?; (3) are there any long-term effects on sexual orientation? Preliminary data is available from three follow-up studies (Ehrhardt, 1979; Money & Schwartz,

1977; Money, Schwartz & Lewis, 1984). The first two reports present data only of the patients and do not include comparisons to appropriate controls, so that their results must be regarded as tentative.

Concerning the first question of the continuation of tomboyism into adolescence and adulthood, it appears that low interest in parentalism persists in adolescence and, probably, throughout adulthood. This is also supported by an earlier report by Ehrhardt, Evers and Money (1968b), who interviewed a sample of 23 women with CAH, ranging in age from 19 to 48 years. They belonged to a group of patients who predated the era of cortisone treatment and, therefore, were exposed not only to high levels of prenatal androgens but also to additional virilization after birth. It is of interest to note that most of these women reported a history of long-term tomboyism in childhood with very little interest in doll play and fantasy rehearsal of motherhood. However, even very strong tomboyism in childhood did not preclude marriage and childbearing. Follow-up on the 23 women showed that 12 had married and 5 had given birth to at least one child. However, attitudinally, having children and raising a family often played a secondary role to interest in career and full-time work. For instance, for 12 of the patients, there was sufficient information regarding the desire to hold and cuddle very small infants. Only two (17%) stated a feminine desire to be affectionate with small infants, whereas the other 10 were noncommittal and preferred children who were at least toddlers. These adults differed in their degree of parentalism from a clinical contrast group that showed a childhood behavior pattern of more stereotypically feminine gender development. These findings suggest, first, that the characteristic pattern of gender-role behavior in prenatally androgenized girls continues beyond childhood and, second, that the gender-role behavior of such girls nevertheless remains within the spectrum or range of acceptable behavior for females in our culture and is usually not considered abnormal or pathological.

The second long-term aspect of behavior development is general adjustment. From preliminary observations, it appears that a subgroup of early-treated CAH females has a problem with social relations. In the follow-up study of 13 adolescents by Ehrhardt (1979), there was a tendency toward being a loner and being socially withdrawn in almost half of the sample. About a third had some symptoms of depression for which they received counseling and psychotherapy. One wonders whether long-term tomboyism predisposes a female to social isolation from both males and females.

The third long-term behavior aspect of interest is sexual orientation. The question is: Does prenatal androgen excess predispose the genetic female to homosexuality? Of the available pertinent studies, all interview-based, three (Ehrhardt & Baker, 1976; Money & Schwartz, 1977; Money et al., 1984) concerned early-treated girls and women with CAH. The majority of these patients were heterosexual, although a number of bisexual or homosexual individuals were also identified; in comparison to controls, this constituted a marked and statistically significant increase of bi- and homosexuality in the CAH women (Money et al., 1984). Of the sample of late-treated CAH women (Ehrhardt et al., 1968b), the majority were heterosexual, some bisexual, and none exclusively homosexual, when classified by overt sociosexual behavior. On the basis of reported erotic dreams and fantasies, at least half of them were heterosexual, the other half bisexual, and none exclusively homosexual. The figures were quite similar to those of Money et al. (1984). Yet the fact that many CAH women were shown to be exclusively heterosexual rules out a rigidly deterministic effect of prenatal androgens on sexual orientation. (For a detailed discussion of the possible role of prenatal hormones in the development of sexual orientation, see Meyer–Bahlburg, 1977, 1979, 1984.)

In conclusion, we can summarize the findings regarding the long-term effects of prenatal androgens on psychosexual differentiation in genetic females as follows:

1. Gender identity is not affected by high levels of prenatal androgens in those females who are consistently raised as girls. However, the combination of ambiguity in prenatal hormones, sex organs, and sex of rearing can result in gender identity confusion.

2. Gender-role behavior appears to be affected by high levels of prenatal androgens resulting in a characteristic pattern of energetic play behavior and low parentalism in childhood with some continuation into adolescence and adulthood. The behavior falls within the normal range of female behavior and is not considered abnormal or psychopathological.

3. Sexual orientation is not dictated by the prenatal endocrine milieu. However, it appears that the frequency of bi- and homosexuality in genetic females is increased after they have been prenatally exposed to high levels of androgens.

Studies of hypoandrogenized genetic males that are discussed elsewhere (Ehrhardt & Meyer–Bahlburg, 1979) have brought analogous results.

PROGESTOGENS AND ESTROGENS

Whereas endocrine syndromes have been very useful in elucidating the role of androgens in fetal differentiation and later behavioral development, there are no endocrine syndromes available for analyzing the effects of prenatal progestogens and estrogens. Instead, we must obtain relevant data by studying offspring from pregnancies that were treated with such hormones. The use of sex hormones in the treatment of problem pregnancies was first introduced in the 1940s, after it had become known that successful initiation as well as maintenance of pregnancy depended, to a large extent, on hormones produced by the mother as well as by the feto-placental unit. High-risk pregnancies—such as those threatened by spontaneous abortion, premature birth, or stillbirth, often in conjunction with pathologic states of the pregnant mother such as diabetes or toxemia of pregnancy—were thought to be linked to deficiencies of hormone production, and hormone supplementation seemed to be the logical approach to treatment. (In the meantime, double-blind controlled studies have shown the ineffectiveness of sex hormone treatment for almost all types of risk pregnancies.) Because most sex hormones and chemically related compounds have some progestational (that is, pregnancy-supporting) properties, a great variety of hormone preparations were tried, especially progestogens and estrogens. Hormone treatment was often prescribed preventively for women with only minor pregnancy problems, and there exist large numbers of people who were prenatally exposed to such exogenous hormones but do not show any gross somatic abnormalities. Thus, one can select subject samples for behavioral research that are free of significant congenital defects as they may occur after more severe pregnancy complications.

Progestogens

One widely used group of drugs included progesterone and progesterone-related progestogens such as medroxyprogesterone acetate (MPA). Extensive animal research led to general models of an interaction of progesterone with other sex steroids in both male and female fetuses (Resko, 1974; Shapiro, Goldman, Bongiovanni, & Marino, 1976). According to this theory, progesterone protects the brain from the masculinizing effects of androgens (and estrogens). There are only three studies that concern such effects in humans. Zussman, Zussman and Dalton (1975, 1977) examined 18 males and 12 females, age 16 to 19 years, who had been exposed in utero to exogenous progesterone administered for the relief of precursor symptoms of pre-eclamptic toxemia in the mother. In a blind interview study, the hormone-exposed subjects were compared to nontreated controls. Progesterone exposure in boys correlated negatively with physical activity level in childhood and also with heterosexual activity level in adolescence. In girls, progesterone exposure was negatively correlated with reports of tomboyism and positively with traditionally feminine activities in childhood. Effects on gender identity were not reported. The data on sex-dimorphic behaviors are compatible with the hypothesized antiandrogenic action of progesterone. Unfortunately, the preliminary reports by Zussman et al. give insufficient information on the subjects' background variables, so that one cannot decide with certainty whether the behavioral differences described are really due to the progesterone treatment itself or to differences in pregnancy conditions or socioeconomic level.

Lynch, Mychalkiw and Hutt (1978) studied another sample of female and male adolescents, age 16 years, with a history of prenatal progesterone exposure, in this case administered for the prevention of pre-eclamptic toxemia. Nineteen hormone-exposed subjects and 13 controls were compared with regard to two personality questionnaires. The only sex-dimorphic scale employed, namely a modified MF (Masculinity–Femininity) subscale of the MMPI, did not show any difference between the samples.

Our own research group had an opportunity to conduct a progestogen study comparing a sample of children from less severe pregnancy conditions to closely matched controls by means of the Buffalo branch of the Collaborative Perinatal Project (CPP; see Niswander & Gordon, 1972). The CPP was a longitudinal developmental study of over 50,000 children who were followed from fetal life to age 7 years; the project was conducted simultaneously at various medical centers of the United States from the late 1950s to the early 1970s. The Buffalo branch was one of the CPP centers with a particularly high rate of prenatal hormone treatment, probably due to the fact that it consisted of a private-patient population. We selected all subjects with hormone exposure for more than 1 week during the second to eighth month after the mother's last menstrual period. For each experimental subject, four matched control subjects with documented lack of hormonal exposure were selected from the same study population. Matching criteria were sex, race, birth date, and socioeconomic status. Subsequently, the study records of the subjects were screened in an effort to match for vaginal bleeding in pregnancy. From equivalent controls, one control subject was chosen for each experimental subject by random selection.

In 1974 to 1976, when they were between 8 and 14 years old, the selected subjects were recalled for a comprehensive psychological follow-up examination involving a battery of psychological tests, questionnaires, and interviews with both mother and child, separately. Details on design, sample characteristics, and results can be found elsewhere (Ehrhardt, Grisanti, & Meyer–Bahlburg, 1977; Ehrhardt, Meyer–Bahlburg, Feldman & Ince, 1984; Meyer–Bahlburg & Ehrhardt, 1982; Meyer–Bahlburg, Grisanti & Ehrhardt, 1977). Interviews were semistructured and covered a variety of sex-dimorphic behaviors. The areas of childhood behaviors studied are largely the same as those that have been previously assessed in other groups of children with abnormal prenatal hormone exposure: toy and game preference, peer relations, physical activity level and athletic skills, marriage and parenting versus career roles, interest in physical appearance, history of tomboyism (in girls) or effeminacy (in boys) labeling, gender-role preference, and aggression. The interviewer rated the information obtained on previously established behavior-rating scales. The interviews were tape-recorded, and a second independent rater repeated the ratings. Disagreements between raters were resolved by discussion. The whole study was done in a double-blind fashion.

The sample included 13 boys, age 9 to 14 years, who had been exposed to the synthetic progestogen, medroxyprogesterone acetate (MPA) only, and their 13 matched controls. All subjects were white and from middle or higher social class, with a mean IQ in the high-average range. MPA-exposed and control subjects were comparable with regard to gestational length, birth weight, birth length, and head circumference at birth. Concerning gender identity, we did not find a difference between the two groups. Differences in gender-role behavior were few and inconsistent, except for aggression where hormone-exposed subjects were lower. To control for general psychopathology, we employed Conners' (1970) Parent Questionnaire that provides eight factor-analytically obtained scales, some of them sex dimorphic, and a summary scale. There was no significant difference on any of these scales. Of clinical interest were two boys with effeminate behavior of a moderate or marked degree, one of them in the MPA-exposed group, the other a control subject. Both had undescended testes. The MPA-exposed boy also had severe congenital heart disease, severe flat feet, and short stature. It is likely that parental-rearing style in conjunction with the general social impact of somatic abnormality, especially in the second case, led to the effeminate behavior.

There were also 15 girls, age 8 to 12 years, who had been exposed to MPA only, and their 15 matched controls. Again, these two groups were highly comparable with regard to background variables. The behavior data showed that all girls were identified as females, and there were no differences in the psychopathology measures. However, there were systematic differences between hormone-exposed girls and controls in gender-role behavior all of which went in the expected direction of demasculinization: The hormone-exposed girls showed an increased interest in stylish clothing, decreases in several aggression measures, and decreased frequency of tomboyism; their mothers described them as being lower in activity level and athletic skills and as having increased interest in girls' toys and games.

Estrogen–Progestogen Combinations

The major other class of hormones used for pregnancy maintenance were the estrogens. Estrogens were rarely used alone for the treatment of problem pregnancies, and behavioral studies of offspring from pregnancies treated solely with estrogens have not yet been published. The more common treatment regimen is a progestogen–estrogen combination. Because we do not have sufficient knowledge of the behavioral effects of the individual estrogens or progestogens, it is impossible to predict with any certainty what their combined effects on sex-dimorphic behavior would be. In subhuman mammals, exogenous estrogens alone exert seemingly paradoxical effects on genital morphology and sex-dimorphic behavior; that is, they tend to masculinize females and to demasculinize males. Thus, progestogen–estrogen combinations can be expected to demasculinize males, whereas their effects on females should be more variable, depending on the dosage and combination.

Regarding the long-term behavioral effects of such progestogen–estrogen combinations, there are only two human studies available. Yalom, Green and Fisk (1973) examined a sample of twenty 16-to-17-year-old males who had been exposed in utero to progesterone plus diethylstilbestrol as a medication for diabetic pregnancy. The subjects were slightly but significantly lower than untreated controls in aggression/assertion (rank-order ratings on the basis of interview data) and in athletic coordination (by observational ratings) and showed tendencies of overall decreased masculine interests and decreased heterosexual experience. Increased gender-identity problems or homosexuality were not noted. The same report (Yalom et al., 1973) covers another group of 20 boys at age 6 years, who had been prenatally exposed to hydroxyprogesterone acetate in combination with the synthetic estrogen, estradiol valerate, again as a treatment for diabetic pregnancy; two of the index subjects had hypospadias. This group of hormone-treated boys showed decreased assertion and decreased athletic ability (by teacher ratings). Unfortunately, these studies did not control for intrauterine history.

In our Buffalo study, we also had samples of children treated prenatally with a variety of progestogen–estrogen combinations. Sample characteristics, selection criteria, design, and assessment methodology were the same as for the MPA groups just described (Erhardt et al., 1984). Also the results were somewhat similar. There were no differences in gender identity between the 22 hormone-exposed boys and their 22 controls. Concerning gender-role behavior, the only differences between hormone-exposed and control boys were of borderline significance and conflicting in direction. There were no differences in psychopathology as assessed by the Conners' Parent Questionnaire. Of clinical interest with regard to gender identity was one boy, prenatally exposed to a combination of progestogens and estrogens, who suffered from severe congenital heart disease. When asked about his choice of gender if he could start all over again, he chose the boy's role if he could live without heart disease and the girl's role if he had to live with heart disease. This boy did not show any effeminate behavior. The female samples—15 girls exposed to progestogen–estrogen combinations and their 15 matched controls—also did not show differences in gender identity. Concerning gender-role behavior, they described themselves in somewhat conflicting terms, whereas their mothers gave a more consistent picture of increased femininity, with increased interest in children over career, increased closeness to mother, decreased athletic skills, increased interest in cosmetics and hair-do, sex preference for female groups, etc. No differences in psychopathology were found.

Summary

In summarizing the available evidence, it seems that prenatal exposure to exogenous progesterone-related progestogens and/or estrogens does not have drastic effects on gender identity or on general psychopathology. Several studies have shown effects on gender-dimorphic behavior, and most of these effects have been in the direction of demasculinization. Generally, the effects were not very strong but surprisingly consistent, especially in females. The results are compatible with predictions based on animal data. In addition, they are in marked contrast to the findings on another class of progestogens, namely, androgen-related progestogens. Some of the latter produced genital masculinization in female offspring, and Ehrhardt and Money (1967; Money & Ehrhardt, 1972), who studied a sample of 10 such girls, found that their behavior was markedly modified in comparison with matched normal controls. The prenatally androgenized girls showed the opposite behavior pattern from those girls who were exposed to progesterone or progestogen–estrogen combinations. Girls with androgen exposure were more often tomboys with a high energy level in outdoor games and athletics and demonstrated a lower level of parentalism. These contrasting findings make it more likely that the demasculinizing effects of progesterone-related progestogens and estrogens are genuine. Data on adolescent and adult adjustment and sexual orientation in offspring from hormone treated pregnancies are not yet available.

CONCLUSION

It appears from the available data that the prenatal endocrine milieu affects the developing brain and subsequent behavior of human beings in a similar way as that of other vertebrates: Androgenic hormones tend to masculinize behavior whereas progesterone-related progestogens and estrogens may act as androgen antagonizers, at least under certain circumstances. Thus, the available observations suggest that prenatal sex hormones contribute to the development of behavioral differences between the sexes in general as it has been demonstrated in animal research. The latter conclusion does not negate that social factors probably have a more important role in human psychosexual differentiation. Yet, it seems likely that the postnatal social factors do not operate on a totally sex-undifferentiated brain. Rather, the prenatal environment has already introduced neurophysiologic biases resulting in temperamental and behavioral tendencies. These tendencies are likely to facilitate or inhibit certain behavior effects of the sex-typing pressures that the developing individual encounters in the social environment.

ACKNOWLEDGMENTS

This work was supported in part by grants from the Spencer Foundation, the Ford Foundation, the Grant Foundation, and the U.S. Public Health Service (# MH 30906).

REFERENCES

Beach, F. A. (1977). Hormonal control of sex-related behavior. In F. A. Beach (Ed.), *Human sexuality in four perspectives*. Baltimore: Johns Hopkins University Press.
Beatty, W. W. (1979). Gonadal hormones and sex differences in nonreproductive behaviors in rodents: Organizational and activational influences. *Hormones and Behavior, 12*, 112–163.

Conners, C. K. (1970). Symptom patterns in hyperkinetic, neurotic, and normal children. *Child Development, 41,* 667–682.

Ehrhardt, A. A. (1969). Zur Wirkung fötaler Hormone auf Intelligenz und geschlechtsspezifisches Verhalten. Unpublished doctoral dissertation, University of Düsseldorf.

Ehrhardt, A. A. (1979). Psychosexual adjustment in adolescence in patients with congenital abnormalities of their sex organs. In H. L. Vallet and I. H. Porter (Eds.), *Genetic mechanisms of sexual development.* New York: Academic Press.

Ehrhardt, A. A., & Baker, S. W. (1974). Fetal androgens, human central nervous system differentiation, and behavior sex differences. In R. C. Friedman, R. M. Richart, & R. L. Vande Wiele (Eds.), *Sex differences in behavior.* New York: Wiley.

Ehrhardt, A. A., & Baker, S. W. (1976, October 28–31). *Paper presented at the International Congress of Sexology,* Montreal. (Data quoted in H. F. L. Meyer–Bahlburg, 1979.)

Ehrhardt, A. A., Epstein, R., & Money, J. (1968a). Fetal androgens and female gender identity in the early-treated adrenogenital syndrome. *Johns Hopkins Medical Journal, 122,* 160–167.

Ehrhardt, A. A., Evers, K., & Money, J. (1968b). Influence of androgen and some aspects of sexually dimorphic behavior in women with the late-treated adrenogenital syndrome. *Johns Hopkins Medical Journal, 123,* 115–122.

Ehrhardt, A. A., Grisanti, G. C., & Meyer–Bahlburg, H. F. L. (1977). Prenatal exposure to medroxyprogesterone acetate (MPA) in girls. *Psychoneuroendocrinology, 2,* 391–398.

Ehrhardt, A. A., & Meyer–Bahlburg, H. F. L. (1979). Prenatal sex hormones and the developing brain: Effects on psychosexual differentiation and cognitive function. *Annual Review of Medicine, 30,* 417–430.

Ehrhardt, A. A., & Meyer–Bahlburg, H. F. L. (1981). Effects of prenatal sex hormones on gender-related behavior. *Science, 211,* 1312–1318.

Ehrhardt, A. A., Meyer–Bahlburg, H. F. L., Feldman, J. F. & Ince, S. E. (1984). Sex-dimorphic behavior in childhood subsequent to prenatal exposure to exogenous progestogens and estrogens. *Archives of Sexual Behavior, 13,* 457–477.

Ehrhardt, A. A., & Money, J. (1967). Progestin-induced hermaphroditism, IQ and psychosexual identity in a study of 10 girls. *Journal of Sex Research, 3,* 83–100.

Gorski, R. A., Gordon, J. H., Shryne, J. E., & Southam, A. M. (1978). Evidence for a morphological sex difference within the medial preoptic area of the rat brain. *Brain Research, 148,* 333–346.

Goy, R. W., & Phoenix, C. H. (1971). The effects of testosterone propionate administered before birth on the development of behavior in genetic female rhesus monkeys. In C. Sawyer & R. Gorski (Eds.), *Steroid hormones and brain function.* Berkeley, CA: University of California Press.

Lee, P. A., Plotnick, L. P., Kowarski, A. A., & Migeon, C. J. (Eds.). (1977). *Congenital adrenal hyperplasia.* Baltimore: University Park Press.

Lynch, A., Mychalkiw, W., & Hutt, S. J. (1978). Prenatal progesterone I. Its effect on development and on intellectual and academic achievement. *Early Human Development, 2,* 305–322.

MacLusky, N. J., & Naftolin, F. (1981). Sexual differentiation of the central nervous system. *Science, 211,* 1294–1303.

McEwen, B. S. (1983). Gonadal steroid influences on brain development and sexual differentiation. In R. O. Greep (Ed.), *Reproductive physiology IV, international review of physiology* (Vol. 27, pp. 99–145). Baltimore: University Park Press.

McEwen, B. S., Lieberburg, J., MacLusky, N., & Plapinger, L. (1976). Interaction of testosterone and estradiol with the neonatal rat brain: Protective mechanisms and possible relationships to sexual differentiation. *Annales de Biologie Animale, Biochimie, Biophysique, 16,* 471–478.

Meyer–Bahlburg, H. F. L. (1977). Sex hormones and male homosexuality in comparative perspective. *Archives of Sexual Behavior, 6,* 297–325.

Meyer–Bahlburg, H. F. L. (1979). Sex hormones and female homosexuality: A critical examination. *Archives of Sexual Behavior, 8*, 101–119.

Meyer–Bahlburg, H. F. L. (1984). Psychoendocrine research on sexual orientation. Current status and future options. *Progress in Brain Research, 61*, 375–398.

Meyer–Bahlburg, H. F. L., & Ehrhardt, A. A. (1980). Neurobehavioral effects of prenatal origin: Sex hormones. In R. H. Schwarz, & S. J. Yaffe (Eds.), *Drugs and chemical risks to the fetus and newborn*. New York: Alan R. Liss.

Meyer–Bahlburg, H. F. L., & Ehrhardt, A. A. (1982). Prenatal sex hormones and human aggression: A review, and new data on progestogen effects. *Aggressive Behavior, 8*, 39–62.

Meyer–Bahlburg, H. F. L., Grisanti, G. C., & Ehrhardt, A. A. (1977). Prenatal effects of sex hormones on human male behavior: Medroxyprogesterone acetate (MPA). *Psychoneuroendocrinology, 2*, 383–390.

Money, J. (1968). Psychologic approach to psychosexual misidentity with elective mutism: Sex reassignment in two cases of hyperadrenocortical hermaphroditism. *Clinical Pediatrics, 7*, 331–339.

Money, J., & Ehrhardt, A. A. (1972). *Man and woman, boy and girl: The differentiation and dimorphism of gender identity from conception to maturity*. Baltimore: The Johns Hopkins Press.

Money, J., Hampson, J. G., & Hampson, J. L. (1955a). Hermaphroditism: Recommendations concerning assignment of sex, change of sex, and psychologic management. *Bulletin of the Johns Hopkins Hospital, 97*, 284–300.

Money, J., Hampson, J. G., & Hampson, J. L. (1955b). An examination of some basic sexual concepts: The evidence of human hermaphroditism. *Bulletin of the Johns Hopkins Hospital, 97*, 301–319.

Money, J., & Schwartz, M. (1977). Dating, romantic and nonromantic friendships, and sexuality in 17 early-treated adrenogenital females, aged 16–25. In P. A. Lee, L. P. Plotnick, A. A. Kowarski, & C. J. Migeon (Eds.), *Congenital adrenal hyperplasia*. Baltimore: University Park Press.

Money, J., Schwartz, M., & Lewis, V. G. (1984). Adult erotosexual status and fetal hormonal masculinization and demasculinization: 46,XX congenital virilizing adrenal hyperplasia and 46,XY androgen-insensitivity syndrome compared. *Psychoneuroendocrinology, 9*, 405–414.

Niswander, K. R., & Gordon, M. (Eds.). (1972). *The collaborative perinatal study of the National Institute of Neurological Diseases and Stroke. The women and their pregnancies*. Philadelphia: W. B. Saunders.

Olioff, M., & Stewart, J. (1978). Sex differences in the play behavior of prepubescent rats. *Physiology and Behavior, 20*, 113–115.

Raisman, G., & Field, P. M. (1973). Sexual dimorphism in the neuropil of the preoptic area of the rat and its dependence on neonatal androgen. *Brain Research, 54*, 1–29.

Resko, J. A. (1974). The relationship between fetal hormones and the differentiation of the central nervous system in primates. In W. Montagna & W. A. Sadler (Eds.), *Reproductive behavior*. New York: Plenum Press.

Rosenblatt, J. S., Siegel, H. I., & Mayer, A. D. (1979). Progress in the study of maternal behavior in the rat: Hormonal, nonhormonal, sensory and developmental aspects. In J. S. Rosenblatt, R. A. Hinde, C. Beer, & M. C. Busnel (Eds.), *Advances in the study of behavior*, (Vol. 10). New York: Academic Press.

Shapiro, B. H., Goldman, A. S., Bongiovanni, A. M., & Marino, J. M. (1976). Neonatal progesterone and feminine sexual development. *Nature, 264*, 795–796.

Toran–Allerand, C. D. (1984). On the genesis of sexual differentiation of the central nervous system: Morphogenetic consequences of steroidal exposure and possible role of alpha-fetoprotein. *Progress in Brain Research, 61*, 63–98.

Yalom, I. D., Green, R., & Fisk, N. (1973). Prenatal exposure to female hormones. *Archives of General Psychiatry, 28*, 554–561.

Zussman, J. U., Zussman, P. P., & Dalton, K. (1975). *Post-pubertal effects of prenatal administration of progesterone.* Presented at the Meeting of the Society for Research in Child Development, Denver, CO.

Zussman, J. U., Zussman, P. P., & Dalton, K. (1977). *Effects of prenatal progesterone on adolescent cognitive and social development.* Presented at the 3rd Annual Meeting of the International Academy of Sex Research, Bloomington, IN.

2 Early Soft Neurological Signs and Later Psychopathology

David Shaffer
Cornelius S. Stokman
Patricia A. O'Connor
Stephen Shafer
Joseph E. Barmack
Suzanne Hess
D. Spalten
Irvin S. Schonfeld

Total population studies, as well as studies of children selected for neurological rather than psychiatric disorders, have shown that children with unequivocal brain damage or epilepsy have considerably higher rates of psychiatric, learning, and cognitive problems than children who are neurologically intact (Rutter, 1977; Rutter, Graham, & Yule, 1970; Shaffer, 1977; Shaffer, McNamara, & Pincus, 1974). However, the relationship between lesser neurological disturbance (i.e., minimal brain dysfunction, or MBD) and psychiatric disorder remains a matter of controversy.

The concept of an MBD syndrome has generally included behavioral deviancy, most commonly taking the form of hyperactivity or inattention, learning difficulties and cognitive abnormalities, and a characteristic response to stimulant treatment. These have been linked to various indicators of neurological impairment, most frequently a history of perinatal morbidity and the presence, on examination, of neurological signs or EEG abnormalities that fall short of being indicative of a classical neurological disease or defect state.

The controversy centers around two issues: first, whether or not the psychological correlates are specific in their relationship to neurological dysfunction, i.e., can they be regarded as pathognomonic, either alone or as a syndrome (see Shaffer, 1980); and second, whether the components are found together with any frequency in the clinical population.

It seems clear that the psychological components of the MBD syndrome cannot be regarded as pathognomonic. Hyperactivity, as it is most commonly observed, is a situation-specific behavior (i.e., occurs either at home or at school), an observation that is in itself inconsistent with a fixed, neurologically based phenomenon. Hyperactivity occurs similarly in both neurologically normal and abnormal children with a behavior disturbance (Shaffer et al., 1974). Both hyperactivity and inattention have biological and environmental correlates (Rapoport & Quinn, 1975; Sandburg, Rutter, & Taylor, 1979), although the relatively less prevalent cross-situational hyperactivity which is observed both at home and at school may be found more often in organically impaired children (Campbell, Endman, & Bernfield, 1977; Schachar, 1979).

Learning difficulties and deviant behavior are commonly associated (Rutter & Yule, 1973; Rutter et al., 1970), and although the presence of this association has been used by some to argue for an underlying brain or neurological abnormality as a causal factor for both, numerous alternative explanations are available. Reading disability could lead to psychiatric disorder (or vice versa), and the common antecedent of both could be some external influence (e.g., poor schooling) rather than brain damage. Further, there is no firm evidence that the association between learning disorder and psychiatric problems is greater in children who have neurological abnormalities. Indeed, the relationship may actually be weaker in neurologically impaired children when schooling is appropriate (Seidel, Chadwick, & Rutter, 1975). Finally, the notion of a characteristic response to stimulants seems unlikely in the light of the work by Rapoport and her colleagues (1978), who have found that improved cognitive performance and diminished motor activity can be produced by amphetamine in nonbrain-damaged and nondeviant children, i.e., that any favorable drug response seen in hyperactive children is a nonspecific phenomenon.

The issue of how often the components of the syndrome go together has been studied in both clinic patients (Routh & Roberts, 1972; Werry, Minde, Guzman, Weiss, Dogan, & Hoy, 1972) and unselected subjects (Nichols & Chen, 1981). These investigations show low correlations among measures of hyperactivity, learning disorder, and neurological abnormality, indicating that these are not commonly found in the same individual. The failure of MBD components to occur together is also suggested by some experiments. Rapoport in a study of the effects of caffeine (Rapoport, Buchsbaum, Weingartner, Zahn, Ludlow, Bartko, Mikkelsen, Langer, & Bunny, 1980) has observed that the stimulant may result in a simultaneous increase in concentration and activity in the same individual.

Taken together, these findings argue strongly against the existence of an MBD syndrome characterized by overactivity and inattention, cognitive difficulties, and some marker of neurological abnormality. Perhaps the notion of MBD as a syndrome is incorrect, and that it is better looked at as an etiological agent in which the forms of psychiatric disorder are varied and shaped by environment and temperament, or perhaps there is a different MBD syndrome with different associated behaviors. If this is so, then identifying a marker of neurological dysfunction and proceeding to seek its behavioral correlates, as has been done in the present study, may be a more appropriate approach to the question "can minor degrees of brain dysfunction influence behavior?" than the traditional approach to research in the field that has consisted of (1) identifying behaviors held to be indicative of brain damage and (2) attempting to establish (without success) their relationship to an index of neurological disorder.

In the present study, neurological soft signs have been chosen as the index of minor neurological dysfunction. There is evidence that they are related to cognitive and psychiatric disturbance, and they can be readily and inexpensively elicited and could thus serve as an accessible marker both for the prediction of later psychiatric disorder and research into the etiology of the dysfunction itself.

The neurological signs include involuntary movements of a choreic or athetoid type, motor abnormalities such as synkinesis (mirror movements), dysdiadochokinesis and general clumsiness, as well as sensory integrative abnormalities, in particular, astereognosis and dysgraphesthesia.

This group of signs is called "soft" not because they cannot be readily and reliably elicited (Rutter et al., 1970; Shaffer, 1978) but rather because they have no reliably identified neuropathological locus and are held to be "developmental" in origin rather than being indicative of any fixed disorder or abnormality. Only a minority of children with soft signs have abnormal EEG's (Capute, Meidermayer, & Richardson, 1968), and by no means all children with neurological disease have soft signs. Their "developmental" nature has been assumed from cross-sectional studies (e.g., Camp, Bialer, Sverd, & Winsberg, 1978; Mikkelsen, Brown, Minichiello, Millican, & Rapoport, 1982; Peters, Romine, & Dykman, 1974) that have found a lower prevalence in older age groups, rather than from longitudinal studies.

The relationship of soft signs to learning problems in young children has been established in a number of studies (Adams, Kocsis, & Estes, 1974; Boshes & Myklebust, 1973; Peters, Romine, & Dykman, 1975; Rutter, Graham, & Birch, 1966; Stine, Saratsiotis, & Mosser, 1975; Wolff & Hurwitz, 1973). Several studies have examined the relationship between neurological signs and behavior in younger children. Among these it has been found that signs are more prevalent in male child psychiatric patients than in normal controls (Peters et al., 1975; Wikler, Dixon, & Parker, 1970); and within a group of disturbed children, soft signs are more common in those who are impulsive, distractable, dependent, and sloppy than in those who are not (Paulsen, 1978; Paulsen & O'Donnell, 1979).

Soft signs have been shown to be related to psychiatric disorder in adolescents and adults by Hertzig and Birch (1966), Hertzig et al. (1968), Rochford, Detre, Bucker, and Harrow (1970), and Mosher, Pollin, and Stabanau (1971), all of whom reported higher rates of soft signs among hospitalized or diagnosed psychiatric patients than among controls; however, the results of those studies were confounded by the inclusion of subjects on medication, by the questionable blindness of the raters, and/or by the inclusion of patients with frank neurological disease. A methodologically satisfactory investigation in adults has been carried out by Quitkin and his colleagues (1976). Two patient groups, schizophrenics with a history of childhood asociality and individuals with "emotionally unstable character disorders," had more soft signs and were more likely to have a history of perinatal morbidity than patients in other diagnostic categories. In all these studies the subjects studied belonged to clinically identified groups. As a result, relative risk for psychiatric problems accruing from soft signs could not be assessed, and the comprehensiveness and generalizability of the findings is likely to be limited. This is so because studies on inpatients (e.g., Hertzig & Birch, 1968, Mosher et al., 1971, Quitkin et al., 1976, and Rochford et al., 1970) may not reveal a relationship between soft sign and a type of psychiatric disorder that does not usually lead to hospital admission. Studies on specialized clinical or institutional populations such as children with hyperactivity or delinquents (Camp et al., 1978; Lewis, Shanok, Pincus, & Glaser, 1979; Lucas, Rodin, & Simson, 1965; McMahon & Greenberg, 1977; Paulsen, 1978; Paulsen & O'Donnell, 1979; Wikler et al., 1979) may not reveal a relationship with other psychiatric conditions, and referral bias in such studies may lead to unrepresentative findings. The few studies in nonreferred populations have been limited to the examination of a single neurological sign (Rutter et al., 1966; and Wolff & Hurwitz, 1966, studied the choreiform syndrome), did not examine behavioral or emotional variables (Adams et al., 1974), or examined only a limited set of behavioral variables so that a full psychiatric diagnosis could not be made (Wolff & Hurwitz, 1973).

The present study examined the relationship between minor neurological signs in childhood and both psychiatric and cognitive disorders in adolescence. Our sample was drawn from the Collaborative Perinatal Project, which has the advantage of contemporaneous documentation of early neurological and psychological measures and of having been initially unselected for either the dependent or independent variables of interest to us. Furthermore, as it is a longitudinal study, we can examine both the predictive strength of soft signs for *later* psychiatric and cognitive problems, and we can examine the issue of developmental changes in soft signs in a longitudinal sample.

The research described in this chapter sets out to examine the following specific issues: first, whether soft neurological signs, as measured at age 7, persist into adolescence, and second, whether a relationship exists between the presence of early signs and later psychiatric diagnosis (at age 17).

METHODS

Subjects ($N = 126$) were drawn from the Columbia Presbyterian Hospital chapter of the Collaborative Perinatal Project (CPP). The CPP, a prospective study coordinated by the National Institute of Neurological and Communicative Disorders and Stroke (NINCDS), was initiated for the purpose of investigating pregnancy wastage (Berendes, 1966) and is described in detail in O'Connor, Shaffer, Stokman, and Shafer (in press). The intent of the CPP was to select a sample clearly independent of the outcome variables of interest, i.e., pregnancy wastage, and to describe the sample sufficiently thoroughly so that findings would be generalizable to similar populations. Fourteen medical centers, including Columbia Presbyterian Hospital, participated in the CPP, yielding data on approximately 55,000 mothers and their offspring. Both mothers and children were repeatedly tested or questioned and data covering a wide range of psychological, neurological, general health, and demographic variables were systematically recorded.

Data collection for the original study began with the initial prenatal visit of the mother to the participating medical center and continued at most centers through the child's seventh year.

The Columbia Presbyterian sample consisted of women admitted to the prenatal clinic between January 1959 and April 1963, with the exception of declared adoption donors and women who had received no more than one prenatal examination. The ratio of participants to registrants was initially 1:6, later reduced so that the average sampling ratio was 1:4.4, with a total of 2235 prenatal clinic registrants (Niswander & Gordon, 1972), of which 2067 were live births. At the time of the 7-year examination, 2019 children had survived, and 83.5% of them attended for reexamination (Gates, 1973). Overall, the loss and attrition rate for the Columbia sample was small, and these rates compare favorably with loss at other centers (generally 70–80% examined, Niswander & Gordon, 1972).

Criteria for Inclusion for Current Study.   This study is a follow-up of black, English-speaking male children born in 1962 and 1963. This cohort, the youngest in the Columbia sample, was chosen because the children would still be in school at the time of follow-up, allowing us to obtain teachers' ratings of behavior and facilitating subject tracing, which could be done through the school system.

Experimental subjects were selected on the basis of the findings at the 7-year neurological examination. A positive rating for any one of 18 specific neurological signs, broadly grouped within the constructs of involuntary movements, coordination, and sensory integration (see Table 2.1 for a complete listing) qualified the subject for inclusion ($N = 63$). A similar number of controls was then matched for sex, race, closest birth date, and the absence of these neurological signs on the 7-year neurological examination.

Psychiatric Evaluation

This report is confined to data obtained from the direct evaluation of the adolescent. A semistructured interview was used to assess the current status of the adolescent and to explore the range and adequacy of current social relationships.

TABLE 2.1
Frequency of Neurological Soft Signs Rated Present
at Age 7 Examination

Involuntary Movements	N	Coordination	N	Sensory Integration	N
Spontaneous tremor	1	Dysdiadochokinesis	35	Astereognosis	9
Tic	1	Awkwardness not otherwise classi-			
Mirror movements	13	fied	12		

The interviewers, as well as the cognitive and neurological testers, were blind with respect to subject status. The presence and severity of somatic, anxiety, affective and psychotic symptoms, antisocial behavior, and delinquency were assessed, and detailed information was obtained about peer and sexual relationships, and about the quality and quantity of family relationships.

The interview includes portions of the Schedule for Affective Disease and Schizophrenia (SADS) (Spitzer & Endicott, 1977), which allowed us to determine whether Research Diagnostic Criteria (Spitzer, Endicott, & Robins, 1978) for affective and psychotic disorders had been met. Sections of the interview developed by Rutter and Graham (1968) cover the adolescent's social relationships and antisocial behavior. Other sections dealing with assessment of sexual behavior and substance and alcohol use were adapted from the SADS (Spitzer & Endicott, 1977) and from forms developed by Kandel, Singer, and Kessler (1976). Ratings of the adolescent's social behavior during the interview have been adapted from the Mental Health Assessment Form (Kestenbaum & Bird, 1978) and include ratings of motor activity, interaction with the interviewer, and emotional responsiveness.

Glossary descriptions and rating scales with defined anchor points were incorporated into the body of the interview.

Overall functioning has been rated on the Global Assessment Scale (GAS) (Endicott, Spitzer, Fleiss, & Cohen, 1976). A psychiatric diagnosis was assigned for cases where the GAS rating was 70 or less. A GAS score ranging between 61 and 70 is defined on the scale as: some mild symptoms (e.g., depressive mood and mild insomnia or some difficulty in several areas of functioning, but generally functioning pretty well, has some meaningful interpersonal relationships and most untrained people would not consider him ''sick'').

Assessment of Reliability.   Intrarater reliability and intrasubject or interrater reliability were assessed. Sessions were conducted at which the interviewers watched and rated videotapes of their respective interviews. All interviewers watched interviewer X with subject A to obtain ratings on the measure used. This procedure constituted the framework for the assessment of reliability (by providing intrasubject and intrarater measures) and furnished additional training.

The GAS rating is a single summary measure that could be used as an indicator of rate of agreement. The rating scale consists of 10 categories on a continuum from 0 to 100 with a continuum nested in each category to permit differential evaluations within a category. Each category, as indicated previously, is clearly defined. Thus, the questions relevant for the purposes of reliability are: Do raters agree with the interviewer on the category of the GAS rating that is given?; do raters (and interviewer) agree on who warrants a psychiatric diagnosis (GAS rating of 70 or less)?

Nine subjects were rated by three to six raters, yielding a total of 41 ratings, with a mean percentage agreement of 38% (rater agreeing with interviewer's categorical placement); however, such a figure may be misleading, because ratings may differ by only one or two points and yet be placed in different categories. With the interview's rating as an index, the mean percentage agreement increased to 59% for all scores within five points of the index rating and to 88.5% for all scores within 10 points of the index rating.

The second question concerns the rate of agreement on the cutting point of 70. Nine subjects were scored by four to seven raters (including index rating), with a 79% rate of agreement on the placement of a subject above or below the GAS score of 70.

Neurological Assessment. The neurological assessment has been described fully elsewhere (Shafer, Stokman, Shaffer, Schonfeld, O'Connor, & Wolfe, in preparation) and was designed both to reevaluate the neurological status of the subjects in ways broadly similar to those used at age 7, and also to identify the significance of the constituents of the particular signs, e.g., speed, errors, rhythmicity of a particular motor task. Ratings in the current study were designed to allow for a more exact determination of the components of each neurological sign and to obtain a greater range of responses.

Our criteria for selecting an age-7 sign to examine persistence were: (1) that the sign had been present in a reasonable number of children—only four signs were present in more than three children (see Table 2.1); and (2) that the sign had been described with sufficient clarity to enable us to replicate the examination in our current protocol—one of the four frequently present at age 7, "awkwardness," did not fulfill this criterion.

Three early signs that fulfill these criteria and that are the subject of the present report are described in more detail.

Astereognosis. As a measure of sensory integration, at age 7, the subject was required to identify, with eyes closed and using only one hand, a bottle cap, a nickle, and a button. At age 17, the items were a quarter, a nickel, a penny, a dime-sized washer, and a penny-sized button. Subjects named each item before testing to ensure familiarity with the objects. At age 7, each item had been presented once and a single positive rating had been given for failure to name any one of the three items. At age 17, each item was presented twice and a positive rating was given for each failure on 10 presentations. Scoring at 17 may be either dichotomous, one or more errors versus no errors, or continuous, as the sum of all items.

Dysgraphesthisia, an alternative measure of sensory integration, was assessed only at age 17. The subject was asked to identify (with eyes closed) a square, a circle, an "X," and the numeral "3," all 1 inch in height, each drawn with a stylus on the palm of the subject's hand. The figures were presented randomly, each one appearing twice. Subjects were asked to name the stimuli before testing, and dysgraphesthesia was considered present if the subject failed to name correctly one or more of the eight stimuli presented.

Mirror Movements.   At age 7, the subject had been asked to perform rapid thumb–forefinger apposition, first with the right, then the left hand. A positive rating had been given if the opposite hand (first the left, then the right) showed similar involuntary movements. At age 17, the testing was expanded to successive rapid thumb–finger apposition for a period of 10 seconds. Finger movements in the opposite hand (order of hands determined by a coin toss) were scored as none, one to six movements, more than six movements within the 10-second period.

Dysdiadochokinesis.   At age 7 and 17, subjects were asked, as a measure of coordination, to alternately pronate and supinate each hand as fast as possible, with the further instruction at 17 that the hand should be lifted up and rotated about the axis of the middle finger, starting with the right hand. Difficulty in executing the rapid alternating movements yielded a positive rating for this sign at age 7. At 17, both irregularity in rhythm and failure to alternate were assessed with scoring for each on a 3-point scale: regular, perceptibly irregular, and grossly irregular, for irregularity in rhythm, and no failure, one failure, and two or more failures, for failure to alternate.

For the analysis in this chapter, signs measured at 17, where possible, were rescored on a present/absent dichotomy to match the dichotomy in the age 7 scoring.

The order of items in the neurological examination was the same for all subjects with the exception that the presentation of certain rapid movement items was counterbalanced.

Assessment of Reliability and Validity.   The assessment of the reliability of the neurological examination involved three groups other than the study population: (1) 10 adolescent inpatients at a nearby psychiatric center, (2) young adult research staff, and (3) 15 normal adolescents. The 10 inpatients were given parts of the examination twice in a 4-week interval. Simultaneous ratings were obtained by two or three of the neurological testers. Inter and intrarater comparisons were made. Rank correlation coefficients (r_s) for total number of positive ratings revealed a high degree of agreement between raters for both test $(r_s = .77)$ and retest $(r_s = .93)$, as well as intrarater test–retest reliability (rater 1: $r_s = .92$ and rater 2: $r_s = .77$; *rater 3 did not test enough subjects for the analysis*).

Cognitive Assessment

Although a broad battery of cognitive tests was given (described in detail in O'Connor et al, in press), this chapter reports only on IQ test results. Full-scale IQ was measured with the Wechsler Adult Intelligence Scale (Wechsler, 1955).

Study Procedures

Tracing. Of the 126 designated subjects, 123 were found. The retrieval procedures utilized information from the original files, such as last-known address and phone number, date of birth of adolescent, name of school subject was attending at age 7, and any other potentially useful information, such as grandparents' addresses and phone numbers. The sources of information that led to the retrieval of subjects are shown in Table 2.2.

Of the 123 identified subjects, 14 had moved out of the New York metropolitan area (to southeastern states, Colorado, and California), four adolescents were incarcerated, and one was in a psychiatric institution.

Testing. The order of testing was partially counterbalanced. All subjects were given the WAIS first, followed by either the neruological assessment or the psychiatric interview. Each parent informant was interviewed on the same day or as close as possible to the day that his/her son or stepson was seen.

When subjects were seen out of town, whether in their homes or in prison, the scheduling order was, of necessity, more flexible, dependent on prison and/or travel schedules.

TABLE 2.2
Source of Information for Retrieval

	N	(%)
Located through phone book	51	(41%)
Located through early school data	32	(25%)
Located through friends or relations	30	(24%)
Located by other means	10	(8%)
Not located	3	(2%)
Total	126	

RESULTS

Social and Family Characteristics

The two groups, early signs present (ESP) and early signs absent (ESA), were compared, at age 17, on the following social and family characteristics: anomalous family composition, mother's educational achievement, dissatisfaction with housing, and ever having been on welfare (Table 2.3). No significant differences among the groups were found.

Persistence of Signs

Of the three signs tested for persistence from age 7 to adolescence, the two motor signs, dysdiadochokinesis and mirror movements, showed significant stability (Table 2.4). More than half the ESP subjects manifested the abnormal sign in adolescence. Both dysgraphesthesia and failure to alternate hands (dysdiadochokinesis) occurred among adolescents who had comparable signs at 7 at more than twice the prevalence rates found among adolescents who were free of signs at age 7.

The finding of persistence did not apply to astereognosis where a high proportion of adolescents in both the ESP and ESA groups misidentified objects. The technique used to elicit astereognosis at 17 was more difficult than that used at age 7. Thus the finding that dysgraphesthesia, a broadly comparable index of sensory integration, differentiated between the two groups (see Table 2.4), suggests that the instability of astereognosis may have been artifactual.

TABLE 2.3
Demographic Characteristics by Sign Group (in percents)

	Signs at 7			
	Present		Absent	
	%	of n	%	of n
Family composition				
Parents separated, divorced, never married, or widowed	58%	60	56%	55
Education of Mother				
Incomplete high school or less	26%	61	20%	55
Housing				
Moderate or severe dissatisfaction	32%	59	27%	55
Welfare				
Ever on welfare	49%	61	44%	55

TABLE 2.4
Persistence of Signs from Age 7 to Age 17 (in percents)

| | A) *Dysdiadochokinesis* Age 7 | | | |
| | *Sign Present* | *No Signs* | | |
Age 17	*(N = 32)*	*(N = 55)*	x^2	p
Irregularity (positive rating)	53%	39%	NS	—
Failure to alternate (positive rating)	55%	26%	7.22	.01

| | B) *Astereognosis* Age 7 | | | |
| | *Sign Present* | *No Signs* | | |
Age 17	*(N = 8)*	*(N = 55)*	x^2	p
Astereognosis (positive rating)	62%	54%	NS	—
Dysgraphesthesia	57%	27%	6.56	.01

| | C) *Mirror Movement* Age 7 | | | |
| | *Sign Present* | *No Signs* | | |
Age 17	*(N = 12)*	*(N = 55)*	x^2	p
Mirror movements				
None	—	20%		
1–6 per 10 seconds	33%	47%		
7 + per 10 seconds	67%	33%		
			5.09	.03

Early Signs and Later Psychiatric Disturbance

Thirty-seven adolescents were given a psychiatric diagnosis on the basis of data obtained from the adolescent interview. The diagnostic criteria were taken from the *Diagnostic and Statistical Manual III* of the American Psychiatric Association. To reduce the number of diagnoses to a manageable set of categories for analysis, five categories were established a priori. These were antisocial, affective/emotional, psychotic, miscellaneous, and no disorder. The proportion of subjects given a diagnosis did not differ by sign group; however, significantly more of the adolescents with early signs fulfilled criteria for an affec-

TABLE 2.5
Mean IQ by Psychiatric Diagnosis by Early Sign
Status

	Sign at 7	
	Present (N)	Absent (N)
No diagnosis	88.86 (39)	95.45 (40)
Antisocial	92.00 (6)	89.75 (8)
Affective/emotional	86.25 (12)	98.30 (3)
Other diagnosis	76.50 (4)	91.25 (4)
(Including 1 schizo.)		
x̄	87.8	94.5

tive/emotional disorder during the 3 months prior to the assessment ($X^2 = 5.4$, df = 1, $p < .05$).

A variety of studies have revealed a relationship between soft signs on one hand and intellectual deficits and learning difficulties on the other. One possibility for our finding of a high prevalence of affective/emotional disorders in the ESP children would be that they had experienced scholastic difficulties and that the disorders were a consequence of persistent failure in school. An analysis of mean IQ differences by sign group and by psychiatric diagnostic group was carried out (Table 2.5). A two-way analysis of variance for unequal cell size (Edwards, 1975) was performed to examine the effects of neurological status and psychiatric diagnosis group on IQ. The results show a significant main effect of neurological status, such that the ESP group had a significantly lower mean IQ than the ESA group ($F = 6.21$, df = 1, 107, $p < .02$). Psychiatric diagnosis, as a main effect, and the interaction were not significant. It is noted that the ESP subjects diagnosed as having an affective/emotional disorder had a lower mean IQ than the ESA subjects within the same diagnostic category.

DISCUSSION

Persistence of Soft Signs

At age 17 two motor signs, mirror movements and dysdiadochokinesis, were found in more than half the subjects known to have had the respective signs at age 7. These rates were significantly higher than rates found within the group of subjects who were sign free at age 7.

The persistence of a third sign, astereognosis, was not supported. At age 17 a high proportion of all subjects performed poorly on this task, and no significant performance differences between subjects with and without signs at age 7 were found. The explanation for this is not clear, although it may have been a result of inappropriate measurement. The task as it had originally been applied at age 7 was, in two respects, altered for use in the adolescent sample. Objects of greater similarity were chosen and a larger number of items was targeted for identification. These changes were designed to make the task more difficult because it was felt that identification of the objects from the age 7 examination would present less of a perceptual challenge at age 17. However, the reformulated task appears to have been equally difficult for both groups, and a high proportion of subjects, regardless of their neurological status, misidentified the objects presented to them. Inappropriate measurement as an explanation is further supported by the finding of a relationship between early astereognosis and later dysgraphesthesia, suggesting that sensory integration difficulty, as well as the motor signs discussed earlier, persist through childhood.

A second finding was of a high base rate of neurological signs at age 17 in the control group. There are at least three competing explanations for this. The first is that there were differences in threshold at Time 1 and Time 2. Thus, it may be that a significant proportion of children who at age 7 were recorded as not having had signs would have been registered as sign positive using the criteria adapted at age 17. It should be noted however that the prevalence of neurological signs in the Columbia chapter of the CPP was higher than at other centers, making it less likely that many false negative assignments were made. The problem of measurement error at Time 2 has been examined through a separate study of the test–retest reliability of neurological signs. Reliability across time was within acceptable ranges.

The second explanation of the high base rate in the controls could be that measurement or recording techniques at ages 7 and 17 are not comparable. The descriptions given of the items measured at 7 with a simple rating of present/absent were not as detailed as those at 17, where several components of each of the signs were measured separately. The result may have been that the positive recording of a sign at age 7 required the presence of a number of different dimensions, although these were not explicitly defined, whereas the positive recording of a sign at age 17 required the presence of a single dimension that might not have qualified the subject for a positive rating in the earlier examination.

A third possible explanation is that neurological dysfunction has been acquired since age 7, and thus signs were acquired de novo after the age of 7. It is the impression of the authors that a high proportion of the subjects frequently smoked marijuana and this may have influenced neurological states. Factors of this sort will be examined in further analyses. This problem will also be approached by examining whether these are different patterns of relationship between signs and disorder for subjects who have had neurological signs present since age 7 and for subjects who were noted only to have signs at age 17. Different relationships within these groups would suggest that the origins of the signs are different.

Regardless of the explanation for these phenomena, the implications are clear, i.e., soft signs persist well after most features of neurological development have been completed. They must be regarded as being potentially stable indications of a neurological difference. Whether the differences matter is of course a function of their correlates.

Correlates of Early Signs—Later Psychiatric Disorder

A second main finding suggests that early signs do indeed matter. Significantly more of the adolescents who had had soft signs in early childhood had recently experienced a depressive episode. Several explanations suggest themselves for this finding.

The first is that despite statistical significance, we have a chance finding. This is always a possibility in a study with small numbers, and it makes some form of replication essential. The data upon which the present chapter is based are derived solely from the psychiatric interview with the adolescent and do not take into account parents' and teachers' reports. Although there is evidence that information about emotional state derived from a direct interview with the adolescents is likely to be more complete and accurate (Carlson & Cantwell, 1980) than that from parents, the available secondary sources will make it possible to test the consistency of the findings. However, it must be further noted that, given the limited congruence between adolescents' and parents' reports of psychiatric disorder in other studies (Gould, Wunsch–Hitzig, & Dohrenwend, 1980), a failure to obtain internal replication would be of only limited value.

A second and more complex explanation might be that, rather than indicating a relationship between an early neurological marker and later psychiatric disorder, the findings indicate continuity of affective psychiatric disorder; that is, there might be an interaction between either the recording or the manifestation of soft signs and psychiatric disorder that has led to systematic bias. It may be that common neurological phenomena, such as the ones studied here, are more likely to be rated present if they are accompanied by some other disturbance of behavior manifest during the examination. Thus seven-year-olds with both signs and disturbed behavior at examination might be reported as having signs at a higher rate and with more consistency than children who have signs but who show normal behavior during examination. Alternatively, it might be that neurological soft signs are latent in many children and simply more likely to emerge under conditions of stress. In this case, children with early disturbance would be more likely to show stress during physical examination and would therefore be more likely to be rated positive for neurological change.

There are a number of strategies open to examine the questions. These include an examination of the psychiatric correlates of *current* signs in both groups and an examination of the subsequent relationships of the ratings made of behavior during testing. These are pursued as our data analysis continues.

A third possibility might be that a true minimal brain dysfunction effect is being noted, i.e., that there is some ill-defined brain dysfunction that is leading to both signs and to a disturbance of affect. The relationship between neurological dysfunction and affective disorder has been reviewed extensively and there is convincing evidence of its importance (see Flor–Henry, 1979; Shaffer, Bijur, Chadwick, & Rutter, submitted for publication; Wexler, 1980). Although the emphasis in most of the research has been on effects of localized cortical dysfunction, the understanding of the anatomical basis for soft signs is so limited that the possibility of a broader relationship cannot be excluded.

Finally, although the relationship between diagnosis and IQ is not significant, there is a suggestion that the depressed and "other" soft signs groups have lower means IQ's (see Table 2.5). An observation of this sort lends itself to at least two interpretations. On the one hand, it might be that low IQ is simply a marker of the extent of brain dysfunction and that affective/emotional disorder is more likely to be found in individuals with more pervasive involvement. The trend could also be interpreted as indicating that soft signs are only indirectly related to psychiatric disorder and that the primary relationship is with the cognitive dysfunction. Children with low IQ scores, regardless of their soft sign status, may have more school difficulties and more difficulties with the stresses of life. Affective/emotional disorders would not be constitutionally determined in this instance but rather would be an expected consequence of the life experiences of the low-IQ group. Albeit with small numbers, the results here do not support this because there is a suggestion that the mean IQ of the affective/emotional disorder soft sign children is low relative to their sign-free counterparts. If this model were correct, it would be expected that the low IQ would apply regardless of soft sign status.

Regardless of the mechanisms that might explain the relationship, the findings suggest the neurological examination of the 7-year-olds yields information of potential value in the prediction of later adjustment difficulties and psychiatric disorder. This alone is important in its implications for preventive psychiatry.

ACKNOWLEDGMENTS

This research is being supported by NIMH Center Grant #MH 30906 and by NIMH Psychiatric Education Grant #MH 07715-17.

The authors wish to express their gratitude to Dr. Stephanie Portnoy, who substantially participated in the cognitive testing.

REFERENCES

Adams, R. M., Kocsis, J. J., & Estes, R. E. (1974). Soft neurological signs in learning-disabled children and controls. *American Journal of Diseases of Children, 128,* 614–618.
Berendes, H. W. (1966). The structure and scope of the Collaborative Project on cerebral palsy,

mental retardation, and other neurological and sensory disorders of infancy and childhood. In S. S. Chipman, A. M. Lilienfeld, B. G. Greenberg, & J. F. Donnelly (Eds.), *Research methodology and needs in perinatal studies*. Springfield, IL: Charles C. Thomas.

Boshes, B., & Myklebust, H. R. (1964). A neurological and behavioral study of children with learning disorders. *Neurology, 14*, 7–13.

Camp, J. A., Bialer, I., Sverd, J., & Winsberg, B. G. (1978). Clinical usefulness of the NIMH physical and neurological examination for soft signs. *Am J Psychiatry, 135*(3), 362–364.

Campbell, S. B., Endman, M., & Bernfeld, G. (1977). A 3-year follow-up of hyperactive children in elementary school. *Journal of Child Psychology and Psychiatry, 18*, 239–249.

Capute, A. J., Meidermayer, E. F., & Richardson, F. (1968). The electroencephalogram in children with minimal cerebral dysfunction. *Pediatrics, 41*, 1104–1114.

Carlson, G. A., & Cantwell, D. P. (1980). *Diagnosis of childhood depression—a comparison of the Weinberg and DSM III criteria*. Paper presented at the annual meeting of the American Psychiatric Association, San Francisco.

Edwards, A. L. (1975). *Experimental design in psychological research*. New York: Holt, Rinehart, & Winston.

Endicott, J. S., Spitzer, R. L., Fleiss, J., & Cohen, J. (1976). The Global Assessment Scale. *Archives of General Psychiatry, 33*, 766–771.

Flor–Henry, P. (1979). Neuropsychological and power spectral EEG investigation of the obsessive-compulsive syndrome. *Biological Psychiatry, 14*(1), 119–130.

Gates, M. J. (1973). *Final report: Collaborative Perinatal Study of National Institute of Neurological Diseases and Stroke*. New York: Columbia University College of Physicians and Surgeons.

Gould, M. S., Wunsch–Hitzig, R., Dohrenwend, B. P. (1980) Formulation of hypotheses about the prevalence, treatment and prognostic significance of psychiatric disorders in children in the United States. In B. P. Dohrenwend, B. S. Dohrenwend, M. S. Gould, B. Link, R. Neugebauer, & R. Wunsch–Hitzig (Eds.), *Mental illness in the United States: Epidemiological estimates*. New York: Praeter Publications.

Hertzig, M. A., & Birch, H. G. (1966). Neurologic organization in psychiatrically disturbed adolescent girls. *Archives of General Psychiatry, 15*, 590–599.

Hertzig, M. A., & Birch, H. G. (1968). Neurologic organization in psychiatrically disturbed adolescents. *Archives of General Psychiatry, 66*, 43–53.

Kandel, D., Singer, E., & Kessler, R. (1976). The epidemiology of drug use among New York State high school students: Distribution, trends and change in rates of use. *American Journal of Public Health, 66*, 43–53.

Kestenbaum, C. J., & Bird, H. R. (1978). A reliability study of the Mental Health Assessment Form for school age children. *Journal of the American Academy of Child Psychiatry, 17*(2), 338–347.

Lewis, D. O., Shanok, S. S., Pincus, J. H., & Glaser, G. H. (1979). Violent juvenile delinquents. *Journal of the American Academy of Child Psychiatry, 18*, 307–319.

Lucas, A. R., Rodin, E. A., & Simson, C. B. (1965). Neurological assessment of children with early school problems. *Develop Med Child Neurol, 7*, 145–56.

McMahon, S. A., & Greenberg, I. M. (1977). Serial neurologic examination of hyperactive children. *Pediatrics, 59*(4), 584–587.

Mikkelsen, E. J., Brown, G. L., Minichiello, M. D., Millican, F. K., & Rapoport, J. L. (1981)- Neurologic status in hyperactive, enuretic, encopretic, and normal boys. *J Am Acad Child Psychiatry, 21*, 75–81.

Mosher, L. R., Pollin, W., & Stabanau, J. R. (1971). Identical twins discordant for schizophrenia. *Archives of General Psychiatry, 24*, 422–430.

Nichols, P. L., & Chen, T. C. (1981). *Minimal brain dysfunction: A prospective study*. Hillsdale, NJ: Lawrence Erlbaum Associates.

Nichols, P. L., Chen, T., & Pomeroy, J. D. (1976). *Minimal brain dysfunction: The association among symptoms.* Paper presented at the annual meeting of the American Psychological Association, Washington, DC.

Niswander, K. R., & Gordon, M. (1972). *The women and their pregnancies.* The Collaborative Perinatal Study of the National Institute of Neurological Diseases and Stroke, DHEW Publication No. (NIH), 73-379.

O'Connor, P. A., Shaffer, D., Stokman, C., & Shafer, S. (in press). A neuropsychiatric follow-up of children in the Collaborative Perinatal Project population. In S. Mednick, & M. Harway (Eds.), *Longitudinal research in the United States* (tentative). Boston: Martinus Nijhoff.

PANESS, MH-9-41, National Institute of Mental Health, Department of Health, Education, and Welfare, United States Government Printing Office, 490-127.

Paulsen, K. (1978). Reflection-impulsivity and level of maturity. *J Psychol, 99,* 109-112.

Paulsen, K., & O'Donnell, J. P. (1979). Construct validity of children's behavior problem dimensions: Relationship to activity level, impulsivity, and soft neurological signs. *J of Psychol, 101,* 273-278.

Peters, J. E., Romine, J. S., & Dykman, R. A. (1975). A special neurological examination of children with learning disabilities. *Developmental Medicine and Child Neurology, 175,* 63-75.

Quitkin, F., Rifkin, A., & Klein, D. F. (1976). Neurologic soft signs in schizophrenia and character disorder. *Archives of General Psychiatry, 33,* 845-853.

Rapoport, J. L., Buchsbaum, M. S., Weingartner, J., Zahn, T. P., Ludlow, C., Bartko, J., Mikkelsen, E. J., Langer, D. H., & Bunney, W. E. Jr. (1980). Dextroamphetamine: Cognitive and behavioral effects in normal and hyperactive boys and normal adult males. *Archives of General Psychiatry, 37,* 933-946.

Rapoport, J. L., Buchsbaum, M. S., Zahn, T. P., Weingartner, H., Ludlow, C., & Mikkelsen, E. J. (1978). Dextroamphetamine: Cognitive and behavioral effects in normal prepubertal boys. *Science, 199,* 560-563.

Rapoport, J., & Quinn, P. (1975). Minor physical anomalies (stigmata) and early developmental deviation: A major biologic sub-group of "hyperactive children." *International Journal of Mental Health, 4,* 29-44.

Rochford, M. M., Detre, T., Bucker, G. J., & Harrow, M. (1970). Neuropsychological impairments in functional psychiatric disease. *Archives of General Psychiatry, 22,* 114-119.

Routh, D. K., & Roberts, R. D. (1972). Minimal brain dysfunction in children: Failure to find evidence for a behavioral syndrome. *Psychological Reports, 31,* 307-314.

Rutter, M., & Brown, G. W. (1966). The reliability and validity of measures of family life and relationships in families containing a psychiatric patient. *Social Psychiatry, 1,* 28-53.

Rutter, M., & Graham, P. (1968). The reliability and validity of the psychiatric assessment of the child: I. Interview with the child. *British Journal of Psychiatry, 114,* 563-579.

Rutter, M., Graham, P., & Birch, H. G. (1966). Interrelations between the choreiform syndrome, reading disability and psychiatric disorder in children of 8-11 years. *Devel Med Child Neurol, 8,* 149-159.

Rutter, M., Graham, P., & Yule, W. (1970). *A Neuropsychiatric study in childhood.* London: Spastics International Medical Publications.

Rutter, M., & Yule, W. (1973). Specific reading retardation. In L. Mann, & D. Sabatino (Eds.), *The first review of special education.* Philadelphia: Buttonwood Farms.

Rutter, M. (1977). Brain damage syndrome in childhood: Concepts and findings. *J Child Psychol Psychiat 18,* 1-22.

Sandberg, S. T., Rutter, M., & Taylor, E. (1978). Hyperkinetic disorder in psychiatric clinic attenders. *Dev. Med. Child Neurol. 20,* 279-299.

Schachar, R., Rutter, M., & Smith, A. (in press). Of situationally and pervasively hyperactive children: Implications for syndrome definition. *Journal of Child Psychology and Psychiatry.*

Seidel, U. P., Chadwick, O. F., & Rutter, M. (1975). Psychological disturbance and physically disturbed children. *Developmental Medicine and Child Neurology, 17,* 563–573.

Shafer, S. Q., Stokman, C. J., Shaffer, D., Schonfeld, I., O'Connor, P. A., & Wolfe, R. (in preparation). *Ten-year consistency of neurological test performance in boys without focal neurological deficit.*

Shaffer, D. (1977). Brain injury. In M. Rutter, & L. Hersov (Eds.), *Child psychiatry: Modern approaches.* London: Blackwell Scientific Publications.

Shaffer, D. (1978). "Soft" neurological signs and later psychiatric disorder—A review. *Journal of Child Psychology and Psychiatry, 19,* 63–65.

Shaffer, D. (1980). An approach to the validation of clinical syndromes in childhood. In S. Salinger, J. Antrobus, & J. Glick (Eds.), *The ecosystem of the sick kid.* New York: Academic Press.

Shaffer, D., Bijur, P., Chadwick, O. F. D., & Rutter, M. D. (Submitted for publication). *Localized cortical injury and psychiatric symptoms in childhood..*

Shaffer, D., McNamara, N., & Pincus, J. (1974) Controlled observations on patterns of activity, attention, and impulsivity in brain-damaged and psychiatrically disturbed boys. *Psychological Medicine, 4,* 4–18.

Spitzer, R. L., & Endicott, J. (1977). *Schedule of affective disorders and schizophrenia (SADS,* 3rd ed.). New York: Biometrics Research, New York State Psychiatric Institute.

Spitzer, R. L., Endicott, J., & Robins, E. (1978). *Research diagnostic criteria for a selected group of functional disorders* (3rd ed.). New York: Biometrics Research, New York State Psychiatric Institute.

Stine, O. C., Saratsiotis, J. M., & Mosser, R. S. (1975). Relationships between neurological findings and classroom behavior. *American Journal of Diseases of Children, 129,* 1036–1040.

Wechsler, D. (1955). *Wechsler Adult Intelligence Scale.* New York: Psychological Corporation.

Werry, J. S., Minde, K., Guzman, A., Weiss, G., Dogan, K., & Hoy, E. (1972). Studies on the hyperactive child: VII. Neurological status compared with neurotic and normal children. *American Journal of Orthopsychiatry, 42,* 441–450.

Wexler, B. E. (1980). Cerebral laterality and psychiatry: A review of the literature. *American Journal of Psychiatry, 137*(3), 279–291.

Wikler, A., Dixon, J. F., & Parker, J. B. Jr. (1970). Brain function in problem children and controls: Psychometric, neurological and electroencephalographic comparisons. *Amer J Psychiatry, 127*(5), 94–105.

Wolff, P. H., & Hurwitz, J. (1966). The choreiform syndrome. *Dev Med Child Neurol, 8,* 160–165.

Wolff, P., & Hurwitz, J. (1973). Functional implications of the mentally brain-damaged syndrome. *Seminars in Psychiatry, 5,* 105–115.

3 Prospective Longitudinal Study of Firstborn Neonates

Elsie R. Broussard

Generally somebody has a promising idea about what constitutes a high-risk population. This may be on the basis of a theoretical hypothesis or one's own observations or observations made by others. Through a series of steps—these promising ideas are developed—research programs evolve to test the merit of these ideas. Findings are shared with others who in turn develop similar programs, sometimes modifying or adding to what has been done originally. Thus in small increments—bit by bit—the state of the art advances.

Attempts to identify factors that place neonates at risk for subsequent psychosocial disorder and developmental deviations are numerous. The most often studied risk factors have been those associated with organic impairment (Kopp & Krakow, 1983). Attention has been drawn to preterm infants, multiple births, offspring of teenage mothers, infants with physical anomalies, and those evidencing symptoms of perinatal distress (Cohen & Parmelee, 1983; Sameroff, 1981). Risk factors have also included socioeconomic variables; infants born into environments associated with poverty, malnutrition, or emotional and cognitive deficiency are often regarded as being at risk (Parnas, J., Schulsinger, F., Schulsinger, H., Mednick, S., & Teasdale, T.). In these instances the potentially handicapping factors are quite readily apparent.

The prospective longitudinal studies of Pittsburgh Firstborns conducted since 1963 have focused on quite a different population selected from healthy full-term infants. These studies have demonstrated the relationship of the mother's perception of her newborn to the child's subsequent psychosocial development at ages 4½ and 10/11 years of age. This chapter provides a report of the preliminary data analysis of the most recent phase of the studies—an evaluation of the firstborns at age 15 years.

Previous publications have described the details of the longitudinal studies of the Pittsburgh Firstborns of 1963 and are not repeated here (Broussard, 1976, 1979; Broussard & Hartner, 1970, 1971;). However, some background information is indicated.

BACKGROUND INFORMATION

During clinical practice I had noted that mothers of healthy newborns demonstrated a wide range of responses to their newborns and their needs. Some mothers made a smooth transition from pregnancy to motherhood and required little guidance. They had pride and pleasure in raising their infants and their infants thrived. Others lacked pride in their infants and evidenced little pleasure in motherhood, although their infants were found upon pediatric examination to be clinically healthy and appealing.

It became apparent to me, as it had to others, that the way a mother relates to her child is influenced by her perception of him, and that his behavior is affected by her handling of him. These observations led me to develop an instrument to measure the mother's perception of her neonate and to conduct longitudinal studies of healthy neonates. This instrument made it possible to assess further the relation between maternal perception of the neonate and the child's subsequent development.

Instrument of Measure

The Broussard *Neonatal Perception Inventories* (NPI) were devised to measure the mother's perception of her newborn as compared to her concept of the average infant. The NPI consist of two forms, the Average Baby form and Your Baby form. Each form consists of six single-item scales: crying, spitting, feeding, elimination, sleeping, and predictability. These items were selected because past clinical experience indicated these to be concerns mothers expressed about their babies as well as areas that reflect the state of functioning of the mother–infant system during the neonatal period.

The six scales are rated from 1 (signifying none) to 5 (signifying a great deal) for each of the inventories. The lower values on the scale represent the more desirable behavior. The scales are totaled for each of the forms separately with no attempt at weighting the scales. Thus, a total score is obtained for the Average Baby form and a total score is obtained for the Your Baby form.[1] The total score

---

[1]On the basis of 318 primiparae delivering normal, full-term, single births, the total scores range from 7 to 23 out of a possible score of 6 to 30, the differences between the scores range between +9 to −9.

of the Your Baby Perception form is then subtracted from the Average Baby Perception form. The discrepancy constitutes the NPI score. For example: Given a total Average Baby score of 17 and a total Your Baby score of 19, the NPI score is −2. Given a total Average Baby score of 15 and a total Your Baby score of 14, the NPI score is +1. One-month-old infants rated by their mothers as better than average (+ score) are considered at Low-Risk. Those infants *not* rated better than average (− or 0 score) are considered at High-Risk for subsequent development of emotional difficulty.

The NPI may be viewed as a projective measure because the mother is presented with a set of ambiguous stimuli that provide a gestalt upon which she projects her concept of what most little babies are like and her expectations of what her newborn will be like. Understandably, this will vary from mother to mother and is dependent on her past experiences.

The NPI provide a measure of the *Adaptive Potential* of the mother–infant system. The NPI do not predict the precise nature of the psychosocial disorder. The complexity of human development makes such predictive specificity impossible. The NPI can serve to screen for potential failures in psychosocial adaptation stemming from disorders in the earliest mother–infant relationship, disorders that may exist undetected at an early stage.

The Study Population

The study population consisted of 318 primiparae all delivering single, live, full-term healthy infants weighing 5.5 pounds or more during a specified 2½-month time period in 1963. Infants were examined in the delivery room, upon admission to the newborn nursery, and again at time of discharge. If any complication occurred during the hospital stay, the infant was excluded from the study. Selection of healthy neonates, weighing 5.5 pounds or more, was an attempt to ensure that infants were within the range of normal endowment so that the infant was biologically equipped to elicit response from the mother and not handicapped in his ability to respond to maternal care.

The educational background of the parents ranged from grammar school to postgraduate training. Occupations included skilled and unskilled industrial work, white collar, and professional. On the Hollingshead Index of Social Position (Education and Occupation of Father), the population distribution was as follows: Class I = 1.9%; Class II = 13.5%; Class III = 29.8%; Class IV = 48.1%; Class V = 6.7%.

At the time of delivery, one mother was single and one widowed.[2] All others were married and living with their husbands. White respondents comprised 93.6% of the study population. The ages of the mothers at the time of delivery ranged from 14–41 years with the median, 21.8 years.

---

[2]Mothers giving their infants up for adoption were excluded from the study.

Based upon the NPI score, infants were categorized at approximately 1 month of age as being at High-Risk or Low-Risk for possible development of psychosocial disorders. One hundred and ninety five (61%) infants were rated as better than average and were considered to be at Low Risk; the one hundred and twenty three (39%) who were not rated as better than average constituted a group at High-Risk.

Follow-Up Study at Age 4½ Years

When the children reached 4½ years of age, 120 of the original population were evaluated during a single clinical examination by one of two child psychiatrists.[3] Neither examiner had any knowledge of the children's predictive NPI risk ratings. Except for racial distribution due to the loss of the 20 black subjects in the original population, the demographic data for the original population were comparable with the data for the subpopulation evaluated at each age. The proportion of children rated at High-Risk was almost identical in the original and follow-up groups. There was no statistically significant difference between the groups with regard to other descriptive data (e.g., health of mother, type of delivery). With respect to these data, the children evaluated at 4½, 10/11, and 15 years were judged representative of the original 318. The follow-up data reported in this chapter apply to Caucasian children.

The classification proposed by the GAP Committee on Child Psychiatry was used as a frame of reference to formulate a diagnosis (Group for the Advancement of Psychiatry, 1966). Seven children were judged to require intervention related to a circumscribed event (i.e., the death of a parent, possible brain damage with established etiology, situational anxiety with a clearly defined acute precipitating event, e.g., recent surgery). Twenty-eight children were judged to need additional clinical study in order to determine whether psychopathology was present. Because further study was precluded by funding restrictions, the data analysis was restricted to the remaining 85 children. Thirty four of these children were judged to have a degree of psychopathology sufficient to warrant therapeutic intervention. Fifty one were considered to be healthy children.

There was a statistically significant association between the NPI predictive risk rating and the evaluation at age 4½. Infants predicted to be at high risk at 1 month of age were more likely to have psychosocial disorder at age 4½ than those who were at low risk ($X^2 = 18.50$; 1df; $p < .00002$).

---

[3]Because psychiatrists were only available on a part time basis, and research subjects were unpaid volunteers with many other commitments, it was not possible to arrange a fixed assignment of a specific case number to a specific psychiatrist. To maximize the opportunity for subjects to participate in the continued study, office appointments were scheduled on a 7-day-week basis and with whichever psychiatrist was available for the clinical interview. This, of course, meant that the ultimate number of cases seen by a given psychiatrist, as well as the distribution of high-risk cases were left entirely to chance.

Follow-Up at Age 10/11 Years

When the firstborns were between 10 and 11 years of age, 104 were evaluated clinically during a single office interview by one of three psychiatrists, none of whom had previously evaluated the children. None had prior knowledge of the child's predictive risk rating at 1 month nor of the previous evaluation conducted at age 4½. Based on a summary of hospital birth records, developmental data previously gathered by parent interviews, history of school performance obtained by teacher interview, and on his office interview with the child, the psychiatrist constructed a diagnostic profile using Anna Freud's Metapsychological Profile (Freud, 1965).

In assessing the psychosocial functioning of the firstborns, the clinicians studied the intrapsychic functioning and adaptive capacity of the children functioning in their respective environments, considered their coping mechanisms, and looked at their tendencies towards progressive development as well as the regressive tendencies that were operant. The children were also rated according to the Probability of Mental Disorder, using a 4-point confidence level scale adapted from Leighton, D., Harding, J., Macklin, D., Hughes, C., Leighton, A. (1963). The scale was: A-High Confidence Mental Disorder; B-Probable But Less Certain; C-Doubtful But Suspicious; D-High Confidence No Mental Disorder. The A, B, and C categories were considered by the author as probably representing gradations of Mental Disorder. For statistical analysis, the A, B, and C categories were pooled into one group and compared with the D category, representing No Mental Disorder. There was a statistically significant association between the NPI predictive risk rating at 1 month of age and the psychiatric rating of the child at age 10/11 years ($X^2 = 5.68$, 1df; $p < .017$). The findings indicate that the mother's perception of her 1-month-old firstborn continued to be predictive of a higher incidence of psychopathology.

It is important to note that not one of the children who had been judged as having psychopathology at age 4½ was considered to be free of disorder when evaluated by different psychiatrists at age 10/11. This provides evidence that when there has been no treatment children do not tend to "outgrow" the problems.

The reverse was not true, however. Among those children who had been considered to be free of psychosocial disorder at 4½, there were those who were considered to have difficulty at 10/11. This is as one would expect in view of what we know about the many stresses encountered during the developmental process of growing up.

PSYCHIATRIC EVALUATION AT ADOLESCENCE

When the children reached adolescence, 99 (56 males and 43 females) were evaluated clinically by one of four psychiatrists following the same format used

TABLE 3.1
Percentage Distribution of Mental Disorder Among 99 15-Year-Old
Firstborns According to Sex

Psychiatric Ratings	Males		Females		Total	
	No.	%	No. %	No.	No.	%
A	15	26.78 (60%)	10	23.25 (40%)	25	25.25
B	18	32.14 (62.06%)	11	25.58 (37.93%)	29	29.29
C	11	19.64 (61.11%)	7	16.3 (38.88%)	18	18.18
D	12	21.42 (44.44%)	15	34.9 (55.55%)	27	27.72
Total	56	56.56	43	43.43	99	100.0

( ) represents row percentages

at the 10/11-year age evaluation.[4] At the time of the evaluation, one subject was 16 years and 3-months-old. The remaining 98 ranged in age from 14 years 7 months to 15 years 9 months. The distribution of psychiatric ratings is given in Table 3.1.

In order to study the relationship of the NPI risk rating at 1 month of age to the psychiatric ratings at age 15, the A, B, and C categories were again pooled into one group and were compared with D category. Table 3.2 contains the data for the total group and for males and females separately.

For the 99 children, there was a significant relationship between the NPI risk rating at 1 month of age and subsequent mental disorders ($X^2 = 4.14, p < .042$). The phi correlation coefficient was .20 and the odds ratio was 2.7 to 1. The odds ratio indicates that those 1-month-old infants viewed negatively by their mothers

---

[4]Attrition is always a factor in longitudinal research. Following the 1-month postpartum home visit, we had no contact with subjects until children were 4½ years old. At that time, 155 were located and asked to participate in another home visit interview. Twelve refused and one child had died. Home interviews were conducted with 142 mothers. Of these 121 brought the children for office evaluations (the one black subject was omitted from data analysis). We subsequently located children who had previously moved, thus increasing our available pool of subjects. *A total of 162 different firstborns* came in for one or more psychiatric evaluations. The number of subjects seen for office evaluation at each time point varied. Parents often willingly participated with home interviews or permitted us to interview school personnel about their firstborn, yet were not able to bring the child to the office. At age 9, we completed 150 home visits, 127 school visits at age 9½, and 104 office evaluations at 10/11 years. At age 13 we completed 141 home visits, at 13/14 years 135 school visits, and 99 office visits at age 15.

TABLE 3.2

The Relationship Between the NPI and Subsequent Psychiatric Ratings by Four Raters at Age 15 for Males, Females, and Total

NPI Ratings	Males			Females			Total		
	Mental Disorder	No Mental Disorder	Total	Mental Disorder	No Mental Disorder	Total	Mental Disorder	No Mental Disorder	Total
Negative	21	1	22	14	6	20	35	7	42
Positive	23	11	34	14	9	23	37	20	57
Total	44	12	56	28	15	43	72	27	99
	$X^2 = 6.14\ p < .013$ $\emptyset = .33$ Odds Ratio = 10.04/1			$X^2 = .39\ p < .531$ $\emptyset = .10$ Odds Ratio = 1.50/1			$X^2 = 4.14\ p < .042$ $\emptyset = .20$ Odds Ratio-2.7/1		

were 2.7 times more likely to have a diagnosis of mental disorder at age 15 than those infants who had been positively viewed by their mothers.

Further analysis of the data for all the raters according to sex revealed that the relative odds ratio for males is 10.04, meaning that a negatively viewed infant male is 10 times more likely to have a diagnosis of mental disorder than a positively viewed male. In regard to females the odds ratio was 1.5, meaning that a negatively viewed female was 1.5 times more likely to have a diagnosis of mental disorder than a positively perceived female.

Examination of the distribution of ratings by each of the psychiatrists indicated that one rater was discrepant in the evaluation of negatively perceived (High-Risk) females. That rater diagnosed all the high-risk females as being free of disorder and placed them in the D category. Because this was discrepant from the distribution of ratings of the other three raters, the author subsequently chose to analyze the data eliminating the 18 children evaluated by the fourth rater. Table 3.3 contains the distribution of psychiatric ratings for the 81 children examined by the other three raters.

Analysis of data for the 81 adolescents shows that there is still a significant relationship between the NPI risk rating and Mental Disorder at age 15 ($X^2 = 7.29$, 1df, $p < .007$) as shown in Table 3.4.

The discrepancy between males and females with the total is much less than when all 99 children are included (see Table 3.2). Although the odds ratio for the males is higher (8.42/1) than for the females (4.08/1), the difference is not significant ($Z = .437$, $p < .662$). Those children with negative NPI risk ratings are more likely to have a diagnosis of mental disorder at age 15 than those who had been positively perceived. The correlation between the two variables is .30.

TABLE 3.3
Percentage Distribution of Mental Disorder Among 81 15-Year-Old
Firstborns According to Sex

Psychiatric Ratings	Males		Females		Total	
	No.	%	No.	%	No.	%
A	11	23.91 (52.38%)	10	28.57 (47.61%)	21	25.92
B	14	30.43 (58.33%)	10	28.57 (41.66%)	24	29.62
C	10	21.73 (62.50%)	6	17.14 (37.50%)	16	19.75
D	11	23.91 (55%)	9	25.71 (45%)	20	24.69
Total	46		35		81	

( ) represents row percentages

TABLE 3.4
The Relationship Between the NPI and Subsequent Psychiatric Ratings by Three Raters at Age 15 for Males, Females, and Total

NPI Rating	Males			Females			Total		
	Mental Disorder	No Mental Disorder	Total	Mental Disorder	No Mental Disorder	Total	Mental Disorder	No Mental Disorder	Total
Negative	16	1	17	14	2	16	30	3	33
Positive	19	10	29	12	7	19	31	17	48
Total	35	11	46	26	9	35	61	20	81
	$X^2 = 4.82$ $p < .028$ $\emptyset = .32$ Odds Ratio $= 8.42/1$			$X^2 = 2.69$ $p < .101$ $\emptyset = .28$ Odds Ratio $= 4.08/1$			$X^2 = 7.29$ $p < .007$ $\emptyset = .30$ Odds Ratio $= 5.48/1$		

TABLE 3.5
The Relationship Between the NPI and Subsequent Psychiatric Ratings at Ages 4 ½, 10/11, and 15

NPI Ratings	Age 4 ½			Age 10/11			Age 15		
	Mental Disorder	No Mental Disorder	Total	Mental Disorder	No Mental Disorder	Total	Mental Disorder	No Mental Disorder	Total
Negative	24	12	36	37	5	42	30	3	33
Positive	10	39	49	42	20	62	31	17	48
Total	34	51	85	79	25	104	61	20	81

Age 4 ½: $X^2 = 18.50$, $p < .00002$, $\emptyset = .47$, Odds Ratio ~7.8/1

Age 10/11: $X^2 = 5.68$, $p < .017$, $\emptyset = .23$, Odds Ratio = 3.5/1

Age 15: $X^2 = 7.29$, $p < .007$, $\emptyset = .30$, Odds Ratio = 5.48/1

Comparisons Between Evaluations at Ages 4½, 10/11, and 15 Years

The NPI rating at 1 month of age was significantly related to the psychiatric rating at each of the three later ages (4½, 10/11, and 15). To further study the effect of the NPI rating over time, the psychiatric rating was also dichotomized at ages 4½ and 10/11. For completeness, Table 3.5 contains the three 2 by 2 cross tabulations.

A significant relationship is evident at each of the three time points. In each case, a positive relationship exists between the mother's rating at 1 month of age and the child's subsequent psychosocial development. However, as the child becomes older, more life variables evidently come to play an important part in his development. Needless to say, there is no possible way to account for the diversity of uncontrollable life experiences that these children encounter as they grow. The closest relationship does exist at age 4½ ($X^2 = 18.50$, $p < .00002$) where the phi coefficient is .47. At age 10½, the phi coefficient is .23 ($X^2 = 5.68$; $p < .017$). The phi coefficient at age 15 is .30 for the 81 children rated by the three psychiatrists. (If the ratings of the fourth psychiatrist are included, then phi is equal to .20.)

The number of children evaluated clinically at each age varied. This phenomenon is not unusual in logitudinal research studies. Additional insight can be gained by examining the data pertaining to those children ($N = 42$) evaluated at all three of the time points. The relationship between the NPI and psychiatric ratings can be determined and the idea of transitivity can be considered; that is, can one account for the correlations between the NPI and psychiatric evaluations at age 10/11 and at age 15 in terms of the correlations between the psychiatric evaluations at ages 4½ and 10/11 and at ages 10/11 and 15? This can be restated in the following way. Transitivity for the 10/11 age data would mean that the correlation between the NPI and age 10/11 evaluation is equal to the product of the correlation between the NPI with the 4½ year evaluation and the correlation of age 4½ and 10/11. Similarly, the correlation between the NPI and the age 15 evaluation would equal the product of the three earlier correlations, i.e., NPI with 4½, 4½ with 10/11, and 10/11 with 15.

Forty-two children were evaluated at all three of the time points. Table 3.6 contains the correlation matrix for the four measures.

The correlations between the NPI rating and each of the three psychiatric ratings are somewhat higher for the subpopulation of 42 children than for the total population evaluated at each age. Data contained in Tables 3.5 and 3.6 show the following comparison: .50 versus .47 for age 4½; .36 versus .23 for age 10/11; .39 versus .30 for age 15. All three are still statistically significant and the correlation at age 4½ is still the largest. The correlations in the off diagonal represent the closest time points and these would be expected to be larger. This is true for Table 3.6, where r_{12} = .50 for NPI and age 4½, r_{23} = .47 for age 4½ and age 10/11, and r_{34} = .46 for age 10/11 and age 15.

To check for transitivity for age 10/11 data, the correlation between NPI and 10/11 (r_{13}) is compared with the product of the correlation between NPI with 4½ (r_{12}) and 4½ with 10/11 (r_{23}). It can be seen that r_{13} = .36, which is greater than (r_{12}) (r_{23}) = .2350. Similarly, for the age 15 data r_{14} is compared with the product of r_{12}, r_{23}, and r_{34}. This indicates that r_{14} = .39, which is greater than (.50) (.47) (.46) = .1081. This implies that the relationship between NPI and the psychiatric ratings at ages 10/11 and 15 is more than can be accounted for by the explanation that the mother's rating affected development only during the early years. The correlation of the NPI with the age 15 psychiatric rating is over three times as large as would be expected if there were no carry-over effect beyond age 4½.

Another way to look at the relationship between NPI and subsequent development is as follows. Among the 42 children for whom a psychiatric rating was available at each time point, 16 (38.09%) had been rated negatively on the NPI and 26 (61.90%) rated positively. Examination of the frequency distribution of the number of psychiatric ratings of disorder at ages 4½, 10/11, and 15 revealed that seven of the children had been diagnosed as free of disorder at all three of the evaluations. All these children had positive NPI scores. Table 3.7 summarizes this data. As noted in Table 3.7, only positively rated NPI children were diagnosed as free of mental disorder at all three of the evaluations. None of the negatively rated NPI children were found to be free of mental disorder at all three of the evaluations. The X^2 value for this table is 9.51; 3df; $p < .025$, indicating a significant association between the two variables. Because the categories can be considered as ordered, the gamma coefficient is also appropriate. In this instance the gamma is .80, which again indicates a strong positive relationship between the variables. Children rated positively on the NPI are much more likely to be

TABLE 3.6
Correlation Matrix for NPI and Psychiatric Ratings at Ages 4 ½, 10/11, and 15 (N = 42)

		Psychiatric Ratings		
	NPI	*4½*	*10/11*	*15*
NPI	1.0	.50	.36	.39
		($p < .001$)	($p < .021$)	($p < .012$)
4½		1.0	.47	.28
			($p < .003$)	($p < .071$)
10/11			1.0	.46
				($p < .003$)
15				1.0

TABLE 3.7
Cross Classification of NPI Rating and Subsequent Diagnostic History at
Ages 4½, 10/11, and 15 Years

NPI Rating	Number of Times Diagnosed As Free of Mental Disorder				
	Three	Two	One	None	Total
Positive	7	6	9	4	26
	26.92%	23.07%	34.61%	15.38%	
Negative	0	1	5	10	16
		6.25%	31.25%	62.5%	
Total	7	7	14	14	42

$X^2 = 9.51$; 3df; $P < .025$

rated free of mental disorder over the three evaluations than are children rated negatively. Those children rated negatively on the NPI are more likely to have had a diagnosis of mental disorder at all three of the evaluations than those who had been rated positively on the NPI at 1 month of age (62.5% vs. 15.38%). The distribution was similar for males and females alike.

The Relationship of Other Selected Variables to Psychosocial Development and the NPI Risk Rating

No association was demonstrated between either the NPI Risk Rating or the Psychiatric Ratings and the following variables: the type of delivery, religious preference, maternal age at delivery, educational level of the parents, the father's occupation, prenatal or postpartum complications, moves or deaths of significant others during the year prior to pregnancy or after delivery, the frequency of hospitalization of the child, illness within the nuclear family, changes in income since delivery, or the sex of the child.

SUMMARY DISCUSSION

The Pittsburgh Firstborn project began in 1963 as a study of the natural history of the developmental outcome of firstborns. When the study began, the author asked the parents if they would be willing to share their experiences in raising their firstborns in order that more could be learned about their parenting experiences and the children's development as they grew. Parents were told that findings from the study of their experiences in raising firstborns might be of help to other parents in the future.

This chapter represents a report of the data analysis of the evaluation of psychosocial development of firstborns during midadolescence. The data indicate that the association between the maternal perception of the neonate and the subsequent psychosocial development of the child has persisted over time and is predictive of the probability of mental disorder at age 15 among the firstborns. The experience to date indicates that the Neonatal Perception Inventories have shown construct and criterion validity and provide an easily administered screening measure that can predict the adaptive potential of a given infant–mother pair and identify a population of infants at high risk for subsequent psychosocial difficulty.

The presence of a positive maternal perception during the first month of life does not guarantee that there will be no difficulties in the child's subsequent development. The absence of a positive maternal perception of the neonate is associated with a very high rate of subsequent psychopathology. When things do not go well between a mother and child, this does not imply a conscious rejection on the part of the mother. There may be a variety of factors involved in the actual life situation (e.g., a mother being upset over a distressing family event, a physical illness, or a lack of confidence in her ability to be a mother). It can be postulated, on one hand, that the unique personality characteristics of the neonate, or innate genetic characteristics, are detected very early by the mother and that her rating represents a "true" picture of the child. On the other hand, it can be postulated that the mother's expectations may influence the child's behavior to the extent that these become a self-fulfilling prophecy. The fact that these infants were considered to be "normal" by the physicians providing health care tends to support the latter, that is, maternal perception has an influence on development. In either event, the fact that as early as 1 month of age we can predict a population of infants at higher risk offers a basis for planning programs aimed at primary prevention.

Any research can be considered an intervention in that there is some impact by virtue of the subjects having been chosen for intensive study. Whatever impact there may have been was consistent for all subjects. Through the years, I respected the original agreement with the subjects: that my role was one of researcher. I did not assume the role of an active practitioner of medicine. These families did not live in isolation and many professional resources were available to them through the usual channels available to families. They did not consider me to be responsible for providing primary health care. Occasionally, a parent would express some concern about a child and ask for an opinion. In these instances, the families were referred back to their source of pediatric care with the statement that the physician who had been providing care over time knew the children best. In a few instances, parents called again after having talked with their family physician and specifically asked for a psychiatric referral or referral to a mental health clinic. When this occurred, the request was honored. It was interesting to note that even when I responded to the parents' specific request for referral, there was little follow through with obtaining that help. The author was aware that pathology in the child was often syntonic within the family system and aware that parents often did not consider problems in their child as being problems about which they wished to take action. If at anytime I had been concerned that the firstborn (or parent) was in danger of harming himself or others, I would have intervened.

In a number of instances, a parent sought psychiatric help for him or herself. There is no way to know what impact a parent's treatment had on his or her relationship to the child and the child's subsequent development. One might anticipate that the parent's treatment would be beneficial to all family relationships and to the firstborn's development as well. Further data analysis and careful study of individual subjects is currently in process in order to assess the relative contribution of respective life variables to developmental outcome.

The author is often asked, ''Surely, you do not mean that 75% of the population of 15-year-old firstborns have some kind of psychosocial disorder?'' Indeed, this is what the author means. This is not to say that 75% are psychotic or extremely impaired. This author believes that within the total continuum of psychosocial functioning, a significant portion of firstborns are functioning less than optimally. It is important to note the outcome measures used at each of the three evaluations were clinical assessments conducted by a psychiatrist who had no knowledge of the NPI risk ratings or of the previous psychiatric evaluation. When we look clinically, the magnitude of psychosocial disorder is impressive.

Leon Eisenberg, in a thought provoking article asked the question: ''Is the prevention of mental illness possible in any meaningful sense?'' He contended that it is and cited examples of effective preventive measures (Eisenberg, 1962). I echo his sentiments that efforts at prevention of psychosocial disorder are essential and end this chapter by quoting the title of his paper ''If Not Now, When?''

ACKNOWLEDGMENTS

This research was supported by the Staunton Farm Foundation, Pittsburgh, PA, NIH General Research Support Grant FR5451, and the University of Pittsburgh.

The author would like to express appreciation to Ching Chun Li, Ph.D., University Professor of Biometry and Human Genetics, Department of Biostatistics, Graduate School of Public Health, and Charles Stegman, Ph.D., Associate Professor of Education, Department of Educational Research Methodology, for their consultation regarding statistical analysis of the data.

REFERENCES

Broussard, E. R. (1976). Neonatal prediction and outcome at 10/11 years. *Child Psychiatry and Human Development, 7*, 85–93.

Broussard, E. R. (1979). Assessment of the adaptive potential of the mother–infant system: The neonatal perception inventories. *Seminars in Perinatology, 3* (1), 91–100.

Broussard, E. R., & Hartner, M. S. S. (1970). Maternal perception of the neonate as related to development. *Child Psychiatry and Human Development, 1*, 16–25.

Broussard, E. R., & Hartner, M. S. S. (1971). Further considerations regarding maternal perception of the firstborn. In J. Hellmuth, (ed.), *Exceptional infant. Studies in abnormalities* (Vol. 2). New York: Brunner/Mazel.

Cohen, S. E., & Parmelee, A. H. (1983). Prediction of five-year Stanford–Binet scores in preterm infants. *Child Development, 54* (5), 1242–1253.

Eisenberg, L. (1962). If not now, when? *American Journal of Orthopsychiatry, 32,* 781–793.

Freud, A. (1965). *Normality of pathology in childhood.* New York: International Universities Press.

Group for the Advancement of Psychiatry, Committee on Child Psychiatry (1966). *Psychopathological disorders in childhood: Theoretical considerations and a proposed classification.* New York: Jason Aronson.

Kopp, C. B., & Krakow, J. B. (1983). The developmentalist and the study of biological risk: A view of the past with an eye toward the future. *Child Development, 54* (5), 1086–1108.

Leighton, D. C., Harding, J. S., & Macklin, D. B., Hughes, C. C., Leighton, A. H. (1963). Psychiatric findings of the Stirling County Study. *American Journal of Psychiatry, 119,* 1021–1026.

Parnas, J., Schulsinger, F., Schulsinger, H., Mednick, S., & Teasdale, T. (1982). Behavioral precursors of schizophrenia spectrum. *Archives of General Psychiatry, 39,* 658–670.

Sameroff, A. J. (1981). Longitudinal studies of preterm infants: A review of chapters 17–20. In S. L. Friedman & M. Sigman (Eds.), *Preterm birth and psychological development.* New York: Academic Press.

4

Discussion of Chapters 1–3

Rachel Gittelman

DISCUSSION

The three chapters approach the problem of early predictors of later psychopathology from very different perspectives. They share the common characteristic of reporting on adolescent status, therefore affording the opportunity to compare results.

Disregarding methodological considerations, one is puzzled by differences across the three investigations in rate of identified psychiatric disorder. Thus, at the age of 15, 54 of 99 (53%) of Broussard's subjects are considered ill (eliminating the doubtful cases), whereas only 33% of the sample in Shaffer et al.'s study are. The contrast is even more striking if only boys are considered in Broussard's cohort, because, among the males, 59% were evaluated to be psychiatrically ill in adolescence. True, the two samples were very different because in one instance it was all black (Shaffer et al.), and in the other practically all white (Broussard). Furthermore, there are clear social class differences. But, surprisingly, the group at higher risk for behavioral problems, the lower class disadvantaged group, is the one in which the lower prevalence of psychiatric problems was found.

In contrast, Meyer–Bahlburg et al. do not report any serious psychopathology in their groups of adolescents exposed to sex hormones in utero. These authors did not conduct systematic diagnostic interviews, but it seems that through parental and direct interviews they obtained a very good sense of the youngsters' adjustment. Their seemingly negative findings with regard to psychiatric disorders is not problematic because, of necessity, they were studying small groups of adolescents and it is quite possible to obtain groups of 20 or 30 individuals free of diagnosable mental disorder.

Broussard may have found a greater prevalence of deviance because her concerns were not limited to the identification of mental disorder but encompassed broader and subtler issues of interpersonal adjustment. From the report, this does not appear to be the case because Dr. Broussard explicitly states that psychiatric interviews were geared to elicit the presence of mental disorder.

The great advantage of the Shaffer study is the availability of objective diagnostic criteria, which did not exist when Dr. Broussard conducted her studies. The existence of stipulated behavioral characteristics for various mental disorders certainly will not eliminate vexing inconsistencies such as those found in these chapters, but it is hoped that it will do much to reduce them. At the least, diagnostic definitions enable easier implementation of reliability estimates. The lack of reliability data on the mothers' ratings of their infants, and of the psychiatric evaluation, is indeed unfortunate in the study by Dr. Broussard. Another substantial omission concerns the nature of psychiatric disorders at various age levels; this information is altogether lacking. Given the importance of this measure in the investigator's work, it is curious that no attention is given to it. In view of the theoretical underpinnings of the study, different patterns of psychological dysfunction would be expected in the low- and high- risk groups.

The results are most impressive, and at the same time most troubling, with regard to the continuity of psychiatric disorder from age 4 on. Thus, it is reported that not a single child diagnosed at the age of 4½ was free of a psychiatric disorder later on. Even infantile autism, the most tenacious of early childhood mental disorders, has some, though admittedly very modest, rate of recovery. The reported unanimity in early and late dysfunction is not consistent with a now large literature that, as it accumulates, reveals a great deal more discontinuity in development than had been hitherto anticipated (for some of this work see Shaffer & Dunn, 1979).

Thus, even if the real methodological limitation of attrition is discounted, not a trivial concern because at age 15 only 31% of the original children were reexamined, the results are surprising. If they are substantiated by further investigations, where more explicit criteria for the presence of mental disorders are included, and an acceptable proportion of the original cohort is retrieved at follow-up, Dr. Broussard will have made an extremely important contribution.

Dr. Shaffer's group has conducted a systematic, careful investigation in an area that has been of great interest, but which has generated very little empirical data. Professional attitudes toward neurological soft signs have varied from attributing to them specific diagnostic significance to discounting them altogether. The results of the study are important, if only because they indicate that soft neurological signs may be relatively stable phenomena. This is in itself a useful contribution. Puzzlingly, they are found to predict affective disorders— the type of psychiatric condition one would least expect to be associated with neurological impairment because mood disorders so far have not been linked to various developmental disorders of childhood. Much of the adult literature on characteristics of CNS function in adult depressives does not document that positive findings are trait, rather than state, phenomena. In other words, among adults, though depression may be associated with certain right hemisphere abnormalities, those have not been shown to predict the occurrence of depressive disorders, nor to persist beyond the clinical mood disorder.

The association between depression and stable neurological abnormality is all the more unexpected because, in the study of adult inpatients by Quitkin, Rifkin, and Klein (1976), quoted by Shaffer et al., where similar measures were obtained without knowledge of the patients' diagnoses, neurological soft signs were not overrepresented among depressed patients. The association between neurological soft signs and current or recent depressive disorders is weakened somewhat by the application of more stringent standards for the presence of such disorders. For instance, of the 15 patients included among those with recent depressive disorders, five received diagnoses that are equivocal in their relationship to affective symptomatology (two were diagnosed as schizoaffective, two as panic disorder, one as overanxious). The distribution in the remaining 10 patients with affective disorder (6 manic–depressive patients, 1 atypical depressive, 3 adjustment reactions with depression) is still disproportionate—8 are in the soft sign and 2 in the control group. However the difference between the two groups is no longer significant, but a trend persists (uncorrected $X^2 = 3.40$, $p = .066$). Of great interest is the presence of six cases of bipolar illness, all in the neurological soft sign group. A rate of 10% of bipolar illness in this group of boys who are below the age-risk period is most unusual. Provocatively, Quitkin et al. (1976) found that patients they called "emotional unstable character disorders," had significantly more soft signs than other patient groups. There are similarities between the bipolar and emotionally unstable groups. Both are described as experiencing periods of marked mood shifts, the difference being that emotionally unstable patients have rapid alternations between high and low moods. Clinical descriptions of the patients with depressive disorders in the adolescent sample would enable comparison between the two studies' results.

It is conceivable that early onset manic–depressive disorder has its origin in deviant brain development in a subgroup of patients. This provocative finding clearly calls for replication. It is hoped that the authors are proceeding to explore this important issue, because confirmation of this unexpected finding would generate new explorations among adolescent manic–depressive disorders.

The review by Meyer–Bahlburg and associates is most interesting not only in documenting the effects of prenatal sex hormones on later deviant behavior, but also in illuminating possible mechanisms for the genesis of normal gender differentiated behavior, and its maintenance over time. Though gender identity is unaffected by in utero exposure to androgens, more subtle aspects of gender-role function seem to be. The report of increased energetic play levels for exposed individuals is consistent with the literature that has documented higher motor activity levels in boys than in girls. This difference does not appear to be a function of cultural expectations (Maccoby & Jacklin, 1974). The effect of prenatal androgens on play patterns is somewhat more surprising given the findings of no differences in the level of nurturing behavior in boys and girls (Maccoby & Jacklin, 1974). However, there are differences in play patterns between the two sexes, especially as age increases. The team led by both senior investigators, Drs. Meyer–Bahlburg and Ehrhardt, has provided the best executed investigations of this developmental issue. Their results strongly suggest that biological factors contribute to what always has been assumed to be socially determined behavior, either through behavioral shaping, i.e., little girls are reinforced for behaving like Mommy and little boys like Daddy, or through unconscious psychological mechanisms, such as defensive identification. The fact that some behaviors may be established more readily in one sex than in the other needs to be considered. Wisely, the authors do not suggest that there is direct hormonal influence on behavior. The model of biological "preparedness for learning" (Seligman & Hager, 1972), wherein the organism is viewed as biologically more amenable to establish certain associations rather than others, seems potentially relevant to an understanding of the influence of sex hormones on complex gender-related activity.

In view of the triad associated with prenatal androgens in women—higher motor activity level, low parentalism, and, less certainly, bisexuality—it would be interesting to learn whether these covary. Are low parentalism and energetic play correlated? Is bisexuality likely to occur in those with more vigorous play and less "playing house" activity? If low parentalism and high energy level coexist, the question arises whether both are an outcome of a substrate, gender dimorphic, process, or whether increased activity is the characteristic that leads to behavior incompatible with quiet games such as "playing house." These alternate patterns can be elucidated. If energy level were the primary factor in role-imitative behaviors, low parentalism would be a mere epiphenomenon of activity level. If so, low parentalism should occur only in children with elevated energy levels. In contrast, if both behaviors were independent products of a third process, the two should occur singly and together with more or less equal frequency. A delineation of these mechanisms would do much to refine our understanding of unsatisfactorily defined terms such as *masculinizing* and *feminizing* influences.

The same questions arise with regard to the effect of prenatal exposure to estrogens on subtle gender-related behaviors. Is the feminizing hormone effect of these compounds a broad one affecting multiple aspects of personality, or are separate individual behaviors affected? Is there a specific characteristic that is influential in determining the appearance of others?

These questions are difficult to answer only because the investigators, perforce, are dependent on experiments of nature, and the number of affected individuals available for study is unavoidably restricted; and, unfortunately, clear conclusions from the application of multivariate approaches require large subject pools. However, considering the excellent track record of the Meyer–Bahlburg and Ehrhardt team, we may feel confident that they will undertake further well-executed studies that will clarify these issues.

REFERENCES

Maccoby, E. E., & Jacklin, C. N. (Eds.). (1974). *The psychology of sex differences*. Stanford: Stanford University Press.

Quitkin, F., Rifkin, A., & Klein, D. F. (1976). Neurologic soft signs in schizophrenia and character disorders. *Archives of General Psychiatry, 33,* 845–853.

Seligman, M. E. P., & Hager, J. L. (Eds.). (1972). *Biological boundaries of learning*. Englewood Cliffs, NJ.: Prentice–Hall.

Shaffer, D., & Dunn, J. (Eds.). (1979). *The first year of life*. London; Wiley.

5 Discussion: Causal Models in Life-Span Research on Psychopathology

Sheppard G. Kellam

The importance of early neurological soft signs, prenatal endocrine milieu, and mother's perception of her newborn are the subjects of the three chapters presented in this volume. The long-term outcomes of these three very different domains of investigation are reported for a variety of populations at risk. The underlying research model implicit in all of these chapters is my subject in this discussion, whereas Dr. Gittleman's discussion is focused on specific aspects of each chapter.

Each of these chapters can be viewed from a life-span developmental perspective. The age span extends from perinatal or thereabouts to adolescence and later. These studies, drawn from widely different arenas, report meaningful antecedents to outcomes that include psychopathology, learning, social-role function, and gender identity. The purpose of such studies is, of course, to understand and thereby to be able to prevent or alter the paths leading to specific outcomes. The long period of life-span between antecedents and outcomes in these studies and others similar in design and purpose calls attention to the potential complex effects of intervening events and conditions on the clarity of the long-term relationships between early origin and adolescent or adult outcome. It is remarkable that these and other recent longitudinal studies, with little attention to such intervening variables, yield results that may be important to causal models.

There are two reasons, however, for changing the strategy in the next stage to one of more complex causal modeling, complex in the sense of including measures of social structure, social adaptational status, psychological, and biological conditions as these evolve during the intervening period of the life cycle. The first reason is that such intervening conditions, if not included in the equation, probably attenuate the strength of relationships we find between early conditions

71

and later outcomes. The second reason is that only rarely are early conditions without intervening or developmental conditions a sufficient explanation of later outcomes. For example, a genetic predisposition for being tall is only part of the explanation of that outcome. Nutrition and the conditions that enhance or inhibit its quality add greatly to the genetic explanation.

CAUSAL MODELS THAT CROSS DISCIPLINES

My thesis is that complex causal models are now necessary and possible and include longitudinal or periodic measures of social structure and social adaptational, psychological, and biological status. The family provides us an example of social structure later in this discussion. In the prior stage of life-span research, far more important work has been done in methodology than in successful theory building in many disciplines. Far more investigators have been trained to work in narrow areas than to collaborate across disciplines important to psychiatric research. We can now develop a much higher level of integration across biological, social, and psychological disciplines than we have been able to do in the past.

Between social structure and the individual is a highly interactive process involving social task demand and the individual's behavioral response. In the Woodlawn studies we have named this demand/response process social adaptation. In each social field at each stage of life there is an individual (occasionally more than one) who defines the social tasks and rates the responding performance of people in that social field. We have termed such individuals natural raters, and their ratings of the adequacy of performance we have named measures of social adaptational status (Kellam, Branch, Agrawal, & Ensminger, 1975; Kellam & Ensminger, 1981). The raters and social fields include parents in the home, teachers in the classroom, supervisors at the work place, and so on. The importance of each social field and the specific nature of the tasks vary as a function of the stage of the life cycle. Chance, the fit of the individual with others in the same social field and with the natural rater, as well as earlier experience, learning, and biological endowment, all may play a role in an individual's social adaptational status in a particular social field. Terms such as *promoted* or *fired, passed* or *failed,* even *married* or *divorced* all carry elements of success and failure in our society and are social adaptational terms. Measures of success or failure in specific stages of life in specific fields may be important in the evolving paths leading to long-term outcomes.

Causal model's whether they involve genetic, early neurological, early endocrine, or early child-rearing characteristics require the inclusion of measures such as evolving family structure, evolving social adaptational status in fields such as school, peer group, or work, and psychological and physical status. Such complex analytic models allow for more clear explanation of the conditions under which early contributions may be enhanced or inhibited by later conditions in relation to outcomes such as depressive illness, for example.

Causal Models and Sex Differences

Sex differences in almost all outcomes relevant to psychiatry have now been demonstrated repeatedly. This variable must also be more often included in the next stage of our causal models. Women at certain stages of life appear to be more at risk of depression than men. Violent behavior and heavy drug and alcohol use are more characteristic of men than women. Many other behaviors that occur more often in one sex than the other could be cited. In recent developmental epidemiological studies, including our own but spanning a variety of laboratories and populations, it appears that these sex differences are important sufficiently to be taken into account in almost all life-span developmental research. In the Meyer–Bahlburg et al. chapter on the endocrine milieu, for example, sex differences appeared again to be important in the long-term outcomes. Indeed, any explanation of a psychopathological outcome that does not at the same time explain the sex differences can be said to be an incomplete explanation. Ensminger and Harris in discussing research on delinquency have separately made this point (Ensminger, Brown, & Kellam, 1982; Harris, 1977).

Causal Models and Periodic Measures:
The Short-Hop Strategy

Genetic and early biological, psychological, and social characteristics will in many if not most cases be more clearly visible in their impact on short-term outcomes early in the life-span than on long-term adolescent or adult outcomes. This hunch is based on the proposition that the longer the age span from the time of the initial early variable the less the contribution of the early variable to later outcome will be clear. Clarke and Clarke (1976) have made this hypothesis in regard to the importance of early family experience. By short-term outcomes I am referring to antecedents found in preschool or in first grade or soon thereafter. Such outcomes become antecedents of later outcomes in adolescence or early adulthood. The search for such short-term outcomes is now proceeding with considerable speed in developmental epidemiology. The search, in turn, for their origins should become an important strategy as more is learned about the consequences of such early antecedents. Studies of genetic contribution to such early predictors as aggressiveness (fighting, breaking rules, truancy) in young male children, for example, may provide an important part in a causal model intended to explain later outcomes.

The strategy implication is to build models that predict to early outcomes, and from early outcomes to longer term outcomes, rather than to jump directly from a

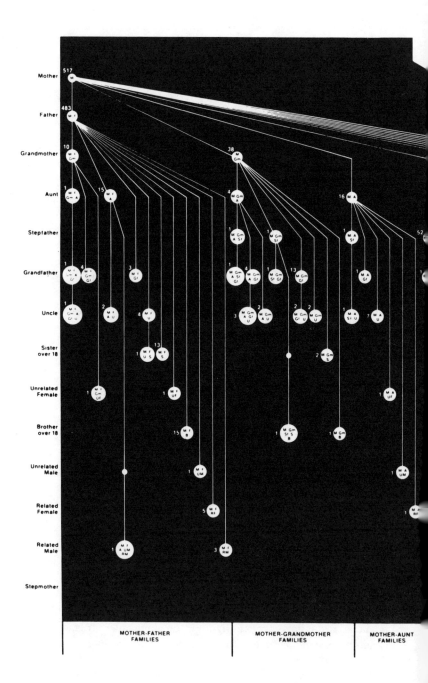

FIG. 5.1.   Variation in fami

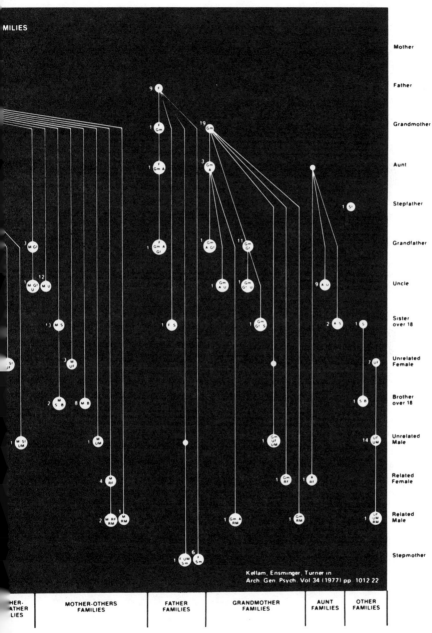

Mother

Father

Grandmother

Aunt

Stepfather

Grandfather

Uncle

Sister
over 18

Unrelated
Female

Brother
over 18

Unrelated
Male

Related
Female

Related
Male

Stepmother

Kellam, Ensminger, Turner in
Arch. Gen. Psych. Vol 34 (1977) pp. 1012 22

| HER-ATHER LIES | MOTHER-OTHERS FAMILIES | FATHER FAMILIES | GRANDMOTHER FAMILIES | AUNT FAMILIES | OTHER FAMILIES |

wn first grade children (1966–1967).

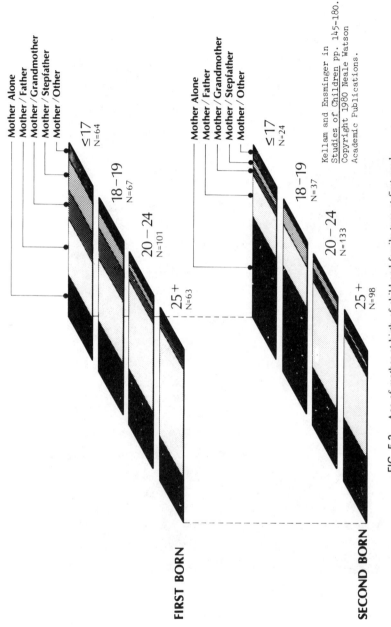

Mother Alone
Mother / Father
Mother / Grandmother
Mother / Stepfather
Mother / Other

≤17
N=64

18–19
N=67

20–24
N=101

25+
N=63

Mother Alone
Mother / Father
Mother / Grandmother
Mother / Stepfather
Mother / Other

≤17
N=24

18–19
N=37

20–24
N=133

25+
N=98

FIRST BORN

SECOND BORN

Kellam and Ensminger in
Studies of Children pp. 145–180.
Copyright 1980 Neale Watson
Academic Publications.

FIG. 5.2. Age of mother at birth of child and family type at first grade.

genetic contribution to an adult outcome such as psychosis. Such predictors as early aggressive behavior (fighting and breaking rules) in first grade or shyness (i.e., tendency to sit alone and not speak up much in the classroom) may well be more easily discernable in relation to their genetic or early developmental origins than an adult diagnostic category may be to genetic origins. There is now considerable evidence for the prediction from antisocial behavior early in life to adolescent and adult delinquency, drug, alcohol, and cigarette use, psychopathology, and adult mental health clinic attendance (e.g., Ensminger, Kellam, & Rubin, 1983; Kellam, Ensminger, & Simon, 1980; Kellam, Brown, & Fleming, 1982; Kellam, Brown, Rubin, & Ensminger, 1983; Robins, 1981; Watt, 1978).

Causal Modeling and Measures of Family Structure

For illustration of the kind of social structure measures I have referred to, let me describe the variations of family types we found raising the first-grade population of Woodlawn, a poor, urban, black community on the south side of Chicago in the school year 1966–67. In that year there were 86 different combinations of adults raising first-grade children. In a prior study (of the 1964–65 population) there had been 79 different combinations with an almost identical taxonomic classification. These types may be collapsed into several major categories for analytic purposes. Mother/father, mother/grandmother, and mother/aunt households were more effective in the Woodlawn child's social adaptation to school and psychological well-being. Mother alone, mother/stepfather, and others were far less effective. These results were replicated in both of these two cohorts (Kellam, Ensminger, & Turner, 1977).

Family types were classified in terms of the adults present at home on the basis of information obtained in the family interview with the mothers (or mother surrogates) of the first-grade children. A taxonomy of the various combinations of adults present in the households of the 1966 population of first-graders' families is shown in Fig. 5.1. We found 10 different adult relatives present in the families, plus four residual categories of relatives and nonrelatives, male and female. These are listed in the left and right margins in the order of their frequency in the Woodlawn families.

The figure is cumulative from top to bottom. If one begins at the upper left-hand corner with mother alone and descends directly downward to mother/father and then to mother/father/grandmother, it may be seen that mother-alone families occur 517 times, mother/father 483 times, mother/father/grandmother 10 times, and mother/father/grandmother/aunt only once. When a combination does not contain the next relative listed in the margins, it is shown by a line moving laterally and downward to the next included relative. Thus, there are 38 mother/grandmother families, four mother/grandmother/aunt families, and so on. Although the number of families in many of the combinations is too small to analyze, the taxonomy illustrates the diversity that exists in the households of first-grade children in this community.

Eight major classes of families, plus a residual "other" category, may be seen in the cone-like clustering of family types. These are named across the bottom of the figure. These nine, plus mother-alone families, yield the 10 major classes of families raising first-grade children in 1966 in Woodlawn.

In two separate total populations of Woodlawn first-grade children, we found mother-alone households the highest risk for the child's maladaptation to first grade and poor psychological well-being. Mother/father, mother/grandmother, and mother/aunt were about equal and were the most effective family types. The absence of the father was not the risk factor, but rather the aloneness of the mother (Kellam et al., 1977).

This illustration conveys the great variation in family environment in which early mother–child interaction, prenatal endocrine milieu, or soft neurological signs will play out their effects on later behavior and psychiatric conditions. In the next stage of research causal models should include such family conditions, along with social adaptational, psychological, and biological status. We can specify far better than previously the kinds of environment in which the child develops and is socialized. Such conditions will add power to our causal analyses in regard to such outcomes as depression or criminality.

A second figure further illustrates this point by including along with family structure the simple variables of whether the mother began child-rearing in her teenage years, and whether the first-grade child in 1966 was her first or second born (Kellam & Ensminger, 1980; Kellam et al., 1983). Each large rectangle in Fig. 5.2 represents the distribution of family types for each age group of mothers for either first-born or second-born first-grade children. From this figure we can see that if the first-grade child is the mother's firstborn, the likelihood of being in a mother-alone (high-risk) family is about the same regardless of her age at her first birth. However, there is a considerable reduction in mother/father (low-risk) families among teenage mothers, with an increase in mother/grandmother (also low-risk) households.

Consider now the family structure of the mother and child if the child is her second born. Here we see that teenage mothers with the advent of a second birth dramatically increase their risk of being in a mother-alone household, with the frequency of both mother/father and mother/grandmother households markedly decreased. Note that the stability is considerable among mother/father households in which mothers began child-rearing when they were older.

SUMMARY

Such specifications allow us to examine the children along a variety of biological, social structural, social adaptational, psychological, and physical characteristics taking into account the interplay of early antecedents and subsequent environment of the child.

Not only can point-in-time classification be done, but longitudinal classification should and can be made of family structure and other social contextual characteristics. Mother-alone households that remain mother alone can be specified, along with mother/father that remain mother/father, mother/father that separate, and mother/grandmother that remain mother/grandmother or split. Change or stability in these family structures and in the other intervening measures can be classified.

I have argued in this discussion that, in order to understand the relationships of early biological and social characteristics to outcomes in adolescence or adulthood, the next generation of causal models must include systematic specifications of intervening variables in which the interplay of the biological, social structural, social adaptational, and psychological variables can be assessed. Otherwise, these intervening variables in all likelihood will attenuate and confuse us as to any contributions that the early variables make to the later outcomes.

REFERENCES

Clarke, A. M., & Clarke, A. D. B. (Eds.). (1976). *Early experience: Myth and evidence* (Chapter 1). New York: The Free Press.

Ensminger, M. E., Brown, C. H., & Kellam, S. G. (1982). Sex differences in antecedents of substance use among adolescents. *Journal of Social Issues 38*, 25–42.

Ensminger, M. E., Kellam, S. G., & Rubin, B. R. (1983). School and family origins of delinquency: Comparisons by sex. In K. T. Van Dusen & S. A. Mednick (Eds.), Prospective studies of crime and delinquency (pp. 73–97). Boston: Kluwer-Nijhoff.

Harris, A. R. (1977). Sex and theories of deviance: Toward a functional theory of deviant type scripts. *American Sociological Review, 42*, 3–16.

Kellam, S. G., Branch, J. D., Agrawal, K. C., & Ensminger, M. E. (1975). *Mental health and going to school: The woodlawn program of assessment, early intervention, and evaluation.* Chicago: University of Chicago Press. Reprinted in paperback by same publisher, 1979.

Kellam, S. G., Brown, C. H., & Fleming, J. P. (1982). Social adaptation to first grade and teenage drug, alcohol, and cigarette use: Developmental epidemiological research in Woodlawn. *Journal of School Health*, 301–306.

Kellam, S. G., Brown, C. H., Rubin, B. R., & Ensminger, M. E. (1983). Developmental paths leading to teenage psychiatric symptoms and substance use: Developmental epidemiological studies in Woodlawn. In S. B. Guze, F. J. Earls, & J. E. Barrett (Eds.), *Childhood psychopathology and development* (pp. 17–51). New York: Raven Press.

Kellam, S. G., & Ensminger, M. E. (1980). Theory and method in child psychiatric epidemiology. In F. Earls, (Ed.) *Studying children epidemiologically,* International Monograph Series in Psychosocial Epidemiology, Vol. 1 (pp. 145–180). New York: Neale Watson Academic Publishers.

Kellam, S. G., Ensminger, M. E., & Simon, M. B. (1980). Mental health in first grade and teenage drug, alcohol, and cigarette use. *Drug and Alcohol Dependence, 5*, 273–304.

Kellam, S. G., Ensminger, M. E., & Turner, R. J. (1977). Family structure and the mental health of children: Concurrent and longitudinal community-wide studies. *Archives of General Psychiatry, 34*, 1012–1022.

Robins, L. N. (1981). Epidemiological approaches to natural history research. *Journal of the American Academy of Child Psychiatry, 20*, 556–580.

Watt, N. F. (1978). Patterns of childhood social development in adult schizophrenics. *Archives of General Psychiatry, 35*, 160–165.

6 Children at High Risk for Schizophrenia: Predictions From Infancy to Childhood Functioning

Yvonne Marcuse
Barbara Cornblatt

The offspring of schizophrenics are known to have a greatly increased risk for becoming schizophrenic—as high as 40% for children with two schizophrenic parents and 10–15% for those with a single affected parent, compared to only 1% in the general population. This increased rate of morbidity makes it economically feasible to conduct longitudinal research on preschizophrenics. Such studies have two main objectives. One important goal is to obtain a natural history of the premorbid period, uncontaminated by knowledge of eventual outcome. Another, perhaps even more critical, objective is to identify early predictive indicators that may clarify the etiology of the disorder and serve as targets for preventive intervention.

In this chapter we consider the prediction of childhood characteristics in the offspring of schizophrenics from observations made during infancy. We concentrate on two types of indicators that have been examined in the literature on high-risk children in the infant age range. The first issue, that of obstetrical and perinatal complications, has received considerable attention since Mednick and Schulsinger (1968) described a high incidence of pregnancy and birth complications in the disturbed offspring of schizophrenic parents. The second type of indicators, neurological "soft signs," includes a variety of motor dysfunctions, visual–motor deficits, right–left confusion, and other subtle, nonlocalizing neurological abnormalities. Soft signs in high-risk infants have long been the focus of Barbara Fish's work (1977, in press; Fish & Alpert, 1962), but other research on such infants has both corroborated and failed to corroborate her findings. Following a brief review of the literature on each of these two areas, we discuss data on infants born to schizophrenic parents in the New York sample of a nationwide prospective study on pregnancy, infancy, and early childhood.

Obstetric Complications

McNeil and Kaij (1978) reviewed over 80 papers relating to obstetric factors in the development of schizophrenia. Most of these studies used fairly reliable prospectively recorded data, such as birth certificates or hospital records; several used prospective data from the Collaborative Perinatal Project (CPP) of the National Institute of Neurological and Communicative Disorders and Stroke (see METHODS, following, for a description of the CPP). However, the studies differ greatly in the kinds of complications, psychiatric diagnostic criteria, comparison groups, and results obtained. Table 6.1 summarizes the results of the studies that have examined obstetric complications in offspring of schizophrenics compared to control groups. Terms used in the table and elsewhere in this chapter are those that McNeil and Kaij (1978) defined in their review paper as follows:

1. *Pregnancy complications* (PC's) are all unusual somatic events occurring between conception and the onset of labor.
2. *Birth complications* (BC's) include all complications of labor and delivery.
3. *Neonatal complications* (NC's) are those conditions occurring in the newborn from birth through 2–4 weeks postpartum.
4. Overall *obstetric complications* (OC's) is a summary score combining PC's, BC's, and NC's.

The table does not distinguish between comparisons of high-risk children with offspring of normal parents and comparisons with offspring of parents with nonschizophrenic psychiatric disorders (i.e., a significant difference indicates that the schizophrenics' offspring are different from *all* controls).

The outcomes of these studies show few significant differences between the high-risk children and their controls in birthweight, PC's, BC's, NC's, or overall OC rates. In two studies, however, fetal and neonatal deaths were significantly more frequent in index pregnancies. Also in contradiction to the pattern of generally negative results are several findings of low birthweight among offspring of schizophrenics, and the 1978 report by McNeil and Kaij of increased NC's and OC's in a high-risk sample studied in Sweden. In recent work, Mednick and colleagues continue to find obstetric complications in Danish (Feldman, Mednick, Schulsinger, & Fuchs unpublished manuscript) and Finnish (Wrede, Mednick, Huttunen, & Nilsson in press) samples of children born to schizophrenics.

Mednick's first high-risk study (Mednick, 1970; Mednick & Schulsinger, 1968) remains the only attempt to relate OC's in the offspring of schizophrenics to their adult psychiatric outcome. A subgroup of high-risk offspring, who were judged to be severely disturbed in 1968 as teenagers, were reported to have been

TABLE 6.1

Differences Reported in the Literature Between Offspring of Schizophrenics and Controls in Pregnancy and Perinatal Complication Rates

	Low Birthweight	PC's	BC's	NC's	OC's	Fetal/Neonatal Deaths
Paffenbarger et al., 1961	*					NS
Sobel, 1961						*
Mednick & Schulsinger, 1968					NS	
Yarden & Suranyi, 1968	NS					
Lane & Albee, 1970	NS					
Mednick, 1970					*	
Mednick et al., 1971	NS	NS	NS	NS	NS	
McNeil & Kaij, 1973	NS	NS	NS	NS	NS	
Mednick et al., 1973	*					
Sameroff & Zax, 1973		NS	NS	NS	NS	
McNeil et al., 1974	NS				NS	
Mizrahi et al., 1974	NS					
Rieder et al., 1975	NS	NS	NS	NS	NS	*
Schachter et al., 1975	NS	NS	*	NS	NS	
Hanson et al., 1976	NS	NS	NS	NS	NS	NS
Rieder et al., 1977		NS	NS	NS	NS	
Zax et al., 1977	*	NS	NS	*	*	NS
McNeil & Kaij, 1978			NS	NS	NS	
Wrede et al., in press		*	NS	NS	NS	
Feldman et al., unpublished		*			*	

*Complications more prevalent in offspring of schizophrenics ($p < .05$)

83

characterized both by anomalous autonomic responses when tested several years earlier and by high rates of obstetrical complications. However, these relationships are unclear because later examination (H. Schulsinger, 1976) of the high-risk group showed that some members who had been called "sick" in 1968 were no longer disturbed, whereas others who had been considered to be "well" in 1968 had become disturbed in the meantime.

Motor Development and Neurological Soft Signs

Like the research on obstetrical factors, which has yielded mixed results, investigations of neurological and motor signs in high-risk infants have produced inconsistent findings. Beginning with Barbara Fish's (1971, in press; Fish & Alpert, 1962) studies on babies born to schizophrenic mothers, there are many suggestions in the literature that subtle neurological disturbances in childhood may be related to eventual schizophrenia. These defects do not take the form of overt brain damage or localized nervous system dysfunction. Instead they appear as generalized deficits of motor performance, visual–motor integrations, muscle tone, growth, and sensitivity to stimuli—a complex that Fish (1977) has labeled *pandevelopmental retardation*. Fish has found these signs in infants who became schizophrenic during childhood and therefore manifested what she considers to be the most extreme pathology in the schizophrenic spectrum (Fish, 1975). However, many workers do not agree with Fish's assumption that there is a clear genetic continuity between childhood and adult schizophrenia. Furthermore, Fish's study has yielded an unusually high percentage of childhood schizophrenics compared to other studies of the offspring of schizophrenics, making her findings somewhat difficult to assess.

Other evidence of deviant neurological development in high-risk infants has been reported by Mednick and colleagues (Mednick, Mura, Schulsinger, & Mednick, 1971) in their "OB" study of children in a large Danish birth cohort, by Ragins, Schachter, Elmer, Preisman, Bowes, & Harway (1975) studying infants of schizophrenic mothers in Pittsburgh, and by Marcus and coworkers in Israel (1981). But three further studies do not show differences in neurological development between infants of schizophrenics and other infants. Ragins et al. (1975) found no significant differences between the retrospective reports of schizophrenic and normal control mothers about their children's neuromotor development in infancy or their ages at attainment of developmental milestones. Using the Minnesota sample of the Collaborative Perinatal Project, Hanson, Gottesman, and Heston (1976) found no differences between infants of schizophrenic parents and infants of normal parents or parents with other psychiatric disorders on a variety of measures, including neurological variables. McNeil and Kaij (1984) in Sweden, too, have failed to find high-risk infants to be excessively deviant neurologically, with "clear neurological abnormalities" occurring at higher rates among babies whose mothers had other psychiatric disorders and groups of babies with normal control mothers.

Neurological dysfunctions have been reported more consistently in school-age children of schizophrenic parents. In the Israeli study initiated by Rosenthal (1971), Marcus (1974) found high frequencies of soft signs, including disorders of fine motor coordination and left–right orientation, among the high-risk subjects; these signs were especially prevalent among high-risk boys under the age of 11. A recent neurological and behavioral study of high-risk infants by Marcus and colleagues (1981) appears to support the earlier results on older children, and these investigators indicate that a striking feature common to both the Israeli school-age study and the infant study, as well as to Mednick's Danish data that Marcus reanalyzed (Marcus, Wilkinson, Burack, Mednick & Schulsinger, 1980), is that a substantial subgroup of the high-risk sample falls below the range of scores exhibited by the controls.

Although Hanson et al. (1976) were unable to identify any neurological problems of significance in high-risk infants, they noted poor motor skills in a substantial proportion of these subjects at later ages and, interestingly, that poor motor skills were combined with large intraindividual variability on psychological tests and with "schizoid" behavior at age 7 in 17% of the high-risk children. Rieder and Nichols (1979), also working with a sample (Boston) of the Collaborative Perinatal Project, described an association between hyperactivity and soft signs, especially poor coordination, in the male offspring of schizophrenic parents.

In an ongoing prospective study of children of schizophrenic parents in the New York metropolitan region, Erlenmeyer–Kimling and colleagues (Erlenmeyer–Kimling, 1975; Erlenmeyer–Kimling, Marcuse, Cornblatt, Friedman, Rainer, & Rutschmann, 1984) have observed deficiencies in gross and fine motor skills—especially in the latter—in each of two independent samples. High-risk subjects in both samples showed impaired motor functioning on a modified version of the Lincoln–Oseretsky test of motor impairment. High-risk subjects in the first sample were not significantly different than children of depressed or normal parents on the pediatric neurology examination, but there was a nonsignificant trend suggesting that younger (below age 11) high-risk males had poor neurological functioning compared to other subjects in the sample. Subjects in the second sample were given an improved version of the neurological examination that included more soft sign items, and between-group differences were accordingly stronger than in the first sample. As in the first sample, the neuromotor deviations were most noticeable in high-risk boys below the age of 11, a finding similar to that reported by Marcus (1974).

As a whole, the studies of neuromotor functioning in children of schizophrenic parents point to the presence of disturbances in such children at young ages. Why the studies of infancy are discrepant is unclear, but the studies that have examined high-risk children of school age clearly indicate that neuromotor deviations occur in a subgroup of these children. The relationship between neuromotor development in childhood and the later emergence of psychopathology in such samples is, however, not yet known.

OC's in Relation to Soft Signs

The relationship between obstetric factors and neurological signs in high-risk children is also unresolved. Only in a handful of studies has the nature of this association been examined, and those studies that have addressed this issue reveal a very inconsistent picture. For example, Fish (1977) reported no relationship at all between obstetric factors and neurological signs: None of the children with pandevelopmental retardation, including two childhood schizophrenics, had histories of OC's (overall obstetric complications) and none of the children with OC's had developmental problems in childhood. By contrast, both the Marcus infant study (Marcus et al., 1981) and the Mednick "OB" project (Mednick et al., 1971) showed an association between low birthweight and developmental dysfunctioning in the first year among high-risk, but not among control, subjects; these projects unfortunately lack childhood outcome data at this time.

Most studies that have examined OC's in high-risk children have simply neglected the question of neurological sequelae. Conversely, studies that have reported an excess of soft signs usually have only retrospective data, or none at all, on the obstetric histories of the mothers. To avoid the biases associated with retrospective data and also to relate OC's to childhood neurological status, it is necessary to collect data prospectively from the earliest possible point in the mother's pregnancy until the child reaches an age such that his development may be reliably assessed. We have attempted to do this by investigating the relationship between PC's (pregnancy complications) and neurological outcome in a sample of children with schizophrenic parents from the Collaborative Perinatal Project (see METHODS, later), which recorded prospective obstetrical information on more than 55,000 pregnancies along with thorough neurological follow-up of the offspring from birth to age 7.

METHODS

The Collaborative Perinatal Project

Data were collected during 1959–1973 by the Collaborative Perinatal Study on Cerebral Palsy, Mental Retardation, and other Neurological and Sensory Disorders of Infancy and Childhood, a nationwide study conducted by the Perinatal Branch of the National Institute of Neurological and Communicative Disorders and Stroke (Berendes, 1966; Niswander & Gordon, 1972). In the Collaborative Perinatal Project (CPP), detailed histories were recorded on approximately 55,000 women and their pregnancies at 12 participating hospitals across the country, and the children of these pregnancies were followed with thorough medical and behavioral examinations at prescribed intervals through the age of 7 years. Three of the 12 hospitals participating in the CPP are located in New York State: Buffalo Children's Hospital in Buffalo and Columbia Presbyterian and New York Hospitals in New York City. The study reported here was confined to the 5800 pregnancies that were followed in these three collaborating hospitals, and data from the three hospitals are combined to form the New York State subsample of the CPP.

Although not intended to be a study of psychopathology, the CPP collected prospective data on many areas of child development that have received close attention in the search for antecedents of schizophrenia. Specifically, there is excellent information on the maternal and familial health history, the mother's past and present obstetrical history, labor, and delivery, the baby's neonatal status and follow-up observations from 4 months to 7 years, emphasizing the child's physical health (including neurological status), and the development of motor, linguistic, perceptual, and intellectual skills. Neurological examinations were performed by staff neurologists in the collaborating hospitals. The soft signs that were evaluated included those reported most frequently in the schizophrenia and high-risk literature: locomotor and postural development, fine and gross motor coordination, lateral dominance and left–right identification, muscle tone and reflexes. The fact that schizophrenia was not the focus of the CPP suggests that these data are relatively free of examiner biases that may occur when the purpose of a study is known to the observers.

Subjects

A sample of 22 children at high risk for schizophrenia was ascertained by screening the CPP files for children from the New York State subsample whose parents (one or both) reported any history of treatment for a psychiatric disorder. Children were eliminated from the study if their parents belonged to racial groups other than white or black and if a language other than English was spoken in the home. Hospitalizations in New York State psychiatric facilities were confirmed through the state's Department of Mental Hygiene, and records were obtained from the admitting institutions.

It proved possible to locate and secure access to the records of 66 State hospital patients and 44 Presbyterian Hospital patients. Of these 110 sets of records, 49 were eliminated from further consideration because they seemed unlikely to support a diagnosis of schizophrenia. These exclusions were either (1) uncomplicated cases of organic disorder, alcoholism, or narcotics addiction or (2) clinic patients who were seen only intermittently as outpatients and whose

TABLE 6.2
Interrater Agreement on RDC Diagnoses of Parents

1. *Agreement on strict diagnosis:*	
Schizophrenia or schizoaffective (mainly schizophrenic)	20
Schizoaffective (mainly affective) or other affective disorder	18
Other diagnosis	19
2. *Disagreement on strict* and *agreement on intent diagnosis:*	
Schizophrenia or schizoaffective (mainly schizophrenic)	1
Schizoaffective (mainly affective) or other affective disorder	1
Other diagnosis	0
3. *Disagreement on both strict and intent diagnoses:*	2
Total:	61

records gave no evidence of psychiatric hospitalization or serious functional impairment.

The remaining 61 cases were diagnosed according to the Research Diagnostic Criteria (Spitzer, Endicott, & Robins, 1978) by two raters trained in the use of the RDC by the Spitzer-Endicott research group at Psychiatric Institute. Results of the diagnostic review are shown in Table 6.2. In addition to the strict RDC diagnosis, which requires a very literal interpretation of available information, each rater gave an "intent" diagnosis based upon her impression of what the RDC diagnosis would most probably be if specific additional information were available. However, interrater agreement was high for strict RDC judgments and it proved unnecessary to rely upon intent diagnoses in all except one of the cases reported here.

The two raters agreed on the strict diagnosis in 57 cases out of the total of 61, i.e., with 93.4% agreement. Twenty cases whose ratings agreed at the strict level and one case with agreement at the intent level received diagnoses in the "schizophrenia spectrum," which for our purposes includes all subtypes of schizophrenia as well as the RDC diagnosis "schizoaffective disorders, mainly schizophrenic." The 22 children of these 21 parents comprise the high-risk sample. Tables 6.3 and 6.4 show the distributions by sex and race of the parents and children in the high-risk group. It should be noted that the parent sample

TABLE 6.3
Distribution by Sex and Race of Index Parents

	White	Black	Total
Schizophrenic Fathers:	2	1	3
Schizophrenic Mothers:	7	11	18
Total:	9[a]	12	21

[a]Includes 2 pairs of schizophrenic spouses

TABLE 6.4
Distribution by Sex and Race of Index
Children

	White	Black	Total
Males:	6	4	10
Females:	2	10	12
Total:	8[a]	14[b]	22

[a]Includes 1 pair of opposite-sex siblings
[b]Includes 1 pair of opposite-sex siblings and 1
pair of sisters

includes two pairs of schizophrenic spouses, each having one child in the sample, and also that three of the other parents have two children each. The sample of high-risk children includes 10 boys and 12 girls, and the largest single category is black girls.

A comparison group consisting of 88 low-risk children with no family history of mental illness was selected from the total pool of CPP cases who passed the screening for race and language. Four comparison children were matched to each high-risk child on the basis of hospital where born, race, sex, mother's age, and socioeconomic index. Five high-risk children dropped out of the study before age 7. This report includes analyses of data on 17 high-risk children and their 68 matched controls.

Procedure

The initial data set contained nearly 500 variables from the CPP. These included items on family history, SES, maternal health history, pregnancy and delivery, as well as data on the child's behavior, health, and neurological status from birth to age 7. Items were eliminated if they showed no variation among the study children; most of these were items pertaining to serious illnesses and abnormalities that were not present in the sample. Of the remaining items, those dealing with the mother's health history, pregnancy and birth complications, and with the child's neonatal status were combined into six mean scale scores weighted by the reliability of the mean. The items in each of the initial four scales are shown in Table 6.5. In addition to the PC, BC, NC, and MH (maternal health history) scores, weighted means were also generated for total obstetrical complications (MHOC) to form two additional scales.

Four factor scores derived from items in the 7-year data were computed and made available by Dr. Paul Nichols and colleagues at NINCDS. These scores, which measure *School Achievement, Immaturity, Hyperactivity,* and *Neurological signs,* represent the first four factors to emerge from a principal compo-

TABLE 6.5
Items in Obstetrical and Perinatal Complication Scales

Pregnancy Complications (PC's)	Birth Complications (BC's)
Weight gain $\geq$ 30 lb.	FHR $\geq$ 161 (1st Stage)
Hemoglobin $\leq$ 9.3 gms.	FHR $\leq$ 139 (" ")
Hematocrit $\leq$ .30	Duration 1st Stage
Vomiting	Forceps
Fever	Meconium
Swelling of hands/face	Vaginal bleeding at admission
Vaginal bleeding	Nonvertex delivery
Anemia	Induction of labor
KUB infection	Augmentation of labor
	Placental complications
	Abruptio placenta
	Placenta previa
	One umbilical artery
	Arrested progress of labor
	Anesthesia at delivery
	Gaseous agents at delivery
	Intravenous agents at delivery
	Conduction agents at delivery

Neonatal Complications (NC's)	Maternal History Items(MH)
Gestational age < 36 wks.	First child and age $\geq$ 35 yrs.
Birthweight $\leq$ 2500 gms.	Height < 60 in.
1-min. Apgar $\leq$ 5	At least 1 prior fetal death
5-min. Apgar $\leq$ 5	At least 1 prior stillbirth
Bilirubin $\geq$ 10mg.	Confining illnesses in last year
Hemoglobin $\leq$ 12.0 gm/100 ml	Inadequate pelvic dimensions
Hematocrit $\leq$ .49	
Direct Coombs test: Positive	
Significant respiratory events	

nents factor analysis of the 25 items chosen by Nichols in an independent study of the total CPP population of white and black children with IQ's above 80 and lacking major neurological impairment. The 25 items are as follows:

Behavioral Items: hyperactivity, hypoactivity, impulsivity, short attention span, emotional lability, socioemotional immaturity, and withdrawal.

Cognitive and Perceptual-Motor Items: low verbal IQ, low performance IQ, scores on Bender–Gestalt, Draw-a-Person, and Illinois Test of Psycholinguistic Abilities lower than those predicted by IQ.

Academic Items: spelling, reading, and arithmetic achievement scores lower than predicted by IQ and grade.

Neurological Items: poor coordination, abnormal gait, impaired position sense, astereognosis, nystagmus, strabismus, abnormal reflexes, mirror movements, other abnormal movements, and abnormal tactile finger recognition. The procedures used to derive the four factor scores from these items for this analysis are more fully described in Nichols, Chen & Pomeroy, (1976), and Rieder and Nichols (1979). In addition to the factor scores, data on growth, cognitive, behavioral, and neurological performance at 8 months, 4 years, and 7 years were also analyzed.

RESULTS

Obstetrical Data

Three-way factorial analyses of variance were computed for the four obstetrical and perinatal mean scale scores and for maternal history in combination with obstetrical complications (MHOC). In comparisons between the 17 high-risk infants and their matched controls, none of the scales showed a significant group difference (see Table 6.6). The high-risk group had a lower mean birthweight than the controls, but the difference was not significant.

Comparisons of males and females also were not significant, except that mothers with adverse prenatal histories tended to have sons instead of daughters ($p = .044$). However, there were two group by sex interactions, with male high-risk infants having more NC's and total OC's than the other subgroups of infants. Black infants as a group had lower birthweight than whites ($p = .013$) and there was also a tendency for black infants of schizophrenics to have more NC's than whites or than black controls ($p = .004$). These results are summarized in Table 6.6.

Outcome Variables at 8 Months, and 1, 4, and 7 Years

Analyses of the outcome data (behavioral and neurological variables and physical development) are summarized in Table 6.7. Group comparisons on the many outcome variables were, by and large, not significant with the following exceptions: The high-risk group was markedly deficient in School Achievement ($p = .014$) and specifically in reading ($p = .006$). The differences approached significance for the Auditory–Vocal Association subtest of the Illinois Test of Psycholinguistic Abilities ($p = .066$) at age 7 and for the Graham block-sort test ($p = .062$) at age 4. The poor performance of the high-risk group in reading and in overall achievement as measured by the School Achievement factor score at

TABLE 6.6
Obstetric Variables: Direction of Differences by Group, Sex, and
Race

	High Risk vs. Control	Male vs. Female	White vs. Black	Group/ Sex Interaction	Group/ Race Interaction
Birthweight	2	1	1*		
PC's	2	2	2		
BC's	2	1	1		
NC's	1	1	2	3[b]	4[b]
OC's	2	1	1	3[a]	
MH	1	1*	1		
MHOC	—	1	1		

[a] $p < .05$
[b] $p < .01$
Note: 1: High Risk > Control; Male > Female; White > Black
2: Control > High Risk; Female > Male; Black > White
3: Male High Risk > Other Groups
4: Black High Risk > Other Groups
Note: PC's = Pregnancy Complications
BC's = Birth Complications
NC's = Neonatal Complications
OC's = Total Obstetric Complications
MH = Adverse Maternal History
MHOC = Maternal History + Obstetric Complications

age 7 cannot be accounted for by differences in IQ. The reading score is a residual score controlled for IQ and, furthermore, the high-risk group actually had a mean IQ two points higher than that of the control group.

The high-risk children also tended to score poorly, compared to the controls, on the other 7-year factor scores, i.e., they showed more Hyperactivity, Immaturity, and Neurological soft signs, but the differences were not significant. Surprisingly, their motor performance prior to age 7 was superior to that of the controls: The directions of differences on the 8-month Bayley Motor test and the 4-year tests of fine and gross motor abilities favored the high-risk children, though not to a statistically significant extent. In terms of physical development, the high-risk children appear to "catch up," following initial deficits in gestational age and birthweight. Starting at 1 year, group differences in height and weight were not significant.

Significant sex differences were present in both groups, with males scoring more poorly than females on all variables in the School Achievement factor, except for arithmetic, and exhibiting more neurological signs, as seen in the

Neurological Factor score. There were no significant differences between black and white children, except on the Graham block-sorting test, which favored blacks ($p = .043$), and group by race interactions were directionally inconsistent.

Correlations Between Obstetric and Neurological Variables

Although group differences were notable mainly in their absence, both for the set of obstetrical scales and for most of the childhood outcome variables, this lack of significant differences does not necessarily reveal whether there is a possible association between the two sets of variables or whether they are related differently in the two groups. In order to examine the relationships more carefully, correlations between all obstetrical scales and soft sign variables were computed within each group. In the large matrix of resulting correlation coefficients, only a few (10) correlations were significantly different from zero in the control group, and these were small in magnitude. Twice as many correlations were significant in the high-risk group, and the magnitude of these correlations was considerably larger than in the control group. Moreover, the correlations that were significant in the high-risk group were almost entirely exclusive of those that were significant in the control group. Although it is possible that some of the significant values were obtained by chance, given the size of the correlation matrix, the fact that the two groups yielded such different patterns of relationship between obstetric and neurological variables merits further probing. Path analysis could be used to look at differences between the two groups on the level of processes that may affect whole systems of variables differently in these groups, but the number of subjects involved here is too small for such analyses.

A feasible approach with this sample is to recognize that the rather large correlations in the high-risk group suggest that there may be a subgroup of subjects scoring poorly on *both* OC's and neurological variables and to concentrate attention on identifying the individual members of this deviant subgroup. Because OC's and neurological deficits have both sometimes been reported in the retrospective histories of adult schizophrenics, it is possible that high-risk children having both indicators may be especially vulnerable. The high-risk sample contains five children who score in the uppermost (i.e., poorest) 25% of the group on at least one obstetrical indicator and also score abnormally on several neurological signs. The soft signs appearing most frequently in this subgroup are poor coordination, low scores on the Neurological factor score at age 7, on the Bayley motor test at 8 months, and mixed dominance. Table 6.8 shows the concordance between obstetric complications and neurological abnormality in these five children.

TABLE 6.7
Outcome Variable: Direction of Differences by Group, Sex, and Race

	High Risk vs. Control	Male vs. Female	White vs. Black	Group/ Sex Interaction	Group/ Race Interaction
One-Year Data					
Bayley mental (8 mos.)	1	2	—		
Bayley motor (8 mos.)	1	2	2		
Height (1 yr.)	2	1	2		
Weight (1 yr.)	2	1	1		
Four-Year Data					
Graham block sort	2	2	2[a]		3[a]
Gross motor	1	2	2		4[a]
Fine motor	1	1	1		
Full scale IQ	2	1	1		
Height	2	2	2		
Weight	2	2	1		

Seven-Year Data

Full scale IQ	1	1	1
Bender–Gestalt	1	1	1
Draw-a-person	2	1	2
I.T.P.A.	2	2	1
Spelling	2	2^b	2
Reading	2^b	2^b	2
Arithmetic	2	2	1
School achievement factor	2	2	2
Hyperactivity factor	1	1	1
Immaturity factor	1	2	1
Neurological factor	1	1^a	1
Height	2	2	2
Weight	1	2	2

$^a p < .05$
$^b p < .01$
Note: 1: High Risk > Control; Male > Female; White > Black
      2: Control > High Risk; Female > Male; Black > White
      3: Black High Risk < Other Groups
      4: White Controls < Other Groups

TABLE 6.8
Concordance Between Obstetric and Neurological Indicators in Five High-
Risk Children

	Child				
	#1	*#2*	*#3*	*#4*	*#5*
Obstetric Indicators Present[a]					
Birthweight	X	X	X	X	
PC's	X		X		
BC's	X	X		X	X
NC's		X	X	X	
OC's		X	X		
MH	X		X		
MHOC	X	X	X		
Neurological Indicators Examined[b]					
Coordination	X		X		
Gait					
Position sense					
Astereognosis					
Nystagmus					
Strabismus					X
Abnormal reflexes					X
Mirror movements					
Other abnormal movements					
Tactile finger recognition					
Neurological factor score	X		X		X
Right–left identification					
Mixed dominance	X	X	X	X	
Bayley motor	X	X		X	

[a]Child is among the 25% of high-risk sample showing the highest number of indicators.
[b]Child's score is abnormal or, for continuous variables, among the worst 25% of the sample.

DISCUSSION

The literature on obstetric and perinatal complications in infants of schizophrenic parents remains controversial. Most studies show few or no significant differences between high-risk and normal control infants, but a few investigators have emphasized positive findings. The positive findings themselves are difficult to interpret. A tendency toward low birthweight in high-risk infants compared to controls is the most frequently reported finding among birth variables and occurs, at a nonsignificant level, in the CPP sample reported here. The importance of low birthweight in high-risk infants is not clear, however, as no relationship between low birthweight and the occurrence of schizophrenia has been demonstrated. Moreover, both McNeil and Kaij (1973) and Sameroff and Zax (1978) have reported no differences between infants born to schizophrenic women and infants born to women with other psychiatric diagnoses with respect to obstetric and perinatal complications, so that there appears to be nothing specific to risk for schizophrenia in this class of variables.

Neurological findings on children at risk for schizophrenia are more promising. Although the results are mixed in comparisons involving high-risk and control infants, nearly every attempt to examine motor functions and soft signs in childhood has produced either statistical group differences or a trend in this direction or, in the data reported here, associative patterns that distinguish between the high-risk and control children.

It is tempting to conclude from this consistency of findings that neurological signs represent a fundamental (perhaps genetic) vulnerability indicator in children at risk for schizophrenia. It is important to note, however, that studies in which neurological signs have been examined in children of parents with other psychiatric disorders as well as in children of schizophrenic parents have often found no differences between these groups. Thus far, the only prospective work relating early neurological signs to adult psychiatric outcome are Fish's (1977 in press) follow-up of infants of schizophrenic mothers and the follow-up by Shaffer and colleagues (this volume) of subjects from the Columbia Presbyterian sample of the CPP who had soft neurological signs at the 7-year examination. In Fish's sample, high-risk infants who showed neurointegrative retardation were the ones who developed schizophrenia at later ages. In the study by Shaffer et al., however, soft signs at age 7 were not predictive of schizophrenia in young adulthood although they did appear to be related to other forms of psychopathology, thus once again raising the problem of nonspecificity for schizophrenia.

The objective of this chapter was to consider the possibility that obstetric and perinatal complications might predict to the emergence of neurological signs in childhood in the offspring of schizophrenic parents. Few differences were found in either set of variables between the high-risk and normal control subjects of the New York CPP sample. Nevertheless, correlations between the obstetric and neurological variables were more frequent and larger in the high-risk subjects, and a subgroup of children consisting of approximately 22% of the high-risk subjects, was identified as being positive for both obstetric and neurological variables. Both Marcus (Marcus et al., 1981) and Mednick (Mednick et al., 1971) have reported an association between an obstetric-perinatal variable (low birthweight) and developmental problems in the first year of life in high-risk subjects, but Fish (1977) found no relationship between obstetric complications and poor neurological development in her subjects. Thus, whereas the data on the subgroup of high-risk children in the New York CPP sample are suggestive as indicating vulnerability to schizophrenia, they remain to be corroborated with further studies, including comparisons with offspring of parents with other psychiatric disorders.

ACKNOWLEDGMENTS

Research reported in this chapter was supported in part by an NIMH postdoctoral fellowship, MH 015955, to the first author under the sponsorship of L. Erlenmeyer–Kimling and in part by the Department of Mental Hygiene of the State of New York.

REFERENCES

Berendes, H. W. (1966). The structure and scope of the collaborative project on cerebral palsy, mental retardation, and other neurological and sensory disorders of infancy and childhood. In S. S. Chipman, A. M. Lilienfeld, B. G. Greenberg, & J. F. Donnelly (Eds.), *Research methodology and needs in perinatal studies* (pp. 118–138). Springfield, IL: Charles C. Thomas.

Erlenmeyer–Kimling, L. (1975). A prospective study of children at risk for schizophrenia: Methodological considerations and some preliminary findings. In R. Wirt, G. Winokur, & M. Roff (Eds.), *Life history research in psychopathology* (Vol. 4). Minneapolis: University of Minnesota Press.

Erlenmeyer–Kimling, L., Marcuse, Y., Cornblatt, B., Friedman, D., Rainer, J. D., & Rutschmann, J. (1984). The New York High-Risk Project. In N. F. Watt, E. J. Anthony, L. C. Wynne, & J. Rolf (Eds.), *Children at risk for schizophrenia: A longitudinal perspective*. New York: Cambridge University Press.

Feldman, P. M., Mednick, S. A., Schulsinger, F., & Fuchs, F. (unpublished manuscript). *Schizophrenia in children of schizophrenics: Pregnancy and birth complications*.

Fish, B. (1971). Contributions of developmental research to a theory of schizophrenia. In J. Hellmuth (Ed.), *Exceptional infant*. New York: Brunner/Mazel.

Fish, B. (1975). Biological antecedents of psychosis in children. In D. Freedman (Ed.), *The biology of the major psychoses: A comparative analysis*. Association for Research in Nervous and Mental Diseases Publication (No. 54), Raven Press.

Fish, B. (1977). Neurobiologic antecedents of schizophrenia in children. *Archives of General Psychiatry, 34,* 1297–1313.

Fish, B. (in press). Offspring of schizophrenics from birth to adulthood. In N. F. Watt, E. J. Anthony, L. C. Wynne, & J. Rolf (Eds.), *Children at risk for schizophrenia: A longitudinal perspective*. New York: Cambridge University Press.

Fish, B., & Alpert, M. (1962). Abnormal states of consciousness and muscle tone in infants born to schizophrenic mothers. *American Journal of Psychiatry, 119,* 439–445.

Hanson, D. R., Gottesman, I. I., & Heston, L. L. (1976). Some possible childhood indicators of adult schizophrenia from children of schizophrenics. *British Journal of Psychiatry, 129,* 142–154.

Lane, E. A., & Albee, G. W. (1970). The birth weight of children born to schizophrenic women. *Journal of Psychology, 74,* 157–160.

Marcus, J. (1974). Cerebral functioning in offspring of schizophrenics: A possible genetic factor. *International Journal of Mental Health, 3,* 57–73.

Marcus, J., Auerbach, J., Wilkinson, L., & Burack, C. M. (1981). Infants at risk for schizophreniz: The Jerusalem infant development study. *Archives of General Psychiatry, 38,* 703–713.

Marcus, J., Wilkinson, L., Burack, C. M., Mednick, S., & Schulsinger, F. (1980). *Neurologic dysfunction in offspring of schizophrenics: A preliminary and informal report of work in progress*. Paper presented at the High-Risk Consortium Plenary Meeting, San Juan, Puerto Rico.

McNeil, T. F., & Kaij, L. (1973). Obstetric complications and physical size of offspring of schizophrenic, schizophrenic-like, and control mothers. *British Journal of Psychiatry, 123,* 341–348.

McNeil, T. F., & Kaij, L. (1978). Obstetric factors in the development of schizophrenia: Complications in the births of preschizophrenics and in reproduction by schizophrenic parents. In L. C. Wynne, R. L. Cromwell, & S. Matthysse (Eds.), *The nature of schizophrenia*. New York: Wiley.

McNeil, T. F., & Kaij, L. (1984). Offspring of women with nonorganic psychoses: Progress report. In H. F. Watt, E. J. Anthony, L. C. Wynne, & J. Rolf (Eds.), *Children at risk for schizophrenia: A longitudinal perspective*. New York: Cambridge University Press.

McNeil, T. F., Persson–Blennow, I., & Kaij, L. (1974). Reproduction in female psychiatric patients: Severity of mental disturbance near reproduction and rates of obstetric complications. *Acta Psychiatrica Scandinavica, 50,* 23–32.

Mednick, S. A. (1970). Breakdown in individuals at high risk for schizophrenia: Possible predispositional perinatal factors. *Mental Hygiene, 54,* 50–63.

Mednick, S. A., Mura, E., Schulsinger, F., & Mednick, B. (1971). Perinatal conditions and infant development in children with schizophrenic parents. *Social Biology, 18,* S103–S113.

Mednick, S. A., Mura, E., Schulsinger, F., & Mednick, B. (1973). Erratum and further analysis: "Perinatal conditions and infant development in children with schizophrenic parents." *Social Biology, 20,* 111–112.

Mednick, S. A., & Schulsinger, F. (1968). Some premorbid characteristics related to breakdown in children with schizophrenic mothers. In D. Rosenthal & S. S. Kety (Eds.), *The transmission of schizophrenia*. Oxford: Pergamon Press.

Mizrahi Mirdal, G. K., Mednick, S. A., Schulsinger, F., & Fuchs, F. (1974). Perinatal complications in children of schizophrenic mothers. *Acta Psychiatrica Scandinavica, 50,* 553–568.

Nichols, P. L., Chen, T. C., & Pomeroy, J. D. (1976). *Minimal brain dysfunction: Association among symptoms*. Presented at 84th annual meeting of the American Psychological Association, Washington, DC.

Niswander, K. R., & Gordon, M. (1972). *The Collaborative Perinatal Study of the National Institute of Neurological Diseases and Stroke: The Women and their Pregnancies*. Washington, DC, U.S. Government Printing Office.

Paffenbarger, R. S., Steinmetz, C. H., Pooler, B. G., & Hyde, R. T. (1961). The picture puzzle of the postpartum psychoses. *Journal of Chronic Diseases, 13,* 161–173.

Ragins, N., Schachter, J., Elmer, E., Preisman, R., Bowes, A. E., & Harway, V. (1975). Infants and children at risk for schizophrenia. *Journal of Child Psychiatry, 14,* 150–177.

Rieder, R. O., Broman, S. H., & Rosenthal, D. (1977). The offspring of schizophrenics II: Perinatal factors and IQ. *Archives of General Psychiatry, 34,* 789–799.

Rieder, R. O., & Nichols, P. L. (1979). Offspring of schizophrenics III: Hyperactivity and neurological soft signs. *Archives of General Psychiatry, 36,* 665–674.

Rieder, R. O., Rosenthal, D., Wender, P., & Blumenthal, H. (1975). The offspring of schizophrenics I: Fetal and neonatal deaths. *Archives of General Psychiatry, 32,* 200–211.

Rosenthal, D. (1971). A program of research on heredity in schizophrenia. *Behavioral Science, 16,* 191–201.

Sameroff, A. J., & Zax, M. (1973). Perinatal characteristics of the offspring of schizophrenic women. *Journal of Nervous and Mental Disease, 157,* 191–199.

Sameroff, A. J., & Zax, M. (1978). In search of schizophrenia: Young offspring of schizophrenic women. In L. C. Wynne, R. L. Cromwell, & S. Matthysse, *The nature of schizophrenia: New approaches to research and treatment*. New York: Wiley.

Schachter, J., Kerr, J., Lachin, J. M. & Faer, M. (1975). Newborn offspring of a schizophrenic parent: Cardiac reactivity to auditory stimuli. *Psychophysiology, 12,* 483–492.

Schulsinger, H. (1976, October). *Clinical outcome of a 10-year follow-up of children of schizophrenic mothers.* Paper presented at the meeting of the Society for Life History Research in Psychopathology, Fort Worth, Texas.

Sobel, D. E. (1961). Infant mortality and malformations in children of schizophrenic women. *Psychiatric Quarterly, 35,* 60–65.

Spitzer, R. L., Endicott, J., & Robins, E. (1978, February). *Research Diagnostic Criteria (RDC) for a selected group of functional disorders* (3rd ed.).

Wrede, G., Mednick, S. A., Huttunen, M. O., & Nilsson, C. G. (in press). *Pregnancy and delivery complications in the births of an unselected series of Finnish children with schizophrenic mothers.*

Yarden, P. E., & Suranyi, I. (1968). The early development of institutionalized children of schizophrenic mothers. *Disorders of the Nervous System, 29,* 380–384.

Zax, M., Sameroff, A. J., & Babigian, H. M. (1977). Birth outcomes in the offspring of mentally disordered women. *American Journal of Orthopsychiatry, 47,* 218–230.

7 Children at High Risk for Schizophrenia: Predictions from Childhood to Adolescence

Barbara Cornblatt
Yvonne Marcuse

In the previous chapter, we evaluated the evidence suggesting that pregnancy and birth complications have long-term effects on a child's subsequent neurological development. We concluded that the link between these difficulties in infancy and later childhood disorders is a relatively weak one. In the current chapter, we have redirected our focus to difficulties in cognitive functioning, but we are asking a similar question—namely, whether there is any evidence for a link between early cognitive dysfunctions and subsequent disturbances, where the disturbances in question are behavioral and are expected to be the first clinical manifestations of adult schizophrenia.

The evidence we are considering has been generated by studies of children at risk for schizophrenia. Across all these studies, risk is defined by virtue of having one or two parents who are schizophrenic. This definition of risk is derived from previous research on adult offspring of schizophrenic parents (Erlenmeyer–Kimling, 1968, 1970), which indicates that children of one schizophrenic parent will be between 10 and 15 times more likely (and children of two schizophrenic parents closer to 40 times more likely) to develop schizophrenia as adults than children in the general population.

As mentioned in the previous chapter, a major goal of high-risk research is to identify "predictive indicators" of future schizophrenia in preschizophrenic children many years before the actual onset of the disorder—with hope that this will lead to preventive intervention.

In several of the prospective studies of children at risk for schizophrenia, attentional processing has been selected as a promising area to search for "predictive indicators." This choice is based on the following considerations: First, an impressive body of accumulated research literature demonstrates that, across a wide variety of testing situations, adult schizophrenics do not perform as well on tests of attention and information processing as do a number of comparison groups (cf. Kornetsky & Mirsky, 1966; McGhie, Chapman, & Lawson 1965; Nuechterlein, 1977). Second, experimental results have been further supported by clinical observations and by introspective reports of schizophrenic patients describing various attentional dysfunctions (cf. Bleuler, 1950; Freedman & Chapman, 1973; McGhie & Chapman, 1961). Third, in the search for childhood predictors of adult psychopathology, it is most logical to look first for subtle disturbances in those areas that have been found to be most grossly dysfunctional in affected adults.

In this chapter, we argue that, viewed overall, the preliminary findings of the high-risk studies suggest that childhood attentional deficits may well be early warning signals of pathology in adolescence and possibly of schizophrenia in adulthood. Our discussion focuses first on findings that show that at least some children at risk are deficient in attention and information processing in areas compatible with those reported in the adult literature. Second, we present recent data from the program of studies being conducted at New York State Psychiatric Institute that indicate that attentional dysfunctions do, in fact, predict adolescent behavioral disturbances, which in turn may be reflective of eventual schizophrenia.

ATTENTIONAL DYSFUNCTIONS IN HIGH-RISK CHILDREN

Attention and information-processing variables have been included in five high-risk studies, namely: (1) the Massachusetts Intervention Project (Grunebaum), (2) the Waterloo–McMaster high-risk project (Asarnow & MacCrimmon), (3) the Minnesota series of risk studies (Garmezy), (4) the New York program of longitudinal studies (Erlenmeyer–Kimling), and (5) the Stony Brook Project (Weintraub & Neale). In all but the latter project, attention and information processing have been major emphases of the research. The five studies are quite heterogeneous in the measures used and the specific processes that they have studied. Although this diversity imposes limitations on the extent to which data can be generalized across the studies, several important observations can be made.

As a whole, the studies demonstrate that, as a group, children at risk for schizophrenia characteristically perform more poorly than their respective normal controls across a variety of attentional measures. The question, however, is whether specific attentional dysfunctions that predict vulnerability to schizophrenia can be identified by comparing the deficits established for adult schizophrenics and those identified thus far in children at risk. There is a clear overlap between the measures used in high-risk research and those used in studies of adult schizophrenics in three areas of attentional functioning: (1) speed of reaction time, (2) sustained attention, and (3) heightened susceptibility to distraction. Each area is discussed briefly in the following sections.

Reaction Time Measures

Measures of reaction time have been perhaps the most widely used procedure in the experimental study of schizophrenia and have proved to be effective in detecting attentional deficits in affected adults. (A thorough overview of this complex area of attentional research can be found in Nuechterlein's (1977) review of the reaction time literature on schizophrenia.) Reaction time procedures have not been similarly successful in differentiating high-risk children from normal controls, however. In only one study—a substudy by Marcus (1972) in Garmezy's Minnesota series—were high-risk children found to have significantly slower reaction times than normal control children, and Nuechterlein (1977) has discussed some reservations about these findings. By contrast, no differences between groups were seen in the Waterloo–McMasters project (Asarnow, Steffy, MacCrimmon, & Cleghorn, 1977; Asarnow, Steffy, MacCrimmon, & Cleghorn, 1978), in a second substudy by Phipps–Yonas (1979) in the Minnesota series, or in two independent samples in the New York high-risk project (Rutschmann, Cornblatt, & Erlenmeyer–Kimling, 1977). Thus, reaction time does not appear to be a promising measure for high-risk research.

Measures of Sustained Attention

Adult schizophrenics have been found to show impaired performance on measures of sustained attention compared to normal controls and to patients with other psychiatric conditions (Kornetsky, 1972; Kornetsky & Mirsky, 1966; Orzak & Kornetsky, 1966) not only during overt psychotic states but during remission as well (Asarnow & MacCrimmon, 1978; Wohlberg & Kornetsky, 1973). All five of the high-risk projects mentioned earlier have included measures of sustained attention. As in the studies of adult schizophrenics, all but one (the Stony Brook project) of the high-risk studies used versions of the Continuous Performance Test (CPT). Versions of the CPT that were sufficiently difficult for the age group being tested showed significant deficits in sustained performance, similar to those reported in adult schizophrenics, among the at-risk children in two samples in the New York study by Erlenmeyer–Kimling and colleagues (cf. Cornblatt & Erlenmeyer–Kimling, 1984; Erlenmeyer–Kimling & Cornblatt, 1978; Erlenmeyer–Kimling, Marcuse, Cornblatt, Friedman, Rainer, & Rutschmann, 1984; Rutschman et al., 1977), in a dissertation study carried out by Nuechterlein in the Minnesota series (Nuechterlein, 1979; Nuechterlein, Phipps–Yonas, Driscoll, & Garmezy, 1980), and in an early report from the Massachusetts Intervention Project (Grunebaum, Weiss, Gallant, & Cohler,

1974). In subsequent reports from the latter study (Cohler, Grunebaum, Weiss, Garner, & Gallant, 1977; Grunebaum, Cohler, Kauffman, & Gallant, 1978; Herman, Mirsky, Ricks, & Gallant, 1977), as well as those from the Waterloo–McMaster project (Asarnow et al., 1978), the CPT failed to show significant differences between high-risk and normal control groups. It is likely, however, that the difficulty level of the tasks was inappropriate for the age groups under study, and that this accounted for the negative results.[1]

Signal detection analysis was used in the New York study and in Nuechterlein's substudy of the Minnesota series to generate d', an index of sensitivity to differences between stimuli, and β, an index of response bias. In both studies, the high-risk subjects had lower d's,[2] indicating reduced stimulus sensitivity in comparison to the normal controls. There were no differences between groups in the β measure, however. Thus, overall, the results of the two studies show: (1) that high-risk children have less ability than normal controls to discriminate between critical and irrelevant stimuli for sustained periods of time and (2) that these differences are due to lower stimulus sensitivity (d') in the high-risk group rather than to differences in motivation or task-taking approaches, as measured by β.

The Stony Brook project (Oltmanns, Weintraub, Stone, & Neale, 1978; Winters, Stone, Weintraub, & Neale, 1981), in which the CPT was not used, also included a measure of a type of sustained attention, the Visual Search Task, in which subjects search through arrays of letters of either high or low confusability to detect a designated target letter. Compared to normal controls, high-risk subjects were found to take significantly longer to search through the more difficult arrays to find the target letter. Thus, the findings from this project are in line with those reported by Nuechterlein and by the Erlenmeyer–Kimling group.

Measures of Distraction

Distractibility is the third aspect of attention that is of particular interest to high-risk investigators. Clinical research has indicated that schizophrenic patients experience feelings of being flooded by stimuli from the surrounding environment and of not being able to selectively screen irrelevant stimuli out of con-

---

[1]The inability of the investigators in the Massachusetts series to replicate their inital findings in later studies is inconclusive in any event because of a number of other methodological problems, including: (1) frequent changes in subjects and diagnostic criteria for the high-risk samples from study to study, (2) small sample sizes (also a serious problem in the McMaster–Waterloo study), (3) data combined over too wide an age range, and (4) biased attrition rates, in that continued cooperation in the study favored retention of the healthier mothers—and, therefore presumably healthier children.

[2]In the case of Nuechterlein's study, HR subjects had lower scores on the factor considered to measure d' across CPT conditions.

scious awareness (Freedman & Chapman, 1973; McGhie & Chapman, 1961). Experimental findings have corroborated these subjective reports and have demonstrated that a heightened susceptibility to distraction is characteristic of many schizophrenic patients (Chapman & McGhie, 1962; Lawson, McGhie, & Chapman, 1967; Oltmanns & Neale, 1975). Data from the high-risk studies, however, are reported to be somewhat less consistent in showing similar tendencies in children at risk.

Two types of distraction paradigms have been used in high-risk research—auditory distraction combined with a visual task (usually a version of the CPT) and auditory distraction combined with an auditory task (some type of digit span measure). In both cases, the variable of interest is the extent of deterioration in performance on the basic task after the onset of distraction.

Auditory distraction combined with a visual task (the CPT) was used in the Massachusetts Intervention Project (Grunebaum et al., 1978) and in the first of two samples studied in the New York high-risk project (Cornblatt & Erlenmeyer–Kimling, 1984: Erlenmeyer–Kimling & Cornblatt, 1978: Rutschmann et al., 1977). In the Massachusetts study, distraction had no effect on task performance in either the high-risk or the normal control group, but, as noted previously, the CPT task may simply have been too easy for the subjects at the ages at which they were tested. Distraction was more effective in disrupting performance in the New York study: Although the effect of distraction was not statistically significant, performance differences between the high-risk and normal control subjects increased during distraction.

Auditory distraction during an auditory task has been studied in both the Stony Brook and the New York projects. In both studies, the task required recall of auditorially presented stimuli—digits or letters. The Stony Brook investigators (Oltmanns et al., 1978) reported that there were no differences between groups on a digit span task without distraction, but that, on the distraction trials, high-risk subjects recalled fewer digits than did normal controls. On a follow-up retesting (Winters, Stone, Weintraub, & Neale, 1981), the same results emerged and the impaired performance of the high-risk subjects under distraction was traced to a "primacy" defect, i.e., the higher rate of errors in this group applied only to the first two, out of five, digits presented.

In the first sample of the New York project, no group differences in performance were found on trials involving distraction, although this may have been due to the fact that the distraction condition was too difficult, resulting in very poor performance in both the high-risk and control groups. (Other processes tapped by the primary attentional task are discussed subsequently.)

Thus, the evidence with respect to heightened vulnerability to distraction in high-risk children is too equivocal to allow definite conclusions to be drawn. Auditory distraction had no effect on performance on the simple visual task (CPT) used in the Massachusetts study and was only moderately effective in disrupting performance on the CPT in the New York project. Auditory distraction, which had no effect on the recall of auditory stimuli in the New York project, did however impair recall in high-risk subjects in the Stony Brook project. In passing, it should be added that preliminary analyses of a new test—a test of auditory distraction and information overload—added to the battery of the New York project during the third round of testing of the first of the two samples under study do appear to support the hypothesis of heightened sensitivity to distraction in children at risk for schizophrenia (Cornblatt & Erlenmeyer–Kimling, 1984; Erlenmeyer–Kimling et al., 1984).

Clearly, more research needs to be directed to the question of differential distractibility. In the Stony Brook and New York projects, efforts have been made to develop distraction paradigms that take into account the criticisms that Chapman and Chapman (1978a,b; Chapman, 1979) have raised about experimental studies of schizophrenia. The Chapmans have argued that to study differential distractibility in schizophrenic patients the distraction and no-distraction conditions of a given test must first be equated for level of difficulty and reliability. Otherwise, the finding that schizophrenics perform more poorly than normal controls on experimental tests of distraction may be a psychometric artifact reflecting a generalized performance deficit, rather than heightened susceptibility to distraction, per se. (It should be noted, however, that as Chapman (1979) has himself pointed out, this criticism is most applicable to patient populations and may not be appropriate for populations of individuals who are not ill and do not yet show a generalized deficit, as is the case with high-risk subjects.) Investigators in the New York project have refined their attentional test battery and extended it to include measures of distraction, which combine both auditory and visual distraction with both auditory and visual tasks, and information overload, in addition to short-term memory capacity, speed of processing, and sustained attention. The expanded test battery recently has been administered to both samples and will be readministered to the second sample in the near future to provide longitudinal as well as cross-sectional data on the processes under study.

Other Measures of Information Processing

In addition to the measures falling into the three broad categories of attention discussed earlier, other types of attention/information-processing measures have been included in the test batteries of the high-risk studies. Major findings on these measures can be summarized briefly.

Selective Attention. Measures of selective attention were administered in the Massachusetts and Waterloo–McMaster projects as well as in a substudy by Driscoll in the Minnesota series. In the Massachusetts study, Grunebaum and coworkers initially found that 5-year-old, but not 6-year-old, high-risk subjects performed more poorly than normal controls on an Embedded Figures Test (Grunebaum et al., 1974), but on subsequent testing, no differences were found between high-risk and control subjects of any age (Cohler et al., 1977; Grune-baum et al., 1978). (This same pattern of results was also reported for the CPT in the Massachusetts study.) Asarnow and colleagues (Asarnow et al., 1977, 1978) in the Waterloo–McMaster study did find differences between their high-risk and control subjects: The high-risk subjects detected significantly fewer target letters than controls on the most complex condition of a Span of Apprehension task and showed a similar trend on the most difficult condition of a Competing Voices test. By contrast, though, Driscoll (1979) found no differences between subject groups in the Minnesota project on an incidental learning task that was considered to measure selective attention. Thus, once again the picture is unclear concerning the potential of a particular type of attentional task for differentiating high-risk children.

Sorting Tasks.   Sorting tasks have been included in the test batteries of both the McMaster and the Stony Brook projects, and in both cases, high-risk subjects have been reported to perform significantly more poorly than normal control subjects.

Speed of Information Processing and Short-Term Memory.   The auditory attentional task that was used in the first sample of the New York high-risk project to assess the effects of distraction on auditory attention also measured speed of processing and short-term memory. Both were found to be affected in the high-risk group. These subjects showed less improvement than the normal controls when going from the more difficult to the easier of the presentation rates, and they also showed greater deficiencies in recalling letters from a presented sequence (only the longer sequence, 5 letters, was affected). The short-term memory deficit was subsequently observed in a different task of recall given to the second sample (Cornblatt & Erlenmeyer–Kimling, 1984) and in still a third task administered to the first sample at older ages (Rutschmann, Cornblatt, & Erlenmeyer–Kimling, 1980).

Although speed of processing and STM capacity, per se, have not been tested explicitly by any of the other high-risk investigations concerned with attentional processing, dysfunctions in both areas have been reported in adult schizophrenics (cf. Hawks & Robinson, 1971, McGhie et al., 1965, Slade, 1971). Both areas are currently being explored further in children at risk by the New York team of investigators.

IDENTIFICATION OF DEVIANT SUBJECTS

Given the variability of findings generated by the individual attentional measures from study to study, even among tests considered to measure the same attentional process, the question asked earlier—namely, whether comparisons between the deficits established for adult schizophrenics and those reported for children at risk would point to predictors of vulnerability—must be answered with a qualified "not yet." However, investigators in some of the projects have turned to a different approach to the analysis of the data that yields considerably more consistency in the findings.

In the alternate strategy, the primary concern is to identify those subjects who perform most deviantly across a number of attentional measures. The search for a subgroup of deviant subjects is based on the assumption that only about 15% of the high-risk subjects will develop the disorder themselves and that it will be primarily this subgroup that will display the attentional deficits under study. The strategy of looking for deviant subgroups was enunciated in the early days of high-risk research (Erlenmeyer–Kimling, 1972; Hanson, Gottesman, & Meehl, 1977), but, in practice, many investigators expected that the "vulnerable" subgroup would perform sufficiently poorly to pull the mean level of performance for the entire high-risk group significantly below that of the normal control group on any test of attention that tapped a core dysfunction. Analysis of group differences was then expected to provide substantial clues about predictive indicators.

The use of group differences to validate attentional indicators has turned out to be far more problematic than originally envisioned. As indicated in the preceding discussion, differences between groups on the individual measures of attention are often neither clear nor consistent. Thus, it is likely that only the most sensitive of measures is capable of detecting the subtle fluctuations in attention that significantly discriminate the children who are at true risk for schizophrenia from the remainder of their group who are not truly at risk or from normal control children.

Consequently, investigators in four of the five high-risk projects (excepting the Massachusetts Intervention Project) have focused with increasing intensity on the identification of a subgroup of the most deviant performers within their respective samples. Quite different techniques have been used in the four studies to identify subjects who perform most poorly across several attentional measures, but in each of the studies a higher incidence of deviant performers has been found in the high-risk group than in the normal control group.

In the Minnesota series of studies, three dissertation students, Nuechterlein, Phipps–Yonas, and Driscoll (Nuechterlein et al., 1980), attempted to find subgroups of deviant performers on their respective measures. Principal components analysis was used to generate factors in each of the three substudies, and subjects were defined as being deviant on a factor if their scores were in the poorest 10% of the distribution for the normal controls. Phipps–Yonas and Driscoll—using a reaction time factor and two learning factors (one for intentional and one for incidental learning), respectively—were unable to identify a distinct subgroup of extreme-scoring high-risk subjects. These results are not surprising in view of the fact that neither reaction time nor the learning tasks have been found to discriminate well between high-risk and control subjects. By contrast, on a d' factor derived from signal detection analysis of CPT data, Nuechterlein found a significant excess of poor performers among high-risk subjects (29%) compared to normal controls (9%). The deviant subject analysis is consistent with the group data on d' mentioned earlier. Also consistent is the fact that the signal detection index of response bias, β, which showed no group differences, failed to yield a distinct subgroup of extreme scorers.

Asarnow and colleagues (Asarnow et al., 1977, 1978) in the Waterloo–McMaster study factor analyzed the eight measures in their attentional/information-processing battery and then used cluster analysis on the five factor scores that were obtained for each subject. Four clusters of subjects resulted. Two of these, which represented good to superior performance across the measures, included all but one of the 20 control subjects and 4 of the 9 high-risk subjects. A third cluster contained only 1 subject, a high-risk child who was deviant on all the measures in the battery. The remaining cluster had 4 high-risk subjects and 1 control subject who showed poor performance on 3 of the attentional tasks, a pattern that the investigators interpreted as indicating a deficiency in ability to detect target from background stimuli as the amount of information to be processed increases.

Investigators in the Stony Brook group (Oltmanns et al., 1978, Stone, Neale, & Weintraub, 1977; Winters et al., 1981) began their search for a subgroup of deviant performers by selecting six variables that had best differentiated the high-risk and normal control groups—namely, one index from each of four cognitive tests and both verbal and performance IQ. The four cognitive indices were standardized after being controlled for age, IQ, and age by IQ interaction. Deviance was defined as any score falling more than one-half a standard deviation from the mean in the direction of poor performance. The number of deviant measures was tallied for each subject, and a series of chi-square tests were performed on the distributions for the high-risk and normal control group to determine the deviance score that maximally discriminated between groups. A subgroup of subjects who were deviant on three or more of the six variables was thus identified and was found to contain 32% of the children of schizophrenic parents (diagnosed according to DSM II) and close to 20% of the normal controls. Subsequently, when schizophrenia was diagnosed more narrowly (Winters et al., 1981) in the parents, the proportion of the high-risk subjects falling into the deviant performance subgroup rose to nearly 44%. Although the refinement in the diagnosis of the schizophrenic parents appears to have improved the differentiation between the high-risk and control groups, the relatively high percentage of normal control subjects located in the deviant subgroup in this study most likely reflects an overly loose definition of deviance.

A different type of strategy was used in the New York high-risk project to assign deviance scores. Fifteen response indices were selected from the CPT (8 indices), the auditory Attention Span Test (5 indices), and the Digit Span (2 indices) subtest of the Wechsler Intelligence Scale for Children, after controlling for age and sex. A cut-off point, which identified the most poorly performing 5%

of the normal control group, was assigned to each response index so that all subjects with scores falling below the cut-off were classified as deviant on that particular index. The number of indices on which a subject was deviant was then tallied, and the distributions of deviance scores were examined separately for the two groups of subjects. Based on the distributions, a score of four or more deviant indices was selected to define a deviant subgroup. Thus, scores of three or less were considered to represent random fluctuations in attentional performance, whereas scores of four or more were thought to be indicative of a true attentional deficit displayed across a number of different measures. In the normal control group, 60% of the subjects were not deviant on any attentional index, 35% had one to three deviant scores, and 5% had scores of four or more. In contrast, in the high-risk group, 35% of the subjects had no deviant scores, 40% had one to three deviant scores, and 25% had four or more deviant scores and were classified as constituting a special subgroup of subjects.

The findings across the four studies are in relatively good agreement in showing a considerably larger percentage of high-risk than normal control subjects in a deviant performance subgroup. The compositions of various deviant subgroups are, of course, affected by the discriminating power of the individual tests in the different project batteries, the number of subjects tested, and the criteria used to define deviance. Nevertheless, it is apparent that, by eliminating the noise associated with the individual measures of attention, composite deviance scores that reflect a global attentional deficit across several indices offer promising means for detecting subgroups of children at risk for schizophrenia.

PREDICTIVE VALIDITY OF ATTENTIONAL DEVIANCE: DATA FROM THE HIGH-RISK PROJECT

Despite the consistency of the finding across high-risk projects that global attentional deficits are primarily characteristic of subjects at risk for schizophrenia, the validity of this approach for identifying future schizophrenics cannot be determined until the subjects being followed in the longitudinal studies are well into the schizophrenia risk period. Nevertheless, support for the predictive validity of composite attentional scores in relation to psychopathological development in adolescence is provided by the New York study, the only one of the high-risk projects under review that has compared laboratory deviance scores from childhood assessments with evaluations of global adjustment at later ages.

The New York High-risk Project: Description

The New York program consists of two independent samples: an initial sample (Sample A) of 208 children first tested in the laboratory between 1971–72 and a replication sample (Sample B) of 150 children who were first tested between

1977–79. At the time of first testing all the children in both samples were between the ages of 7–12 years and met the following additional criteria: They were white, English-speaking, and came from homes with intact marriages between the biological parents. Both samples include a high-risk (HR) group—children of one or two schizophrenic parents—a psychiatric control (PC) group—children of parents with affective disorders—and a normal control (NC) group—children of psychiatrically normal parents. Children of schizophrenic or affective parents were originally located through their parents' admissions to one of several state psychiatric facilities in the New York metropolitan area. Consecutive admissions were screened to identify patients who had one or more children aged 7–12 and who did not have a diagnosis of chronic alcoholism, drug addiction, brain trauma, or psychosis of toxic origin. Diagnostic screening in Sample A was initially done by two project psychiatrists on the basis of hospital records, and, subsequently, SADS-L interviews were administered and RDC diagnoses assigned. Diagnoses for Sample B were based on the RDC from the beginning at intake.

For Sample A, children in the normal control group were recruited through two large school districts; for Sample B they were selected in conjunction with an independent sampling firm. In both samples, normal control children were eliminated from the study if their parents were found to have had treatment for a major psychiatric disorder.

More detail about sample selection and descriptions of diagnostic procedures can be found in Erlenmeyer–Kimling, et al. (1984) and Erlenmeyer–Kimling, Cornblatt, and Golden (1982).

The balance of this chapter focuses on the relationship between the attentional data collected from Sample A during the first round of testing[3] and behavioral ratings completed several years later. Similar comparisons cannot yet be made for Sample B because these children are still too young to be exhibiting the types of problems that began to emerge in late adolescence in Sample A subjects.

Behavioral Ratings

For Sample A subjects, behavioral disturbances have been measured according to a five-point Behavioral Global Adjustment Scale (BGAS). The BGAS ratings are based primarily on information obtained from the parents of the children during routine follow-up telephone calls that have been made every 3 to 6 months since Sample A was recruited in 1971. Three major areas of functioning are taken into consideration in assigning the BGAS ratings: (1) family relationships and the

---

[3]The data collected from Sample A during the first round of testing has been emphasized throughout this chapter because it is these data that have been most thoroughly examined with respect to prediction of subsequent behaviors. Discussion of the Sample A data collected during the later testing rounds can be found in Erlenmeyer–Kimling et al. (1984), and Cornblatt & Erlenmeyer–Kimling (1984).

TABLE 7.1
Behavioral Global Adjustment Scale (BGAS) Sample A Results

Group	BGAS 78				BGAS 79			
	N	$\bar{X}$	S.D.	F Value	N	$\bar{X}$	S.D.	F Value
HR	(72)	3.29	.99	26.58[a]	(72)	3.14	1.01	25.54[a]
NC	(84)	4.00	.68		(92)	3.81	.69	

[a] $P < .001$

child's general development, (2) peer interactions, and (3) school functioning. Ratings are scored in the direction of health—that is, the higher the score, the healthier the overall behavior is considered to be. The rating categories range from gross behavioral disturbance requiring hospitalization (a rating of 1) to above-average functioning (a rating of 5).

To date, two sets of ratings have been completed for Sample A, the first based on behavioral data collected up until August of 1978 (BGAS 78) and the second based on information obtained through August of 1979 (BGAS 79). A third set, including information through August of 1980, is in process of being completed. As can be seen in Table 7.1, high-risk subjects received significantly lower (more deviant) scores for both BGAS 78 and BGAS 79 than did members of the NC group. Furthermore, when BGAS categories 1 (severely impaired) and 2 (markedly impaired) are combined, a substantially higher proportion of high-risk subjects (24%) than normal controls (2%) fall into this seriously impaired subgroup of subjects.

Comparison Between Attentional Deviance Scores and Behavior Ratings

Table 7.2 shows the correlations between the attentional deviance scores and the two sets of behavioral ratings for the HR and NC groups. It is clear that the relationship between early attentional deviance, measured at least 7 years prior to the first set of BGAS ratings, and subsequent behavioral disturbances is very different for the two subject groups. In the normal control group, the correlations between attentional deviance in the laboratory and both sets of behavioral ratings is essentially zero. By contrast, the HR group shows a significant relationship between the laboratory scores and both BGAS 78 and BGAS 79 scores. Furthermore, for subjects in the high-risk group, the correlation between the attentional

TABLE 7.2
Relationship Between Deviance on Attentional
Measures and Behavioral Ratings

	Correlations with Attentional Deviance Scores	
	BGAS 78	BGAS 79
High Risk	$-.30^a$	$-.42^b$
	($n = 65$)	($n = 65$)
Normal control	0.00 (n.s)	$-.13$ (n.s.)
	($n = 84$)	($n = 90$)

$^a P < .01$
$^b P < .001$

TABLE 7.3
Comparison of Deviant and Nondeviant Attentional Responders on
BGAS Scores

			BGAS 79		
		N	$\bar{X}$	S.D.	t value
HR GROUP	Deviant responders	16	2.50	0.89	
	Nondeviant responders	56	3.32	0.97	3.03[a]
NC GROUP	Deviant responders	5	3.60	0.55	
	Nondeviant responders	87	3.83	0.70	0.71 (ns)

[a]$P < .01$

and behavioral scores has increased as the behavioral ratings have been updated (i.e., from BGAS 78 to BGAS 79) and, presumably, have become more accurate.

To examine the predictive potential of the attentional deviance scores a little more closely, a comparison can be made between the deviant and nondeviant responders within each group. As indicated earlier, subjects were considered to be deviant responders if they had a composite attentional score of 4 or more. This yielded a deviant subgroup of 5 subjects within the NC group and 16 subjects in the HR group. Table 7.3 compares BGAS 79 scores for the deviant versus nondeviant responders in each of the two groups. As expected from the correlations, the deviant responders in the HR group have a significantly lower mean BGAS rating than do the remaining nondeviant high-risk subjects. By contrast, there is no difference in the BGAS means between the deviant and nondeviant responders in the normal control group.

The importance of the observed relationship between early attentional deviance and poor BGAS scores in adolescence depends on our being able to demonstrate in the future that the BGAS scores are, in themselves, fairly accurate predictors of continuing psychopathology. However, if this expectation is borne out, it will be clear that attentional dysfunctions in childhood can serve as "predictive indicators" of adult behavioral disturbances.

SUMMARY AND CONCLUSIONS

The data generated by the high-risk projects concerned with attentional processing have indicated that three major areas of functioning appear most fruitful for continued study. These are: (1) sustained attention, (2) distractibility and ability to process information under conditions of overload, and (3) attention span and short-term memory. All three of these areas have been shown to be impaired in schizophrenic adults. By contrast, reaction time deficits, which also have been consistently demonstrated in schizophrenic adults, have not been detected in children at risk. Thus, it can be concluded that studies of reaction time are of less promise in high-risk research than studies of other types of attentional processes.

Problems in high-risk research arise, however, when attempts are made to base specific predictions on any one attentional measure; that is, although high-risk subjects as a group differ from normal control subjects as a group on many measures falling into the three categories of attention listed previously, no single measure of attention or even single domain of attention has yet yielded data that can be used to predict which subjects within the high-risk group are most likely to become ill. And, given the variety of measures used from study to study as well as inconsistencies between studies presumably using the same measure (e.g., the CPT), it may not be feasible to attempt to use specific measures to make predictions in this stage of high-risk research.

Instead, the evidence reviewed in this chapter supports the use of an alternate predictive strategy that involves the detection of a global attentional deficit—that is, a deficit that is displayed across a number of attentional measures. The four high-risk studies discussed in this chapter that identified subjects with such global deficits were consistent in finding these subgroups to consist largely of subjects at risk for schizophrenia. Furthermore, data from the New York high-risk project have demonstrated that the deviance scores obtained from the early test battery on clinically normal children predict, to a significant extent, subsequent behavioral problems as the children reach late adolescence, 7 to 8 years after the initial testing. On the basis of this evidence, it can be proposed that composite deviance scores that result from assessing poor performance in several attentional domains may be both more reliable and more valid than are scores derived from individual attentional measures.

Although the findings from the New York project clearly show that attentional dysfunctions in childhood are indicators of behavioral problems appearing during late adolescence and early adulthood, the caveat remains that, only with further follow-up, will it be possible to establish that early attentional deficits actually predict to schizophrenia.

REFERENCES

Asarnow, R. F., & MacCrimmon, D. J. (1978). Residual performance deficit in clinically remitted schizophrenics: A marker of schizophrenia? *Journal of Abnormal Psychology, 87,* 597–608.

Asarnow, A. F., Steffy, R. A., MacCrimmon, D. J., & Cleghorn, J. M. (1977). An attentional assessment of foster children at risk for schizophrenia. *Journal of Abnormal Psychology, 86*(3), 267–275.

Asarnow, R. F., Steffy, R. A., MacCrimmon, D. J., & Cleghorn, J. M. (1978). An attentional assessment of foster children at risk for schizophrenia. In L. C. Wynne, R. L. Cromwell, & S. Matthysse (Eds.), *The nature of schizophrenia.* New York: Wiley.

Bleuler, E. (1950). *Dementia praecox or the group of schizophrenias* Trans. J. Zinkin, New York:International Universities Press. (Original work published 1911)

Chapman, L. J. (1979). Recent advances in the study of schizophrenic cognition. *Schizophrenia Bulletin, 5,* 568–580.

Chapman, L., & Chapman, J. (1978a). The measurement of differential deficit. *Journal of Psychiatric Research, 14,* 303–311.

Chapman, L., & Chapman, J. (1978b). When should schizophrenic and normal groups be compared? *Journal of Psychiatric Research, 14,* 321–325.

Chapman, J., & McGhie, A. (1962). A comparative study of disordered attention in schizophrenia. *Journal of Mental Science, 108,* 455.

Cohler, B. J., Grunebaum, H., Weiss, J., Gamer, E., & Gallant, D. (1977). Disturbances of attention among schizophrenic, depressed and well mothers and their young children. *Journal of Child Psychology and Psychiatry, 18,* 115–135.

Cornblatt, B., & Erlenmeyer–Kimling, L. (1984). Early attentional predictors of adolescent behavioral disturbances in children at risk for schizophrenia. In N. Watt, E. J. Anthony, L. C. Wynne, & J. Rolf (Eds.), *Children at risk for schizophrenia: A longitudinal perspective.* (pp 198–211) New York: Cambridge University Press.

Driscoll, R. (1979). *Incidental and intentional learning and social competence in high-risk children.* Paper presented at the 17th Annual Convention of the American Psychological Association, New York.

Erlenmeyer–Kimling, L. (1968). Studies on the offspring of two schizophrenic parents. In D. Rosenthal & S. S. Kety (Eds.), *The transmission of schizophrenia.* New York: Pergamon Press.

Erlenmeyer–Kimling, L. (1970). A prospective study of children of schizophrenic parents. USPHS (NIMH) Grant-MH 19560.

Erlenmeyer–Kimling, L. (1972). Gene environment interactions and the variability of behavior. In L. Ehrman, G. S. Omenn, & E. Caspari (Eds.), *Genetics, environment and behavior.* New York: Academic Press.

Erlenmeyer–Kimling, L., & Cornblatt, B. (1978). Attentional measures in a study of children at high-risk for schizophrenia. *Journal of Psychiatric Research, 14,* 93–98. Also in L. Wynne, & R. Cromwell (Eds.), *The nature of schizophrenia* (pp. 359–365). New York: Wiley.

Erlenmeyer–Kimling, L., Cornblatt, B., & Golden, R. (1982). Early indicators of vulnerability to schizophrenia in children at high genetic risk. In S. B. Guze, F. J. Earls, & J. E. Barrett (Eds.), *Childhood psychopathology and development.* New York: Raven Press.

Erlenmeyer–Kimling, L., Marcuse, Y., Cornblatt, B., Friedman, D., Rainer, J. D., & Rutschmann, J. (1984). The New York high-risk project. In N. F. Watt, E. J. Anthony, L. C. Wynne, & J. E. Rolf (Eds.), *Children at risk for schizophrenia: A longitudinal perspective.* New York: Cambridge University Press.

Freedman, B., & Chapman, L. J. (1973). Early subjective experience in schizophrenic episodes. *Journal of Abnormal Psychology, 82,* 46–54.

Grunebaum, H., Cohler, B. J., Kauffman, C., & Gallant, D. (1978). Children of depressed and schizophrenic mothers. *Child Psychiatry and Human Development, 8*(4), 219–228.

Grunebaum, H., Weiss, J., Gallant, D., & Cohler, B. J. (1974). Attention in young children of psychotic mothers. *American Journal of Psychiatry, 131,* 887–891.

Hanson, D. R., Gottesman, I. I., & Meehl, P. E. (1977). Genetic theories and the validation of psychiatric diagnoses: Implications for the study of children of schizophrenics. *Journal of Abnormal Psychology, 86,* 575–588.

Hawks, D. V., & Robinson, K. N. (1971). Information processing in schizophrenia: The effect of varying the rate of presentation and introducing interference. *British Journal of Social and Clinical Psychology, 10,* 30–41.

Herman, J., Mirsky, A. F., Ricks, N. L., & Gallant, D. (1977). Behavioral and electrographic measures in attention in children at risk for schizophrenia. *Journal of Abnormal Psychology, 86*(1), 27–33.

Kornetsky, C. (1972). The use of a simple test of attention as a measure of drug effects in schizophrenic patients. *Psychopharmacologia, 24*, 99–106.

Kornetsky, C., & Mirsky, A. F. (1966). On certain pharmacological and physiological differences between schizophrenics and normal persons. *Psychopharmacologia, 8*, 309–318.

Lawson, J. S., McGhie, A., & Chapman, J. (1967). Distractibility in schizophrenia and organic cerebral disease. *British Journal of Psychiatry, 113*, 527–535.

Marcus, L. M. (1972). *Studies of attention in children vulnerable to psychopathology*. Unpublished doctoral dissertation, University of Minnesota, Minneapolis.

McGhie, A., & Chapman, J. (1961). Disorders of attention and perception in early schizophrenia. *British Journal of Medical Psychology, 34*, 103–117.

McGhie, A., Chapman, J., & Lawson, J. S. (1965). The effect of distraction on schizophrenic performance (I): Perception and immediate memory. *British Journal of Psychiatry, 111*, 383–390.

Nuechterlein, K. N. (1977). Reaction time and attention in schizophrenia: A critical evaluation of the data and theories. *Schizophrenia Bulletin, 3*, 373–428.

Nuechterlein, K. (1979). *Sustained attention and social competence among offspring of schizophrenic mothers*. Paper presented at the 87th Annual Convention of the American Psychological Association, New York.

Nuechterlein, K., Phipps–Yonas, S., Driscoll, R., & Garmezy, N. (1980). *Attentional functioning among children vulnerable to adult schizophrenia: Vigilence, reaction time and incidental learning*. Paper presented at the Risk Research Consortium Plenary Conference, San Juan, Puerto Rico.

Oltmanns, T. F., & Neale, J. M. (1975). Schizophrenic performance when distractors are present: Attentional deficit or differential task difficulty level? *Journal of Abnormal Psychology, 84*, 205–209.

Oltmanns, T. F., Weintraub, S., Stone, A., & Neale, J. M. (1978). Cognitive slippage in children vulnerable to schizophrenia. *Journal of Abnormal Child Psychology, 6*(2), 237–245.

Orzak, M. H., & Kornetsky, C. (1966). Attention dysfunction in chronic schizophrenia. *Archives of General Psychiatry, 14*, 323–326.

Phipps–Yonas, S. (1979). *Reaction time, peer assessment, and achievement in vulnerable children*. Paper presented at the 87th Annual Convention of the American Psychological Association, New York.

Rutschmann, J., Cornblatt, B., & Erlenmeyer–Kimling, L. (1977). Sustained attention in children at risk for schizophrenia. *Archives of General Psychiatry, 34*, 571–575.

Rutschmann, J., Cornblatt, B., & Erlenmeyer–Kimling, L. (1980). Auditory recognition memory in adolescents at risk for schizophrenia: Report on a verbal continuous recognition task. *Psychiatry Research, 3*, 151–161.

Slade, P. D. (1971). Rate of information processing in a schizophrenic and a control group: The effect of increasing task complexity. *British Journal of Social and Clinical Psychology, 10*, 152–159.

Stone, A. A., Neale, J. M., & Weintraub, S. (1977). *Using information-processing tasks to form groups of vulnerable and invulnerable children of schizophrenic parents*. Paper presented at the 85th Annual Convention of the American Psychological Association, San Francisco.

Weintraub, S., & Neale, J. M. (1980). *The Stony Brook high-risk project*. Paper presented at the Risk Research Consortium Plenary Conference, San Juan, Puerto Rico.

Winters, K. C., Stone, A. A., Weintraub, S. & Neale, J. M. (1981). Cognitive and attentional deficits in children vulnerable to psychopathology. *Journal of Abnormal Child Psychology, 9*, 435–453.

Wohlberg, G. W., & Kornetsky, C. (1973). Sustained attention in remitted schizophrenics. *Archives of General Psychiatry, 28*, 533–537.

8 MMPI Profiles in Adolescence as Indicators of Achievement and Adjustment in Young Adulthood

Joseph Lowman
M. David Galinsky

Life history research has commonly focused on the antecedents and outcome factors associated with psychopathology (e.g., Clausen, 1975; Erlenmeyer–Kimling, 1975; Feldman & Orford, 1980; Roff, 1975; Rosenthal, 1974), although studies have increasingly taken a broader perspective including longitudinal studies of early development (Bell, 1974), vocational behavior (Jordaan & Super, 1975), and factors associated with retirement (Streib, 1975) and aging (Martin, 1975). In general, studies have shown striking continuities in development, although the occurrence of psychopathology has not always been followed or preceded by indications of dysfunctionality. For example, studies of treated children (Robins, 1966, 1972, 1979) and adolescents (Hafner, Quast, & Shea, 1975) have shown that the presence of psychological dysfunctionality is not universally predictive of later difficulties.

The research to be reported here attempts to integrate interest in psychopathology and in normative development by studying a population of adolescents, eighth graders to be exact, whose Minnesota Multiphasic Personality Inventory (MMPI) profiles collected as part of a normative study of schoolchildren suggested an unusually high degree of psychopathology, but whose teachers and peers reported observing few unusual behavior patterns or personality characteristics. This benign impression of the group was supported by research interviewers who also saw the youngsters as being reasonably well adjusted to their surroundings. The sample under study is also unusual in that the social background of its members is not typical of those commonly studied, being from an unaffluent part of the rural south and consisting of equal numbers of black and white subjects.

Any longitudinal study of psychopathology that takes adolescence as its starting point faces certain theoretical pitfalls, primarily resulting from the high base rate of subjective distress and inadequately developed impulse control frequently found in this developmental period. Thus, measures of personality taken during adolescence should be interpreted in the light of age-specific norms, although this does not occur with regularity. Individual differences in degree of subjective discomfort, perceived disturbance, and dysfunctionality within this generally turbulent period do exist, however, and may be indicative of underlying social, constitutional, or psychological factors related to differences in vulnerability to stress. As Felner, Farber, & Primavera (1983) and others, and as Dohrenwend's (1978) model proposes, such psychological mediators are likely to be related to the probability of maladaptation during subsequent periods of stress. Her perspective would argue that adolescence is a good period for such initial study in that differences among subjects at that time may provide valid indicators of risk for later difficulties.

The research presented here speaks to this issue in that several different methods of analyzing and categorizing our subjects' eighth-grade MMPI profiles are reported in an attempt to determine to what extent the striking degree of elevation represented measurement error arising from the use of this instrument with adolescent subjects or reflected the presence of underlying personality predispositions that, although not surfacing in observable distress at the time, were predictive of eventual dysfunctionality.

Our findings are subject to further qualification because of the social atypicality of our sample. The fact our sample is equally balanced for race and sex creates the possibility of systematic biases because higher rates of psychopathology among lower social strata have been found reliable (Dohrenwend & Dohrenwend, 1969). In light of this, we compare our findings between black and white and between male and female subjects, but it is unfortunate that our sample did not contain sufficient numbers of subjects to permit separate analyses for each race by sex combination. The reader is therefore advised to keep the potential advantages and limitations of our sample in mind when interpreting our results.

Before presenting the specific aims of this research, we briefly describe the larger research from which this study emerged.

BACKGROUND OF THE PRESENT RESEARCH

In the early 1960s, Earl Baughman and Grant Dahlstrom (see *Negro and White Children,* 1968) conducted an ambitious psychological study of children attending four segregated schools (two black and two white) in a rural area of piedmont North Carolina. Their findings revealed racial differences on achievement and intelligence as reported by others (Loehlin, 1975) and indicated that a variety of family and personality variables were associated with intelligence and school achievement as well. It was the portentous MMPI data that they collected and the inconsistency between these data and the external observer impressions that prompted us to follow up only the 262 eighth graders in their larger sample.

In our follow-up study of their eighth-grade subjects (see Lowman, Galinsky, & Gray–Little, 1980), interview data gathered from our subjects at young adulthood (ages 23–25), indicated that they turned out remarkably well in light of the data collected on them earlier. For example, in spite of the fact over half the subjects had pathological MMPI profiles, their average educational attainment was slightly over high school graduation, most were married (70%) with few separations or divorces (10%), and few reported arrests (5%) or outpatient (9%) or inpatient (2%) treatment for psychological difficulties. Standing out among our findings was the predominance of Stanford–Binet Intelligence Scale (Terman & Merrill, 1960) IQs as predictors of achievement. Of noteworthy contrast to this finding was the lack of significant racial differences in educational attainment, an especially surprising outcome given the average difference of 15 IQ points between racial groups found earlier.

Weighted indices of overall disturbance (DSI) computed on their MMPI profiles (see Cooke, 1967a,b; Dahlstrom, Welsh, & Dahlstrom, 1972, 1975) were not found to be significantly related to very many of the outcome variables in our original study, although many of the subjects' DSIs (44%) fell above the cutting score for a pathological profile. The DSI scores were significantly correlated with several of the eighth-grade measures reflecting intellectual ability (e.g., Stanford–Binet IQ, $r = -.32$, and Stanford Achievement Test, $r = -.32$). Correlation coefficients between DSIs and the study's achievement variables, education, occupational status, and income, were not significant (r's $= -.16$, .10, and .00, respectively). A secondary procedure in which we divided our subjects into those scoring above and below the pathology cutting score on the DSI did find more relationships, but not of a sufficient quantity nor magnitude to demonstrate a relationship between elevated adolescent MMPI profiles and subsequent achievement or adjustment. The research to be reported here was undertaken because of the belief our previous method of classifying MMPI profiles may not have been sufficiently sensitive to adequately evaluate the predictive validity of elevated MMPI profiles during adolesence as predictors in longitudinal studies.

Specific Study Aims

Specific aims of this study were (1) to determine the extent to which elevated scores on the MMPI among a nontreatment group of adolescents are valid risk indicators of eventual psychopathology and inadequate functioning; (2) to evalu-

ate the differential ability of various methods of analyzing elevated MMPI profiles to predict later difficulties; and (3) to discover any differential patterns in
these relationships over time associated with sex and race.

METHODS

Description of Located Sample

The original sample of 262 eighth graders contained 23% black males, 32%
black females, 22% white males, and 23% white females. Using a combination
of school records, telephone directories, personnel listings at major local employers, and interviews with previously located subjects, we were able to locate
61% of the black males, 60% of the black females, 77% of the white males, and
72% of the white females, for an overall rate of 67% (incidentally, no one
refused to participate). Thus our methods were apparently more successful at
locating white subjects but equally successful in finding both sexes. This differential rate may have been a function of greater migration among the blacks
and/or of less likelihood of blacks having telephones or working for major
employers in the area. Nonetheless, the differences in follow-up rate were not
considered sufficiently great to pose major problems for our analyses or conclusions. A more critical question was whether there was a systematic difference in
predictor measures, especially the MMPI, between those subjects we found and
those we were unable to locate. The final section of this discussion of our
methods reports such comparisons.

Follow-up Interview and Measures

A follow-up interview taking approximately 30 minutes was given to our subjects face-to-face whenever possible, but most often over the telephone. It assessed a broad range of variables dealing with their lives from the time they were
in the eighth grade. The specific measures of achievement and adjustment to be
presented here are as follows:

Achievement Variables
1. *Educational Attainment:* the total number of years of formal schooling of
any type (e.g., college, vocational) a person reported receiving.
2. *Occupational Status:* a five-point scale based on just the occupational
rankings from the Hollingshead and Redlich (1958) scale of social position.
(Note: inverse directionality for this scale results in the value 1 representing the
highest status stratum and 5 the lowest.)
3. *Income:* a seven-point scale representing the subjects' report of their individual weekly incomes before taxes beginning with $50.00 and proceeding in
$50.00 increments to over $300.00 per week.

Adjustment Variables

1. *Health Opinion Scale:* (HOS, Leighton, Leighton, & Danley, 1966) a 22-item weighted scale of personality adjustment assessing primarily the physiological and behavioral symptoms of depression and anxiety. (Note: higher scores on the HOS indicate greater psychopathology.)

2. *Marital Status:* a classification into single, married, and separated or divorced subjects.

3. *Arrests:* subjects' reporting having been arrested since in the eighth grade.

4. *Outpatient Treatment:* subjects' reporting of receiving outpatient treatment for psychological difficulties.

5. *Psychiatric Hospitalizations:* subjects' reporting of ever being hospitalized for psychological problems.

The MMPI profiles collected by Baughman and Dahlstrom were the primary data from the eighth-grade assessment that were used although Stanford–Binet IQ scores were used in one analysis as a covariate. Concerning the MMPI scores, it is important to note that Baughman and Dahlstrom collected these data using a tape-recorded rather than a written administration in order to insure maximum validity.

Classification of MMPI Profiles

The MMPI produces normative scores on numerous empirically developed scales of personality. Because of the wealth of validational data and clinical experience available on it (see Dahlstrom et al., 1972, 1975; Dahlstrom & Dahlstrom, 1980), the MMPI has been for many years the standard objective personality instrument in use throughout the world. The 10 standard clinical scales are labeled according to the different diagnostic criterion groups used in their construction. For example, several scales are commonly used representing various forms of neurosis (such as hypochondriasis or obsessive compulsive) and psychotic disorders (such as schizophrenia or mania). In addition, one scale was constructed for the character disorder diagnosis of psychopathic or antisocial personality. The absolute elevation on specific MMPI scales is an important factor to consider in interpreting a subject's scores, but the overall configuration, or relative elevation, among the standard scales is of more importance and clinical utility. Subtleties in profile configuration and classification are the MMPI's primary strength, although these are difficult to capture in research applications.

The first step in analyzing the MMPI data was to rescore them according to adolescent norms, norms unavailable when Baughman and Dahlstrom conducted their study. This resulted in a reduced estimation of the level of pathology present in the sample during the eighth grade, although it was still considerable, with 37% of the sample (as compared to 61% based on adult norms) having elevations on at least one of the clinical scales. Thus, some of the data distortion resulting from the base rate of distress during adolescence was reduced at the outset by using age-specific norms.

Two different methods of classifying the array of MMPI scales were used in this study in an attempt to capture more of the configural subtlety of the test. One of these simply classified subjects according to the number of scales on which they had elevations, or T scores of over 70 (or 95th percentile). This simple method produced three groups, Normal, One-Point, and Two-Point (all but five subjects in this group had only two scales elevated) containing 106, 30, and 33 subjects, respectively. This method, then, represented a division of our sample based on how many scales were elevated above the accepted pathological cuttoff point.

In an attempt to capture additional complexity, profiles were also classified into Normal, Neurotic, Character Disorder, and Psychotic configurations. The same subjects constituted the group of normals in both analyses, but subjects with scale elevations were recombined based on their particular elevated scale(s) to achieve the final classifications used. The system of so classifying elevated MMPI profiles developed by Lachar (1974) was used with a slight modification by Dahlstrom (1979) to assign classifications to some subjects whose particular configurations could not be classified using Lachar's system (six profiles were still unable to be classified). This resulted in 106 profiles being classified Normal (those with no elevations), 16 Neurotic, 18 Character Disorder, and 23 Psychotic. These classifications indicated which group of normal or diagnostic patients the subjects' eighth-grade profiles most resembled. An assumption of this approach to profile classification is that the configurations found in a normal adolescent population that are similar to those of actual adult patients will be differentially predictive of outcome 10 years later.

Comparison of Lost and Found Subjects

As was mentioned earlier, slightly more white than black subjects were successfully located. The lost subjects were quite similar overall on the eighth-grade variables to those located, however. Of particular relevance to this study, however, was the fact that the groups differed on DSIs, with the lost subjects having significantly higher DSIs. Even after the data were recorded using adolescent norms, this differential follow-up rate is apparent. Table 8.1 presents race and sex data on all subjects, lost and found, in the elevation and diagnostic code type groups. As can be seen, the lost subjects, as compared to those located, had 54 versus 65% classified Normal, 11 versus 10% classified Neurotic, 11 versus 11% classified Character Disorder, and 25 versus 14% classified Psychotic. Thus, the lost subjects appeared to have contained relatively fewer normal subjects and more of those subjects whose eighth-grade profiles were similar to persons

TABLE 8.1
Frequency, Sex, and Race of Subjects in MMPI Groups

Elevation Groups

	Normal		One-Point		Two-Point		Totals	
	f	%	f	%	f	%	f	%
Males								
Blacks	20	(12)	7	(4)	8	(5)	35	(21)
Whites	31	(18)	4	(2)	6	(4)	41	(24)
Females								
Blacks	26	(15)	9	(5)	13	(8)	48	(28)
Whites	29	(17)	10	(6)	6	(4)	45	(27)
Totals	106	(63)	30	(17)	33	(20)	169	(100)

Diagnostic Code Types

	Normal		Neurotic		Character		Psychotic		Totals	
	f	%	f	%	f	%	f	%	f	%
Males										
Blacks	20	(12)	3	(2)	7	(4)	4	(2)	34	(21)
Whites	31	(19)	6	(4)	3	(2)	0	(0)	40	(25)
Females										
Blacks	26	(16)	3	(2)	5	(3)	12	(7)	46	(28)
Whites	29	(18)	4	(2)	3	(2)	7	(4)	43	(26)
Totals	106	(65)	16	(10)	18	(11)	23	(14)	163	(100)

assigned psychotic diagnoses. This slight bias needs to be kept in mind when our results are presented in the following section.

RESULTS

The achievement and adjustment data were evaluated using eight separate but nonindependent analysis of variance (ANOVA) tests over time. The desire to compare these two methods of profile categorization and a theoretical interest in each of the four outcome measures (three achievement and one adjustment) precluded the use of single comparisons using a multivariate model. Our sample was also of insufficient size to compare race, sex, and MMPI groups using 3-way ANOVAs; thus, we evaluated sex and race effects separately in 2-way tests.

Achievement Variables

The results of the ANOVAs on the achievement variables are presented in Table 8.2 for all subjects. As can be seen, the elevation groups were not significantly different from each other on any of the achievement outcome variables. The difference on Educational Attainment came so close to significance ($p < .06$) that orthogonal contrasts were computed to test differences between the specific groups. These showed the group having elevations on two or more scales to have attained significantly less education than those whose profiles were within normal limits. There was a trend ($p < .06$) approaching significance for the One-Point group to have attained more education than the Two-Point group. Thus, the data suggest that simply having one MMPI scale in the pathological range does not predict attaining fewer years of formal education but that having two or more elevated scales is suggestive of less educational attainment.

Categorization by diagnostic groups was more predictive of differences at young adulthood on achievement variables. Both the measures of educational attainment and weekly income as shown in Table 8.2 were significantly different across the four groups. An inspection of the group means indicated that the four diagnostic groups were ranked similarly for both these variables. Subsequent contrasts on the education variable indicated that the Neurotics were not significantly different from the Normals (although they were consistently higher on both achievement variables), but that the Neurotics and the Normals had higher achievement indices than the Psychotics on both variables. The Character Disorders occupied an intermediate position and were not significantly different from the Normals and Neurotics nor from the Psychotics. A similar pattern of significant contrasts was obtained for income with the exception that the Neurotics' income scores were significantly higher than the Normals. Thus, categorization of the elevated MMPI profiles by diagnostic types revealed an interesting pattern suggesting moderately anxious subjects with Neurotic profiles are likely to

TABLE 8.2
Follow-Up Variable Means, SDs, and ANOVA Statistics for MMPI Groups—All Subjects

| | Elevation Groups | | | | | | | | |
| | Normals | | One-Point | | Two-Point | | | | |
Variables	M	SD	M	SD	M	SD	F	df	p <
Adjustment									
HOS	25.6	(4.0)	25.2	(3.7)	26.6	(4.4)	1.26	(2,171)	.31
Achievement									
Education	12.4	(2.2)	12.8	(3.4)	11.4	(2.0)	2.77	(2,171)	.06[a]
Occupational									
Status	3.6	(1.1)	3.3	(1.3)	3.9	(1.3)	1.69	(2,139)	.19
Income	2.9	(1.0)	3.1	(1.1)	2.7	(1.2)	1.03	(2,136)	.36

| | Diagnostic Code Types | | | | | | | | | | |
| | Normals | | Neurotic | | Character Disorder | | Psychotic | | | | |
Variables	M	SD	M	SD	M	SD	M	SD	F	df	p <
Adjustment											
HOS	25.6	(4.0)	26.3	(4.5)	24.5	(2.5)	27.0	(4.7)	1.51	(3,164)	.21
Achievement											
Education	12.4	(2.2)	13.4	(4.1)	11.7	(2.3)	11.4	(1.9)	2.58	(3,165)	.05[b]
Occupational											
Status	3.6	(1.1)	3.2	(1.7)	3.8	(1.4)	3.8	(1.1)	.85	(3,132)	.47
Income	2.9	(1.0)	3.6	(1.8)	2.8	(.7)	2.3	(.8)	3.26	(3,130)	.02[c]

[a]Contrasts on Education: Normals versus One-Points, p < .54; Normals versus Two-Points, p < .02; One-Points versus Two-Points, p < .06.
[b]Contrasts on Education: Normals versus Neurotics, p < .14; Normals versus Character Disorders, p < .26; Normals versus Psychotics, p < .03; Neurotics versus Character Disorders, p < .16; Neurotics versus Psychotics, p < .05; Character Disorders versus Psychotics, p < .62.
[c]Contrasts on Income: Normals versus Neurotics, p < .05; Normals versus Character Disorders, p < .59; Normals versus Psychotics, p < .04; Neurotics versus Character Disorders, p < .14; Neurotics versus Psychotics, p < .04; Character Disorders versus Psychotics, p < .15.
Note: Higher HOS scores indicate greater psychological distress and higher Occupational Status scores reflect lower status jobs.

achieve at somewhat higher levels than normals and that those with the more disturbed thinking and behavior associated with psychotic profiles were least likely to achieve.

Table 8.3 presents means on outcome variables for all female, male, black, and white subjects. These nonindependent means are only for the race and sex comparisons individually and do not represent specific race by sex groups. The patterns of rank ordering of the means within each of these comparisons is quite similar to that displayed in Table 8.2 for all subjects. Neurotics tended to have the highest average achievement scores, Normals followed at a close second, and Psychotics were clearly lower than the others. Subjects whose profiles resembled Character Disorders fell somewhere between Neurotics and Psychotics. ANOVAs comparing males with females showed significant sex effects both on Occupational Status (F (1) = 4.81, p < .03) and on Income (F (1) = 8.11, p < .005) with females reporting lower status jobs earning less income. Although mean education for females was higher than that of males, the ANOVA testing this difference approached but did not attain significance (F (1) = 3.32, p < .07). None of the interaction effects were significant between race or sex for either of the two methods of MMPI classification. Thus, the pattern of means for the race and sex groups constituting our overall sample did not appear to be systematically different from the whole.

Because of previous findings in the Lowman et al. (1980) study that MMPI scores were negatively correlated with intellectual measures, the ANOVAs showing significant differences between the elevation and diagnostic groups were recomputed using an analysis of covariance (ANACOVAR) model controlling for eighth-grade Stanford–Binet IQ scores. The results of these ANACOVARs are presented in Table 8.4. As can be seen, the combined models using MMPI elevation group and IQ and using diagnostic code types and IQ were both significantly related to education (p < .005 for elevations, p < .004 for diagnostic type) and to income (p < .05 for elevations, p < .04 for diagnostic types). It appears that the combined models predicted a greater proportion of variance for education scores (R^2s = .19 for elevation and .24 for diagnostic types) than for income scores (R^2s = .15 for elevation and .20 for diagnostic types). The diagnostic code type method of profile classification, then, appeared to account for more variance than using simply the number of elevations. More important, the unique effects attributable to IQ and to the MMPI groupings were clearly different from each other, with IQ accounting for the significance of the overall models. Neither elevation groups nor diagnostic groups significantly predicted education or income when the effects of IQ were partialed out. Most of the p values for the MMPI groups alone were far from significant and the controlled test of diagnostic groups predicting education (p < .12) was as close as any came. IQ clearly appears to be the more powerful of the two variables, as effects attributable to MMPI scores disappear when IQ is partialed out.

Adjustment Variables

Tables 8.2 and 8.3 also present descriptive and ANOVA statistics on the HOS, the self-report measure of adjustment used. These scores were not significantly different for any of the elevation or diagnostic groups. The rank ordering of the HOS means was similar to those for education and income except that the Neurotics and the Psychotics appeared to report more distress than the Normals or Character Disorders, whereas the latter group reported the least anxiety. In addition, none of the race and sex comparisons were significant. Thus, the elevated MMPI profiles at adolescence were not predictive of differences in adjustment at young adulthood as measured by the Health Opinion Survey.

Because the equivalence of measures gathered at various points in time is important to longitudinal studies, the lack of equivalence between the MMPI and the HOS is a serious weakness in the design of the study reported here. Even though the content of the two scales is similar, the fact that they are not identical weakens somewhat the conclusions about the lack of relationship over time between the two adjustment measures. In an attempt to estimate consistency over time on a more limited but equivalent measure, data were rescored using only 16 of the 22 HOS items, items almost identical in content and wording to 16 of the 566 MMPI items. A Pearson correlation coefficient computed on the two sets of these 16 identical items produced a coefficient of .16 ($p < .01$). Although this degree of similarity is statistically significant, it is not especially meaningful or useful given the large number of subjects involved (169) and the small percentage of variance accounted for (3%). This finding lends support to the conclusion about the lack of relationship between the two adjustment measures, because even when an attempt was made to produce equivalent measures, the selected eighth-grade MMPI responses were not related in any meaningful way to the HOS scores gathered at young adulthood.

The categorical nature of the other adjustment variables and the small size of our sample severely limited the kinds of statistical tests and inferences we could make from them. It was possible to compare elevation group and diagnostic code type differences in marital status using Chi Square analyses, and these were not significant (elevation group $X^2(6) = 8.54$, $p < .20$). Thus, the eighth-grade MMPI elevations were not associated with subsequent marital status.

The small number of subjects reporting arrests ($n = 9$) precluded inferential statistics but MMPI profiles did not appear to be related to this outcome variable. Only one of the nine subjects had an elevated score on any of the scales compared to one out of three for the subjects overall.

Psychiatric treatment appeared slightly related to previous MMPI scores. For example, 5 of the 15 subjects reporting outpatient treatment had elevated scales and 4 of those 5 had two elevations. Those profiles with multiple elevations were of a psychotic code type and the single elevation fell into the Character Disorder

TABLE 8.3

Means on Outcome Variables by MMPI Groups, Race, and Sex, Diagnostic Code Type[a]

Elevation Groups

	Males			Females		
Variables	Normal	One-Point	Two-Point	Normal	One-Point	Two-Point
HOS	25.1	24.9	26.1	25.8	25.4	27.0
Education	12.2	11.8	11.7	12.5	13.3	11.3
Occupational Status	3.7	3.8	4.0	3.3	2.8	3.8
Income	3.1	3.4	3.2	2.6	2.8	2.1

	Blacks			Whites		
	Normal	One-Point	Two-Point	Normal	One-Point	Two-Point
HOS	26.2	24.8	26.2	24.9	25.7	27.4
Education	12.5	12.9	11.1	12.2	12.6	12.0
Occupational Status	3.8	3.5	3.9	3.3	3.0	4.0
Income	2.7	2.6	2.4	3.0	3.6	3.1

Diagnostic Code Types

Males

	Normal	Neurotic	Character Disorder	Psychotic
HOS	25.1	26.5	24.1	27.0
Education	12.2	12.3	11.8	10.2
Occupational Status	3.7	3.2	4.1	4.7
Income	3.1	4.2	2.7	2.7

Females

	Normal	Neurotic	Character Disorder	Psychotic
HOS	25.8	26.0	25.0	27.0
Education	12.5	14.7	11.6	11.6
Occupational Status	3.3	3.0	3.2	3.5
Income	2.6	2.2	2.8	2.2

(Blacks)

Males

	Normal	Neurotic	Character Disorder	Psychotic
HOS	26.2	24.0	24.6	26.9
Education	12.6	13.5	11.7	11.2
Occupational Status	3.8	2.5	3.8	4.0
Income	2.8	3.0	2.4	2.3

Females

	Normal	Neurotic	Character Disorder	Psychotic
HOS	24.9	27.7	24.3	27.2
Education	12.2	13.3	11.8	11.9
Occupational Status	3.3	3.4	3.8	3.0
Income	3.0	3.8	3.5	2.5

(Whites)

[a]Insufficient numbers of subjects did not allow independent Race by Sex means.

Note: Higher HOS scores indicate greater psychological distress and higher Occupational Status scores reflect lower status jobs.

TABLE 8.4

Analysis of Covariance on Education and Income for MMPI Groups—Controlling for IQ

Variable	Effect	Unique Effects			Overall Model Effects			
		F	df	$p <$	F	df	$p <$	R^2
Education	Elevation							
	Groups	1.29	(2)	.28	4.72	(3,61)	.005	.19
	IQ	9.06	(1)	.004				
	Diagnostic							
	Code Types	2.01	(3)	.12	4.41	(4,56)	.004	.24
	IQ	5.79	(1)	.02				
Income	Elevation							
	Groups	.23	(2)	.80	2.86	(3,48)	.05	.15
	IQ	8.53	(1)	.005				
	Diagnostic							
	Code Types	.87	(3)	.46	2.71	(4,44)	.04	.20
	IQ	5.16	(1)	.03				

category. The other 10 subjects with outpatient histories had normal profiles. Of the 3 subjects reporting psychiatric hospitalizations, 1 had had a normal profile and the other 2 had two-point elevations of a psychotic variety. Thus, there was the slightest of suggestions that subjects reporting subsequent psychiatric treatment were more likely to have had psychotic-appearing profiles when in the eighth grade than the base rate of such profiles would predict. It must be emphasized, however, that this suggestion is based on a very small number of subjects and that most persons with psychotic profiles did not report a history of treatment and that most persons receiving treatment were those with normal eighth-grade profiles.

DISCUSSION

The analyses reported here indicate clearly that elevated MMPI profiles collected during adolescence should *not* be considered valid predictors of later psychopathology or inadequate functioning based on the presence of scale elevations alone. There can be no question that using adult norms for adolescents is highly likely to overestimate the extent of future disability. But even using elevated scores based on adolescent norms as risk predictors in longitudinal research cannot be recommended without qualification based on the data reported here. There is reason to believe that a sophisticated method of categorizing MMPI profiles based on similarity to diagnostic groups is more likely to give valid predictions, especially for those individuals with psychotic patterns. The strong relationship observed here between these patterns and IQ suggest, however, the psychotic profiles be used as predictors with caution and that substantial additional research is needed on the relationship between cognitive deficit as revealed in intelligence and personality measures.

The data and analyses reported here clearly support the need for adjusting risk indicators of psychopathology for both the stage of the life cycle (Dahlstrom, 1983) and the specific cultural groups (Gynther, 1972) from which they were collected. Even though no differential race or sex effects were found for the lower SES black and white subjects studied here, the importance of qualifying risk predictors over time for different groups has in no way been diminished.

ACKNOWLEDGMENTS

Appreciation is expressed to Earl Baughman and to Grant Dahlstrom for the use of data collected by them in previous research. Dahlstrom's assistance in developing the diagnostic classification system we used was especially helpful. Appreciation is also expressed to the Carolina Population Center for financial support used to collect follow-up data from Baughman and Dahlstrom's subjects. Dorene Goodfriend's efforts at rescoring and classifying the subjects' MMPI data are also greatly appreciated. Correspondence concerning this chapter should be sent to Joseph Lowman, Department of Psychology, Davie Hall 013-A, University of North Carolina, Chapel Hill, NC, 27514.

REFERENCES

Baughman, E. E., & Dahlstrom, W. G. (1968). *Negro and white children: A psychological study in the rural south*. New York: Academic Press.

Bell, R. (1974). The Bethesda longitudinal study: The overall study and some specific findings. In R. D. Wirt, G. Winokur, & M. Roff, (Eds.), *Life history research in psychopathology* (Vol. 4). Minneapolis: University of Minnesota Press.

Clausen, J. (1975). The impact of mental illness: A twenty-year follow-up. In R. D. Wirt, G. Winokur, & M. Roff (Eds.), *Life history research in psychopathology* (Vol. 4). Minneapolis: University of Minnesota Press.

Cooke, J. K. (1967a). Clinician's decisions as a basis for deriving actuarial formulae. *Journal of Clinical Psychology, 23*, 232–233.

Cooke, J. K. (1967b). MMPI in actuarial diagnosis of psychological disturbance among college males. *Journal of Counseling Psychology, 14*, 474–477.

Dahlstrom, W. G. (1983). The development of psychological testing. In G. Kimble & K. Schlesinger (Eds.), *Topics in the history of psychology*. Hillsdale, NJ: Lawrence Erlbaum Associates.

Dahlstrom, W., G., & Dahlstrom, L. (Eds.). (1980). *Readings on the MMPI: A new selection on personality measurement*. Minneapolis: University of Minnesota Press.

Dahlstrom, W. G., Welsh, G., & Dahlstrom, L. (1972). An MMPI Handbook (Vol. I: Clinical Interpretations). Minneapolis: University of Minnesota Press.

Dahlstrom, W. G., Welsh, G., & Dahlstrom L. (1975). An MMPI Handbook, Vol. II: Research Applications. Minneapolis: University of Minnesota Press.

Dohrenwend, B. P., & Dohrenwend, B. S. (1969). Social status and psychological disorder. In *A causal inquiry*. New York: Wiley.

Dohrenwend, B. S. (1978). Social stress and community psychology. *American Journal of Community Psychology, 6*, 1–14.

Erlenmeyer–Kimling, L. (1975). A prospective study of children at risk for schizophrenia: Methodological considerations and some preliminary findings. In R. D. Wirt, G. Winokur, & M. Roff, (Eds.), *Life history research in psychopathology* (Vol. 4). Minneapolis: University of Minnesota Press.

Feldman, P., & Orford, J. (1980). *Psychological problems: The social context*. New York: Wiley.

Felner, R. D., Farber, S. S., & Primavera, J. (1983). Transitions and stressful life events: A model for primary prevention. In R. D. Felner, L. A. Jason, J. N. Moritsugu, & S. S. Farber (Eds.), *Preventive psychology: Theory, research, and practice*. New York: Pergamon Press.

Gynther, M. D. (1972). White norms and black MMPI's: A prescription for descrimination. *Psychological Bulletin, 78*, 386–402.

Hafner, A., Quast, W., & Shea, M. (1975). The adult adjustment of one thousand psychiatric and pediatric patients: Initial findings from a twenty-five-year follow-up. In R. D. Wirt, G. Winokur, & M. Roff, (Eds.), *Life history research in psychopathology* (Vol. 4). Minneapolis: The University of Minnesota Press.

Hollingshead, A. B., & Redlich, F. C. (1958). *Social class and mental illness: A community study*. New York: Wiley.

Jordaan, J. P., & Super, D. E. (1974). The prediction of early adult vocational behavior. In D. G. Ricks, A. Thomas, & M. Roff (Eds.), *Life history in psychopathology* (Vol. 3). Minneapolis: The University of Minnesota Press.

Lachar, D. (1974). *The MMPI: Clinical Assessment and Automated Interpretation*. Los Angeles: Western Psychological Services.

Leighton, A. M., Leighton, D. C., & Danley, R. A. (1966). Validity in mental health surveys. *Canadian Psychiatric Association Journal, 11,* 167–178.

Loehlin, J. C., Lindzey, R., & Spuhler, J. N. (1975). *Race differences in intelligence*. San Francisco: W. H. Freeman Company.

Lowman, J., Galinsky, M. D., & Gray–Little, B. (1980). *Predicting achievement: A ten-year follow-up of black and white adolescents*. Chapel Hill: Institute for Research in Social Science Monograph Series.

Martin, C. (1975). Marital and sexual factors in relation to age, disease, and longevity. In R. D. Wirt, G. Winokur, & M. Roff, (Eds.), *Life history research in psychopathology* (Vol. 4). Minneapolis: University of Minnesota Press.

Robins, L. N. (1966). *Deviant children grown up*. Baltimore: Williams & Wilkens.

Robins, L. N. (1972). An actuarial evaluation of the causes and consequences of deviant behavior in young black men. In M. Roff, L. N. Robins, & M. Pollack, (Eds.), *Life history research in psychopathology* (Vol. 2) Minneapolis: University of Minnesota Press.

Robins, L. N. (1979). Follow-up studies. In H. C. Quay & J. S. Werry (Eds.), *Psychopathological disorders of childhood*. New York: Wiley.

Roff, J. (1975). Long-term outcome for a set of schizophrenic subtypes. In R. D. Wirt, G. Winokur, & M. Roff (Eds.), *Life history research in psychopathology* (Vol. 4). Minneapolis: University of Minnesota Press.

Rosenthal, D. (1974). Issues in high-risk studies of schizophrenia. In D. F. Ricks, A. Thomas, & M. Roff (Eds.), *Life history research in psychopathology* (Vol. 3) Minneapolis: The University of Minnesota Press.

Streib, G. (1975). Changing perspectives on retirement: Role crises or role continuities. In R. D. Wirt, G. Winokur, & M. Roff (Eds.), *Life history research in psychopathology* (Vol. 4). Minneapolis: The University of Minnesota Press.

Terman, L. M., & Merrill, M. A. (1960). *Stanford–Binet Intelligence Scale: Manual for the Third Revision, Form L–M*. Boston: Houghton–Mifflin.

9 Methodological Issues in the Prediction of Psychopathology: A Life-Span Perspective

Erich W. Labouvie

The empirical studies presented in this volume are concerned with relatively small segments of the human life-span and are likely to be inspired by age-specific theories of psychopathology. However, taken together they do extend over the total life-span. Therefore, it seems quite reasonable to focus a discussion of methodological issues onto those problems that are common to developmental investigations regardless of the age ranges studied and that become particularly salient within a life-span framework.

Given the necessary and unavoidable selectivity of any such discussion, the reader is advised to consult the existing literature on life-span developmental psychology (Baltes, 1973; Baltes, Cornelius, & Nesselroade, 1979; Baltes, Reese, & Lipsitt, 1980; Baltes & Schaie, 1973; Goulet & Baltes, 1970; Huston–Stein & Baltes, 1976, Nesselroade & Reese, 1973), on developmental research design and methodology (Adam, 1978; Baltes, 1968; Baltes, Reese, & Nesselroade, 1977; Buss, 1974; Labouvie, 1978, 1982; Wohlwill, 1973), and on analytical procedures and models that have been proposed in the context of confirmatory multivariate analysis and causal modeling of time-ordered or longi-tudinal data (Bielby & Hauser, 1977; Heise, 1975; Humphreys & Parsons, 1979; Jöreskog & Sörbom, 1977; Kenny, 1975; Labouvie, 1974; Simonton, 1977; Skinner, 1978; Strauss Marmor & Marmor, 1978).

It seems fair to warn the reader not only of the selectivity built into the ensuing discussion but also of the biases that permeate it. One of those biases, in particular, may run counter to a position that is rather common among behavioral scientists. Often the argument can be heard that the context of behavioral obser-vations is generally so noisy that relatively crude and insensitive measurements as well as rather simple analytical and statistical devices are sufficient to extract from the data whatever information is considered relevant. The position taken here is just the opposite; that is, the noisier the overall context of the phenomenon studied, the more sophisticated and sensitive our devices and analytical tools and filters have to be to separate signals from noise.

The following presentation and discussion of issues is arbitrarily but intentionally divided into two sections corresponding to the distinction between description and explanation (e.g., Baltes, 1973; Baltes et al., 1977). The distinction is arbitrary because the boundaries between what constitutes a description versus an explanation of a given phenomenon are quite fluid and not absolute. However, the distinction is maintained intentionally in order to avoid the kind of conceptual confusion that is likely to arise whenever the two tasks are not sufficiently separated from each other.

DEFINITIONS OF PSYCHOPATHOLOGY:
THE EMPIRICAL DATA CONTEXT

A discussion of methodological issues becomes more meaningful if it is accompanied by a working definition of the phenomenon or class of phenomena that are the object of one's description and explanation. As far as the topic of psychopathology is concerned, there is certainly enough evidence to attest to past difficulties in obtaining commonly acceptable definitions as well as reliably replicable empirical procedures associated with those definitions (e.g., Achenbach & Edelbrock, 1978; Anthony, 1970; Eme, 1979; Goldfarb, 1970; Pfeiffer, 1977; Schaie & Schaie, 1977). Rather than trying to join that debate—which would be beyond the expertise of this author—it seems sufficient for present purposes merely to propose a general description of empirical data contexts that are most likely to elicit inferences and judgments about the potential or actual presence of some form of psychopathology. In other words, if clinical inferences and decisions are based on the observation of empirical events, one may want to define, at least in a general sense, the kind of empirical observations that tend to influence the content of those inferences.

According to this line of reasoning, the following definition is advanced as a general framework for the subsequent discussion of issues:

1. If the form, intensity level, frequency level, or persistence level of a behavior and/or its consequences fall outside the range that is considered acceptable for the population to which a given individual is assigned, notions of a potential or actual presence of psychopathology are more likely to emerge.

2. If the form, intensity level, frequency level, or persistence level of an environmental event or characteristic fall outside the range that is acceptable for the population to which a particular individual is assigned, notions of a potential

presence or development of psychopathology are also more likely to be advanced.

That this represents a definition of relevant data contexts rather than psychopathology per se should be quite evident. First, it is recognized that different clinicians and researchers may sample different sets of behaviors and environmental events to obtain what they consider to be relevant information. Second, it is left open how one may proceed to specify acceptable ranges of behaviors and environments as well as the reference population to which a given individual belongs. Ideally, such specifications are derived from theories that may or may not include developmental assumptions. In practice, however, they are often based on statistical norms and distributions. Third, the explicit reference to environmental events is intended to point out their relevance for the prospective study of historical or distal antecedent-consequent relationships in the development of psychopathology. In other words, a consideration of environmental characteristics is important when defining individuals or populations that are "at risk" of developing pathological developmental patterns.

Although it is not expected that this definition is acceptable to every behavioral scientist interested in the area of psychopathology, it seems to be general enough to encompass different forms of psychopathology and, more importantly perhaps, basic enough to allow a separate consideration of descriptive and explanatory issues.

THE DESCRIPTION OF PSYCHOPATHOLOGY:
CRITERIA AND PREDICTORS

In this context description is viewed as the systematic recording of empirical events according to specified procedures that are reliable and replicable. Typically, the events that are of interest to behavioral scientists are measured in terms of response variables (R), organismic variables (O), and environmental or stimulus variables (S). According to the general paradigm $R = f(R, O, S)$ (e.g., Baltes, 1973), predictors or antecedents are sampled from all three categories whereas criteria are, of course, obtained from the class of response variables.

Measurement

According to classical views of the measurement process (e.g., Lord & Novick, 1968), the construction of tests is always preceded by the invention or construction of a concept that prescribes a certain form of relational structure among all members of a specified population of individuals or events. If this conceptualization is in the form of mutually exclusive categories without any intrinsic quantitative order, corresponding measures are constructed as nominal scales. On the other hand, if the relational structure is conceptualized as a quantitative ordering, the resulting scales are constructed as ordinal, interval, or ratio scales. Thus, in the first case, psychopathology would be viewed as a qualitative discontinuity between normal and abnormal behavior and would be measured by nominal scales. In the second case, it would be conceptualized as a quantitative continuum ranging from normal to abnormal and assessed by quantitative scales.

However, the classical view of measurement describes only part of the overall picture. Specifically, it does not take into account the possibility that, because the relationship between an invented conceptual structure and an empirical scale structure is always obtained for a finite set of individuals, that relationship is subject to change whenever the empirical scale is applied in new or different populations of individuals. Consequently, it is not infrequent to find that the application of a measurement instrument precedes the invention of underlying concepts and associated relational structures. Moreover, whereas the classical view suggests a one-to-one relationship between conceptual and empirical relational structures, the alternative view allows greater flexibility; that is, the quantitative structure of an empirical scale may be translated into a conceptual structure that is either quantitative or qualitative, and vice versa. For instance, the translation of observed quantitative differences into underlying qualitative differences is attempted whenever quantitative cutoff points are selected to assign individuals to qualitatively different categories or stages. The formulation of relationships between quantity and quality has been formalized more systematically in areas such as catastrophe theory (e.g., Fararo, 1978) and multistructure models (e.g., Baltes & Nesselroade, 1970; Bentler, 1976; McDonald, 1978, 1979).

Although the two views of measurement seem to represent opposites to each other, it is more appropriate to regard them as interactive and complementary components of the business of description, with either one alone representing only a one-sided view of measurement activities. Taken together the two approaches lead to a distinction between four types of relationships that may characterize the linkage between empirical and conceptual relational structures (see Table 9.1). However, the present discussion is biased in favor of measures

TABLE 9.1
Possible Relationships between Measures and Concepts and Their
Associated Relational Structures

Relational Structure of Measures	Relational Structure of Concepts
Nominal Scale	Categorical Concept
Quantitative Scale	Quantitative Concept

with quantitative empirical structures. In other words, nominal scales, though not nominal concepts, are viewed here as measurement that lacks detail, sensitivity, and precision.

Single and Joint Distributions of Empirical Events

Systematic description of empirical events in terms of one or more measures results in single and joint frequency distributions. Analytical procedures and methods that can be used to analyze information contained in these distributions may, by and large, be grouped into two categories: (1) parametric methods that are based on the assumption of uni or multinormal distributions, and (2) nonparametric procedures that are distribution free. Proponents of the first category like to assure us that their methods are quite robust with regard to violations of the normality assumption. Proponents of nonparametric methods suggest that it is not necessary to pay attention to the particular forms and types of distributions that are found. In either case, it seems that the specific characteristics of single and joint distributions within and across different populations are essentially discarded as irrelevant and of little information value.

Although it is impossible to consider this issue in any great detail here, it is at least possible to raise it as a question that probably deserves more systematic attention from behavioral researchers. A more detailed consideration of the characteristics of single and joint distributions may be particularly important if the focus is on low-frequency events as suggested by the working definition introduced at the beginning. Specifically, distributional characteristics of measures may be useful with regard to (1) the formulation of norms of and boundaries between different populations including definitions of normal and abnormal (e.g., Moran, 1966), (2) the detection of systematic differences or changes in the relationships between measures as a function of their level, and (3) the systematic sampling of variables according to the type of distribution they exhibit in a given population.

Figures 9.1 and 9.2 try to illustrate these points more concretely. In a purely descriptive sense, empirical distributions of single variables do not only indicate the low-frequency ranges of some phenomenon but suggest also which operational definitions of norms and boundaries may be appropriate depending on the symmetry–asymmetry and uni versus multimodality of the obtained distributions. Figure 9.2 presents examples of joint distributions where the strength of the relationship between two variables varies as a function of their levels. The possibility of such interdependence between level and strength of association has been empirically investigated in the area of intellectual performance. According to the performance-differentiation hypothesis (e.g., Reinert, 1970), the degree of differentiation of intellectual abilities is dependent on the absolute level of intellectual performance. In the present context, similar phenomena may be obtained not only among sets of behavioral criterion variables, but also when considering

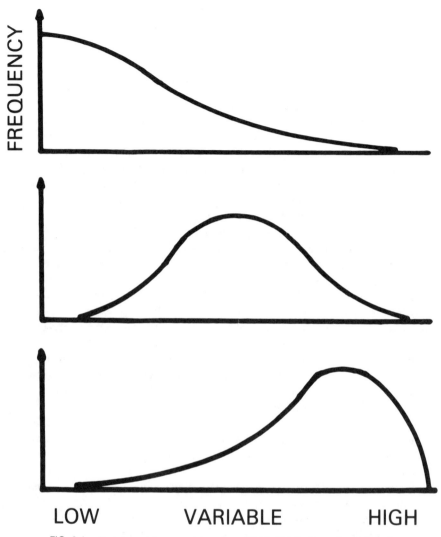

FIG. 9.1. Prototypes of asymmetric and symmetric distributions of criteria and predictors.

FIG. 9.2. Prototypes of joint distributions. The strength of association between variables varies with the level on each. A = areas of no relationship, B = areas of positive relationships.

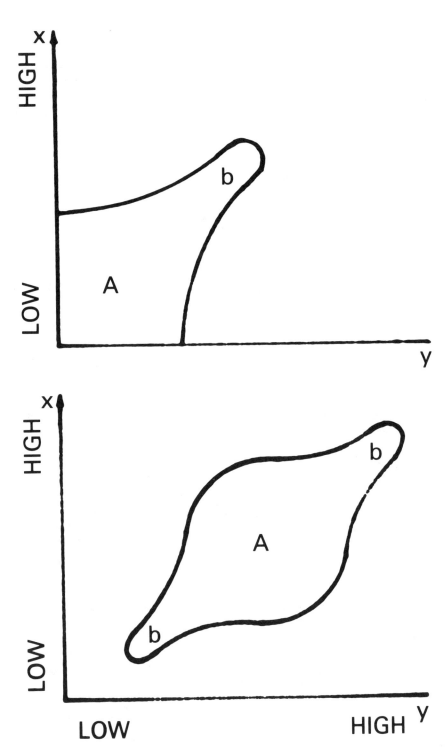

relationships between predictors and criteria. Clearly, changes in relationships as a function of level, if found, are useful and relevant with respect to the issue of continuity–discontinuity between normal and abnormal. Finally, it may be useful to consider different forms of distributions (see Fig. 9.1) as a potentially important facet for the sampling of variables to describe both low- and high-frequency events (e.g., Foa, 1965; Mellenbergh, Kelderman, Stijlen, & Zondag, 1979). If for no other reason, this consideration is likely to be helpful in selecting analytical procedures that are compatible with the empirical distributions.

Developmental Considerations

From a developmental point of view the task of description and measurement is compounded by several additional issues, among them (1) the problem of equivalence, (2) the possibility of changes in distributions and norms as a function of age and cohort, and (3) the choice of studying *sequences of differences* between individuals or groups over a series of occasions or of comparing individual *patterns of change* over a similar series of occasions.

1. Equivalence. The most basic issue that faces the study of psychopathology from a developmental viewpoint is the problem of functional equivalence of measures in relation to underlying concepts. Equally applicable to criteria and predictors, to behavioral, organismic, and environmental variables, the issue involves the following questions: (1) How do we know or how do we determine whether the same, formally identical measure relates to the same concept in different age or cohort groups, and (2) how do we know or how do we determine whether formally different measures are related to the same concept, either in the same or in different populations? As Rock, Werts, and Flaugher (1978) have pointed out (see also Labouvie, 1980b), the issue of equivalence when applied to comparisons of predictor-criterion relationships across different populations involves a consideration of four assumptions.

(1). Corresponding measures, be they formally identical or different, are conceptually equivalent.

(2). Conceptually equivalent measures have equal scale metrics or units of measurement across populations.

(3). Conceptually and metrically equivalent measures have equal reliabilities across populations.

(4). The systematic errors of conceptually and metrically equivalent and equally reliable measures are equal across groups, that is, there is consistency between observed and true mean differences between groups.

Unless the validity of each of these assumptions can be tested empirically, interpretations of population-related differences in predictor-criterion relationships may lead to ambiguous or even erroneous conclusions. In general, strategies that allow such a test require the use of multiple sets of measures for each concept that is being considered in order to establish systematic patterns of convergent and discriminant validity (Campbell & Fiske, 1959). From a developmental perspective the issue of equivalence may be most salient in relation to the variables of age and cohort. However, it should be pointed out that the issue can be raised whenever different groups of individuals including different experimental treatment groups are compared on empirical measures.

2. Changes in Distributions and Norms.   As suggested by our working definition, inferences about the possible presence of one or the other form of psychopathology are not only dependent on assumptions involving relationships between empirical measures and underlying concepts, but also on the standard of reference that is used to judge whether a particular behavioral or environmental event falls outside acceptable ranges. Consequently, it becomes important to specify one's choice of a reference group used to compare an individual's behavior or environment. The most obvious comparative parameters for a life-span perspective are chronological age and cohort or time of birth. The cohort variable is used to define populations of individuals that enter the continuously changing flow of historical conditions at different points in time (e.g., Baltes et al., 1979). Chronological age simply indicates the amount of time passed between birth and the point in time at which individuals of a particular cohort are observed. Defining reference groups in terms of age and cohort assumes, of course, that distributions of empirical variables are subject to change as a function of variations in age and cohort. Such changes may involve shape, range, and modality of both single and joint distributions. Thus, the same behavioral event may be variously interpreted as either a high-frequency or a low-frequency event depending on the actual or assumed normative distributions that are employed as a reference system. As far as the task of description is concerned, it is, therefore, necessary to recognize that the use of age- and cohort-specific norms may lead to systematic biases in the description and measurement of psychopathology when applied to age and cohort groups other than those for which they were obtained in the first place.

3. Individual Differences and Intraindividual Changes.   It is probably fair to state that the bulk of behavioral research, regardless of whether it is concerned with normal or abnormal phenomena, has focused on the study of differences between individuals and groups of individuals. This is true even in the case of so-called longitudinal studies that follow the same individuals over some time interval in order to obtain repeated observations. Although such studies can provide information about the change exhibited by each individual over successive points in time, the bias in favor of individual differences is evident by the fact that methodological paradigms used to analyze such data are typically based on the idea of relating differences observed at an earlier point in time to differences observed at a later occasion.

The rather one-sided emphasis on individual differences and their sequencing over differential individual change patterns is perhaps the result of a misunderstanding of the classical experiment. Viewed by many as the scientific method par excellence, it utilizes random assignment of individuals in order to achieve equality of groups before the onset of different experimental conditions. Because of this initial equality, differences observed on a single posttest will stand in a one-to-one relationship to the differential changes that are the result of the different treatments. Thus, although the classical experiment uses only a single posttest, it is more appropriately interpreted as a study of differential change than of differences at a single point in time.

In conjunction with this more general misconception of the classical experiment, psychometricians have repeatedly warned against the direct empirical description and measurement of intraindividual changes in the form of difference scores (e.g., Cronbach & Furby, 1970). Although the criticism of difference scores is based on untested and, therefore, unwarranted assumptions (Labouvie, 1980a; Williams & Zimmerman, 1977), it is unfortunate that most behavioral scientists have somewhat prematurely accepted the validity of those conclusions. Finally, a preference for individual differences rather than intraindividual changes is often motivated by the fact that the use of formally identical measures across a series of occasions is not always desirable or possible. In that instance it is relatively convenient to express sequential relationships between individual differences in the form of synchronous, crosslagged, and autocorrelations (e.g., Kenny, 1975). However, the representation of individual change patterns and sequences, in comparison, becomes methodologically more difficult and cumbersome.

The issue of whether to choose differences or changes as the target of description is of course not limited to the category of criteria or response variables. It applies equally well to organismic and environmental variables. As far as environmental measures are concerned, it is not uncommon to represent individual changes in terms of the occurrence of certain specific and well-defined events such as graduating from high school, getting married, having a child, losing a spouse, getting divorced, etc. Although it is comparatively easy to achieve a high degree of reliability in the recording of such events, the validity and equivalence of those measures across different age and cohort populations remains debatable (e.g., Dohrenwend & Dohrenwend, 1974).

Whenever the focus is on differences between individuals or groups, the representation of change is accomplished in terms of average trends and the stability–instability of differences over time. In either case the information that is extracted from the data represents averaged characteristics of a group of individuals rather than of each individual separately. Ultimately, the developmental relevance of a distinction between individual differences and differential intraindividual changes lies in the fact that they imply different representations of the notion of developmental *sequentiality*. More specifically, intraindividual change defines sequentiality at the individual level; in contrast, individual differences define sequentiality at the group level.

THE EXPLANATION OF PSYCHOPATHOLOGY: PREDICTION AND UNDERSTANDING

Given the title of this volume it would be inappropriate to discuss the task of explanation without distinguishing between two different purposes that may be pursued somewhat independently of each other. Specifically, one may consider developmental explanations to be aimed either at the prediction or the understanding of behavioral phenomena. Prediction is always possible without understanding. In comparison, understanding typically, though not always, implies the possibility of prediction.

Prediction is seen here as the explication of relationships between a set of criteria and sets of predictors in order to maximize predictive accuracy as defined by formal principles such as the principle of least squares fit (e.g., Bentler & Woodward, 1979; Skinner, 1978). Given a reliable and valid set of criteria, predictors may be sampled more or less systematically from sets of antecedent conditions including response variables, organismic variables, and environmental variables. Prediction paradigms such as multiple linear regression or canonical correlation (Bentler & Woodward, 1979; Cohen & Cohen, 1975; Pruzek & Frederick, 1978; Wainer, 1978) require essentially only that the predictor variables are reliable. In other words, it is not necessary that their construct validity is known or established as long as they exhibit predictive validity. Furthermore, even if their construct validity were established, a high degree of predictive accuracy should not lead to the conclusion that the formal prediction model, usually in the form of a linear additive equation (e.g., Anderson & Shanteau, 1977; Birnbaum, 1973; Dawes & Corrigan, 1974; Weeks & Bentler, 1979), represents a theoretically meaningful model of the phenomenon studied.

A particular example that helps to illustrate the distinction between prediction and understanding relates to the employment of multiple regression procedures either for the mere purpose of maximizing predictive accuracy or in the context of path analysis and causal modeling (e.g., Bentler, 1978; Bielby & Hauser, 1977; Heise, 1975; Jöreskog, 1970, 1973, 1974; Jöreskog & Sörbom, 1977; Labouvie, 1974; Werts & Linn, 1970). The latter requires not only explication of the construct validity of both criteria and predictors but also an explication of predictor-criterion relationships in terms of postulated mechanisms and processes.

A closer look at currently available theories of development (e.g., Overton & Reese, 1973; Reese & Overton, 1970) suggests that developmental understanding of a phenomenon generally implies more than just specification of causal antecedent–consequent relationships. Failure to explicate implicit notions of the quality of these cause–effect relationships is likely to lead not only to unnecessary confusion in the study of both normal and abnormal development but also to the possible use of inappropriate methodologies. The need for greater clarity seems to be directly related to the concept of multiple causation and the fact that most behavioral outcomes of interest cannot be linked to a single antecedent that is both necessary and sufficient for their occurrence. Instead, it is more likely that most antecedents either alone or in combination are at best either only a necessary but not sufficient or a sufficient but not necessary condition for the presence of a specified outcome event. The difference between these two types of antecedent conditions, as illustrated in Table 9.2, is often of theoretical importance but not necessarily always considered in one's choice of data collection and data analysis strategies.

For instance, if some antecedent conditions, $x \geq x_c$, are hypothesized to be necessary but not sufficient for the occurrence of psychopathology, $y \geq y_c$, the frequency f_b of observing $y \geq y_c$ given $x < x_c$, should be equal to zero and the frequency f_a of observing $y < y_c$ given $x < x_c$, should be equal to the frequency of observing $x < x_c$. The magnitude of the frequencies f_c and f_d is logically irrelevant to support or reject the hypothesis (see Table 9.2). In comparison, if the goal is to identify a set of antecedents, $x \geq x_c$, as sufficient but not necessary for the occurrence of psychopathology, $y \geq y_c$, the frequency f_c of observing $y <$

TABLE 9.2
Qualities of Causal Relationship:
Expected Frequencies

Antecedent	Consequent	
	$y < y_c$	$y \geq y_c$
H_o: $x \geq x_c$ is necessary and sufficient for $y \geq y_c$.		
$x < x_c$	$f_a > 0$	$f_b = 0$
$x \geq x_c$	$f_c = 0$	$f_d > 0$
H_o: $x \geq x_c$ is necessary but not sufficient for $y \geq y_c$.		
$x < x_c$	$f_a > 0$	$f_b = 0$
$x \geq x_c$	irrelevant	irrelevant
H_o: $x \geq x_c$ is sufficient but not necessary for $y \geq y_c$.		
$x < x_c$	irrelevant	irrelevant
$x \geq x_c$	$f_c = 0$	$f_d > 0$

Note: f_a, f_b, f_c, and f_d are expected frequencies.

y_c given $x \geq xc$, should be zero and the frequency f_d of observing $y \geq y_c$ given $x \geq x_c$, should equal the frequency of observing $x \geq x_c$. Here, the frequencies f_a and f_b are irrelevant in reference to the hypothesis.

Most empirical studies of psychopathology focus on a simultaneous analysis of all four frequencies f_a through f_d whenever the rate of psychopathology in some target population is compared with that in a so-called base-line population. It should be recognized, however, that such an analysis of complete contingency tables is only appropriate if the specified antecedent condition is assumed to be both necessary and sufficient for the occurrence of psychopathology. In all other cases, it is more appropriate and informative to consider only certain subsets of frequencies in order to determine the causal status of the antecedent.

From a life-span developmental perspective any antecedent must be viewed as embedded within a larger developmental matrix and sequence of antecedents. Consequently, the status of a given antecedent as either necessary or sufficient or both in relation to a specified outcome is not necessarily absolute and invariant but may depend on that broader context. Because the developmental history of individuals is subject to historical change, the causal status of a particular set of antecedents is not only always defined relative to a particular developmental history or population of such histories, but also subject to historical change. For instance, sexual intercourse, at one time, was a necessary but not sufficient antecedent to the conception of a human being. However, with recent medical advances, it has achieved the status of being neither necessary nor sufficient, at least in modern cultures. Thus, it may well be that most antecedents and predictors that are considered in studies of both normal and abnormal development are only weak causes in the sense that they are necessary or sufficient or both in reference to only a small and limited range of developmental histories.

Explanatory Paradigms

Translation of the task of explanation into a research paradigm involves numerous issues. Among those that are perhaps more salient for a life-span framework are the following: (1) choice of time lags between predictors and criteria, (2) focus on differences or changes in both antecedents and consequents, and (3) degree of specificity with which antecedents and consequents are defined and measured.

1. Proximal and Distal Relationships. In a developmental context any set of criteria can be related to antecedents/predictors that vary along the time dimension and represent a continuum ranging from concurrent or proximal to historical or distal relationships. As far as predictive purposes are concerned, it is quite common to find that relationships decrease in strength as time lags increase, forming so-called simplex patterns among correlations (e.g., Humphreys, 1960). Consequently, concurrent or short-term predictors are likely to yield greater accuracy than long-term predictors. However, it is not precluded that adding distal to proximal predictors may increase the amount of criterion variance that is accounted for. Whereas it is quite simple and straightforward to enter sets of short- and long-term predictors either simultaneously or successively into prediction models such as multiple linear or nonlinear regression (e.g., Cohen & Cohen, 1975), the resulting solutions are not necessarily very useful for the conceptualization or understanding of the processes that underlie the particular phenomenon.

As far as the modeling of causal mechanisms and relationships is concerned, it can be expected that the internal validity of empirical evidence is generally more suspect with regard to distal as compared to proximal relationships. In the case of correlational data, longer time intervals imply typically a greater number of intervening events and, thus, a greater number of competing hypotheses and explanations for the observed long-term relationships. Therefore, it would seem desirable to explicate such distal relationships in the form of chains and sequences of several relatively short-term relationships (e.g., Labouvie, 1974). In the case of experimental strategies such as multiple time series (e.g., Campbell & Stanley, 1963; Labouvie, 1978; Simonton, 1977), longer time intervals generally imply a decrease in experimental control, increased intrusion of history, and possibly an increased lack of equivalence between treatment and control groups due to differential testing and instrumentation effects or due to differential selectivity of factors such as experimental dropout and attrition (Baltes, 1968; Campbell & Stanley, 1963; Wohlwill, 1973).

2. *Differences Versus Changes.*   As mentioned once before most behavioral scientists seem to rely primarily on the observation of individual or group differences when formulating their predictor–criterion or antecedent–consequent relationships. Specifically, differences observed at one time point are explicated in relation to differences observed at earlier and/or later points in time. Important is the fact that most of these differences describe differences in level or status at selected points in time with very little reference to individual change and differences in those changes. As suggested by the simulation studies of Baltes and associates (Baltes & Nesselroade, 1973; Baltes, Nesselroade, & Cornelius, 1978), an exclusive focus on differences and their sequential relationships across time may be unnecessarily one-sided and restrictive. In fact, it can be shown at the level of formal models (Labouvie, 1981) that the representation of criterion variables in terms of sequences of individual differences versus differential intraindividual changes leads to causal models that are not equivalent and not reducible to each other.

Figure 9.3 attempts to illustrate this distinction more concretely. Suppose that some environmental intervention x_1 at time T_1 is inversely related to individual differences on some criterion y_1 also observed at time T_1. Furthermore assume that differences in x_1 produce differential rates of linear change from T_1 to T_2 to T_3.

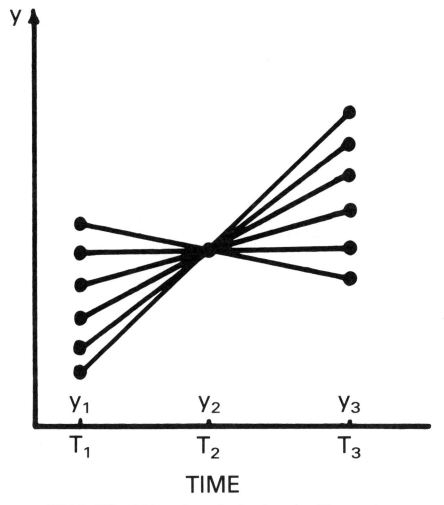

FIG. 9.3.   Differential changes in y as a function of antecedent differences at time T_1. It is corr(x_1, y_1) = 1.0.

According to those assumptions the correlation between x_1 and y_1 is corr(x_1, y_1) = -1.0. Information about predictor–criterion relationships, if based on individual differences, is obtained in the form of corr(x_1,y_2) = 0.0 and corr(x_1,y_3) = 1.0. A corresponding causal interpretation may suggest that criterion differences at T_2 are not influenced but those at T_3 are determined by differences in x_1 at T_1. In contrast, if the focus is on differential changes in the criterion variable, the relevant information is obtained in the form of corr(x_1, y_2-y_1) = 1.0 and corr(x_1, y_3-y_2) = 1.0, and a causal interpretation would more appropriately conclude that differential changes in y over the time interval $[T_1, T_3]$ were determined by differences in x_1 at T_1. Of course, it is not suggested that a focus on individual change will always lead to a more appropriate causal interpretation. Instead, it is implied that whenever there is empirical evidence to suggest the presence of substantial differential changes, rather than merely average change, a focus on changes in the criterion measures may be useful to gain a better understanding of the underlying processes. Besides, an exclusive emphasis on differences is more likely to promote the formulation of stability-oriented and single-sequence models of developmental phenomena over that of change-oriented and multiple-sequence models.

4. Specificity of Criteria and Predictors.   According to Fishbein and Ajzen (1975), criterion variables can be defined as single-act criteria, repeated-observation criteria, or as multiple-act criteria. Of course, a similar classification can be introduced for the predictor variables. If predictors are provided in the form of response variables, the same terminology applies. If environmental variables are used as predictors, one may distinguish between single-event predictors, repeated-observation predictors, and multiple-event predictors. It is not the purpose of this discussion to delineate these categories in any detail. Whether or not one agrees with the particular classification is less important than the fact that predictors and criteria, antecedents and consequents, can be defined, conceptualized, and operationalized along a dimension of specificity generality.

The question of specificity of predictors and criteria is relevant in two regards. First, the observation and identification of distal relationships is likely to be inversely related to the level of specificity at which both antecedents and consequents are measured; that is, the more specific the predictors and criteria are in terms of time and space, the less likely it will be to observe relatively strong distal relationships. Second, the kind of specificity that is important from a developmental point of view concerns the definition of predictors and criteria in reference to either narrow time points or more extended time intervals. Quite often conceptual formulations and empirical investigations fail to explicate with sufficient clarity the time frames that are associated with the predictors and criteria of interest. The selection of more or less time-specific measures will depend on the properties that are assumed to characterize the underlying change processes. For instance, if considerable instability and rapid rates of change are expected, time-specific measures in conjunction with densely spaced observation points along the time dimension are probably more appropriate than measures that ''average'' across wider time frames.

In sum, the previous considerations suggest that a successful explication of antecedent–consequent relationships is not likely without a reasonable match between the specificity of concepts and the specificity of measures. Besides this match that represents a feature of one's measurement model, there is the question of matching appropriately the specificity generality of predictors with that of the criteria at both the conceptual and operational level.

SUMMARY

The issues discussed previously are certainly not unfamiliar or new ones to the study of either normal or abnormal patterns and outcomes of development. However, perhaps because they are so basic, they have often been overlooked in empirical investigations with age-specific perspectives. It is hoped that the previous discussion has made clear that these issues cannot be ignored once a life-span developmental framework is adopted. The various issues were selected and considered in relation to two scientific tasks, namely those of description and explanation. More important than this distinction is, however, the assumption on which the interpretation of these issues was predicated. That assumption postulates that, whenever we compare different populations of individuals and whenever we investigate relationships, we are not interested in describing and explaining those differences and relationships at the level of specific and arbitrary measures but at the level of more abstract concepts.

ACKNOWLEDGMENTS

The writing of this chapter was facilitated in part by a grant from the National Institute on Alcohol Abuse and Alcoholism (Grant No. AA 3509–02).

REFERENCES

Achenbach, T. M., & Edelbrock, C. S. (1978). The classification of child psychopathology: A review and analysis of empirical efforts. *Psychological Bulletin, 85,* 1275–1301.

Adam, J. (1978). Sequential strategies and the separation of age, cohort, and time-of-measurement contributions to developmental data. *Psychological Bulletin, 85,* 1309–1316.

Anderson, N. H., & Shanteau, J. (1977). Weak inference with linear models. *Psychological Bulletin, 84,* 1155–1170.

Anthony, E. J. (1970). The behavior disorders of childhood. In P. H. Mussen (Ed.), *Carmichael's manual of child psychology* (Vol. II). New York: Wiley.

Baltes, P. B. (1968). Longitudinal and cross-sectional sequences in the study of age and generation effects. *Human Development, 11,* 145–171.

Baltes, P. B. (1973). Prototypical paradigms and questions in life-span research on development and aging. *The Gerontologist, 13,* 458–467.

Baltes, P. B., Cornelius, S. W. & Nesselroade, J. R. (1979). Cohort effects in developmental psychology. In J. R. Nesselroade & P. B. Baltes (Eds.), *Longitudinal research in the study of behavior and development.* New York: Academic Press.

Baltes, P. B., & Nesselroade, J. R. (1970). Multivariate longitudinal and cross-sectional sequences for analyzing ontogenetic and generational change: A methodological note. *Developmental Psychology, 2,* 163–168.

Baltes, P. B., & Nesselroade, J. R. (1973). The developmental analysis of individual differences on multiple measures. In J. R. Nesselroade & H. W. Reese (Eds.), *Life-span developmental psychology: methodological issues.* New York: Academic Press.

Baltes, P. B., Nesselroade, J. R., & Cornelius, S. W. (1978). Multivariate antecedents of structural change in development: A simulation of cumulative environmental patterns. *Multivariate Behavioral Research, 13,* 127–152.

Baltes, P. B., Reese, H. W., & Nesselroade, J. R. (1977). *Life-span developmental psychology: Introduction to research methods.* Monterey, CA: Brooks/Cole.

Baltes, P. B., Reese, H. W., & Lipsitt, L. P. (1980). Life-span developmental psychology. *Annual Review of Psychology, 31,* 65–110.

Baltes, P. B., & Schaie, K. W. (Eds.). (1973). *Life-span developmental psychology: Personality and socialization.* New York: Academic Press.

Bentler, P. M. (1976). Multistructure statistical model applied to factor analysis. *Multivariate Behavioral Research, 11,* 3–22.

Bentler, P. M. (1978). The interdependence of theory, methodology, and empirical data: Causal modeling as an approach to construct validation. In D. B. Kandel (Ed.), *Longitudinal research on drug use: Empirical findings and methodological issues.* New York: Wiley.

Bentler, P. M., & Woodward, J. A. (1979). Regression on linear composites: Statistical theory and applications. *Multivariate Behavioral* Research Monographs (No. 79-1).

Bielby, W. T., & Hauser, R. M. (1977). Structural equation models. *Annual Review of Sociology, 3,* 137–161.

Birnbaum, M. H. (1973). The devil rides again: Correlation as an index of fit. *Psychological Bulletin, 79,* 239–242.

Buss, A. R. (1974). A general developmental model for interindividual differences, intraindividual differences, and intraindividual changes. *Developmental Psychology, 10,* 70–78.

Campbell, D. T., & Fiske, D. W. (1959). Convergent and discriminant validation by the multitrait–multimethod matrix. *Psychological Bulletin, 56,* 81–105.

Campbell, D. T., & Stanely, J. C. (1963). *Experimental and Quasiexperimental Designs for Research.* Chicago: Rand McNally.

Cohen, J, & Cohen, P. (1975). *Applied multiple regression/correlation analysis for the behavioral sciences.* Hillsdale, NJ: Lawrence Erlbaum Associates.

Cronbach, L. J., & Furby, L. (1970). How should we measure "change"—or should we? *Psychological Bulletin, 74,* 68–80.

Dawes, R. M., & Corrigan, B. (1974). Linear models in decision making. *Psychological Bulletin, 81,* 95–106.

Dohrenwend, B. S., & Dohrenwend, B. P. (Eds.). (1974). *Stressful life events; Their nature and effects.* New York: Wiley.

Eme, R. F. (1979). Sex differences in childhood psychopathology: A review. *Psychological Bulletin, 86,* 574–595.

Fararo, T. J. (1978). An introduction to catastrophes. *Behavioral Science, 23,* 291–317.

Fishbein, M. & Ajzen, I. (1975). *Belief, attitude, intention and behavior: An introduction to theory and research.* Reading, MA: Addision–Wesley.

Foa, U. G. (1965). New developments in facet design and analysis. *Psychological Review, 72,* 262–274.

Goldfarb, W. (1970). Childhood psychosis. In P. H. Mussen (Ed.), *Carmichael's manual of child psychology* (Vol II). New York: Wiley.

Goulet, L. R., & Baltes, P. B. (Eds.). (1970). *Life-span developmental psychology: Research and theory.* New York: Academic Press.

Heise, D. R. (1975). *Causal analysis.* New York: Wiley.

Humphreys, L. G. (1960). Investigations of the simplex. *Psychometrika, 25,* 313–323.

Humphreys, L. G., & Parsons, C. K. (1979). A simplex process model for describing differences between cross-lagged correlations. *Psychological Bulletin, 86,* 325–334.

Huston–Stein, A., & Baltes, P. B. (1976). Theory and method in life-span developmental psychology: Implications for child development. *Advances in Child Development and Behavior, 11,* 169–188.

Jöreskog, K. G. (1970). A general model for analysis of covariance structure. *Biometrika, 57,* 239–251.

Jöreskog, K. G. (1973). Analysis of covariance structures. In P. R. Krishnaiah (Ed.), *Multivariate analysis* (Vol. III). New York: Academic Press.

Jöreskog, K. G. (1974). Analyzing psychological data by structural analysis of covariance materials. In D. H. Krantz, R. C. Atkinson, R. D. Luce, & P. Sappes (Eds.), *Contemporary developments in mathematical psychology* (Vol. 2). San Francisco: Freeman.

Jöreskog, K. G., & Sörbom, D. (1977). Statistical models and methods for analysis of longitudinal data. In D. J. Aigner & A. S. Goldberger (Eds.), *Latent variables in socioeconomic models.* Amsterdam: North–Holland.

Kenny, D. A. (1975). Cross-lagged panel correlation: A test for spuriousness. *Psychological Bulletin, 82,* 887–903.

Labouvie, E. W. (1974). Developmental causal structures of organism-environment interactions. *Human Development, 17,* 444–452.

Labouvie, E. W. (1978). Experimental sequential strategies for the exploration of ontogenetic and sociohistorical changes. *Human Development, 21,* 161–169.

Labouvie, E. W. (1981). The study of multivariate change structures: A conceptual perspective. *Multivariate behavioral research, 16,* 23–35.

Labouvie, E. W. (1980a). The measurement of individual differences in intraindividual changes. *Psychological Bulletin, 88,* 54–59.

Labouvie, E. W. (1980b). Identity versus equivalence of psychological measures and constructs. In L. W. Poon (Ed.), *Aging in the 1980s: Psychological issues.* Washington, DC: American Psychological Association.

Labouvie, E. W. (1982). Issues in life-span development. In B. B. Wolman (Eds.), *Handbook of developmental psychology.* Englewood Cliffs, NJ: Prentice–Hall.

Lord, F. M., & Novick, M. R. (1968). *Statistical theories of mental test scores* (with contributions by A. Birnbaum). Reading, MA: Addison–Wesley.

McDonald, R. P. (1978). A simple comprehensive model for the analysis of covariance structures. *British Journal of Mathematical and Statistical Psychology, 31,* 59–72.

McDonald, R. P. (1979). The structural analysis of multivariate data: A sketch of a general theory. *Multivariate Behavioral Research, 14,* 21–38.

Mellenbergh, G. J., Kelderman, H., Stijlen, J. G., & Zondag, E. (1979). Linear models for the analysis and construction of instruments in a facet design. *Psychological Bulletin, 86,* 766–776.

Moran, P. A. (1966). The establishment of a psychiatric syndrome. *British Journal of Psychiatry, 112,* 1165–1171.

Nesselroade, J. R., & Reese, H. W. (Eds.). (1973). *Life-span developmental psychology: Methodological issues.* New York: Academic Press.

Overton, W. F., & Reese, H. W. (1973). Models of development: Methodological implications. In J. R. Nesselroade & H. W. Reese (Eds.), *Life-span developmental psychology: Methodological issues.* New York: Academic Press.

Pfeiffer, E. (1977). Psychopathology and social pathology. In J. E. Birren & K. W. Schaie (Eds.), *Handbook of the psychology of aging.* New York: Van Nostrand Reinhold.

Pruzek, R. M., & Frederick, B. C. (1978). Weighting predictors in linear models: Alternatives to least squares and limitations of equal weights. *Psychological Bulletin, 85,* 254–266.

Reese, H. W., & Overton, W. F. (1970). Models of development and theories of development. In L. R. Goulet & P. B. Baltes (Eds.), *Life-span Developmental Psychology: Research and Theory.* New York: Academic Press.

Reinert, G. (1970). Comparative factor analytic studies of intelligence throughout the human life-span. In L. R. Goulet & P. B. Baltes (Eds.), *Life-span developmental psychology: Research and theory.* New York: Academic Press.

Rock, D. A., Werts, C. E., & Flaugher, R. L. (1978). The use of analysis of covariance structures for comparing the psychometric properties of multiple variables across populations. *Multivariate Behavioral Research, 13,* 403–418.

Schaie, K. W., & Schaie, J. P. (1977). Clinical assessment and aging. In J. E. Birren & K. W. Schaie (Eds.) *Handbook of the psychology of aging*. New York: Van Nostrand Reinhold.

Simonton, D. K. (1977). Cross-sectional time-series experiments: Some suggested statistical analyses. *Psychological Bulletin, 84*, 489–502.

Skinner, H. A. (1978). The art of exploring predictor-criterion relationships. *Psychological Bulletin, 85*, 327–337.

Strauss Marmor, G., & Marmor, M. (1978). Comment on Simonton's "Cross-sectional time-series experiments: Some suggested statistical analysis." *Psychological Bulletin, 85*, 1102–1105.

Wainer, H. (1978). On the sensitivity of regression and regressor. *Psychological Bulletin, 85*, 267–273.

Weeks, D. G., & Bentler, P. M. (1979). A comparison of linear and monotone multidimensional sealing models. *Psychological Bulletin, 86*, 349–354.

Werts, C. E., & Linn, R. L. (1970). Path analysis: Psychological examples. *Psychological Bulletin, 74*, 195–212.

Williams, R. H., & Zimmerman, D. W. (1977). The reliability of difference scores when errors are correlated. *Educational and Psychological Measurement, 37*, 679–689.

Wohlwill, J. F. (1973). *The study of behavioral development*. New York: Academic Press.

10 Improving Prediction in Longitudinal Research: Equivalence, Developmental Stages, and Other Issues

Denise B. Kandel

The chapters in this section represent two very different intellectual endeavors. The first is a broad and brilliant review of methodological issues, with a strong but not exclusive focus on developmental research; the other three are empirically based longitudinal analyses. The two studies described in the three empirical chapters are representative of most longitudinal research in which an individual's later outcome is predicted on the basis of earlier attributes. In Labouvie's terminology, they are studies of "sequences of differences between individuals or groups over a series of occasions". The New York State follow-up study of children at high risk for schizophrenia, reported in the chapters by Cornblatt and Marcuse, represents a most difficult type of longitudinal research to carry out because of the rarity of the outcome of interest and the complexities of selecting the proper sample. Despite the enormous difficulties involved in gathering such a sample, this investigation is also notable for the inclusion of a replication sample and the richness of the data collected that cover the spectrum from biological to psychological and social variables.

Because of its broad sweep and its emphasis on formal methodological principles, Labouvie's chapter provides a convenient framework around which to organize a discussion of empirical longitudinal research. I take the Labouvie chapter as a reference point to accomplish two tasks: (1) to focus on data from the chapters by Lowman and Galinsky and those by Cornblatt and Marcuse to provide a concrete illustration of the analytical difficulties created by one of the problems described by Labouvie, namely the lack of equivalence in measurement and (2) to address myself more directly to the Labouvie chapter by elaborating on two specific points. I also discuss an additional issue, that of developmental stages, which is crucial to the study of human development within a life-span perspective. Thus I develop four points related to improving prediction in longitudinal research.

The Principle of Equivalence

Labouvie asks us to consider to what extent problems arise in longitudinal research because of violations in the principle of equivalence. "The issue involves the following questions: (a) how do we know . . . whether the same, formally identical measure relates to the same concept in different age or cohort groups, and (b) how do we know or how do we determine whether formally different measures are related to the same concept, either in the same or in different populations?" It should be recognized that the problem of equivalence arises in all research, whether longitudinal or cross-sectional, although it may be more acute in longitudinal research because of the strong effects associated with age in all areas of functioning. The problem of equivalence confronts the two studies. The chapter by Cornblatt and Marcuse illustrates the problems that arise because of changes in measures resulting from changes in the scientific orientation of investigators over time. These changed measures preclude comparisons between initial and subsequent individual scores. Because of technological advances, the New York State investigators had to modify one of the attention measures in order to computerize it and make it compatible with psychophysiological recordings. The resulting test, however, was easier than the initial one and did not differentiate between groups. The vigilance test used at the later testing when respondents were older did not have the same discriminatory power as the earlier version had at the initial interview. As a result, no over-time comparison on vigilance was possible for members of Sample A.

Both issues of equivalence singled out by Labouvie, noncomparability across age groups and noncomparability across measures, create tensions in the Lowman and Galinsky's chapter. The problem of nonequivalence, derived from noncomparability of measures of psychological functioning at each of the two time periods is discussed by Lowman and Galinsky. Because MMPI measurements were not available in the adult period, psychological adjustment in adulthood was measured by the Health Opinion Scale. As noted by the authors, this 22-item scale measures mainly the physiological and behavioral symptoms related to depressive mood and anxiety as contrasted to the multiscale, 566 item, MMPI instrument. Obviously, the HOS and the MMPI are very different from each other, both in their conceptual and psychometric properties. Within the limitations of their data, the authors carried out an ingenious analysis in which they compared the correlations over time of duplicate items in both sets of measures. The results of this methodological analysis lend greater confidence to their conclusion that there is very little relationship between measures of adjustment taken between the two different phases of the life cycle under investigation.

However, a more serious problem in that chapter is that of nonequivalence across groups. Lowman and Galinsky themselves point to the importance of equivalence across age groups in their discussion of the degree of psychopathology in their adolescent cohort. The proportion defined as psychopathological decreased by about half, from 61 to 37%, when the criteria applied to identify psychopathological subjects on the MMPI were changed from norms developed on adults to norms developed on adolescents. This illustrates the very point made by Labouvie when he cautions that the use of norms "obtained for a specific age cohort group may lead to systematic biases in the description and measurement of psychopathology when applied to other age and cohort groups". Because of concern with a life-span developmental perspective, Labouvie stresses in particular nonequivalence due to differences in chronological *age:* Groups sampled over time are at different stages of development and measures do not necessarily have the same meaning at different chronological ages. However, I suggest that it is crucial also to consider equivalence in terms of criteria other than age, criteria such as sex or ethnicity that identify a person's position in the social structure.

Certain results obtained by Lowman and Galinsky, such as the relatively high proportion of respondents classified as psychopathological (despite the application of revised adolescent norms) and the low predictive power of psychopathology in adolescence for predicting functioning in young adulthood, may be ameliorated if the principle of equivalence incorporates the factor of race. The MMPI was initially validated on a Midwestern sample of white adult males. We are not told in the present chapter the sociodemographic characteristics of the adolescent group on which the youth norms were developed. I assume that it is also a white sample. Yet, it is instructive to refer to another series of studies done, not on psychopathology, but on cognitive functioning of children. More than a decade ago, Gerald Lesser carried out a series of cross-sectional and longitudinal studies on the development of cognitive abilities in children in diverse cultural groups. Four mental abilities were measured: space conceptualization, verbal ability, number facility, and reasoning ability. Four different groups of children were studied initially: Chinese, Jews, Blacks, and Puerto Ricans. Striking differences were found not only in the absolute levels of each mental ability but also in the configuration of scores among the four areas (Stodolsky & Lesser, 1967). The Chinese scored especially high on spacial ability, Jews especially high on verbal ability (Fig. 10.1). The interesting finding is that the group-specific patterns or configurations were invariant across social class groups, although the absolute levels of scores on each ability tended to be depressed in the lower as compared to the middle-class groups. (See Figs. 10.2 and 10.3 for an example in two groups). The study originally carried out on first-grade children in New York City was subsequently replicated in Boston and extended to include white Catholic children. Retest 5 years later of the original New York City cohort indicated great consistency over time in the patterns of mental abilities (Stodolsky & Lesser, 1967).

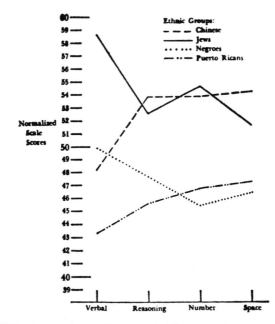

FIG. 10.1. Pattern of normalized mental-ability scores for each ethnic group (Stodolsky & Lesser 1967).

I suggest as a possibility to be systematically tested that the same organizational principle may apply to personality attributes as to cognitive abilities: There may be group-specific profiles of personality characteristics, with certain configurations having different meanings regarding psychopathology for individuals of different groups, whether defined according to sex, ethnicity, social class, or age. The sample included in the Lowman and Galinsky study is evenly split between black and white children. Carrying out analyses in which the same MMPI norms were applied to each group may have in fact obscured the identification of truly psychopathological subjects and may have reduced the potential predictive power of the earlier adolescent scores for later functioning in adulthood. The identification and application of norms based on race-specific groups, on the other hand, could have improved the definition of a subject as falling within a psychopathological range and could thereby have ameliorated the prediction and discriminatory power of the earlier score.

As a sociologist, I am naive about the MMPI. However, my suspicion about the crucial importance of defining race-specific norms for the MMPI scores, norms that would incorporate configurations of responses, was confirmed when in an attempt to learn something quickly about the MMPI, I subsequently consulted one of the standard anthologies on mental tests and measurements and found statements that echo almost exactly the point just mentioned. Thus, Mal-

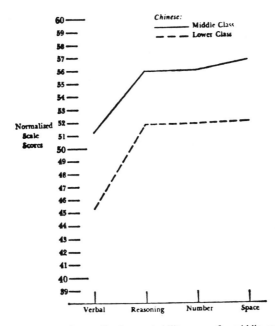

FIG. 10.2.   Patterns of normalized mental-ability scores for middle- and lower-class Chinese children.

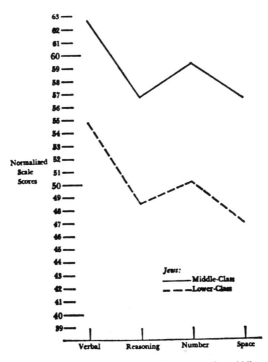

FIG. 10.3.   Patterns of normalized mental-ability scores for middle- and lower-class Jewish children. (Stodolsky & Lesser 1967).

com Gynther (1975), citing results from his own work, writes that because the rules derived to develop clinical diagnoses were developed on samples of white males:

> If one attempts to apply the . . . rules for discriminating psychotic from neurotic profiles to the incoming patients of a typical urban mental health center, only about 10–15 percent are even potentially suitable for analysis . . . The explanation for this apparent anomaly is that the rules are not applicable to the vast majority of patients—females, Negroes, those diagnosed organic or behavior disorder. (p. 458)

Some paragraphs later he adds: "It is now clear that MMPI's cannot be evaluated satisfactorily without this information [about the effects of social status, age, intelligence, and especially race]. The grossest case of neglect involved knowledge of Negro performance in the MMPI" (p. 459). Gynther (1975) then proceeds to quote from his own work again to the effect that

> profiles given by Negroes tend to be higher than those given by whites . . . The unwary interpreter thus is apt to label Negroes as sicker than they actually are. More dramatic differences were disclosed by later studies which focused on *patterns* of item endorsement, as opposed to the traditional scale score analysis . . . Some new evidence indicates that the inapplicability of white norms is so great, especially if limited education and rural residence are added to the race factor, that MMPI's should not be used with Negroes. (p. 459)

This is exactly the group included in the sample studied by Lowman and Galinsky: black rural youths. The problem of unreliability of scores is compounded by the fact that respondents are adolescents. In another article on the MMPI, David Rodgers (1975) warns that adolescent respondents "show considerable discrepancy between verbal self-descriptions and life-situation behavior, such that they can, and often do in typical assessment settings, produce test results that either grossly overstate or understate the emotional pathology or upset that is clinically observable" (p. 460).

I do not believe that carrying out two-way analyses of variance in which race is used to partition subjects handles the problem of nonequivalence because the misclassification as to psychopathology is already embedded in the scoring system for persons in each group. The low predictive power of the MMPI performance in adolescence for achievement 10 years later may be related to violations in the principle of equivalence.

It is clear from examining the research presented in this section that the issue of equivalence is, as stressed by Labouvie, one of the most important to be resolved in longitudinal research.

Labouvie raises many other issues besides equivalence. I focus on two of these issues for further but brief elaboration. One issue is the definition of psychopathology; the other is the definition of distal versus proximal variables. Finally, I introduce for consideration an issue that is ignored in Labouvie's chapter.

Psychopathology Versus Deviance

The definitions of psychopathology in the Labouvie chapter are stated at a very high level of abstraction. The attribution of psychopathology is made if characteristics of a behavior or characteristics of an environmental context are such that their "form, or intensity level, or frequency level or persistence level . . . fall outside the range that is considered acceptable for the population to which a given individual is assigned". I have some problems with those definitions in two respects. First, without further elaboration or explanation, the inclusion of characteristics of environmental factors in the definition seems to be defining the consequence (individual pathology) by one of its causes (environmental context).

Second, it seems that the definitions, because of their generality, would apply to two different types of behaviors: psychopathology, on the one hand, and deviance, on the other. As a result, important distinctions would be obscured, distinctions that apply to etiology, developmental characteristics, and consequences attending on each type of behavior. Psychopathology carries with it the notion of psychological disturbance. Yet, some of the very behaviors that would fall under the definitions cited earlier, i.e., "behaviors that fall outside the range that is considered acceptable for the population to which a given individual is assigned," would simply be deviant behaviors. Richard and Shirley Jessor, for example, stress the age-graded nature of many norms that define certain behaviors as "deviant" or "problematic" when engaged at the inappropriate phase in the life cycle but not when engaged in at some other time (Jessor & Jessor, 1977). For example, drinking or smoking at age 14 would certainly be defined as falling outside the range that is considered acceptable for populations of adolescents although the same behaviors would be acceptable for adults. The same point applies to sexual behavior. Yet, I do not believe that we would want to assign a priori a pejorative psychopathological label to adolescents who engage in such behaviors. Whether or not they are psychopathological is a matter for empirical testing. Such deviant behaviors, however, differ from psychiatric disturbances as would be reflected in high scores on the MMPI. In part, the difference derives from a difference in the degree of control that the individual has over the generation of the behavior itself. I cannot, at this time, develop a systematic analysis of these two types of behavior. I do, however, call attention to the fact that it may be useful to distinguish the criteria and the conditions as well as the behaviors that are defined as falling outside an acceptable range. Some behaviors may simply be deviant; whether or not they also involve psychopathology should remain an open question. The attribution of psychopathology should perhaps be reserved for those behaviors that deviate from expectations involving cognitive or psychological development. The usefulness of this distinction is that it may call our attention to different classes of factors as being involved both in predicting the development of these behaviors and their subsequent consequences. Biological factors may play a more preeminent role for one class of behavior (psychopathology) than the other (deviance), whereas the reverse would hold for social factors.

Distal versus Proximal Variables

The second theme in the Labouvie chapter that I comment on is the distinction between distal versus proximal variables. I bring attention to another meaning of the distinction than the one presented here. Labouvie has in mind differences in the timing of events and their temporal proximity to the events and states being currently measured in a particular study. The same terminology, however, has been used in a different way by another psychologist involved in longitudinal research. Jessor (Jessor, 1979b; see also Jessor, 1979a; Jessor & Jessor, 1977) uses the terminology to distinguish between levels of "conceptual proximity to experience, to perception, to interpretation, or to psychological response" (p. 6). For Jessor, the distal-proximal distinction in the perceived environment refers to ego's perceptions of characteristics of significant others' attributes (behaviors and values) that vary in the extent to which they are related to the particular behavior of ego under study. Jessor's work has been concerned with adolescent involvement in various problem behaviors, such as drinking or marihuana use (Jessor & Jessor, 1977). Distal variables are those variables that describe the general nature of the social environment of the adolescent, such as the closeness of the parent–adolescent bond and the extent of social controls exercised by parents and peers; the proximal variables are social variables that pertain specifically to the behavior at issue, specific parental disapproval for certain problem behaviors or the extent of friends' role models for the behavior.

Thus, the terms distal or proximal can refer to different kinds of distances, distances defined according to time, or space, or psychological meaning and experience.

Developmental Stages in the Study of Life-Span Development

I have saved for last what I consider to be the most important point, a point that in fact I developed at the 1979 meeting of the Society for Life History Research on Psychopathology. This concerns the absence in Labouvie's review of any attention to a true developmental perspective in longitudinal research and the attendant strategies it implies. Because of the emphasis on a life-span perspective, it is all the more important that such a perspective be introduced. A developmental perspective entails many conceptual and methodological implications. I single out the notion of developmental stages.

At one of the first meetings of the Society for Life History Research on Psychopathology, Ricks (1974) pointed out that major contributions of "life history investigations are dynamic descriptions of sequential developmental patterns leading into the different psychopathological syndromes" (p. 351). These descriptive contributions may be as important as the predictive studies of later behaviors from knowledge of earlier events. In fact, I propose that adequate prediction cannot take place in the absence of prior identification of the developmental phases in a behavior. Whether psychopathological or not, most aspects of human development proceed along well-defined developmental sequences. Piaget identified steps in cognitive development and Kohlberg subsequently identified steps in moral development based on a Piagetian cognitive model. Our own work on adolescent involvement in legal and illegal drugs has sensitized me to the occurrence of these developmental phases in drug behavior. We found that the use of legal drugs, such as tobacco and alcohol, almost always preceded the use of illegal drugs, such as marijuana or the psychedelics (Kandel, 1975, 1980; Kandel & Faust, 1975; Yamaguchi and Kandel, 1984a,b). Similarly, Robins (1979) identified stages in narcotic addiction among former Vietnam veterans: use of narcotics in Vietnam, continuation after return, and addiction if use continued after return.

The identification of stages carries with it important methodological implications. The methodological implications concern the analytical strategies to be followed both in studying the predictors and the consequences of a particular behavior (Kandel, 1980; Kandel, Margulies, & Davies, 1978; Kandel, Kessler, & Margulies, 1978). In such developmental sequences, especially those involving deviant or psychopathological outcomes, the population at each subsequent stage is smaller than the population at the earlier stage. The strategy involves decomposing samples into appropriate groups at risk for involvement in the next phase in the sequence. Such partitioning, in turn, makes it possible to identify with greater accuracy the predictors and consequences of various patterns of use of specific drugs and favors the development of optimal intervention strategies. In our own analyses, we did not predict marijuana use simply by starting with all nonusers of marijuana at a particular point in time and comparing those young people who subsequently began to use marijuana and those who did not. Rather, analysis of initiation was confined to the population at risk for initiation, namely those adolescents at the first interview who had already reached the prior stage of alcohol use. We found that different factors were relevant at different stages. Failure to decompose the longitudinal sample into stages and populations at risk for progression to the next stage of drug use would have led to misleading conclusions in the attribution of particular causal factors. Robins makes similar points about the importance of decomposing samples into steps. She (Robins, Davis, & Wish, 1977) stresses that: "There is nothing new about defining the 'population at risk' in which one is to search for predictors of an outcome. What is less common is sequentially defining successively diminishing populations at risk" (p. 380). As Robins et al. conclude later on in the same article, unless the sample had been decomposed, several of the findings would not have come to light "because no single variable is a strongly positive predictor at all stages of the development of addiction" (p. 397).

What I find rather interesting, from the perspective of the sociology of science, is that although the usefulness of developmental stages has now been emphasized repeatedly in the meetings of the Society of Life History Research in Psychopathology, because the comments I have cited were made at meetings in 1973, in 1976, and in 1977, (See Kandel, 1979; Ricks 1974; Robins, et al., 1977), the notion is still ignored in much of our discussions of longitudinal research, even within a life-span perspective. However, the identification of sequential phases in the development of psychopathology and the decomposition of samples into groups appropriately defined as being at risk for psychopathology may help improve the success we have in our predictive endeavors.

ACKNOWLEDGMENTS

Work on this manuscript was partially supported by Research Grants DA00064, DA02867 and DA03196 and Research Scientist Award DA00081 from the National Institute on Drug Abuse and a grant from the John D. and Catherine T. MacArthur Foundation.

REFERENCES

Gynther, M. D. (1975). Minnesota Multiphasic Personality Inventory. In O. K. Buros (Ed.), *Personality: Tests and Reviews II, A Monograph Consisting of the Personality Sections of the Seventh Mental Measurements Yearbook (1972) and Tests in Print II (1974).* Highland Park, NJ: The Gryphon Press.

Jessor, R. (1979a). Marihuana: A review of recent psychosocial research. In R. Dupont, A. Goldstein, & J. O'Donnell (Eds.), *Handbook on drug abuse.* Washington, DC: National Institute on Drug Abuse.

Jessor, R. (1979b, June). *The perceived environment and the study of adolescent problem behavior.* Paper presented at the Symposium on the Situation in Psychological Theory and Research at LOVIK, Stockholm.

Jessor, R., & Jessor, S. L. (1977). *Problem behavior and psychosocial development—A longitudinal study of youth.* New York: Academic Press.

Kandel, D. (1975). Stages in adolescent involvement in drug use. *Science, 190,* 912–14.

Kandel, D. B. (1979). Convergences in prospective longitudinal surveys of drug use in normal populations. In S. Sells, W. Pollin, J. Strauss, & M. Roff (Eds.), *Life history research in psychopathology* (Vol. 6). Baltimore: Williams & Wilkins.

Kandel, D. (1980). Developmental stages in adolescent drug involvement. In D. Lettieri (Ed.), *Drug theories.* Washington, DC: U.S. Government Printing Office. Reprinted in E. Walther (Ed.), *Rapture and reality—Drugs in cross-cultural comparison.* Cologne, Germany: Museum Für Völkerkunde.

Kandel, D., & Faust, R. (1975). Sequence and stages in patterns of adolescent drug use. *Archives of General Psychiatry, 32,* 923–932.

Kandel, D. B., Kessler, R. C., & Margulies, R. Z. (1978). Antecedents of adolescent initiation into stages of drug use: A developmental analysis. In D. B. Kandel (Ed.), *Longitudinal research in drug use: Empirical findings and methodological issues.* Washington, DC: Hemisphere–Wiley.

Kandel, D. B., Margulies, R. S. & Davies, M. (1978). Analytical strategies for studying transitions into developmental stages. *Sociology of Education, 51,* 162–76.

Ricks, D. F. (1974). Life history research: Retrospect and prospect 1973. In D. F. Ricks, A. Thomas, & M. A. Roff (Eds.), *Life history research in psychopathology* (Vol.3). Minneapolis: University of Minnesota Press.

Robins, L. N. (1979). Addict careers. In R. I. Dupont, A. Goldstein, & J. O'Donnell (Eds.), *Handbook on Drug Abuse.* Washington, DC: U.S. Government Printing Office.

Robins, L. N., Davis, D. H., & Wish, E. (1977). Detecting predictors of rare events: Demographic, family and personal deviance as predictors of stages in progression toward narcotic addiction. In J.S. Straus, B. Haroutun, & M. Roff (Eds.), *The origins and course of psychopathology.* New York: Plenum Press.

Rodgers, D. A. (1975). Minnesota Multiphasic Personality Inventory. In O. K. Buros (Ed.), *Personality: Tests and Reviews II, A Monograph Consisting of the Personality Sections of the Seventh Mental Measurements Yearbook (1972) and Tests in Print II (1974).* Highland Park, NJ: The Gryphon Press.

Stodolsky, S. S., & Lesser, G. (1967). Learning patterns in the disadvantaged. *Harvard Educational Review, 37,* 546–593.

Yamaguchi, K. & Kandel, D. B. (1984a). Patterns of Drug Use from Adolescence to Early Adulthood-II. Sequences of Progression. *American Journal of Public Health, 74,* 668–672.

Yamaguchi, K. and Kandel, D. B. (1984b). Patterns of Drug Use from Adolescence to Early Adulthood-III. Predictors of Progression. *American Journal of Public Health, 74,* 673–681.

11

A Life-Span Developmental View of Childhood Predictors of Later Psychopathology: Commentary

Richard M. Lerner

The once little-challenged view that the longitudinal research design is the sine qua non of developmental methodology has met with increasing criticism in recent years. Because of problems of internal and external validity, simple longitudinal designs have been increasingly criticized. More powerful and general sequential designs, which in many cases may be the design of choice, have been often suggested as more useful (see Nesselroade & Baltes, 1979).

A simple longitudinal design typically involves repeatedly studying a group of people born in or near a single point in time. In other words, people from a single *birth cohort* are repeatedly assessed. However, this is where problems of internal and external validity are introduced. For example, when the same measures are repeatedly applied across age levels, issues of instrument decay, of level of measurement, and of measurement equivalence are raised (Baltes, Reese, & Nesselroade, 1977). In addition, being from a single birth cohort, subjects can only be one age at a specific point in time. Thus, in a simple longitudinal design two components of developmental change functions (age and time) may not be separable. Inferences about the role of age changes would thus be limited by such a problem of internal validity. In turn, focus on one cohort may limit generalizability to others, and therefore simple longitudinal studies also may have problems of external validity, problems that may increase with repeated testing and sample attrition. Loman and Galinsky's data are a case in point: The "re-tested" and "lost" groups were found to differ on the MMPI and may be assumed to have been different on other key variables, some of which may be related to the "time-two" data. In short, unless longitudinal studies include retest and drop-out control groups (Baltes et al., 1977), many validity problems of this sort cannot be addressed adequately.

All the chapters presented in this section include procedures and/or recommendations that recognize the limits of conventional longitudinal research. Yet, what often goes unrecognized, by those who heed many life-span developmentalists' calls for developmental research designs that attempt to appraise the unconfounded contributions to developmental change, is that these calls are primarily based on a metatheoretical model of development that contrasts from the traditional mechanistic and organismic ones used in human development (Lerner, 1982; Lerner & Busch–Rossnagel, 1981; Overton & Reese, 1973; Reese & Overton, 1970). A developmental contextual paradigm is associated with life-span developmental psychology (Lerner, 1984; Lerner & Busch–Rossnagel, 1981; Lerner & Kauffman, in press). This paradigm draws attention to the roles of history-graded and nonnormative influences on development, in addition to just age-graded ones (Baltes & Reese, 1984), because of the assumption that development is an outcome of a bidirectional relation between the changing organism and its changing biocultural context (Lerner, 1984); variables such as time-of-measurement and cohort are often marker variables, then, of changes in the changing context of an organism, and this context is part of the causal matrix of covariation that provides a basis of development. From this perspective then, antecedent–consequent relations found with one cohort, at one age, and at one time are not necessarily applicable to other combinations of cohort, age, and time because the historical context may have changed significantly. Labouvie, in his chapter, makes a similar point, noting that "use of age- and cohort-specific norms may lead to systematic biases in the description and measurement of psychopathology when applied to age and cohort groups other than those for which they were obtained in the first place." Thus, from this perspective Loman and Galinsky used the MMPI with an inappropriate population; and because their rescoring on the basis of adolescent norms was not coupled with explicit documentation of the correspondence between the standardization population and their sample, there was little done to remedy this problem.

Thus, not only may simple longitudinal designs have the problems of external validity I outlined previously, but, seen in the light of a developmental contextualistic, life-span framework, the validity of the definitions and measures of psychopathology that may be used are limited by the specific contextual factors acting on the sample. Labouvie has appropriately cautioned researchers about this issue, and Lowman and Galinsky have suggested that in addition to age, one must look at other demographic variables, such as sex or race, as potential markers of status-specific person-context relations, in order to understand variation in the role of particular psychopathological symptoms at one point in life for later functioning. For example, the generally positive adjustment and performance characteristics of both their white and black subjects at the time of the 10-year follow-up may have been due to a cohort-specific, but nonassessed, intervention that, perhaps, enhanced the functioning of all subjects in such a way as to reach some near maximum level for that point in time; alternatively, it may have acted on the blacks, more so than on the whites, to move them to a level compatible to the whites.

Of course, such possibilities could only be appraised if measures of the context, as well as the person, were included. However, it is fair to say that most psychological and psychiatric research is personological in focus (Bronfenbrenner, 1979). Yet, a developmental contextual, life-span view, in sensitizing researchers to the potential role of historical and non-normative influences, also indicates that measures of the changing context, and of the *relations* between individuals and contexts have to be included in developmental research (see Lerner & Lerner, 1983, for an example of the application of this perspective to the study of temperament). Thus, the descriptive identification of the medical, physiological, and behavioral characteristics of children of schizophrenic versus nonschizophrenic parents, as presented in the chapters by Marcuse and Cornblatt, is useful; nevertheless, the work needs to be extended by a focus on *processes* of child–context, and particularly child–parent, *interaction* that differentiate schizophrenic from nonschizophrenic families.

The type of research I am suggesting then requires multidisciplinary expertise in order to capitalize on knowledge of levels of analysis other than the individual/psychological. In addition, such research, in studying relations between individuals and their contexts, must be attentive to the possibility, previously implied, that all elements in this relation, and the relation itself, may change. For example, age-graded influences, related to biological maturation, may play their most salient role in the etiology of psychopathology in infancy and early childhood, early adolescence, and old age. Normative, history-graded influences occur when the sociocultural context plays its major role, and such factors may be most salient in the problems of middle-to-late adolescents and young adults. In turn, non-normative life events, such as death of a spouse, onset of serious illness, or divorce, may play their major role in the adult and, again, in the aged years. Thus, the same measures may be differentially associated with the prevalence of psychopathology at different times in life because the nature of the person–context relation has altered substantially (Lerner & Lerner, 1983).

In a general sense, then, we may note that useful measures of psychopathology, mental health, or their antecedents need to be devised in ways sensitive to the particular portions of life within which they are to be applied. Thus, the issue of measurement equivalence is raised. Labouvie's excellent discussion of this issue has cautioned us to be sure that our measures have consistent meaning across the age range within which they are applied; as a sample case, Lowman and Galinsky's data can be seen as an instance of no equivalence being found between two measures, the MMPI (measured at Time 1) and the HOS (measured at Time 2), the authors believed were of similar personality characteristics. Moreover, the MMPI, as used by Loman and Galinsky, is perhaps better seen as a measure of intellectual differences among particular groups of adolescents measured at a specific point in time. Further, given the verbal admin-istration of the MMPI with these subjects, and given the finding that "effects attributable to MMPI scores disappeared when IQ is partialled out" (Loman & Galinsky, this volume), it may have been that the MMPI scores were biased by variables associated with the verbal functioning of the subject, the tester, and/or the interaction between the two.

Thus, to Labouvie's caution I add that measurement equivalence needs to be established not only across ages, but also across samples, contexts, and times as well. Although a formidable task, techniques suitable for the establishment of measurement equivalence exist in the human individual-difference literature (Lerner, Palermo, Spiro, & Nesselroade, 1982), for example, in regard to the well-known multitrait–multimethod matrix approach for establishing convergent and discriminant validity. However, an age comparative approach is not concep-tually dissimilar from cultural or animal comparative approaches. Thus, in our attempts to establish measurement equivalence we should borrow from these other specialities, and for example, begin to control across age by systematic variation as well as by systematic equation.

Moreover, providing convergent and discriminant validation in this way should aid in addressing the issue of level of measurement (Baltes et al., 1977). As implied by Labouvie (this volume), the appropriate level of measurement may change when an instrument is applied to "new or different populations of individuals." A choice of instruments, from among an array resulting from an instrument's × levels crossing, would be made on the basis of data consistent with theoretically specified convergent and discriminant validation expectations. This notion highlights the need to have a well-articulated theory guiding the choice and application of one's measures and methodologies and leads to a final point I wish to emphasize.

All the conceptual and methodological revisions in the longitudinal study of psychopathology, forwarded by a developmental contextual, life-span perspec-tive, need to be embedded in well-articulated theoretical models that link chang-ing people to their changing worlds (Lerner & Lerner, 1983). Thus, I applaud Labouvie's call for the increased use of causal modeling techniques. Although quite complex such methods are simply quantitative procedures for translating verbally specified, theoretical relations into empirically verifiable relations. Wider employment of these techniques will have at least two positive features. First, they will require researchers to specify the nature of the relations among the variables they measure, both within and across time, and thus to empirically assess whether their specific structural model can be supported. Second, it will force researchers to indicate the measurement model they associate with the variables under scrutiny. As such, other researchers, who may adopt comparable structural models but alternative measurement ones or use comparable measures but see them as indexes of conceptually different variables, may begin to have clear quantitative bases for understanding the divergence or compatibility among data sets.

However, despite the method of analysis one may use in a particular study, the general point is that theory-guided research is essential if we are to significantly move towards correcting many of the deficits in extant longitudinal research. Indeed, the substantive chapters in this section could have been improved by using theory to guide method. For example, Loman and Galinsky never precisely indicate why or if they had theoretical or rational expectations that the MMPI would relate to any specific variables measured at Time 2. Similarly, Marcuse and Cornblatt did not communicate any theoretical basis for the variables they selected for study. Use of large numbers of measures with small samples is likely to result in unreliable information, that is, results that capitalize on chance. Thus, if we are to move beyond normative prediction, or prediction based on empirical generalizations from extant data sets, and move towards deductive prediction, which as Labouvie (this volume) suggests is often tied to understanding, better use of theory needs to be made in future longitudinal research.

In sum, both theoretical and empirical integration among scientists may be gained if precise measures and powerful analytic techniques are combined with clear theoretical specification of the character of human change in a changing context. Both a developmental contextual, life-span view and our interests in understanding the bases of psychopathology and in optimizing human development suggest that we do not do less in our future research efforts.

ACKNOWLEDGMENTS

The preparation of this chapter was supported in part by grants from the John D. and Catherine T. MacArthur Foundation and from the William T. Grant Foundation.

REFERENCES

Baltes, P. B. (1979, Summer). On the potential and limits of child development: Life-span developmental perspectives. *Newsletter of the Society for Research in Child Development,* 1–4.

Baltes, P. B., & Reese, H. W. (1984). The life-span perspective in developmental psychology. In M. H. Bornstein & M. E. Lamb (Eds.), *Developmental psychology.* Hillsdale, NJ: Lawrence Erlbaum Associates.

Baltes, P. B., Reese, H. W., & Nesselroade, J. R. (1977). *Life-span developmental psychology: Introduction to research methods.* Monterey, CA: Brooks/Cole.

Bronfenbrenner, U. (1979). *The ecology of human development.* Cambridge, MA: Harvard University Press.

Lerner, J. V., & Lerner, R. M. (1983). Temperament and adaptation across life: Theoretical and empirical issues. In P. B. Baltes & O. G. Brim, Jr. (Eds.), *Life-span development and behavior* (Vol. 5). New York: Academic Press.

Lerner, R. M. (1982). Children and adolescents as producers of their own development. *Developmental Review, 2,* 342–370.

Lerner, R. M. (1984). *On the nature of human plasticity.* New York: Cambridge University Press.

Lerner, R. M., & Busch–Rossnagel, N. A. (1981). Individuals as producers of their development: Conceptual and empirical bases. In R. M. Lerner & N. A. Busch–Rossnagel (Eds.), *Individuals as producers of their development: A life-span perspective* (pp. 1–36). New York: Academic Press.

Lerner, R. M., Palermo, M., Spiro, A., III, & Nesselroade, J. R. (1982). Assessing the dimensions of temperamental individuality across the life-span: The Dimensions of Temperament Survey (DOTS). *Child Development, 53,* 149–159.

Lerner, R. M., & Kauffman, M. B. (in press). The concept of development in contextualism. *Developmental Review.*

Nesselroade, J. R., & Baltes, P. B. (Eds.). (1979). *Longitudinal research in the study of behavior and development.* New York: Academic Press.

Overton, W. F., & Reese, H. W. (1973). Models of development: Methodological implications. In J. R. Nesselroade & H. W. Reese (Eds.), *Life-span developmental psychology: Methodological issues* (pp. 65–86). New York: Academic Press.

Reese, H. W., & Overton, W. F. (1970). Models of development and theories of development. In L. R. Goulet & P. B. Baltes (Eds.), *Life-span developmental psychology: Research and theory* (pp. 115–145). New York: Academic Press.

12 A 15- to 20-Year Follow-Up of Married Adult Psychiatric Patients

John A. Clausen

Recent reviews of the literature on long-term outcomes in psychosis, particularly schizophrenia, appear to be in agreement that features of the disorder, the person, the person's history, and the social milieu to which the patient returns may all influence outcome (Beck, 1978; Möllor, Zerssen, Werner–Eilert, & Wuochner–Stockheim, 1983; Strauss & Carpenter, 1978; Vaillant, 1978). In general, if one follows a cohort of formerly hospitalized patients, the best predictor of rehospitalization is the number of times that the patient has previously been hospitalized. As a consequence, any study that follows up a cohort of successive discharges from a mental hospital (which will contain first admissions and readmissions) will tend to give a more negative picture of outcome than one that starts with a cohort of first admissions. This chapter reports findings of an intensive follow-up study of a cohort of patients who were first admitted to a mental hospital in the 1950s with diagnoses of schizophrenia, affective psychosis, severe psychoneurosis, or character disorder.[1]

METHODS

The long-term follow-up was built on a short-term longitudinal study started at the Laboratory of Socioenvironmental Studies, NIMH, in the 1950s to delineate how families—especially spouses—defined and responded to symptoms of men-

---

[1] A very preliminary report on the follow-up study that is the source of this data here presented was given at the fourth meeting of the Society for Life History Research in Psychopathology (Clausen, 1975). At that time we had only partially coded and punched our data, and the diagnostic classifications that were used for presenting the data were those given by hospital staff at the time of the patient's discharge from initial hospitalization.

tal disorder prior to the patient's initial admission to a mental hospital. The families selected for the study were those of married white persons between the ages of 20 and 49 years who had entered a public mental hospital in the Washington, D.C. area and who had not previously been hospitalized for mental disorder. Inclusion in the sample depended on the availability of an interviewer at the time of the patient's admission and the willingness of the patient's spouse to be interviewed. Fewer than 10% of the wives of male patients and roughly 20% of the husbands of female patients either refused to participate in the study or left the area before we were able to interview them. In general, then, our sample should be reasonably representative of white married patients experiencing an initial hospitalization for the specified categories of mental disorder in the 1950s in the Washington area.

Sixty-three Washington-area patients who met all the sampling specifications were included in the follow-up. In addition, we followed up 17 married women who were first admitted to a California state mental hospital in the late 1950s. All had been diagnosed schizophrenic; they are described in the book, *Schizophrenic Women* (Sampson, Messinger, & Towne, 1964), the product of a much more intensive study somewhat parallel to the one we carried out at NIMH.

In 1971, we began to trace and secure information on these 80 patients and their families.[2] Although the focus of our research was on the impact of mental illness on the family and our primary respondent was the spouse, we attempted to secure data on the current functioning of the patient, the history of treatment during the 15 to 20 years intervening since the initial hospitalization (both from spouses and from clinical records), and data on the occupational careers and intervening life histories of patient and spouse. Although we do not have clinical assessments of the patients, except as these were available through later treatment records, our outcome data go considerably beyond those available for most patients in long-term follow-ups.[3]

Interviews with the spouse, the patient, or another family member were the source of reasonably current data (or data on the patient's activities up to death) for 66 of the 80 patients. We have limited data from clinical records or informants for all but six of the other patients. We have been unable to find any trace of these six—all female schizophrenics—in recent years.

Because the original diagnoses were in many instances suspect, we prepared clinical summaries, drawing on interviews and hospital records, as a basis for rediagnosis. The summaries detailed the presenting complaint, the circumstances surrounding it, the evolution of the disorder, and salient features of the life history prior to hospitalization. Our psychiatric consultant rediagnosed about half the sample, giving particular attention to the diagnosis of schizophrenia and

---

[2]The earlier preliminary report on the follow-up dealt with a total sample of 105, which included a number of patients who had initially appeared to meet our sampling specifications but did not in fact do so.

[3]A more detailed description of follow-up procedures is given in Clausen (1975).

using the criteria developed for the International Pilot Project on Schizophrenia. Budget stringencies precluded completion of the rediagnoses by our consultant, but Dr. Carol Huffine and I then independently reviewed and assessed the entire series using the Research Diagnostic Criteria (Spitzer, Endicott, & Robins, 1978). There was substantial agreement between us and, for those cases that our consultant had previously diagnosed, among the three of us. To be classified as "definitely schizophrenic" both judges had to agree that the criteria were met. If the criteria for schizophrenia were largely met and there were not contraindications, the final classification was "probably schizophrenic." Cases on which there was disagreement or ambiguity but in which the criteria were partially met and there was substantial evidence of psychosis were classified as "possibly schizophrenic."

Reclassification of original diagnoses was frequent. For example, of the 17 women diagnosed as schizophrenic in the California study, we classified seven as definitely or probably schizophrenic, seven as possibly schizophrenic, and three as not psychotic but neurotic. The latter three later received outpatient treatment, and two were then diagnosed psychoneurotic. Of the seven women whom we classified as "possibly schizophrenic," five are known to have been rehospitalized; on subsequent readmissions two were diagnosed as involutional, one as manic–depressive, and two as schizophrenic. In the material to be presented, we have in every instance based our final research diagnosis on data available at the end of the initial period of hospitalization, even though subsequent assessments might suggest a different diagnosis.

Overall, of the 20 men originally diagnosed schizophrenic, we regarded 13 as definitely or probably schizophrenic, six as possibly schizophrenic, and one as manic–depressive. Of the 38 women who had originally been diagnosed as schizophrenic, we have classified 15 as definitely or probably schizophrenic, 13 as possibly schizophrenic, 2 as having affective psychosis, and 8 as nonpsychotic. At the same time, it appeared to us that 3 women previously classified as psychoneurotic or as having an affective psychosis qualified for classification as "possibly schizophrenic." Thus, whereas the number of patients classified as definitely or possibly schizophrenic as a result of our research review is less than the number originally diagnosed schizophrenic, in the case of female patients we have made transfers *into* the "possibly schizophrenic" category as well as *out* of it. We have dropped from consideration one male patient originally diagnosed psychoneurotic whose problem was actually Huntington's Disease.

RESULTS

Treatment Status Subsequent to Initial Hospitalization

More than half the men and roughly 90% of the women have had treatment subsequent to their initial hospitalization, but the great majority of both sexes were in the community and functioning 15 to 20 years after their initial hospitalization (Table 12.1). Whether we examine treatment status (Table 12.2) or severity of symptoms presented in the past 5 years (Table 12.3), women in our sample have less favorable outcomes than men except for the group of men with affective psychoses (largely manic–depressives). Even among the women, however, relatively few have remained hospitalized or largely immobilized by symptoms in the most recent 5-year period prior to follow-up.

Perhaps most striking is the finding that of the 13 men who were originally diagnosed schizophrenic and who met rigorous criteria for such a diagnosis, 7 had not received treatment in the 15 to 20 years following initial hospitalization, and 9 were reported to have shown no symptoms beyond occasional mild upsets in the past 5 years. Men who had shown two or more of the most definitive symptoms of schizophrenia actually appear to have had more favorable outcomes than the small group classified as possibly schizophrenic, though the difference could easily be a result of chance, given the small number of cases.

Among female patients, outcomes appear most dismal for those who meet the more rigorous criteria for a diagnosis of schizophrenia; none of these has escaped subsequent treatment and all for whom we have data have experienced at least occasional severe upsets—often entailing symptoms of psychosis—in the past 5 years. On the other hand, 4 of the 16 women classified as possibly schizophrenic had no subsequent treatment, and 4 were asymptomatic except for mild upsets in the past 5 years.

Of the 10 men with affective psychoses—chiefly manic–depressive—3 received no treatment following hospitalization, but all 3 died within 5 years of their release from the hospital. One of the remaining 7 men killed himself after rehospitalization and 5 have had recurrent episodes of severe symptoms, though 2 appear to have been stabilized on lithium at the time of follow-up.

Although most of the patients who had been hospitalized for severe psychoneurosis or character disorders received subsequent treatment, and indeed most of the women were rehospitalized, they were less persistently problematic and had much shorter durations of subsequent hospitalization than either of the schizophrenic groups. Only one of the six nonpsychotic men experienced a rehospitalization, and none appeared to have been persistently symptomatic.

Rates of readmission of female patients to inpatient services declined consistently in each 5-year period, from nearly two-thirds in the first period to less than one-third in the last (10 to 15 years after release from the index hospital). Readmissions of males to inpatient services fluctuated between one-fourth and one-fifth in each 5-year period. Both men and women more frequently sought outpatient treatment in recent years (usually entailing occasional visits for monitoring drug therapy), with rates being much higher for women than for men.

As a basis for classifying outcome, we have reviewed the entire treatment record of each patient and data available on symptoms and role performance since the initial hospitalization. Where data permitted, we have classified the overall level of symptoms as nonexistent or mild, periodic, or persistent. Mild

TABLE 12.1
Current Status of Patients at Follow-Up by Sex and by Research Diagnosis

Current Status of Patient	Male				Female			
	Schizophrenic 13	Poss. Schiz. 6	Affective 10	Nonpsychotic 6	Schizophrenic 15	Poss. Schiz. 16	Affective 4	Nonpsychotic 9
In community, no treatment since release[a]	7	2	—	3	—	3	—	—
In community, has had treatment	5	3	5	3	8	8	3	6
In community, treatment status unclear	—	—	—	—	2	—	—	—
In hospital	1	—	—	—	2	1	—	—
Died—in hospital or after treatment	—	1	3	—	1	1	—	1
Died—without further treatment	—	—	2	—	—	1	—	1
No data	—	—	—	—	2	2	1	1

[a]Except as follow-up to index hospitalization

179

TABLE 12.2
Treatment Subsequent to Initial Hospitalization by Sex
and by Research Diagnosis

Subsequent Treatment	Male				Female			
	Schizophrenic 13	Poss. Schiz. 6	Affective 10	Nonpsychotic 6	Schizophrenic 15	Poss. Schiz. 16	Affective 4	Nonpsychotic 9
None	4	1	1	1	—	3	—	—
Follow up to index hospital only	3	1	2	1	—	—	—	—
Outpatient only	1	—	—	2	2	—	—	1
Rehospitalization	5	3	6	1	10	10	3	6
Patient never re-leased	—	1	—	—	—	—	—	—
Died, no treatment	—	—	1	1	—	1	—	1
No data or treatment status unknown	—	—	—	—	3	2	1	1

TABLE 12.3
Severity of Symptoms in Five Years Prior to Follow-Up by Sex and Research Diagnosis

Frequency and Severity of Symptoms	Male				Female			
	Schizophrenic	Poss. Schiz.	Affective	Nonpsychotic	Schizophrenic	Poss. Schiz.	Affective	Nonpsychotic
Total	13	6	10	6	15	16	4	9
None	4	1	—	3	—	2	1	—
Occasional, mild	5	1	—	1	—	2	—	3
Occasional, severe	1	2	5	2	3	6	1	3
Frequent, severe	1	—	1	—	3	1	—	1
Patient largely immobilized	2	—	1	—	3	—	—	—
In hospital much of period	—	—	—	—	2	1	—	—
No data or patient died	—	2	3	—	4	4	2	2

symptoms were those that were only briefly manifest and did not significantly impair functioning. Patients with occasional severe upsets over the entire 15 to 20 years are classified as periodically symptomatic. Those who have had frequent or long periods of symptoms that produced significant impairment are classified as having "persistent" symptoms. Those classified as essentially symptom free may have had occasional upsets in the early years but have not been markedly impaired for a long period at any time and have been essentially symptom free in the 5 years prior to follow-up.

The Prediction of Outcome

The number of cases is too small for adequate statistical analysis, holding diagnosis constant, but if those diagnosed probable or possible schizophrenia are combined, perhaps we can discern some influences on or predictors of favorable outcome. A number of studies have suggested indicators of favorable prognosis in schizophrenia (Bland, Parker, & Orn, 1978; Strauss & Carpenter, 1974, 1978; Vaillant, 1964, 1978), and it is possible for us to assess at least some of those indicators. Among the items previously found to be good predictors we can examine age at onset, duration of symptoms, premorbid personality, and duration of initial hospitalization. Because our patients were all married, all the men would be classified as showing ability to relate to the opposite sex, so this important prognostic indicator suggests the generally favorable outcome that has been observed. Will the other variables mentioned serve to differentiate groups?

For male patients diagnosed schizophrenic, those whose initial hospitalization came after age 35 were much less likely to be symptomatic in the 5 years prior to follow-up than patients who had been younger at initial hospitalization (1 in 8 vs. 5 in 9). Among female patients, it appears that those admitted after 35 are less likely to be persistently impaired (1 in 7, before age 35 vs. 6 in 12, after age 35).

I had assumed that we would find, as have most other studies, that a short duration of initial hospitalization would be associated with favorable outcome. For schizophrenic males, however, the trend runs in the other direction. All men who were released from the hospital in less than 2 months were seriously or persistently symptomatic in the 5 years preceding follow-up, whereas those hospitalized from 2 months to a year had a predominantly favorable outcome. No such tendency is found for the female patients. From our small sample one cannot conclude that very short hospitalization is either favorable or unfavorable. Patients of both sexes who had initially spent more than a year in the hospital were still episodically or persistently symptomatic 15 to 20 years later.

Duration of symptoms prior to hospitalization, as perceived by spouse, nicely differentiates the symptom free from those with persistent symptoms among men classified definitely or probably schizophrenic. Of seven men whose wives reported that they were first aware of a problem within 3 months of the patients' entry into the hospital, six showed no subsequent symptoms and one was periodically symptomatic. All six of the men whose wives reported longer periods of symptomatic behavior before hospitalization (ranging up to 5 years) were persistently symptomatic or impaired in functioning in the years following hospitalization ($p < .01$). For the six men in our group of possible schizophrenics, those whose symptoms were reported to have been of shortest duration have poorer outcomes, though the differences are not significant. It appears that the psychopathology of these men differed substantially from that of the group classified as definitely or probably schizophrenic. Moreover, there was often evidence of pathology and symptoms long before the wives recognized them.

None of the women classified as definitely or probably schizophrenic was symptom free at follow-up; the mean duration of symptoms recognized by the husbands of these women was well over a year. Among women classified as possibly schizophrenic, the two who were largely symptom free at follow-up had been symptomatic less than 6 months, whereas eight of the 10 who were periodically or persistently symptomatic had a longer duration of symptoms prior to hospitalization.

Social Class

Roughly half our male patients occupied middle-class status prior to hospitalization whereas two-thirds of the female patients had working-class backgrounds. This does not, however, account for the better prognosis of male patients; social class is unrelated to outcome in this sample. Patients with affective diagnoses came from higher status backgrounds than did those diagnosed schizophrenic, but when diagnosis is held constant there is no hint of a trend toward poorer outcomes for lower status men or women.

The Marital Relationship and Later Symptoms

In previous publications (Clausen, 1983; Clausen & Yarrow, 1955; Sampson et al., 1964) we noted that there was a good deal of turmoil in the marital relationship antecedent to the patient's hospitalization. Relationships were somewhat better in the families of male patients than in those of female patients. Moreover, wives were considerably more likely to be sympathetic to their ill husbands (Clausen, 1983). High supportiveness of the spouse predicted voluntary admission; low supportiveness usually connoted commitment. Was spouse's supportiveness associated with outcome over the long run? The answer is a resounding no. Men with a diagnosis of schizophrenia, whose marital relationships were rated poor or very poor, were least likely to have serious symptoms during the 5 years preceding follow-up (Table 12.4). This is not a statistically significant result but it goes opposite to our expectations. For women, there appears to have

TABLE 12.4
Symptoms In Past 5 Years By Preonset Marital Rating For Patients
Classified Schizophrenic

Pre-illness Marital Rating	Males		Females		
	None or Mild Symptoms	Serious or Persistent Symptoms	None or Mild Symptoms	Serious Symptoms	Persistent Symptoms
Total	11	6	4	8	7
Good to very good	1	1	—	1	—
Fairly good	5	5	1	4	3
Fair to poor	4	—	2	2	1
Very poor	1	—	—	1	2
Unable to classify	—	—	1	—	1

been no relationship between preonset marital relationship and subsequent symptoms.

Table 12.5 indicates the current status of the original marriages of our patients, by outcome groups. For both male and female patients, but more strongly for the former, there is a tendency for those who continue to be symptomatic to be separated or divorced. For persons diagnosed schizophrenic, the marital relationship antecedent to hospitalization not only fails to predict outcome but does not even predict whether the couple stayed together. In several of the families where patient and spouse seemed most highly committed to one another at the time of initial admission, the marriage was terminated after one or more additional periods of symptomatic behavior. On the other hand, problematic relationships sometimes improved markedly after the patient's return from the hospital in instances where the patient remained asymptomatic.

Although our assessment of the marital relationship is by no means equivalent to the assessment of "expressed emotion" by Brown and his colleagues (1972), a major source of evidence for our rating of the marriage was based on the spouse's critical comments about the patient in interviews conducted during the patient's hospitalization. Because we are dealing here with first-admission patients, one cannot help but wonder whether the spouse's expression of feelings about the patient after a relatively brief period of hospitalization affords an adequate basis for predicting response to the patient upon his or her return home. This is a matter that we wish to look at much more closely in a new sample of families in which we interviewed patient and spouse 1 month after the patient's return home and again 6 months later, and in which we have systematically assessed emotional involvement and critical attitudes prior to the patient's return home.

TABLE 12.5
Symptoms in Past 5 Years By Current Status Of Marriage For Patients Classified Schizophrenic

Current Marital Status	Males		Females		
	None or Mild Symptoms	Serious or Persistent Symptoms	None or Mild Symptoms	Serious Symptoms	Persistent Symptoms
Total	11	6	4	8	7
Together	10	2	3	6	2
Separated, divorced	1	4	1	1	4
Patient died	—	—	—	1	—
Terminated by hospitalization	—	—	—	—	1

Premorbid Personality

We did not attempt to evaluate the premorbid functioning of the patients in our study except in occupational roles, but we did secure detailed information on the spouse's perception of the patient as a person. Half the men were seen by their wives as essentially healthy, normal persons prior to their breakdown. This was true of only a fifth of the female patients, however. When we examine spouse's perceptions by diagnostic subgroups, they are most positive in the instance of patients diagnosed as having affective psychoses. Seven of the nine men and two of the four women were viewed by their spouses as essentially normal, and, indeed, one of the men was seen as a model of mental health by his wife. Among men classified as schizophrenic, 6 of the 13 were viewed as essentially normal whereas 2 were seen as immature or inadequate, and 3 as excessively nervous and anxious. Among the women classified as schizophrenic, only one-fifth were seen as normal, and more than half were characterized by their husbands as unduly anxious and nervous or suspicious.

Although the men whose spouses regarded them as essentially normal are predominantly found in the group with minimal subsequent symptoms, they do not differ markedly from men regarded as immature or as anxious. Men reported to have a drinking problem at the time of their initial hospitalization, however, and women reported to have been suspicious or withdrawn prior to hospitalization most often show up in the persistently symptomatic group. Again, however, the number of cases involved is too small to be anything more than suggestive.

Employment Histories

There is a significant positive correlation between freedom from symptoms and employment for our male patients, but it is by no means perfect. Several men who have been persistently or episodically symptomatic have nevertheless had reasonably orderly occupational careers; that is, they have been regularly employed with stable or increasing responsibility in a particular field of work. Orderly careers despite recurrent pathology were especially characteristic of patients with affective disorders; all these men were at least episodically symptomatic and most were rehospitalized a number of times, yet three of the five who survived the entire period have had orderly careers and the other two somewhat disorderly careers but reasonably steady employment. Most of the manic–depressives are not only able to maintain orderly careers despite recurrent symptoms; they have been highly successful as salesmen or in other jobs that tend to involve much social contact.

Among men diagnosed schizophrenic, however, episodic or persistent symptoms were most often associated with marginal or intermittent work; usually a succession of short-term jobs at low-skill levels. Nevertheless, one man who retains the delusional system that resulted in his hospitalization in 1952 has been stably employed and several times promoted in his highly technical occupation.

All the men who had received a diagnosis of schizophrenia (definite, probable, or possible) and who remained symptom free after their hospital discharge have had orderly careers. Indeed, they exceed the occupational stability of the husbands of schizophrenic women in our sample. But most of these men have been employed in jobs that do not entail a great deal of contact with others, and with one or two exceptions they have been less outstanding than the affectives.

Those who were steadily employed after hospitalization had been established in an occupation before hospitalization. Indeed, the best predictor of occupational performance in the posthospital period is not subsequent symptoms but demonstrated job competence prior to initial hospitalization (Huffine & Clausen, 1979).

A few of the female patients who have had only periodic symptoms or none at all have been employed, but none of those persistently symptomatic was employed at the time of follow-up. Nevertheless, it does not appear that these symptomatic women are functioning less effectively now than they did 10 to 15 years ago. Quite the contrary: Most husbands of female patients report that their wives can handle problems and crises now as well as, or better than, they could in earlier years, and wives of male patients give them even more positive ratings.

Social Participation

Questions on social participation were asked late in the follow-up interview and were sometimes omitted in instances where interviews had to be curtailed for one reason or another. In all diagnostic groups, very few patients had at follow-up a wide circle of friends or were highly active participants in community affairs, regardless of employment status and symptoms subsequent to hospital release. Only half the schizophrenic males have even one friend who is really close; most confine their close ties to relatives. Women are somewhat more likely to have friends among their neighbors. Many former patients have tended to insulate themselves, largely because of fear of rejection (though few appear to have experienced such rejection (Clausen, 1981)). Some express the desire for more social contacts but lack confidence in their ability to establish new relationships. In general, it appears that male expatients who are functioning well are likely to participate socially with friends of their wives, whereas female expatients are more likely to confine their social participation to family relationships and to friends in the neighborhood.

Although not highly involved with others, most of the former patients, even if recurrently symptomatic, appear to be carrying out expected role functions in the home and community. Some of the men (but almost no women) have been relieved of parental responsibilities by the spouse.

Problems of Classification and Analysis

Because of the heterogeneity and small size of our sample, it does not appear fruitful at this time to conduct elaborate statistical analyses of factors predictive of psychopathology in later life. It is clear that those factors differ somewhat by diagnostic group. In most respects, patients with affective disorders had the characteristics that would lead one to expect a favorable outcome in a schizophrenic. Nevertheless, except as lithium appeared to be bringing stability to a few of the manic–depressives at the time of follow-up, many of these men and women have had so many episodes of symptoms and treatment as to be labeled persistently symptomatic. Yet obviously this is a different kind of persistence than that of the recurrently symptomatic schizophrenic patient who tends to show a degree of impairment most of the time.

We do not have adequate family histories to assess the frequency of affective disorders or schizophrenia in the families of our patients. The tendency to diagnose schizophrenia using a very broad conception in most hospitals from which our cases were selected renders dubious diagnoses of family members who may have received earlier treatment there. For example, one of the men whose diagnosis of acute undifferentiated schizophrenia seems dubious to us had a sister who had been previously hospitalized with a diagnosis of schizophrenia. Yet the patient's wife referred to her sister-in-law's problem as an acute depressive reaction. The patient in our sample was only briefly delusional and has had no recurrence in 20 years, during which he has advanced with the same employer. A review of the full transcript of the diagnostic conferences shows great disagreement as to whether the man was schizophrenic, manic–depressive, or not psychotic at all. Given the diagnosis of schizophrenia, he was hospitalized for 5 months, after which he returned to his old job. To arrive at a usable family history, it would be necessary to attempt rediagnosis of the sister from hospital records. This was beyond the scope of our research.

A comment is in order about the differences between our diagnostic groups, definite or probably schizophrenia and possible schizophrenia. As previously noted, we based rediagnoses on the RDC (Spitzer et al., 1978). Patients classified as definitely or probably schizophrenic had, respectively, at least two or one of the specified types of hallucinations and/or delusions persisting for at least a week, plus a period of illness of at least 2 weeks prior to hospitalization, and either flat or inappropriate affect, derailment, marked illogicality, or marked poverty of speech. (In most instances the period of illness exceeded the 6 months specified in DSM III.) Persons whom we classified as possibly schizophrenic (almost all of whom had been diagnosed schizophrenic on first admission) seldom manifested clear-cut delusions or hallucinations unless for a brief period just before and after hospitalization, nor was their behavior as strikingly bizarre. More often, especially among the women, they seemed physically and mentally retarded, anxious, easily upset, and somewhat incompetent. Affect was flat, for the most part, though in a few instances emotional excitement was at times high.

In several instances the patient simply became mute and never communicated what was going on.

Some Illustrative Cases

It may be useful to give a few examples of cases that cause perplexity. Consider first a man whose diagnosis at discharge from the index hospital was paranoid schizophrenia and whom we have classified as "possible schizophrenia."

> He was 40 years old on initial admission, a skilled worker with a steady work history, and the father of four children. A week prior to admission he had been picked up by police in a neighboring state after he had attempted suicide by driving his car off the side of the road. On admission the staff described him as depressed and disgusted with life. Psychiatric examination found him "oriented in all spheres and possessed of a good memory for both recent and remote events." He was, however, confused and guilty about something he had done or had failed to do. He also believed that he had another wife but could not say who she was.

> He had quit his job 3 weeks prior to admission, in a period when his wife was out of town visiting relatives, but was unable to give a reason for having quit the job. He had thereupon remained at home with no interest in anything until his abortive suicide attempt.

> His wife described her husband as a man who kept his problems to himself and did not discuss his emotions with anyone. He had a "spell" of depression 4 years earlier, during which he could not go to work and stayed home, but he improved spontaneously in 2 or 3 weeks. He had been a heavy drinker but had decided to quit just before the suicide attempt.

> In the 6 months prior to initial admission, his wife described her spouse as doing better than he had in a long time. He had a job he liked, a large garden, enjoyed playing with his children, and had just about stopped drinking.

> During the first week on the ward the patient was suspicious, tense, restless, and rarely took part in activities. Throughout the period of hospitalization it was difficult to get any information from him. He seemed to improve with treatment but would regress after a visit home. He was discharged after 5½ months. A year later, he was readmitted, reporting that he had failed to adjust and could not make himself return to work. According to his wife, he did nothing but sit around the house all day, staring off into space.

> His wife went to work at the time of his first hospitalization and earned enough to support the family. She continued to work after his return home, and it was not until 2 years after his second hospitalization that the patient returned to work. He apparently simply showed up at an employment office, was hired, and worked on a reasonably regular basis for the next 7 years, when he was again hospitalized. On this occasion, he became paranoid about being poisoned, and his delusions led to a display of bizarre behavior that

resulted in his being again committed to the state hospital. Once more he received the diagnosis of schizophrenia, paranoid type.

After 6 months, he was again released. This time he waited the better part of a year before returning to work. He has subsequently been in outpatient treatment, visiting a county mental health clinic once a month. He regularly takes a low dosage of meloril. At follow-up, 4 years after the third hospitalization, he was working regularly as a journeyman on a variety of jobs assigned by the union hiring office. His wife finds him a very stubborn and uncommunicative man, but otherwise reports that their marriage is happy.

Here we have a man who had most of the indicators of favorable outcome and who, indeed, might initially have been diagnosed as having a depressive reaction, but for long periods he seemed less depressed than withdrawn. He had a long period when he was largely immobilized. Yet he became fully functional again.

In comparison with males who developed schizophrenia in adolescence, our sample constitutes a markedly more competent group of men, for the most part able to relate reasonably well to their wives, if not to women in general. Studies of the wives of schizophrenic patients have suggested that these women are often drawn to men who seem "sensitive," shy, and somewhat vulnerable (Planansky & Johnston, 1967). This certainly characterizes the majority of the men who had a definite or probable diagnosis of schizophrenia. For the most part they were seen as meek individuals who withdrew from unpleasant situations. Even among those who have not shown any serious symptoms of mental disorder subsequent to the initial hospitalization, the former schizophrenics tend to participate only minimally in social activities outside the family. When they do, as previously noted, it is primarily with the friends of their wives. Some, indeed, maintain a high degree of isolation from the wives and children with whom they live.

Mr. Rowe, for example, who was hospitalized at 43, regarded himself as sensitive, shy, and not practical. He was physically inept and never able to talk about his feelings. He married at 30 and regarded the children born to the couple as an intrusion. In fact, he avoided interaction with them by spending most of his evenings in his room while the children were young. Periodically, Mr. Rowe felt that people had stolen things from him and that his wife was unfaithful. His acute break came during a summer vacation; he became wilder week by week, drinking, characterizing himself as an FBI agent, fearing arrest, suffering from auditory hallucinations and disorientation. In the hospital he made rapid improvement and was returned home after 4 months.

Fifteen years later, we found Mr. Rowe back in his professional job and in general functioning just as he had before the onset of his initial symptoms. There was improvement in at least one respect, however. He had established a relationship with his son, and they frequently played chess when the son was home from college. His wife characterized him as having had no further symptoms but she accepted the possibility of a recurrence. They still couldn't talk about feelings, and to all intents and purposes they lived in separate worlds under the same roof. There had been no sexual component to their relationship for the previous 5 years, but the wife reported that neither of them had missed it.

We have less information than we would have liked on sexual relationships in the marriages of our schizophrenic patients, but the dominant impression from what we do have is that sex was not of major importance to either partner in most couples with male patients. A number of the women diagnosed schizophrenic felt that their husbands made excessive sexual demands upon them, but our data do not permit us to draw any inferences as to whether or not this would be a significant factor in outcome.

There are a few instances in which all the signs pointed to a favorable outcome, and yet the patient has gone progressively downhill. One man, whose psychotic episode followed an auto accident in which he was at fault, is a case in point.

This man, over 30 at hospitalization, was described by his spouse as having had a happy childhood, normal but perhaps a bit too independent. After the accident, he thought that people were trying to get him to leave his job and that they had access to his thoughts. Voices reminded him of things he must do, and he had visions. He then drove his car 90 miles an hour and hit another car, leading to his arrest for reckless driving and another sequence of bizarre behavior, resulting in commitment.

Upon his return from the hospital the patient no longer talked openly with his spouse. He expressed the feeling that their marital relationship was not satisfactory. Sex, which had been very satisfactory, diminished markedly. A succession of hospital admissions left him in worse shape each time, and he became abusive and assaultive. His wife secured a divorce and he returned to his parents' home.

Finally, his family bought a small hunting lodge for him in a remote wooded area, where he now lives on a small pension. He is antagonistic toward doctors and medication and has essentially no social ties except with a brother who sees him periodically. Obviously, he constitutes a problem for prediction.

DISCUSSION

On the whole, the findings here reported, especially as they relate to schizophrenia, are consonant with those of the studies earlier cited. Favorable outcomes tend to be associated with good "premorbid status," with later age of onset of the first episode of symptoms, with acuteness of onset, and with the existence of precipitating factors. By virtue of the specification that all members of our patient population had been married, this sample would be expected to have more favorable outcomes than if younger, unmarried patients had been included.

The relatively favorable outcomes of our patients are also related to the fact that the population was designated at the time of first admission to a mental hospital. In this respect the sample here studied resembles that of Bland and his associates (1978), who found that nearly three-fifths of their schizophrenic patients followed 10 years after first hospital admission showed no psychiatric impairment when examined. Half the group showed normal economic productivity, a finding closely similar to our own. Follow-up studies of cross sections of patients *discharged* from mental hospitals, without reference to the number of previous admissions, will always lead to a more dismal picture of outcome, because they inevitably constitute a negatively selected sample of first admissions to a mental hospital in some prior period.

The inadequacy of treatment data as an indication of long-term outcome is attested to by the imperfect relationship among treatment, recurring symptoms, occupational performance, and social activities. A number of persistently symptomatic men have been effective occupationally and socially; some have received treatment and others not. We have used a rather stringent basis for assessing recent symptoms and impairment—no major problems in the 5 years immediately preceding follow-up. This perhaps accounts for our finding a higher proportion psychiatrically impaired than did Bland et al. In those instances in which we did more than a single follow-up interview, often at intervals of a year or more, we frequently found marked shifts in the patient's condition and life circumstances. Some patients who had been markedly impaired and were unavailable for interview when we first sought to follow them up subsequently not only became available but appeared to be functioning better than at any time since initial hospitalization.

Discrepancies between being in treatment and showing persisting symptoms were greater for male than for female patients. Men appear to be much more resistant to seeking treatment for later episodes of symptoms. Reversing a tendency found at initial hospitalization, men were more often committed at later hospitalizations. Moreover, wives were much more often involved in getting psychotic husbands back into treatment than were husbands in helping arrange for treatment of their psychotic wives (Clausen, Pfeffer, & Huffine, 1982). It may also be worthy of comment that commitment of the patient to hospitalization subsequent to the initial one was far more often undertaken in the instance of patients whose marriages had broken.

A comment on the more favorable outcome experienced by male than by female patients (other than the affectives) is in order. In general, it appears that favorable prognosis is strongly associated with the acquisition of social competence prior to an incapacitating breakdown. Males who manage to marry and to sustain their marriages for a year or more are likely to have acquired occupational and social skills that are not necessarily required of a married woman. To this extent, the men in our sample are more positively selected for social competence, and their more favorable outcomes were therefore to be expected. In general, in attempts to predict later psychopathology from early adult performance, it would appear that data should be separately analyzed by sex.

When we consider the proportion of patients in our study who have been seriously symptomatic and had treatment subsequent to initial hospitalization, the outcome picture may seem dismaying. On the other hand, if we consider the proportion who are currently functioning reasonably effectively in the community, one has quite a different impression. Moreover, recall that in each successive 5 years, a smaller proportion of the original group of patients has been seriously symptomatic or rehospitalized. In this study of married patients, we can at least agree with Manfred Bleuler that for those patients diagnosed schizophrenic, on the average, one sees no change for the worse but, if anything, improvement beyond the fifth year of psychosis (Bleuler, 1978).

Other recent European follow-up studies reveal similar findings, far more encouraging than the prevailing beliefs about schizophrenia a generation ago (Ciompi, 1980; Huber, Gross, Schuttler, & Linz, 1980; Möller et al., 1983). Is schizophrenia becoming a less severe disorder, as Romano (1977) has suggested, based on his clinical assessments over a long career, or was the earlier pessimistic view of the course of schizophrenia based on a self-fulfilling prophecy? If schizophrenics are not expected to improve, perhaps they will be unlikely to improve. It must be noted, however, that the long-term European follow-up studies deal with schizophrenics who were first hospitalized in an era of pessimism about schizophrenia (Ciompi's patients were all born prior to 1897 and most were hospitalized before 1940), so many schizophrenics obviously recovered despite existing beliefs about the disorder. The group of patients here described were hospitalized in the period when psychoactive drugs were first being employed in the United States. Most spent several months in the hospital, and, despite the negative connotations of admission to a public mental hospital with a functional diagnosis, most of these married patients were subsequently able to perform in normal adult roles most of the time.

ACKNOWLEDGMENTS

The research here reported was supported by Grant MH-19649 from the National Institute of Mental Health. I am indebted to Dr. Carol Huffine for her contributions to all phases of the research and to Shula Gubkin for careful assistance with the computer analysis of a somewhat unwieldy body of data.

REFERENCES

Beck, J. C. (1978). Social influences on the prognosis of schizophrenia. *Schizophrenia Bulletin, 4*, 86–101.

Bland, R. C., Parker, J. H., & Orn, H. (1978). Prognosis in schizophrenia. *Archives of General Psychiatry, 35*, 72–77.

Bleuler, M. (1978). *The schizophrenic disorders: Long-term patient and family studies*. New Haven, CT: Yale University Press.

Brown, G. W., Birley, J. L. T., & Wing, J. K. (1972). Influence of family life on the course of schizophrenic disorders: A replication. *British Journal of Psychiatry, 121*, 241–258.

Ciompi, Luc. (1980). Catamnestic long-term study on the course of life and aging of schizophrenics. *Schizophrenia Bulletin, 6*, 606–617.

Clausen, J. A. (1975). The impact of mental illness: A twenty-year follow-up. In R. T. Wirt, G. Winokur, & M. Roff (Eds.), *Life history research in psychopathology* (Vol. IV). Minneapolis: University of Minnesota Press.

Clausen, J. A. (1981). Stigma and mental disorder: Phenomena and terminology. *Psychiatry, 44*, 287–296.

Clausen, J. A. (1983). Sex roles, marital roles and response to mental disorder. In J. Greenley (Ed.), *Research in community and mental health* (Vol. 3). Greenwich, CT: JAI Press.

Clausen, J. A., Pfeffer, N. G., & Huffine, C. L. (1982). Help-seeking in severe mental illness. In D. Mechanic (Ed.), *Psychosocial epidemiology: Symptoms, illness behavior and help-seeking*. New York: Neale Watson Academic Publications.

Clausen, J. A., & Yarrow, M. R. (Eds.). (1955). The impact of mental illness on the family. *Journal of Social Issues, 11*, (No. 4, entire issue).

Huber, G., Gross, G., Schuttler, R., & Linz, M. (1980). Longitudinal studies of schizophrenic patients. *Schizophrenia Bulletin, 6*, 592–618.

Huffine, C. L., & Clausen, J. A. (1979). Madness and work: Short- and long-term effects of mental illness on occupational careers. *Social Forces, 57*, 1049–1062.

Möller, H. J., Zerssen, D., Werner–Eilert, K., & Wuochner–Stockheim, M. (1983). Outcome in schizophrenia and similar paranoid psychoses. *Schizophrenia Bulletin, 9*, 99–108.

Planansky, J., & Johnston, R. (1967). Mate selection in schizophrenia. *Acta Psychiatrica Scandinavica, 43*, 397–409.

Romano, J. (1977). On the nature of schizophrenia: Changes in the observer as well as the observed. *Schizophrenia Bulletin, 3*, 532–559.

Sampson, H., Messinger, S. L., & Towne, R. D. (1964). *Schizophrenic women: Studies in marital crisis*. New York: Atherton.

Spitzer, R. L., Endicott, J., & Robins, L. (1978). Research diagnostic criteria: Rationale and reliability. *Archives of General Psychiatry, 35*, 773–782.

Strauss, J. S., & Carpenter, W. T. (1974). The prediction of outcome in schizophrenia. II. Relationships between predictor and outcome variables: A report from the WHO International Pilot Study of Schizophrenia. *Archives of General Psychiatry, 6*, 313–320.

Strauss, J. S., & Carpenter, W. T. (1978). The prognosis of schizophrenia: Rationale for a multidimensional concept. *Schizophrenia Bulletin, 4*, 56–67.

Vaillant, G. E. (1964). Prospective prediction of schizophrenic remission. *Archives of General Psychiatry, 11*, 509–518.

Vaillant, G. (1978). A 10-year follow-up of remitting schizophrenics. *Schizophrenia Bulletin, 4*, 78–85.

13 Predictors of Poor and Good Outcome in Schizophrenia

M. T. Tsuang

INTRODUCTION

The overall outcome of mental illness can be used to assess the magnitude of the effect of psychosis over the life-span of a patient and plan some effective measures of coping with the psychiatric disorder. However, the study of outcome is not an end in itself. Psychotics will differ at outcome owing to variables such as response to treatment, constitutional and environmental factors, and differences in the symptom manifestation and diagnosis given at the time of initial assessment. By studying these variables, it may be possible to discover the underlying psychopathological factors that will predict good or poor outcomes.

Langfeldt (1937) laid the cornerstone for research in the predictors for good and poor prognosis in schizophrenia. He found that poor outcome was associated with poor emotional and intellectual development of personality before onset, gradual and insidious onset of illness, absence of precipitating factors, and unfavorable environment before and after onset. Good outcome was associated with atypical features such as depression, elation, preoccupation with physical symptoms, acute onset with confusion, and distinct precipitating events. Vaillant (1962) reviewed the prognostic features that contrasted recovered schizophrenics with chronic, poor-outcome schizophrenics and concurred with Langfeldt's findings. Vaillant selected two cohorts of 30 schizophrenics, one from recovered patients and the other from long-stay patients, and found that good outcome was related to six factors: (1) a family history of depression, (2) acute onset, (3) confusion or disorientation during the acute episode, (4) absence of schizoid premorbid personality adjustment, (5) a clear precipitating event, and (6) presence of symptoms suggesting a psychotic depression.

Although these studies and those that followed them have made a lasting contribution to our understanding of the prognostic features of psychosis, the

195

initial diagnosis of schizophrenia was not defined by operational research criteria and the duration of follow-up did not cover the life-span of the patient. In the Iowa 500 project, we sought to study outcome of schizophrenia by choosing study subjects according to strict operational criteria and following all of them up over the entire life-span, including recovered and deceased patients. We do not claim that these criteria are the only ones to identify schizophrenia, but at least we know what kind of schizophrenia we are studying.

The Iowa 500 project was a 30- to 40-year follow-up and family study of 200 schizophrenics, 100 manics, and 225 depressives selected according to the research criteria of Feighner, Robins, Guze, Woodruff, Winokur, and Munoz (1972), along with a stratified random sample of 160 psychiatrically symptom-free surgical controls. In all, we were able to trace 97% of these study subjects to their current address or to death. We developed the Iowa Structured Psychiatric Interview (ISPI) form for trained research workers to interview subjects blindly. Details on the rationale, reliability, and validity of the ISPI have been reported elsewhere (Tsuang, Woolson, & Simpson, 1980).

We have examined the results of our outcome study to discover whether any of the features of the selection criteria could be used to predict outcome in schizophrenia and affective disorders (Tsuang, Woolson, & Simpson, 1981). Feighner criteria for schizophrenia have three dominant and five optional features. Of the dominant features, the criterion of 6-month duration of illness was met by all patients in our schizophrenia group; thus, this feature was not used in the analysis. The following are the other primary features: (1) delusions or hallucinations in a clear sensorium, or (2) disorganized thoughts. Enough statistical evidence was found to convince us that there was an association between disorganized thoughts and poorer outcome, and between delusions or hallucinations and better outcome. The optional features include singleness at admission, social maladjustment, a family history of schizophrenia, an age of onset before 40, and the absence of alcohol or drug abuse for 1 year before onset. Not one of these optional features, however, was significantly associated with poorer or better outcome.

In the present report, we analyze outcome according to admission variables coded from the original medical records. We have pursued each admission variable using univariate analysis. This means the variables were evaluated independently in terms of the impact on outcome. In addition, because of the statistical problems with multiple comparisons, we also performed a multivariate (stepwise discriminant) analysis with these data.

SUBJECTS AND METHODS

The psychiatric medical charts for the 200 schizophrenic patients in the Iowa 500 project were reviewed by three psychiatrists beginning in 1971 to code systematically admission, family history, and chart follow-up data (Morrison, Clancy,

Crowe, & Winokur, 1972). Included on the charts were verbatim transcripts of staff meetings and interviews with the patients, records of premorbid social adjustment, progress notes, laboratory studies, and discharge summaries. We coded admission data from their charts according to approximately 50 variables. Briefly, these variables were arrayed under demographic information, general clinical and hospital information, and specific clinical and psychiatric data. For example, demographic information included base-line values for age at admission, sex, marital status, employment, residence, and physical health. General clinical and hospital information included age of onset, previous admissions, length of stay, discharge destination, and precipitating factors. Specific symptom variables were arranged according to the functional diagnostic entities—depression, mania, schizophrenia, neuroses, and other personality disorders. Each variable could be easily coded because of the thorough admission records.

Enough information was available at follow-up to rate 186 schizophrenic patients for outcome under all four outcome categories: marital, residential, psychiatric, and occupational. To each patient a categorical rating was given to assess outcome at the time of follow-up based on the definitions spelled out in Table 13.1. With these ratings it was possible to analyze which admission variables were predictive of outcome. Because schizophrenics had a poorer long-term outcome than manic–depressives in our previous follow-up study (Tsuang, Woolson, & Fleming, 1979), we have grouped the good and fair categories together to compare with poor outcome in the present study. Thus, we compared all variables in terms of either better or poorer outcome, using the four outcome categories as defined in Table 13.1.

TABLE 13.1
Definition of Ratings For Outcome*

Status	*Rating*		
	Good = 3	*Fair = 2*	*Poor = 1*
Marital	Married or widowed	Divorced or separated	Single, never married
Residential	Own home or relatives' residence	Nursing or county home	Mental hospital
Occupational	Employed, retired, housewife or student	Incapacitated due to physical illness	Incapacitated due to mental illness
Psychiatric Symptoms	None	Some	Incapacitating

*Tsuang et al., 1979

RESULTS

The following is a discussion of the admission variables that predicted outcome in each outcome category. Table 13.2 systematically arranges those variables that showed statistical significance at less than the 5% level.

Marital. In this category, an age of onset under 30 and the presence of memory deficit predicted poor outcome, whereas a higher percentage of patients with better outcome exhibited symptoms of hyperactivity and flight of ideas. An early age of onset (under 30) appeared in 81.6% of the patients with a poor marital outcome, whereas only 68.9% of those with a better marital outcome had an early onset of illness. Eighteen (14.4%) of the poorer marital outcomes shared the characteristic of memory deficit, whereas only one patient (1.6%) with memory deficit had better results in regard to marriage. In our study a clinical observation of memory deficit signifies objective signs of disorientation as to person, place, and time, or subjective symptoms of complaints about recent or remote memory impairment at the time of admission. It should be noted that the research criteria in this study excluded acute schizophrenics or schizoaffectives, and, therefore, the acute confusional state that may be accompanied by memory loss was not frequently observed in these schizophrenics. In general, memory deficit was present in these patients without clouding of consciousness. In regard to better marital outcome, two improved patients had flight of ideas, whereas it was not found in the group with poorer outcome. Nine schizophrenic patients were hyperactive at admission; seven (11.5%) had better and two (1.6%) had poorer marital outcomes.

Residential. A large group of schizophrenics in our study, totaling 108 patients, experienced blocking of thoughts that led to mutism at admission. In all, 83 (54.2%) of the 153 patients with better residential outcome had this symptom, and 25 (75.8%) of the 33 patients with poorer residential outcome experienced thought blocking.

Occupational. In general, more patients with visual hallucinations, thought blocking, social withdrawal, and memory deficit experienced a poorer outcome, and more patients with euphoric mood and persecutory delusions sustained a better outcome. Out of 79 patients with a better occupational outcome, 75 (94.9%) had persecutory delusions of one kind or another. This is significantly higher than the percentage (81.3%) of patients with persecutory delusions in the poorer outcome category. The numbers of schizophrenics in our study with euphoria on their admission charts were negligible (3). Yet, together with patients showing hyperactivity and flight of ideas, they overwhelmingly predicted overall better outcome.

TABLE 13.2
Prediction of Long-Term Outcome Based on Variables Coded at Admission for Schizophrenia

	Marital Status			
	Good/Fair		Poor	
Admission Variable	(N = 61)	(%)	(N = 125)	(%)
Age of onset (< 30)	42	(68.9)	102	(81.6)[a]
Hyperactivity	7	(11.5)	2	(1.6)[b]
Flight of ideas	2	(3.3)	0	(0.0)[a]
Memory deficit	1	(1.6)	18	(14.4)[b]

	Residential Status			
	Good/Fair		Poor	
	(N = 153)	(%)	(N = 33)	(%)
Blocking, mute	83	(54.2)	25	(75.8)[a]

	Occupational Status			
	Good/Fair		Poor	
	(N = 79)	(%)	(N = 107)	(%)
Euphoric	3	(3.8)	0	(0.0)[a]
Persecutory delusions	75	(94.9)	87	(81.3)[a]
Visual hallucinations	12	(15.2)	37	(34.6)[b]
Blocking, mute	34	(43.0)	74	(69.2)[b]
Social withdrawal	50	(63.3)	85	(79.4)[a]
Memory deficit	3	(3.8)	16	(15.0)[a]

	Mental Status			
	Good/Fair		Poor	
	(N = 86)	(%)	(N = 100)	(%)
Auditory hallucinations	40	(46.5)	60	(60.0)[a]
Visual hallucinations	16	(18.6)	33	(33.0)[a]
Memory deficit	4	(4.7)	15	(15.0)[a]

[a] $p < .05$
[b] $p < .01$

Patients with poorer occupational outcome had more symptoms of visual hallucinations, verbal blocking, social withdrawal, and memory deficit. Visual hallucinations were found in 15.2% of the better outcome individuals and in 34.6% of the poor outcome subjects. Of the 79 subjects in the better outcome group, 34 were positive for verbal blocking, whereas 74 of 107 poorer category people were positive for this variable. The percentage of social withdrawal was higher in the poorer group (79.4%) than in the better category (63.3%). Likewise, memory deficit was significantly more frequent in the poorer group (15.0%) when compared to the better group (3.8%).

Mental.   Under mental status, auditory hallucinations, visual hallucinations, and memory deficit all significantly predicted poor outcome. Auditory hallucinations were present in 60% of poor outcome patients, where 46.5% of better outcome patients had this symptom. Visual hallucinations occurred in 33% of the poor outcome patients, whereas 18.6% of the better outcome subjects had visual hallucinations. Memory deficit was present in 15% of poor-outcome schizophrenics, and it was present in 4.7% of better outcome schizophrenics.

DISCUSSION

Schizophrenia defined by narrow research criteria shows a poor overall outcome. Over 50% of the subjects in our study had incapacitating mental symptoms after 30 to 40 years. The purpose of this study has been to analyze outcome in terms of poor versus good and fair categories to determine which admission variables were predictive of outcome. Memory deficit predicted poorer outcome in three out of four outcome categories. Visual hallucinations and verbal blocking also had the ability to predict poor outcome. In our previous study (Tsuang et al., 1981), we combined delusions or hallucinations as one variable because they were one of the two dominant features required for a diagnosis of schizophrenia according to Feighner criteria. The results showed that delusions and hallucinations together were predictive of good outcome. In the present study, when this variable was divided into delusions and hallucinations separately, we found that delusions were associated with better outcome, but hallucinations seemed to predict poor outcome.

Further analysis based on a subgroup of 52 chronic hebephrenic/catatonic schizophrenics was done to examine the presence or absence of individual symptoms of schizophrenia on a year-by-year basis over a span of 25 years (Pfohl & Winokur, 1982, 1983). Symptoms usually classified as positive symptoms of schizophrenia, such as hallucinations and delusions, were found to have earlier onset and greater tendency to resolve over time than symptoms usually classified as negative such as flat affect, decreased social interaction, and sensorium defects.

As mentioned, memory deficit appeared to be associated with poor outcome in three of four outcome variables. In light of this finding, we examined patients with memory deficit in comparison with schizophrenics without memory deficit from our study (Tsuang, 1982). Out of the 200 schizophrenics in our study, 22 had symptoms of memory deficit on their admission charts. At follow-up 30 to 40 years later, psychiatrists blindly diagnosed the majority of the 22 memory-deficient patients as nonparanoid; 8 were hebephrenic, 10 catatonic, and 2 undifferentiated. Of this group, there was sufficient information on 19 patients to enable us to rate their outcome under all four outcome categories. As the results of this study show, more patients with memory deficit suffered a poor outcome in three outcome categories. Furthermore, at the time of follow-up 30 to 40 years later, a high percentage (42.9%) of the patients with memory deficit at admission still complained of difficulties with memory loss. In contrast, only 22% of the patients in the group without memory deficit at admission complained of an impaired memory. Personal interviewers rated 61.9% of the group with memory deficit at admission as having signs of disorientation with respect to person, place, or time. Substantially fewer (22.7%) in the group without memory deficit at admission presented such signs of disorientation. These indications point out that memory deficit was a highly stable variable over a 30- to 40-year period, and that it predicts poor outcome. Memory deficit may be a manifestation of thought disorder usually found in nonparanoid schizophrenia (Tsuang & Winokur, 1974) or of an organic pathology found in some forms of schizophrenia. It is noteworthy that some researchers using CAT scans have shown that structural brain changes occur in poor outcome, chronic schizophrenic patients (Donnelly, Weinberger, Waldman, & Wyatt, 1980; Golden, Moses, Zelazowski, Graber, Zatz, Horvath, & Berger, 1980; and Johnstone, Crow, Frith, Stevens, Kreel, & Husband, 1978).

In the absence of reliable neuropsychological tests for these patients at admission, a future study of the psychopathology of memory deficit in our schizophrenics should contrast memory-deficit subjects with control subjects, matched for age and sex, who are without memory deficit at admission. At follow-up all patients would be examined with neuropsychological tests and CAT scans. In addition, the entire lifetime information from medical records and interviews should be considered.

From a statistical point of view, univariate analyses present some problems because of the number of independent comparisons that were performed. When analyzing 50 admission variables, we expect a certain number to be significant by chance alone. Therefore, we are currently completing a multivariate analysis (Jennrich, 1977) of these data. This analysis indicates that under the marital-status-outcome category the admission variables of singleness, absence of precipitating factors, private-pay status, and a young age of onset predict poor outcome. In occupational status, we find that the presence of memory deficit, social withdrawal, and the absence of delusions predict poor outcome. Memory deficit predicts poor outcome for mental status at follow-up. Again, the most striking overlap with the univariate analysis is the presence of memory deficit at admission in the poorer outcome category.

SUMMARY

It should be emphasized that this study was a global, cross-sectional measurement of clinical variables at admission and at final outcome 30 to 40 years afterward. To comprehend fully the psychopathological nature and predictive behavior of each prognostic variable would require a study of the entire course of the psychiatric illness. We are presently conducting this type of study using medical records, death certificates, and patient interviews with the hope that we can obtain a clearer picture of the factors that predict poor outcome in schizophrenia.

This chapter has focused on the characteristics of poor outcome in schizophrenia. We studied the outcome of 200 schizophrenics meeting Feighner research criteria, 30 or 40 years after their admission. Features at the time of admission were analyzed. It was found that memory deficit, thought blocking, and social withdrawal, auditory or visual hallucinations, and younger age of onset were predictive of poor outcome. Features associated with good outcome were euphoria, hyperactivity, flight of ideas, and persecutory delusions present at the time of admission.

ACKNOWLEDGMENTS

This study was supported in part by funds from the National Institute of Mental Health, United States Public Service Grants MH24189 and MH31673. Assisting in the preparation of this chapter were Jerome Fleming, M.S., and Bruce McCallum, M.C.S.

REFERENCES

Donnelly, E. F., Weinberger, D. R., Waldman, I. N., & Wyatt, R. J. (1980). Cognitive impairment associated with morphological brain abnormalities on computed tomography in chronic schizophrenic patients. *Journal of Nervous and Mental Disease, 168*, 305–308.

Feighner, J. P., Robins, E., Guze, S. B., Woodruff, R. A., Winokur, G., & Munoz, R. (1972). Diagnostic criteria for use in psychiatric research. *Archives of General Psychiatry, 26*, 57–63.

Golden, C. J., Moses, J. A., Zelazowski, R., Graber, B., Zatz, L. M., Horvath, T. B., & Berger, P. A. (1980). Cerebral ventricular size and neuropsychological impairment in young chronic schizophrenics. *Archives of General Psychiatry, 37*, 619–623.

Jennrich, R. I. (1977). Stepwise discriminant analysis. In K. Enslein, A. Ralston, & H. S. Wilf (Eds.), *Statistical methods for digital computers* (Chapter 5). New York: Wiley.

Johnstone, E. C., Crow, T. J., Frith, C. D., Stevens, M., Kreel, L., & Husband, J. (1978). The dementia of dementia praecox. *Acta Psychiatrica Scandinavica, 57,* 305–324.

Langfeldt, G. (1937). The prognosis in schizophrenia and the factors influencing the course of the disease. *Acta Psychiatrica Scandinavica,* Supplementum *13,* 1–228.

Morrison, J., Clancy, J., Crowe, R., & Winokur, G. (1972). The Iowa 500: I. Diagnostic validity in mania, depression and schizophrenia. *Archives of General Psychiatry, 27,* 457–461.

Pfohl, B., & Winokur, G. (1982). The evolution of symptoms in institutionalized hebephrenic/catatonic schizophrenics. *British Journal of Psychiatry, 141,* 567–572.

Pfohl, B., & Winokur, G. (1983). The micropsychopathology of hebephrenic/catatonic schizophrenia. *The Journal of Nervous and Mental Disease, 171,* 5, 296–300.

Tsuang, M. T. (1982). Memory-deficit and long-term outcome in schizophrenia: A preliminary study. *Psychiatry Research, 6,* 355–360.

Tsuang, M. T., & Winokur, G. (1974). Criteria for subtyping schizophrenia: Clinical differentiation of hebephrenic and paranoid schizophrenia. *Archives of General Psychiatry, 31,* 43–47.

Tsuang, M. T., Woolson, R., & Fleming, J. (1979). Long-term outcome of major psychoses: I. Schizophrenia and affective disorders compared with psychiatrically symptom-free surgical conditions. *Archives of General Psychiatry, 36,* 1295–1301.

Tsuang, M. T., Woolson, R., & Simpson, J. C. (1980). The Iowa structured psychiatric interview: Rationale, reliability and validity. *Acta Psychiatrica Scandinavica,* Supplementum *283* (Vol. 62). Munksgaard, Copenhagen.

Tsuang, M. T., Woolson, R., & Simpson, J. C. (1981). An evaluation of Feighner criteria for schizophrenia and affective disorders using long-term outcome data. *Psychological Medicine, 11,* 1–7.

Vaillant, G. E. (1962). The prediction of recovery in schizophrenia. *Journal of Nervous and Mental Disease, 135,* 534–543.

14 The Chronicity of Depression Among The Elderly

David E. Wilder
Barry J. Gurland
Ruth G. Bennett

Relationships between physical or functional disabilities and depression have been found in many studies (Dovenmuehle & Vervoerdt, 1962: Paykel, 1973), but each of these conditions tends to be temporary in most age groups. Gerontologists have studied chronic disabilities for many years (Katz, Ford, Moskovitz, Jackson, & Jaffee, 1963) but chronicity of depression is seldom discussed (Breslau & Haug, 1983). However, because significant proportions of the elderly suffer from chronic disabilities, one is led to ask whether the depression associated with such disabilities is also chronic. More specifically, one may ask (1) what the relationships may be between chronic disabilities and the incidence, prevalence, and duration of depression in the elderly, and (2) whether chronicity of disability is a confounding factor in predicting depression among the elderly.

High prevalence rates of depression among the elderly are reported in many studies (Busse & Pfeiffer, 1973; Gurland, 1976; Silverman, 1968), but, as Jarvik (1976) has noted, there is considerable confusion about the terminology and the type of depression identified in the literature and there is considerable variance in the details of diagnostic procedures and symptom counts from one study to another. There can be difficulty in distinguishing sadness or melancholy moods from depressive illness for any age group, but this may be especially true for the aged who experience losses in physical strength, health, income, meaningful social relations, and social positions as they grow older. Additionally, it is not clear whether depression with late age of onset should be regarded as the same condition as depression occurring among younger adults. Jarvik (1976) has commented, ''Endogenous vs. reactive, psychotic vs. neurotic, primary vs. secondary, unipolar vs. bipolar are the most popular dichotomies, but not one of them corresponds to an etiologically well-defined category.'' Gurland notes that some studies depend on diagnosis and others use symptom counts to classify subjects as depressed or not depressed, but the exact procedures within each tradition vary considerably. In some studies, existing hospital diagnoses of patients are used, in others new diagnoses are made, and sometimes diagnoses are made for nonpatients (members of the general population) with whom psychiatrists have generally had relatively little experience or training to guide them in making diagnoses. Symptom counts range from self-report questionnaires and inventories of items to items rated from semistructured or unstructured interviews by persons with varying degrees of clinical experience (Gurland, 1976). Clearly, results from studies attempting to predict depression may differ considerably depending on which classifications and procedures are employed.

Dohrenwend and his colleagues (1981) have recently reviewed screening scales used in psychiatric epidemiology and have concluded that, whereas these instruments differentiated psychiatric patients and nonpatients, they were imperfectly related to diagnosed psychiatric disorder in the general population. They have also pointed out that Jerome Frank's concept of demoralization is useful in describing individuals who are identified by the screening scales commonly used in psychiatric epidemiology but who do not fit into traditional psychiatric diagnostic categories. In Frank's (1973) words: ''A person becomes demoralized when he finds he cannot meet the demands placed on him by the environment and cannot extricate himself from his predicament.'' (pp. 316). Frank argues that demoralization is only sometimes related to psychiatric disorders and is more often related to such things as extreme environmental stress, physical illnesses, especially those that are chronic, and ''existential despair'' (Frank, 1973). Because chronic physical illnesses, accumulated losses, extreme environmental stress, and despair are found disproportionately among the elderly and because large numbers of elderly persons do not fit neatly into existing psychiatric categories, demoralization may be an especially appropriate concept to apply to them.

In this chapter, we examine the relationships among depressive symptoms, clinical diagnosis of depression, and chronic disability in a sample of elderly persons who were interviewed twice with an interval of 4 to 5 years between interviews. We use the term demoralized to refer to persons receiving high scores on symptom scales developed from items in the two interview schedules that provided the data for this study, and we suggest that the concept of chronic demoralization is especially appropriate for certain elderly persons. A diagnosis of ''pervasive depression'' (Gurland, Dean, Cross, & Golden, 1980) is distinguished from the demoralization constructs, and disability and dependency are defined and operationalized using an Activities of Daily Living (ADL) scale and a Personal Time Dependency (PTD) scale.

METHODS

Subjects

Data for this chapter were provided by two separate but overlapping surveys of random samples of persons over age 65 residing in New York City. The first survey was a study of the needs and problems of the elderly conducted by the New York State Office for the Aging in late 1971 and early 1972, with support from the Administration on Aging, in which 586 New York City residents were interviewed.[1] The second survey was the US–UK Cross National Geriatric Community Study of the elderly residing in New York City and London (Gurland, Copeland, Kelleher, Kuriansky, Sharpe, & Dean, 1984); 445 randomly selected elderly persons were interviewed in New York during 1975–76. In this study, cooperation was obtained from the New York State Office for the Aging to reconstitute the frame used in their earlier survey. Both studies used probability samples and replicated designs comprising five randomly selected, interpenetrating subsamples. Each subsample was representative of all persons aged 65 or older in all five boroughs of New York City and was randomly drawn from the same randomly selected clusters of households. Response rates were 64 and 70%, respectively, for the two household surveys.

Of 161 individuals who fell into both study samples, 110 (or 68.3%) were located and interviewed in both studies. Attrition consisted of 27 refusals, 6 persons who were known to be dead, and 18 who were no longer at the same address and could not be traced. The subsample of 110 persons interviewed in both surveys is very similar to both of the larger samples with regard to distribution of item responses as well as more complex variables or constructs. Differences rarely exceed a few percentage points, and none of these is statistically significant. A few examples, including the variables used in this chapter, are shown in Table 14.1. Thus, although the overlapping subsample is not a deliberately selected random group from each of the two studies, it looks remarkably like both larger random samples, and there are no apparent differences in item or scale scores that might be affecting results.

Disability Measures

The measure of disability in the 1975–76 interview is based on the concept of personal time dependency (PTD) that was developed in the US–UK Cross National Geriatric Community Study (Gurland 1983). PTD individuals are defined

---

[1]We are indebted to the New York State Office for the Aging for permitting us to utilize data from their study. Support for the second survey was provided by grants from the National Institute of Mental Health (Grant # 5RIMH09191) and the Administration on Aging (Grant # 93-P-57467) and by the New York State Office of Mental Hygiene.

TABLE 14.1
Comparisons of 1971–72 and 1975–76 New York City Samples with
Overlapping Subsample on Key Variables

	NYC Portion of Statewide Study 1971–72	Overlapping Subsample Both Dates	NYC Portion of US/UK Study 1975–76
Sex			
Female	58%	61%	60%
Male	42%	39%	40%
Race			
White	82%	81%	80%
Non-white	18%	19%	20%
Age			
65–69	36%	36%[a]	32%
70–74	36%	34%	28%
75–79	15%	18%	21%
80+	13%	12%	19%
ADL			
Low	59%	64%	
Med	18%	17%	
High	23%	19%	
AD Hoc Demoralization			
4+	22%	22%	
Rational Scale Depression			
6+		25%	22%
Diagnosis Depression		15%	13%
PTD		30.9%	30.5%
N =	(585)	(110)	(445)

[a]1971–72 AGES
Note: ADL = Activities of Daily Living scale
　　　PTD = Personal Time Dependency scale

as having mental or physical disabilities that cause the individual to be unable to perform essential tasks that must therefore be provided by someone else, and, further, the withholding of these services would seriously threaten the individual's continued existence in his or her current setting. The PTD concept was operationalized using a set of rater judgments based on applying specific rules to case summaries written by interviewers. Thus, judgments are made as to: (1) whether the respondent receives any of a specified list of services; (2) whether the respondent is able to perform certain tasks, as reported or observed; (3) whether the services correspond with the respondent's disability; (4) whether the inability to perform tasks is the result of mental or physical disability; and (5) whether withdrawal of services would seriously threaten continued existence in the given setting (Gurland, Dean, Gurland, & Cook, 1978). The rating procedures were found to be reliable with 90% agreement and an interrater kappa of 0.78, on 104 cases selected at random. The PTD measure proved useful because it also provided level of care equivalents and cost estimates. The designation of PTD based on rater judgments was also found to be correlated 0.83 with a scale developed from 29 items in the 1976 interview that were thought to be relevant to PTD. This scale was internally consistent (Cronbach's alpha = .94), and virtually all the items it contains are disability related as shown in Table 14.2.

TABLE 14.2
Items Contained in the ADL and PTD Scales

An Indicator Scale of Personal Time Dependency 1975–76	Activities of Daily Living Scale (ADL) 1971–72
Unable to perform essential tasks	Getting about the house
Depends on others for excursions	Going up and down stairs
Physical difficulty getting to doctor	Washing and bathing
Can't care for essential needs	Dressing and putting on shoes
Can't ambulate without assistance	Cutting your toenails
Can't manage essential task because of ambulation	Getting out of the house
Health limits mobility	Feeding yourself
Health limits carrying packages	Watching television
Poor vision impedes tasks	Eating solid foods
Doesn't know phone number	(difficulty doing any of the
Problems handling business by self	above or cannot do them)
Problems dressing by self	
Problems grooming self	
Problems grooming due to physical disabilities	
Does almost no chores by self	
Difficulty doing housework by self	
Problems doing the laundry	
Couldn't survive without help	
Hasn't been out in past week	
Can't prepare own meals	
Has help with shopping	
Because of difficulty spouse does shopping	
Can't do shopping	
Can't cross streets	
Difficulty cutting toenails	
Health limits light chores	
Problems using bath by self	
Could not manage chores without help	
Because of difficulty spouse does chores	

Proportions of individuals who were judged to be PTD in the New York City sample of 445 and in the random subsample of 110 are 30.5 and 30.9%, respectively.

The 1971–72 needs survey contained an Activities of Daily Living (ADL) scale based on the one developed by Shanas, Townsend, Widderburn, Friis, Milhoj, & Stehouwer (1968) and used in their international study, which was derived from the earlier work of Katz (Katz et. al., 1963). Nine items produced a scale with high internal consistency (Cronbach's alpha = .91). These nine items are essentially a subset of the 29 items used in the scale developed to validate PTD in the Cross National study with some minor differences in wording. The two sets of items are presented in Table 14.2.

Depression Measures

Depression was measured in several different ways in the US–UK Cross National Geriatric Community Study. A Rational Scale of Depression was initially developed by selecting items based on their face validity and on information from previous studies. A criterion score of six on this scale was found to identify the cases that raters judged as being substantially depressed. A latent class scale (Gurland et al., 1980) was later empirically developed and was found to identify approximately the same group that scored six or more on the rational scale of depression. Items contained in the rational scale of depression can be found in Table 14.3. Diagnosis of depression was also made by means of explicit and specific rational scale items. These criteria are presented in Table 14.4. The term *pervasive depression* is used to include both the minor and major affective disorders. The diagnosis of pervasive depression was chosen in this epidemiological survey because: (1) It could be reliably made by nonpsychiatrists as well as psychiatrists; (2) it is germane to the public health concern about which elderly persons are in need of psychiatric intervention; and (3) it accorded well with our view that, under survey conditions using nonpsychiatrists for some interviews, it was not possible to subtype the clinical depressions validly, at least not in elderly subjects.

The results of the US–UK Cross National Geriatric Community Study showed that subjects who were diagnosed as pervasive depressives included the cases diagnosed as manic–depressive–depressive and as depressive neurosis (ICD–9) by psychiatrists in face-to-face interviews. (The DSM–III equivalents would presumably be major affective disorder and transient situational neurosis (Gurland et al., 1980).) The use of psychoactive drugs by these subjects distinguished them sharply as a group from the remaining subjects and even from those with high depression-scale scores but not qualifying for the diagnosis of pervasive depression. The group diagnosed as pervasive depressives had an outcome 1 year later that was dramatically different (in the expected direction) from the group diagnosed as dementia, in terms of intellectual deterioration, dependence, institutional admission, and mortality (Gurland et al., 1980).

Figure 14.1 shows the overlap in the number of cases in the New York sample ($N = 445$) of the US–UK study who were identified as depressed by each of the three methods. Pervasive depressive cases are, with a few exceptions, a subset of those identified by both the latent class scale and the Rational Scale of Depression, but about one fifth of the cases identified on each scale are independent of the other scale. Rational Scale of Depression scores of six or higher were obtained by 22% of the entire 1975–76 sample and by 25% of the subsample. Diagnosis of pervasive depression was made for 13 and 15%, respectively.

There was no depression scale in the instrument used in the needs survey of 1971–72. However, items from that instrument were selected on the basis of their face validity and similarity to items used in other depression scales. Ten of these items were found to have high intercorrelations and to form an ad hoc scale with high internal consistency (Cronbach's alpha = .82). A score of four or higher identified 22% of the subsample and was found to be highly correlated with ADL scores obtained from the same interviews ($p < .001$). Items for the ad hoc scale are also presented in Table 14.3.

For the most part, the ad hoc scale items are a subset of the Rational Scale of Depression items (see Table 14.3), and both are subsets of the criteria for diagnosis of depression (Table 14.4). In addition, the two scales contain items that are very much like those in the eight Symptoms Scales from the Psychiatric Epidemiology Research Interview (PERI) that comprise the short scales of demoralization developed by Dohrenwend and his colleagues (Dohrenwend et al., 1981) based on the Jerome Frank concept (Frank, 1973). As Dohrenwend, Shrout, Egri, & Mendelsohn, (1980) suggest, there are many screening scales that seem to be measuring the same thing and to which the demoralization concept may best apply, and demoralization would be expected to be highly related to depression. Moreover, Dohrenwend et al. report severe demoralization rates in general population surveys to run around 25%, a rate almost identical to the one found for both the ad hoc scale and Rational Scales of Depression in this study. Therefore, based on these similarities and on the assumption that these different scales are measuring the same thing, we have adopted the term demoralization to apply to the groups identified on the ad hoc and Rational Scales of Depression.

RESULTS

Disability

A strong relationship was found between ADL scores in 1971–72 and ratings of PTD in 1975–76 (Table 14.5), which suggests that there is a high prevalence of *chronic* disability among the elderly. The severe disabilities identified by elevated ADL scores in 1971–72 are chronic in the vast majority of cases. Seventy-six percent of the persons with ADL scores of three or more in 1971–72 were

TABLE 14.3

Comparisons of Ad Hoc Scale and Rational Scale of Depression Items and Categories with 8 PERI SUBSCALES of Demoralization

Category	Ad Hoc Scale	Rational Scale of Depression	8 PERI SUBSCALE of Demoralization
Dysphoric mood	feels lonely quite often not enough contact with confidant generally not happy satisfaction with life is poor	is not happy depressed mood depressed mood lasts depression worse at particu- lar times recent minor depressive feelings looks sad, mournful, or depressed sounds gloomy or mournful is more irritable lately	sadness
Loss of interest and enjoyment	life generally dull not enough time doing things liked	almost nothing is enjoyed wants to stay away from people	
Worry	worries very often	worries a lot about one or two things is a worrier or worries about almost everything worrying is bothersome cannot stop worrying	
Self-deprecation	feels not useful	unrealistic self-deprecation feels worthless blames self for harm to others self-blame over pecadillos gets angry with self	poor self-esteem

Pessimism and future orientation	usually expects things will not turn out well thinks life will be worse 1 year from now	pessimism about the future future seems bleak or unbearable	hopelessness—helplessness dread
Crying		has felt like crying has cried	
Suicidal		has felt life not worth living has wished to be dead but rejected suicide has fleeting suicidal thoughts has considered a method of suicide	suicidal thoughts
Somatic		has difficulty relaxing admits to being restless awakes more than 2 hours early and cannot get back to sleep has aches and pains without identifiable organic basis undue preoccupation with physical complaints and conditions retarded speech response	psychophysiological symptoms anxiety perceived physical health confused

TABLE 14.4
Criteria for Diagnosis and Severity of Depression

A. *Limited Depression*

1. Depression last only a few hours—can snap out of it
2. Occasional low days
3. Worried about specific problem—can turn mind to other things
4. Cries only when a particular event or situation is discussed
5. Future looks empty

B. *Pervasive Depression*

1. Depression last whole day or longer
2. Cries or feels like crying, often
3. Depression is bothersome and not easily shaken off
4. Future looks bleak or unbearable
5. Can't stop worrying—worry is disproportionate to cause
6. Looks depressed through much of interview

C. *Vegetative Symptoms < Not accounted for by physician*

1. Palpitations
2. Trembling
3. Dizziness
4. Poor appetite
5. Constipation
6. Loss of weight
7. Sleep disturbance
8. Poor concentration
9. Early morning wakening
10. Lies awake with anxious or depressing thoughts
11. Depression worst in mornings
12. Weak or tired
13. Slowed in speech or movement
14. Unexplained aches and pains
15. Subjective complaints of impaired memory

D. *Self-Deprecation*

1. Self-conscious in public
2. Feels a failure
3. Feels guilty

E. *Suicidal or Psychotic (Not accounted for by a nondepressive state)*

1. Actively suicidal (strong impulse, preparations, or attempt)
2. Deluded or hallcinated with a depressive content
3. Mute or immobile
4. Serious injury or ill effect following suicidal attempt
5. Starvation or intercurrent infection
6. Homicidal behavior

(*continued*)

TABLE 14.4 (*Continued*)

F. *Other Features*

1. Stress: a. Irrelevant ( )
       b. Necessary ( ) or Sufficient ( )
       c. Concurrent ( ) or Subsequent ( )
2. Current or Past Excitement: Yes ( ) No ( )
3. Present Episode: Yes ( ) No ( )
4. Past Episode: Yes ( ) No ( )
5. Positive Mood: Yes ( ) No ( )

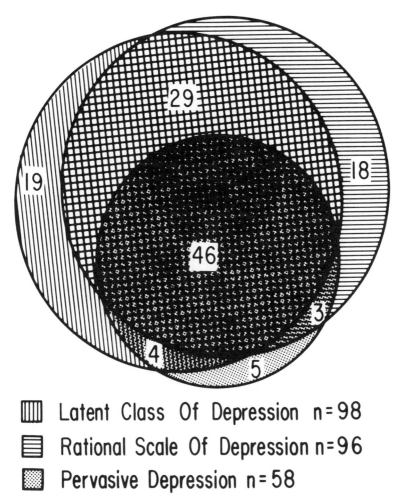

▥ **Latent Class Of Depression n = 98**

▤ **Rational Scale Of Depression n = 96**

▦ **Pervasive Depression n = 58**

FIG. 14.1 Overlap between cases diagnosed as pervasively depressed and those scoring above the cutting points on the Rational Scale of Depression and the Latent Class of Depression.

TABLE 14.5
Relationship Between Disability Levels in 1971–72 and 1975–76

| | 1971–72 Disability Level | | |
| | Not Disabled | Moderately Disabled | Severely Disabled |
1975–76	(ADL = 0)	(ADL = 1&2)	(ADL = 3+)
PTD	14.3%	36.8%	81.0%
NOT PTD	85.7%	63.2%	19.0%
N =	(70)	(19)	(21)

Note: ADL = Activities of Daily Living Scale
PTD = Personal Time Dependency Scale

judged to be PTD in 1975–76 compared with 14.3% of those with scores of zero. Moreover, half of those judged PTD in 1975–76 were in the high-ADL score group in 1971–72, demonstrating that ADL is a good predictor of PTD. General population health surveys have long established the fact that the elderly suffer increasingly from chronic diseases and disabilities compared with younger populations (Givens, 1979), and our findings are consistent with these cross-sectional surveys. However, the distinction between acute and chronic disabilities is not usually made. It is possible that individuals might have had acute disabilities at both data-gathering times in our follow-up study, but examination of the case summaries from the 1975–76 interviews indicated this had not happened with any of the 17 cases we have designated as having chronic disabilities.

Depression

High rates of chronic demoralization among the elderly in the follow-up subsample are also suggested by the strong relationship found between ad hoc scale scores in 1971–72 and the Rational Scale of Depression scores in 1975–76, as shown in Table 14.6. Fifty-eight percent of those with ad hoc scale scores of four or more at the first interview had Rational Scale of Depression scores of six or more at the second interview. The newly demoralized comprise only 15% of those who had 1971–72 ad hoc scores of three or less. Designating the 14 who scored high on both scales as chronic demoralization cases involves the assumption that they also would have scored high *between* the two interviews because, unlike the situation for disability, it is not possible to confirm the chronicity of demoralization from the case summary materials written in 1975–76. However, given that the usual prevalence rates of about 25% in general community populations (Dohrenwend et al., 1981) are replicated in both the 1971–72 and 1975–76 surveys as a whole and in the follow-up subsample of 110 individuals, the low probability of finding so many of the same individuals demoralized at any two points in time is indicated by the statistics contained in Table 14.6.

TABLE 14.6
Relationship Between Demoralization Levels
in 1971–72 and 1975–76

1975–76	1971–72 Demoralization Level	
	Not Demoralized (Ad Hoc Scale 0–3)	Demoralized (Ad Hoc Scale 4+)
Demoralized (Rational Scale 6+)	15.1%	58.3%
Demoralized (Rational Scale < 6)	84.9%	41.7%
Totals	100%	100%
N =	86	24

Relationship between Disability and Depression

Disability in 1971–72 was also found to be highly related to later demoralization as shown in Table 14.7. Because both disability level and prior demoralization were so strongly related to subsequent demoralization, we expected that when the three were considered together, persons who were both severely disabled and previously demoralized in 1971–72 would have the highest rate of demoralization in 1975–76, but this did not turn out to be true. As expected, the lowest rate of demoralization (11.8%) at second interview was found among those who were neither disabled nor demoralized at the first interview (Table 14.8). However, whereas a high rate of demoralization (50%) was found among those who had both prior disability and demoralization, almost as high a rate was found among those with prior disability but who were not previously demoralized (44.2%).

TABLE 14.7
Relationship Between Disability Level in 1971–72 and
Demoralization Level in 1975–76

1975–76	1971–72	
	Not Severely Disabled (ADL = 0–2)	Severely Disabled (ADL = 3+)
Demoralized (Rational Scale 6+)	19.1%	47.6%
Not Demoralized (Rational Scale 0–5)	81.9%	52.4%
Totals	100%	100%
N =	89	(21)

Note: ADL = Activities of Daily Living Scale

TABLE 14.8
Proportions Demoralized or Depressed in 1975–76 by
Demoralization and Disability Levels in 1971–72

1975–76	Not Demoralized (Ad Hoc Score 0–3)		Demoralized (Ad Hoc Score 4+)	
	Not Severely Disabled (ADL = 0–2)	Severely Disabled (ADL = 3+)	Not Severely Disabled (ADL = 0–2)	Severely Disabled (ADL = 3+)
Demoralized and pervasively depressed	9.2%	22.2%	15.4%	16.7%
Demoralized only	2.6%	22.2%	46.2%	33.3%
Pervasively depressed only	1.3%	—	15.4%	—
Not demoralized or pervasively depressed	86.8%	55.6%	23.1%	50.0%
	(76)	(9)	(13)	(12)

Note: ADL = Activities of Daily Living Scale

TABLE 14.9
Number of Demoralized in 1975–76 By 1971–72 Demoralization and
Disability

	Not Disabled in 1971–72		
	Not Demoralized	1976	Demoralized or Depressed
Demoralized 1971–72	3		10
Not Demoralized	66		10
		$X^2 = 25.9$	$P < .001$

	Disabled in 1971–72		
	Not Demoralized	1976	Demoralized or Depressed
Demoralized 1971–72	6		6
Not Demoralized	5		4
			N.S.

The highest rate (61.6%) was found among those previously demoralized but *not* previously disabled. (In addition there were three persons diagnosed as depressed in 1975–76 who were not identified by high Rational Scale of Depression scores. Two of them were also among the group previously demoralized but not disabled.) Stated another way: Among those not disabled in 1971–72, there was a significant relationship between prior and subsequent demoralization, but among those disabled in 1971–72, there was not a significant relationship between prior and subsequent demoralization. Subsequent demoralization was high among the disabled regardless of whether there was prior demoralization (Table 14.9).

DISCUSSION

A number of conclusions are suggested by these findings. First, demoralization appears to be a chronic problem for many aged. This follows from the fact that over half the individuals who were demoralized in 1971–72 and who were located in 1975–76 were also found to be demoralized at the time of the later interview. Moreover, of the subjects who were demoralized in 1975–76, over half had also been demoralized at the first interview. The findings indicate that the high prevalence of demoralization is largely due to chronicity of demoralization and that incidence (new cases) may be much lower. The data also suggest that demoralization is not being treated very well; and if demoralization, like some other conditions, responds best to early intervention, it may be difficult to treat cases that have existed for several years.

A second conclusion is that demoralization and disability are highly related among the aged as they are among younger age groups (Paykel, 1973). This is evident from the fact that although incidence of demoralization (new cases) is very low among the nondisabled and previously nondemoralized, it is high among the disabled who were not previously demoralized. From this it appears that we should be treating both disability and demoralization in common.

Although the time order between disability and demoralization is not always clear from our data, a third conclusion is that it is the acute, not the chronic, cases that are related to disability. Both former cases and new cases are related to disability, and, hence, the incidence of demoralization among the aged may be largely accounted for by disabilities. But the highest rate of chronic demoralization (61.6%) is found among the nondisabled. The high recovery rate among the disabled suggests that the disabled demoralized may be easier to treat and that the difficult cases for treatment may be the demoralized who are not disabled. Another conclusion is that chronicity of condition is a confounding factor in predicting depression.

Whereas nonspecific distress or demoralization has been found to be highly related to depression, it is not clear from our data what this relationship is, and many questions remain unanswered. Because depression is the most prevalent mental disorder among the aged and the relationship with demoralization is so strong, it is tempting to speculate that demoralization is equivalent to mild depression. However, as others have pointed out (Dohrenwend et al., 1980; Gurland, 1976), there is considerable difference between scales developed to measure mental disorder on community populations and diagnosis of mental patient populations. Sometimes little or no relationship is found between item scales and diagnosis of depression (Langner, 1962; Weissman, Myers, & Harding, 1978), and Wing, Mann, Leff, & Nixon, (1978) have found that their depression instrument is clearly not measuring the same thing with patient and community populations. Whether the strong relationship between the demoralization measures and diagnosis of depression found in this study is a result of the specific features of the items and the diagnostic procedures used or is an indication of a more generally strong relationship between depression and demoralization among the aged is not clear. However, it should be noted that, whereas these relationships were very strong, there were some diagnosed cases of depression not detected by any of the demoralization scales used. There were three cases in the follow-up who were not currently high on the demoralization scale but were diagnosed as depressed. None of these was disabled in 1971–72, but two were demoralized at the first interview. Only more closely monitored longitudinal studies with repeated observations can tell us whether depression is typically preceded by demoralization among the aged or whether there are important differences between depressions that are preceded or accompanied by demoralization and those that are not.

REFERENCES

Breslau, L., & Haug, M. (Eds.). (1983). *Depression and aging: Causes, care and consequences.* New York: Springer.

Busse, E., & Pfeiffer, E. (Eds.). (1973). *Mental illness in later life.* Washington, DC: American Psychiatric Association.

Dohrenwend, B. P., Oskenberg, L., Shrout, P. E., Dohrenwend, B. S., & Cook, D. (1981). What psychiatric screening scales measure. In S. Sudman (Ed.), *Health survey research methods* (NCHSR Research Proceedings Series). Washington, DC: DHHS Publication No. (PHS) 81–3268: 188–198.

Dohrenwend, B. P., Shrout, P. E., Egri, G., & Mendelsohn, F. S. (1980). Nonspecific psychological distress and other dimensions of psychopathology. *Archives of General Psychology, 37,* 1229–1236.

Dovenmuehle, R. H., & Vervoerdt, A. (1962). Physical illness and depressive symptomatology. *Journal of American Geriatrics Society, 10,* 932–947.

Frank, J. D. (1973). *Persuasion and healing.* New York, Johns Hopkins University Press. (Orininally published 1961).

Givens, J. (1979). *National Center for Health Statistics: Current Estimates from the Health Interview Survey, United States, 1978.* Vital and Health Statistics (Series 13, No. 130). DHEW Pub. No. (PHS), 80–1551, Washington, U.S. Government Printing Office.

Gurland, B. (1976). The comparative frequency of depression in various adult age groups. *Journal of Gerontology, 31,* 283–292.

Gurland, B., Copeland, J., Kelleher, M., Kuriansky, J., Sharpe, L., & Dean, L. (1984). *The mind and mood of aging: The mental health problems of the community elderly in New York and London*. New York: Haworth Press.

Gurland, B., Dean, L., Gurland, R., & Cook, D. (1978). Personal time dependency in the elderly of New York City: Findings from the US–UK cross-national geriatric community study. In *Dependency in the elderly of New York City (p. 9–45)*. New York: Community Council of Greater New York.

Gurland, B., Dean, L., Cross, P., & Golden, R. (1980). The epidemiology of depression and dementia in the elderly: The use of multiple indicators of these conditions. In J. Cole & J. Barrett (Eds.), *Psychopathology in the aged*. New York: Raven Press.

Jarvik, L. F. (1976). Aging and depression: Some unanswered questions. *Journal of Gerontology, 31*, 324–326.

Katz, S. F., Ford, A. B., Moskovitz, R. W., Jackson, B. A., & Jaffee, M. W. (1963). Studies of illness in the aged—the index of ADL: A standardized measure of biological and psychological functions. *Journal of American Medical Association, 185*, 914–919.

Langner, T. (1962). A twenty-two item screening score of psychiatric symptoms indicating impairment. *Journal of Health and Human Behavior, 3*, 269–276.

Paykel, E. S. (1973). Life events and acute depression. In *Separation and Depression* (Pub. No. 94). Washington, DC: American Association for Advancement of Science.

Shanas, E., Townsend, P., Widderburn, D., Friis, H., Milhoj, D., & Stehouwer, J. (1968). *Old people in three industrial societies*. New York: Atherton Press.

Silverman, C. (1968). *The epidemiology of depression*. Baltimore: John Hopkins Press.

Weissman, M., Myers, J., & Harding, P. (1978) Psychiatric disorders in a U.S. urban community: 1975–76. *American Journal of Psychiatry, 135*, 459–462.

Wing, J., Mann, S. A., Leff, J. P., & Nixon, J. N., (1978). The concept of a "case" in psychiatric population surveys. *Psychological Medicine, 8*, 203–217.

15 Gender, Generations, and Well-Being: The Midtown Manhattan Longitudinal Study

Leo Srole
Anita Kassen Fischer

Among the enduring thematic strands that weave through the long fabric of Western thought has been the certitude that contemporary man is in a condition fallen from an earlier height of simplicity, virtue, and well-being. This retrospective vision harks back to the innocence of scriptural Eden, to serenity in the Golden Age of Hellenic mythology, then to chivalric security in the medieval literature, to quintessential harmony in the Rousseauan "state of nature," and to the earthy wholesomeness of our more recent agrarian past.

One key tenet in this philosophy of history is the pervasive conviction, often accepted as prima facie axiom, that in the population at large mental health has long been on a downhill course and at an accelerating tempo during the modern era. This trend in the psychiatric literature can be referred to as the "Mental Paradise Lost" doctrine. What is required for a credible challenge of this nostalgic doctrine is a series of surveys focusing on the entire spectrum of psychopathology in the general population, replicated over a broad period of time.

The Midtown Manhattan Mental Health Study, launched in 1952 and first fielded in 1954, has taken one step in this direction, having evolved from a cross-sectional epidemiological investigation of a general population into a two-stage longitudinal follow-up study. For labeling convenience, the cross-sectional survey of 1954 is referred to as Midtown I, and the follow-up field research of 1974 as Midtown II.

Methods

Midtown is our code name for an ecologically well-delineated, high-density "Gold Coast and Slum" residential area that in 1954 sheltered some 175,000 inhabitants, 99% of them white. The base-line investigation focused on a

223

rigorous probability sample of 1660 adults between the ages of 20 and 59 that was highly representative of its parent population.

In conceptualizing and designing the Midtown I Study, the investigators did not anticipate the possibility of reexamining the intended subjects at some distant date. Some years later, however, it was determined to be feasible that the original Midtown data set, though not specifically framed for this purpose, could be converted into the base line of a restudy of a large subsample of the original sample.

The hazard overhanging all longitudinal investigations is the certainty of sizeable attrition, e.g., subjects lost to follow-up, with the magnitude of losses tending to be a function of (1) the extent of individual tracking information secured at base line, (2) the number of years intervening, and (3) the degree of residential turnover in the sample's community base. In all three respects, the attritional risks for the Midtown I sample were expectably maximal. In fact, the follow-up search ended with 858 base-line respondents located alive, plus 266 certificated as dead, and a residual 536 (32.6% of the base-line sample) categorized as terminally unlocateable. By actuarial estimate, approximately 100 of the latter were deceased. It was also estimated of the original sample that another 110 were never-married women, then age 20–39, who subsequently married and abandoned their former identifying surname as well as residence, for search purposes becoming anonymous. The terminally unlocateable living figure to an average annual loss of 1.6%, comparing favorably with the rate of many longitudinal studies focused on career-launched adults.

The 858 located survivors, then, comprised the Midtown I subsample accessible for reinterview after a lapse of two decades. In principle, results could be generalized from them as their own 20-year controls. Larger generalizations would also be tenable if the 858 survivors of known address constituted a representative subsample of the total 1294 Midtown I survivors, located and unlocated. Results of comparing the 858 with this total of survivors, in terms of their known characteristics in 1954, indicate that, with few exceptions, the accessible subsample did not deviate significantly from its stated parent universe at that time. Because the subsample could be considered probably representative of its age 40–79 parent universe as well, it was possible to defend the planned Midtown II phase of the study as feasible.

In this light, each of the 858 located survivors was approached individually by experienced health survey field workers, who reinterviewed a total of 695 respondents (the Midtown II panel) scattered through New York City (62%), its surrounding metropolitan region (22%), 28 states beyond (14%), and with 14 respondents located outside the continental United States (2%). On the basis of the 163 nonparticipants' known base-line characteristics, statistical analysis suggests that, had they all been reinterviewed, the study findings would not have deviated markedly from those yielded by the 695 panelists.

The 1954 interview systematically reviewed the presence or absence of 120 manifestations of mental disturbance. These were principally drawn from such established symptom questionnaires as the Minnesota Multiphasic Personality Inventory, The Cornell Medical Index (CMI), and the World War II military screening Neuropsychiatric Adjunct (NSA). The symptom questions in these instruments have been established as both reliable and valid by virtue of their ability to discriminate between diagnostically heterogenous psychiatric patient (criterion) and nonpatient (comparison) groups.

Thomas Rennie, the Midtown I senior psychiatrist, chose 83 of those items for their clinical relevance and their time reference to the recent past, and the remainder, referring to the preadult period, only for lending temporal perspective to the currently visible manifestations of mental health status.

Symptom inventories available at the time reflected major currents in emotional life, rather than criteria of conventional, narrowly circumscribed psychiatric diagnoses. Among the scorable symptom dimensions represented in the interview were the following: generalized psychophysiological "body language" reflecting varying intensities of tension; a series of organ-specific, often psychogenic, dysfunctions; expressions of diffuse or circumscribed anxieties and phobias; depressive states and their reactive corollaries; tendencies to withdraw from others; paranoid ideations; excess intake of liquor and food; signs of maladaptive rigidity and sociopathic orientations; plus the interviewer's observations of the respondent along a series of behavioral dimensions.

Two psychiatrists reviewed and assessed this corpus of symptom information from each subject in terms of overall severity of symptom formation and degree of explicit or implied impairment in social-role functioning. Each psychiatrist independently classified each respondent on a six-fold continuum of general mental health. The continuum was comprised of two major categories, the Unimpaired and the Impaired, each with three classes, respectively. The former category included (1) the nonsymptomatic "Well," (2) the "Mild," and (3) the "Moderate" classes of symptom development. The role-impaired category included these symptomatic grades: (1) the "Marked," (2) the "Severe," and (3) the "Incapacitated," who, except for care-giving kin, would have required hospitalization. This six-grade ordinal schema spanned the entire spectrum of general mental health differences in a noninstitutional population, a comprehensive coverage attempted by no other study of community epidemiology at the time, or, for that matter, since.

Because no firm consensual line had emerged in psychiatry to reliably demarcate the indistinct and historically elastic boundary line of "mental illness," or so-called "caseness," once the classification of subjects had been completed, Rennie accepted the category of the "Impaired" as the Study's operational criterion of functionally significant psychopathology, i.e., morbidity. The investigators were secondarily interested in the class of asymptomatic "Wells," its prevalence relative to that of the Impaired, and the etiological and community health implications of contrasting numerical balances between these two classes in any population or subgroup. The behavioral consequences of such a contrast are apparent by comparing the affective tinderbox found in the slum and the solid middle-class neighborhood as "two worlds" with vastly different mental health "climates."

This stepwise schema of mental health classification had direct antecedents in the thought and clinical practice of Adolph Meyer, as well as in a more recent group of World War II military psychiatrists (Wittson & Hunt, 1955), and coincided in time with the cognate development of a "health-sickness" scale by Karl Menninger and his associates for use with their Topeka Clinic patients (Luborsky, 1962).

Such a unidimensional continuum is a direct parallel of general medicine's own long-standing practice of differentiating progressive grades of "clinical severity" in patients of diverse symptomatologies (Sartwell, 1953). The latter mode of classification has been useful in following patient changes under treatment and is indispensable as a yardstick for the longitudinal investigator's observation of his subjects' shifts in health status, whatever their original diagnostic rubric. (For example, the diagnosis of a subject could be "neurotic" both at time X and time Y, yet he could fall into the "moderate" category of severity at time X and the "incapacitated" category at Y.)

To the criticism of some psychiatrists that the gradient schema of classifying mental disturbances is "primitive," in the sense that it is nosologically non-specific, the following points can be made:

1. Diagnostic specificity and symptom severity are of course indigenous to the clinical information-eliciting context of treating patients. Nevertheless, as Kiev (1978) has noted: "diagnostic specificity may, in fact, not conform to the clusterings of symptoms as they actually appear in large populations." pp. 579

2. In interviewing randomly drawn men and women in their own homes, extreme care had to be taken to stage and arrange the interview with major emphasis on medical and other nonpsychiatric facets of the life history, a requirement essential to minimize the defense-evoking effects of an unexpected intrusion into highly defended sectors of the respondent's psyche (Srole, Langner, Michael, Kirkpatrick, Opler, & Rennie, 1978). Procuring the mass of valid symptom information necessary for differential diagnostic decision making is not possible under such circumstances. The heavy concentration of the structured clinical-type interview on details of psychopathology alerts the sample subject to the fact that, as one, with obvious resentment, declared, "I was cross-examined like a candidate for the booby hatch!" The accuracy of information volunteered under such interviewing circumstances can be seriously questioned. Implied, therefore, is the epidemiological research principle that health examinations and

classifications in a general, nonpatient population must be realistically scaled to what is humanly and temporally possible within the constraints of the more or less neutrally motivated, randomly plucked subject, who in his own home is in effect the host to the interviewer as his guest.

Toward measuring the panelists' mental health changes between 1954 and 1974, multiple regression methods harnessed the computer to reproduce the original psychiatrists' six grade judgmental ratings of the panel's 1954 general mental health, with an accuracy suggested by a Pearson correlation of .83. This compares favorably with a correlation of .75 between the 1660 independent classifications of the two study psychiatrists with one another in 1954. The .83 coefficient suggests that the computer-generated ratings of 1954 were an acceptable surrogate for the psychiatrists' judgmental classifications of that year (Srole, 1975).

Because the identically worded battery of current symptom questions were used in 1974, identical regression methods could be used to produce follow-up mental health ratings that are standardized to the reference model of the computerized 1954 general mental health classification. Such standardization has insured that the degree of concordant reliability between the computerized 1954 and 1974 classifications, hereafter referred to as GMH I and GMH II, respectively, is 100%.

Reliability, however, offers no a priori assurance that GMH II in 1974 is as valid a measure of general mental health as was GMH I in 1954. The issue of a possible shift in validity between GMH I and GMH II had to be confronted. The Midtown panel members had aged by 20 years, and the sampled symptoms might have been less appropriate for older than for younger people. Moreover, in the intervening two decades, semantic and other forms of sociocultural "drift" could have altered the meanings of symptoms through which mental disturbance is projected and verbalized. The latter have been designated as a "time of measurement effect" that can intrude into measures of individual change over time, and the former as an "aging effect."

To test these undismissable possibilities, a series of parallel checks of GMH I and GMH II were carried out, including the discrete correlations of each with a number of classic demographic antecedents like age order, gender, socioeconomic status of family of upbringing, and religious origin. If these time-separated pairs of correlations with the same set of *fixed* background variables proved to be approximately alike, then the inference would be tenable that GMH I and GMH II measured mental health status in essentially the same way. To a striking degree, these and other kinds of checks have supported the plausibility of that inference. Such evidence suggests that GMH II is as valid in 1974 as GMH I had been in 1954, in the special sense of validity as measuring the same construct, free of significant time-of-measurement and aging effects, at two distant points of time (Srole, 1975). This established that in both validity and reliability the two measures were comparable to a satisfactory degree, and therefore adequately standardized yardsticks for discerning change.

Overall Findings

Table 15.1 presents the panel's full distributions in 1954 and 1974 on the Study's six grade continuum of general mental health.

Although by 1974 there are improvements in both a lower Impaired frequency and a higher Well rate, neither of these differences is statistically significant.

It must also be emphasized that the seeming near identity of these two distributions, around the modal class of Mild symptom formation, does not imply predominant individual fixity in mental health status between the two occasions of measurement. On the contrary, only 40% of the entire panel fell into the same GMH grade in 1974 as in 1954, with another 28% of its members slipping one or more classes on that continuum, and 32% improving by moving one or more steps upward.

Thus, the panel's 20-year distribution shifts can be conveyed graphically by the image of a six-step staircase flanked on each side by an escalator. Occupying the same step on the staircase in 1974 as in 1954 are a two-fifths plurality of the panel, whereas on the escalators one third of their fellow members have ascended and slightly more than one fourth have descended. Around the large core of fixity, then, there has been a considerable circulation of mental health changers. (For the same reasons, in the tables to follow, GMH figures for 1974 should be understood to be the net distribution resulting from the panel's post-1954 two-way shifts.)

The findings are hereafter presented in terms of differential frequencies of Impaired GMH, but we emphasize that trends in Well frequencies are usually the

TABLE 15.1
General Mental Health (GMH) Distributions[a] in 1954
and 1974

Symptom Formation Grades	1954, %	1974, %
Well	21.9	25.0
Mild	42.6	42.0
Moderate	21.3	21.1
Marked[†]	9.3	7.5
Severe	4.3	3.5
Incapacitated	0.6	0.9

[a]$N = 695$.

†Impaired subjects (Marked, Severe, and Incapacitated) made up 14.2% of the panel population in 1954 and 11.9% in 1974.

TABLE 15.2
General Mental Health Impaired Rates in Decade-of-Birth Cohorts

	A ± 1900 (N = 134)	B ± 1910 (N = 199)	C ± 1920 (N = 195)	D ± 1930 (N = 167)
1954				
Age, yr	50–59	40–49	30–39	20–29
Rate	22%	16%	14%	7%
1974				
Age, yr	70–79	60–69	50–59	40–49
Rate	18%	12%	10%	8%
Difference	−4%[†]	−4%[†]	−4%[†]	+1%[†]

Note: N = 695.
[†]Not statistically significant using the *t* test of differences between correlated means.

direct mirror image of the Impaired trend; that is, bypassing the numerically more or less unvarying intermediate Mild and Moderate classes of symptom formation, the Impaired rates tend to be high where the Well frequencies are low, and vice versa. Thus, although we must largely confine our discussion to group Impaired frequencies, their apparent epidemiological importance is considerably enhanced when they are viewed in tandem with the reversed trend of the Wells.

In Table 15.2, the panel's four age groups are labeled A, B, C, and D and appear with decade of birth listed, next with the number of panel members in each group, followed by its 1954 (GMH I) and 1974 (GMH II) Impairment rates. By reading the frequencies horizontally from right to left in each row, the figures demonstrate that in both 1954 and 1974 there is an incremental progression in the rates across the successively older groups to the left of D (the youngest), thereby confirming the direction of the age-trend finding reported for the original sample in the Study's first-stage *Mental Health in the Metropolis* monograph (Srole et al., 1978).

The consistent interage trends in both 1954 and 1974 could have been extrapolated to a prediction that at follow-up the general mental health in every age group would have slipped further into more unfavorable Impaired frequencies. To test that prediction, the *vertical* pair of Impaired rates are presented in each Table 15.2 column, where each age group can be compared with *itself* after a span of 20 years.

In none of the four groups is the difference between its GMH I and GMH II percentages statistically significant. With this failed prediction how are we to reconcile the apparent contradiction between the longitudinal (intragroup) null differences in Impaired rates after the passage of two decades, and the cross-sectional (intergroup) age trend, both in 1954 and 1974, toward elevation of those rates at progressively older strata?

To resolve this seeming paradox, attention must be drawn to Table 15.3, focusing on two pairs of cohorts, where age differences have been analytically controlled. The first pair juxtaposes cohort A's Impaired rate in 1954 (MH I) at age 50–59, with cohort C's rate in 1974 (GMH II), also at age 50–59, with highly contrasting frequencies of 22 and 10%, respectively. Thus, paired cohorts A and C are of identical age-since-birth, but were born 20 years apart, i.e., ± 1900 and ± 1920, an interval large enough to consider them as discrete, successive historical generations. In life-cycle terms, when the latter were arriving as neonates, the former were passing into adulthood.

The second pair in Table 15.3 includes cohort B in 1954 at age 40–49 and cohort D in 1974, also at age 40–49, the two presenting generation-specific mental impairment rates of 16 and 8%, respectively, a difference statistically significant at the .05 level of confidence. We must infer that the horizontal intergroup rate differences in Table 15.2 reflect not the assumed consequences of 20 years of aging but, rather, at least among Midtown mid-life adults in matched age-since-birth pairs, of being born into successive *generation-separated cohorts*.

According to the "Paradise Lost" school of psychiatric historiography, the later arrived of two generations should predictably harbor more psychopathology than its predecessor. Table 15.3, however, suggests that in the Midtown panel the opposite has been the case, with the later cohort in both like-age pairs registering an Impaired rate that is *lower* by one half that of the earlier generation. By the standardized yardstick applied to these age-matched cohorts, general mental health seems to have improved rather than declined.

Men versus Women

This finding demands further elaboration in terms of other constituent groups in the Midtown population, the most salient being the two sexes. It should be noted

TABLE 15.3
General Mental Health (GMH) Rates
of Impairment by Generation-
Separated Pairs of Like-Age Cohorts

Cohort A,* GMH I rate	22%
Cohort C,† GMH II rate	10%
Difference	−12%
Significance	$P < .01$
Cohort B,‡ GMH I rate	16%
Cohort D,§ GMH II rate	8%
Difference	−8%
Significance	$P < .05$√

Note: √ Using two sample t tests.

TABLE 15.4

General Mental Health (GMH) Rates of Impairment by Generation-Separated
Pairs of Like-Age Cohorts and Gender Subgroups

	Men	N =	Women	N =
Cohort A,* GMH I rate	15%	(48)	26%	(86)
Cohort C,† GMH II rate	9%	(90)	11%	(105)
Difference	−6%		−15%	
Significance	Not significant		P < .01	
Cohort B,‡ GMH I rate	9%	(79)	21%	(120)
Cohort D,§ GMH II rate	9%	(77)	8%	(90)
Difference	0%		−13%	
Significance	Not significant		P < .02	

*N = 134; age 50 to 59 years in 1954.
†N = 195; age 50 to 59 years in 1974.
‡N = 199; age 40 to 49 years in 1954.
§N = 167; age 40 to 49 years in 1974.

that in none of the four age groups had either of the genders changed significantly in its GMH Impaired rate after the 20-year passage between 1954 and 1974. However, when both sexes are represented in contiguous cohort generations, as in Table 15.4, a different picture emerges.

To judge from the sexist tenor in much of its writings, the "Mental Paradise Lost" school would probably have predicted the preceding table to show a more pronounced intergeneration decline in GMH among the women. If so, the data flatly contradict that expectation.

Examining cohort A at age 50–59 in *1954*, the Impaired frequency is 15% for men, with the appreciably higher rate of 26% for women. In the next horizontal row, however, cohort C, at like-age (50–59) in *1974*, manifest Impairment rates for its two gender groups that are both lower than cohort A's levels, but with a significant decrease only among the women, toward virtual parity with like-age men.

Horizontal comparison of the sexes in cohorts B and D, both at age 40–49, reveals parallel differential intergeneration changes in impairment, from male–female disparity (9 and 21%) in earlier cohort B, to intergender identity (9 and 8%) in the like-age but later cohort D. It seems therefore, that, individual 20-year mental health shifts balance out at net in more or less the same way for the panel's sexes. However, by the scale of generation units, time has dealt rather better with women's mental health than with that of men of the same life-cycle age.

The strength of these unexpected findings would be substantially enhanced if we could marshall evidence of similar diversities on dimensions related to the panel's general mental health, in effect a demonstration of concurrent validity.

For this purpose, a second index of well-being is available, namely a query to the respondent asking whether his/her "general physical health now is excellent, good, fair, or poor?"

The panel's combined self-judged "fair-poor," i.e., ("less than good") responses, rose from 16% in 1954 to 23% in 1974, an increase of almost half again over the Midtown I frequency, with the increase almost entirely concentrated in the panel's oldest group that was at age 70–79 in the latter year.

Turning to Table 15.5, it is clear that cohort A's women have an unfavorable ("less than good") GPH I frequency, which is almost three times higher than the age-matched men. However, by later cohort C, the male "less than good" rate (GPH II) remains virtually identical with that of cohort A men, whereas the cohort C females' frequency in 1974 has dropped to almost half that of the 1954 cohort A women and near parity with age-peer males. Essentially parallel sex-linked patterns obtain in cohorts B and D.

Restated, in the succession of age-matched generation-separated cohorts, self-evaluated general physical health has not changed significantly among panel men. However, among counterpart age-matched women, the "fair–poor" GPH rates have fallen from levels higher than those of their male peers in cohorts A and B to nearly identical levels with the men in cohorts C and D.

Thus, there are strikingly consistent trends in reported intergeneration differences across each of the following sets of variables:

1. Across the two genders.
2. Across two different (but intertwined) indicators of well-being.
3. Across two different, generation-separated mid-life age segments, namely 40–49 and 50–59.

To recapitulate, significant and consistent differential improvements have been discerned, among women only, on both indicators of well-being, as be-

TABLE 15.5
"Fair-Poor" Frequencies of General Physical
Health (GPH) by Generation-Separated Pairs of
Like-Age Cohorts and Gender Subgroups

	Men	Women
Cohort A,* GPH I rate	13%	34%
Cohort C,† GPH II rate	14%	18%
Difference	+1%	−16%
Significance	N.S.	$P < .02$
Cohort B,‡ GPH I rate	16%	24%
Cohort D,§ GPH II rate	11%	9%
Difference	−5%	−15%
Significance	N.S.	$P < .01$

tween the cohorts born in the first two decades of this century and those born in the two decades following.

Discussion: Summary

The Midtown Study has confronted the "Mental Paradise Lost" protagonists with their arch-villain, New York City, and on that most strategic testing ground favorable to their own position, has put the following two of the school's three major articles of faith (Srole et al., 1978, pp. 433–459) under systematic empirical scrutiny:

1. They have held that the trend of mental health in the general population has been on the downgrade over time. Our data have responded in two parts.
    a. After exposure to 20 years of living, mainly in or around the city, the Midtown panelists show no significant net change in mental health composition among any of their four decade-of-birth groups.
    b. On the other hand, by the temporal measure of two generation units, mental health in the later generation, with age controlled, is *not* worse than it had been in the earlier generation, but significantly better.
2. In many cases, women have been viewed as the constitutionally and psychologically fragile gender, their mental health over time being seen as more vulnerable to erosion. Again our data have countered with two generalizations.
    a. After 20 years of living, the Midtown panel of women of all age groups have changed no more in mental health makeup than did their male peers.
    b. On the time scale of generation units, the Midtown panel's intergeneration improvement in mental health is found to be exclusively concentrated in its female respondents. We hypothesize, however, that Midtown's differential intergender progression in well-being between successive generations may be principally concentrated in the big cities.

It is the final responsibility of this report to offer a theory that might articulate the interconnections among (1) the Midtown collectivity units called generations, (2) the overarching macrosocial shifts that occurred in the separate periods of history they passed through, and (3) the sex-specific patterns of changes in well-being delineated previously.

In a classic essay published prior to World War II (Mannheim, 1936), social scientist Karl Mannheim elaborated the concept of generations as of fundamental, cross-cutting importance to sociology, psychology, and history. In a later work (Mannheim, 1940) he asked: "Why did the Middle Ages and the Renaissance produce entirely different types of men?" He urged behavioral scientists to "study the changes of the human mind in an historical setting, in close connection with the changes in the social structure."

In a century of steadily accelerating social and economic changes, interspersed with major macrosocial convulsions speeding up that tempo, successive generation groups have matured in, and navigated through, different temporally definable segments in that 80-year stream of history. The developmental effects, gross and fine, of immersion in different sections of that "engulfing stream" at different stages of the life cycle, are the sources of the proverbial "communication gap" that marks off one generation, with its own uniquely timed sequence of common experiences, from the next. Mannheim refers to the "phenomena of the 'stratification of experience'" in a generation group, arising from exposure to the chronological ordering of imprinting macrosocial configurations. He (Mannheim, 1936) emphasizes the critical distinction between the experiences of preadulthood that:

> happen to make those all important 'first impressions' . . . and those which follow, to form the second, third and other 'strata.' . . Early impressions tend to coalesce into a *natural view* of the world. All later experiences then tend to receive their meaning from this original set. . . The continuous shift in objective conditions has its counterpart in a continuous shift in the oncoming new generations which are first to incorporate the changes in their behavioral systems.[1]

In this light, how are we to explain the differential intergender shifts in well-being between the Midtown A–B generation, born in the two decades before 1915, and the C–D generation appearing during the two decades following? Involved, we hold with Mannheim, is the paramount importance of the sub-culture milieu prevailing during the formative stage of a generation's development.

To face this question adequately, the pages of history must be turned back at least to the last decades of the nineteenth century, which was the temporal locus of the *parents* of Midtown's cohorts A and B. The distinguished historian J. H. Plumb (1973) summarizes the predicament of women in the culminating period of the Victorian era as follows: "Except in the highest ranks of the aristocracy, women . . . were as securely locked in the prison of their households as any convict . . . condemned to a daily treadmill of toil. . . Husbands could be and were tyrants" (pp. 141–143).

"Kinder, Küche, Kirche" fixed the specific confines of a woman's life, with children one-after-the-other pressing the limits of her gestation cycles and emotional reserves. Women were cast as cult symbols of sexless purity upon a public pedestal but privately were locked into a chastity belt, so to speak, of tight sexual repression, and even outright frigidity; all of this, while they were also forced to

---

[1]This striking insight anticipated contemporary cognitive theory in stressing that the individual's current perceptions of reality are filtered through his/her cognitive screen shaped by earlier experiences.

give lip service to the unwritten double standard tacitly enabling men to give their sexuality free rein in or out of the marital bed.

A more pathogenic, culturally patterned design for intergender relationships can hardly be imagined, a point reinforced by Professor Plumb's (1973) reference to the period's:

> agonizing preoccupation with sin, combined with a Jehova-like inflation of the figure of the father. . . Fearful repression of sex was followed, as might be expected, by life-destroying neuroses. . . The whole Victorian scene is littered with broken minds, broken lives and broken careers (pp. 233).

It was this Victorian generation, concludes Plumb, that carried "enormous burdens of anxiety that within this last [20th] century . . . have been lifted off the shoulders of men and women, particularly in the highly industrialized West, to a degree that they can scarcely appreciate" (pp. 199). It is plausible to infer, with Plumb, that during this Victorian period mental disturbance in the general population had been at higher levels of frequency and more severe levels of intensity, above all among its submerged women, than were to ever prevail thereafter.

Members of the last Victorian generation were contemporaries and counterparts of the parents who brought up the Midtown panel's own cohorts A and B, offspring appearing, as already described, with disparities in two indicators of well-being that were manifestly unfavorable to their women.

Plumb goes on to report how the social and psychological currents began to shift on behalf of women in the Edwardian decade (1901–1910), to be accelerated by "that great liberator, World War I." Milestones of female progress were marked by their first entrance into male-monopolized sectors of the labor force (Hesse, 1979) and, by 1920 and the 19th Amendment, into voting booths, representing long-delayed, lowering of previous barriers to feminine economic and political equality.

In a widely acclaimed monograph, a social historian (Fass, 1977) documents that during the decade of the twenties: "American culture was remade . . . by a social transformation of major proportions. It was the change in female behavior that underlined the overall changes that had taken place" (pp. 6).

With this shift, notes Fass, there followed "a democratization of family relations between husband and wife, parents and children, and more latitude for emotional expression for each member of the family" (pp. 54).

A related consequence was "an expanded view of children's welfare," including "a trend toward more equal involvement with, and affection for, each child, regardless of sex." In view of the fact that the Victorian family had previously regarded the preadult son as "a man still growing," and the daughter in effect, as Archie Bunker recapitulates it, "ever my little girl," this new parental "promotion" of the latter toward equality with her brothers probably represented an enormous gain, especially in her own eyes, of socially valued status and personal self-esteem (Friedan, 1981).

This, then, was the context of the generation that emerged during and after World War I, which was first socialized in the "derigidified" family and age-peer milieus of the 1920s, and appeared decades later in the Midtown panel as cohorts C and D.

All the preceding post-World War I milieu developments can be considered sociologically isomorphic with the observed cohort C and D women's quantum jumps in well-being, representing advances over that of their A and B "preliberated" predecessors at like age, and probably even more over that of their late Victorian grandmothers who had suffered the fate of a culturally contrived "Iron Maiden" confinement.

It is a credible hypothesis that isomorphisms on such a three-generation time scale are not mere chance coincidences in the play of history but reflect a cause-and-effect connection between the partial emancipation of women from their 19th-century status of sexist servitude, and their twentieth-century advances in subjective well-being. These inferences would suggest that improvements in a group's social position and role in a society's objective system of status allocations are conducive to improvements in that group's subjective well-being and other dimensions of health.

This chapter foreshadows the establishment of an epidemiological nucleus for the crystallization of the specialty multidisciplinary field of sociopsychiatric history. On its agenda would be a host of research questions, including the following: Will the recently emerged adult generations of the 1980s change in well-being, relative to the base lines of their parents, in a linear or cyclical, pendulum fashion? When is a predominantly affluent society based on eugenic freedom at risk of slipping into a pathogenic, self-destructive system of narcissistic license, an outcome not without historical precedents? What might be the mechanisms inherent in a specific historical macrosocial universe, for variously potentiating the genetic pool of the preadult generation engulfed in it?

Riding on the answers to such questions are prognoses as to the well-being of democracy itself in the new century to be rung in just a few years down the calendar.

REFERENCES

Fass, P. S. (1977). *The damned and the beautiful: American youth in the 1920's*. Oxford, England: Oxford University Press.

Friedan, B. (1981). *The second stage*. New York: Summit Books.

Hesse, S. J. (1979). Women working: Historical trends. In K. W. Feinstein (Ed.), *Working women and families*. Beverly Hills, CA: Sage.

Kiev, A. (1978). The role of expectancy in behavioral change. In J. P. Brady & H. K. Brodie (Eds.), *Controversy in psychiatry*. Philadelphia: Saunders.

Luborsky, L. (1962). Clinicians' judgments of mental health: A proposed scale. *Archives of General Psychiatry, 7,* 407–417.

Mannheim, K. (1936). *Ideology and Utopia: An introduction to the sociology of knowledge.* L. Wirth & E. A. Shils (Trans.). New York: Harcourt Brace Jovanovich.

Mannheim, K. (1940). *Man and society in an age of reconstruction.* New York: Harcourt Brace Jovanovich.

Plumb, J. H. (1973). *In the light of history.* Boston: Houghton-Mifflin.

Sartwell, P. E. (1953). Problems of identification of cases of chronic disease. *Milbank Memorial Fund Quarterly, 31,* 17.

Srole, L. (1975). Measurement and classification in sociopsychiatric epidemiology: The Midtown Manhattan Study (1954) and Midtown Manhattan Restudy (1974). *Journal of Health and Social Behavior, 16,* 347–364.

Srole, L., Langner, T. S., Michael, S. T., Kirkpatrick, P., Opler, M. K., & Rennie, T. A. C. (1978). In L. Srole & A. Fischer (Eds.), *Mental Health in the Metropolis* (revised and enlarged ed.). New York: New York University Press.

Wittson, C. L., & Hunt, W. A. (1955). A rationale for psychiatric selection. *American Psychologist, 10,* 199–204.

16 Discussion of Chapters by Clausen, Wilder, and Srole

Lee N. Robins

These three chapters each provide findings that are surprising in the light of conventional views of psychiatry. The chapter by John Clausen suggests that schizophrenics fare about as well after hospital treatment as do patients with affective disorder, although it is generally thought that schizophrenics remain chronically ill, whereas patients with manic–depressive disease remit. He also found that schizophrenic women fared worse than schizophrenic men. Indeed, nine of the schizophrenic men on whom he reported showed no symptoms or only mild ones in the 5 years prior to follow-up. Schizophrenic men without severe symptoms had reasonably stable although not outstanding occupational careers—more stable indeed than those of the "normal" husbands of schizophrenic women. These findings do not support the usual view that, whereas the severity of symptoms in schizophrenia may fluctuate over time, recovery is virtually impossible. Further he found no association with outcome for either length of time in the hospital or spouse's supportiveness, results that run counter to the view that avoidance of "hospitalism" and presence of social supports are conducive to good outcomes.

Dr. Wilder's results are perhaps less surprising, but he has one finding that might not have been anticipated: that episodes of demoralization (depression) tend to last for at least 5 years in the elderly.

Dr. Srole's chapter presents the surprising finding that aging is not associated with increasing psychiatric symptoms in a general population sample, even though on a cross-sectional basis he finds more symptoms in older subjects. This finding is reminiscent of Schaie's discovery (1970) that the relationship between age and low IQ found on a cross-sectional basis tends to disappear in longitudinal studies following the same persons over time. Schaie argues that cross-sectional

239

studies confound effects of historical increases in educational levels with the effects of aging. Srole argues similarly that cross-sectional studies confound effects of historical changes in women's status with the effects of aging.

The job of the discussant must be two-fold: first, to underscore these novel findings and second, to consider whether they unequivocally call for a revision of our views. Let us take them in the order presented.

Are there special aspects of the methods or the sample in Dr. Clausen's study that might account for his unusual results? The first question one always raises about studies that contrast groups by psychiatric diagnosis is whether the diagnoses are correct. Hospital record diagnoses are notoriously unreliable. Here there seems little to criticize. Dr. Clausen has done yeoman work in attempting to correct hospital diagnoses of schizophrenia to achieve research standards. A more serious question arises about the use of a sample of currently married patients. As Dr. Erlenmeyer–Kimling and colleagues (1980) have shown, schizophrenics, and particularly male schizophrenics, have a low rate of marriage and a high rate of marital dissolution. Thus, currently married male schizophrenics are a particularly rare group. It should not be surprising, then, that almost half the married patients diagnosed schizophrenia by record did not qualify as definite or probable schizophrenics when research criteria were applied. But, surprisingly, rediagnosis was even more common in women than men. Because married schizophrenics are unusual, one must be wary of generalizing these results to *all* schizophrenics. However, this does not make the finding any less interesting that less than half these married schizophrenics were ever rehospitalized and that only four were in hospitals at follow-up. Rather, it prompts us to wonder how married schizophrenics might be expected to differ from other schizophrenics in terms of their long-term outcomes—and why.

Another question that arises is whether those four men who were asymptomatic for 5 years before follow-up were regularly taking antipsychotic medication. One possibility that comes to mind is that married patients may be more compliant with medication regimens than are others, perhaps because there is someone at home to remind them.

The occupational histories of schizophrenic married men were found to be more stable than those of the men married to schizophrenic women. Although this comparison has not been made before, the unstable careers of the husbands of schizophrenics is compatible with the findings of Rosenthal (1975) that antisocial personality is common in the spouses of schizophrenic women. It may be that men with antisocial personality have the insensitivity to lack of responsiveness necessary to accept schizophrenics as spouses. A high proportion of antisocial personalities among these husbands would explain their lack of occupational success, even relative to schizophrenics.

In addition to the surprising new findings in Dr. Clausen's chapter, there are also echoes of the results of others. Like the work by Vaillant (1962) and Astrup (1966), this chapter shows that late onset and short duration of symptoms are favorable predictors of recovery. One reaction that has met these findings of previous studies may apply to the current one: Those dubbed schizophrenic with late and acute onset may actually be atypical cases of manic–depressive disorder who show features of thought disorder. It would be interesting to see whether assignment of diagnoses on the basis of the initial presentation of affective symptoms would produce more clear-cut differentiation at outcome.

Dr. Clausen repeatedly reminds us that this study was not designed to study predictors of outcome, but rather how families respond to psychotic members. The intriguing anecdotes he presents of unique family arrangements give an inkling that that original goal was well met.

Dr. Wilder's principal concern is less with the new finding of a long duration of demoralization than with the association between incapacity for self-care and depression. Among 110 elderly persons previously interviewed in the community, whom he followed for 5 years, nine had limited ability to care for themselves at first interview but were not then "demoralized." Half (4) of these became demoralized by second interview. Among the 75 without limitations who were not initially demoralized, only 12% became demoralized. Although the number with limited ability for self-care at risk of becoming demoralized is too small to trust the results, the discovery of a possible association between physical and mental distress is consistent with findings of other studies of people of varying ages (Hankin & Shapiro, 1980). What Dr. Wilder's study may add is evidence for the causal direction of this relationship because of his longitudinal design. However, we may wonder to what extent his measure of impairment in self-care at Time 1 might actually indicate emotional, rather than physical, disability. Some of the elements such as inability to leave the house alone, lack of grooming, inability to watch television, could be symptoms of depression. It might be useful to divide the scale into items more and less likely to be reflections of psychiatric disorder. Inability to go up and downstairs or eat solid foods might more exclusively indicate physical disability, for instance. If those indicators unlikely to be psychological still predict psychiatric disability, the argument becomes more persuasive.

It would also have been of interest to use his data to learn whether improvement in physical disability over time is associated with improvement in mood. Does physical improvement require freedom from depression or, for persons depressed at Time 1, is improvement in their physical condition followed by recovery from depression? Again the opportunity to explore this area is limited by the very small numbers. Only four severely disabled and 13 moderately disabled at Time 1 were found to have improved sufficiently by Time 2 as to no longer require assistance.

Dr. Srole offers an interesting interpretation of his finding that women now in their 40s and 50s have fewer symptoms than did women those ages 20 years ago. He attributes it to the change in women's status and role over the last 20 years. However, as he recognizes, he has no data that actually supports this explanation of why rates did not rise with aging as expected. But before being concerned with alternative plausible explanations for his finding, we must ask whether the finding itself is solid. Could methodological difficulties have produced a lower rate of problems in women than expected even when the rate actually rose? Dr. Srole devotes considerable time to considering and dismissing possible artifacts, but a number of concerns remain. Three changes in the methods and sample between the two surveys might have contributed to a reduction in rates.

First, there were several changes in data collection methods. The interviewers in the first round of the study had been social workers and social scientists; in the second round, they were employees of the National Opinion Research Center (NORC). NORC interviewers are generally college-educated housewives with no special interest in mental health issues, whereas social workers and psychologists, particularly in the Northeast of 20 years ago, had typically been strongly influenced by Freudian concepts of repression and denial. I can remember my own behavior as an interviewer in that era. I tried hard to maximize rapport in order to get subjects to bare their souls. The more symptoms reported, the more I was convinced that I had done an excellent job of getting the "real" truth. NORC interviewers are trained in a different tradition. Their goal is not confession but reliability. They are taught to be matter-of-fact, friendly but not intimate. They do not attempt to take on a therapist-like role. It would not be surprising if older women respondents reported fewer symptoms to these latter-day interviewers; it would not even be surprising if the very same responses were less often scored positive by modern interviewers who do not view qualifiedly positive answers as only the tip of the iceberg of concealed symptoms.

Second, there was a change in the way in which a decision was made about whether the person interviewed constituted a "case." In the original study, two psychiatrists reviewed a summary of the whole interview, including not only symptoms but also information about childhood symptoms, parents' problems, demographic variables, physical illnesses, and a variety of attitudes and beliefs (Srole, Langner, Michael, Opler, & Rennie, 1962). In the second study, diagnosis was based on computer analysis of a small set of symptoms that were found to be highly correlated with psychiatrists' global judgment in the first round. Srole reports that the correlation between results of applying this computer program and the psychiatrists' judgment was .83 in the first round and claims that this high correlation shows the computer program is an acceptable surrogate for a clinical judgment by the two psychiatrists. However, all that a strong positive correlation tells us is that the same patients ranked high by one diagnostic method are ranked high by the other. It does not tell us whether the *frequency* of high scores is the same. A perfect correlation can still be achieved if scores in one system average higher than scores in the other so long as individuals maintain the same positions relative to each other. Further, the correlation of .83 is based on all subjects taken together. We do not know whether the correlation was that high for women in the age range of interest.

Finally, there is the problem of differential recovery of cases. No follow-up study achieves complete recovery of cases initially interviewed. Some die, some move out of the area, some refuse. Rates of loss can be kept low if there are adequate identifiers collected initially to allow location later on. But this requires foresight. Unfortunately, the Midtown Manhattan Study had not been planned as a follow-up, and so identifiers collected initially were not adequate to achieve high recovery rates. Given this handicap, a recovery rate of 50% is admirable. (Initially there were 1660 subjects, of whom 266 were known to have died, leaving 1394 as potentially reinterviewable. The reinterviewed number is 695, just about half of that potential pool.) Even with such a substantial loss, there is no problem if the loss is random. But we cannot assume it was random. Indeed, the impairment rate at Time 1 for the 695 reinterviewed had been only 14%, whereas the impairment rate for the total Time 1 sample had been 23%. Thus it looks very much as though the impaired were much more likely to be lost to follow-up than were the healthier subjects. Where the sample loss is considerable, as in this case, such selective loss can seriously bias results. Indeed, it would have been possible to obtain Dr. Srole's results even if the mental health of these women had actually *deteriorated* with aging, as he had originally expected. All that is necessary is that recovery of cases be markedly adversely affected by mental disorder, and that recent illness interfere more than earlier illness, a not unreasonable assumption.

Let us assume that the truth is that, with aging, the proportion moderately or severely impaired rises from 25 to 30%. This increase might result from 60% of those impaired at first interview remaining impaired, whereas 20% of those well at first interview become sick and remain so at time of follow-up. Assuming 1000 survivors to simplify calculation, the true frequencies would then be the following:

	Time 1			
	Impaired	Not Impaired	Total	
Time 2	f	f	N	%
Impaired	150	150	300	30
Not Impaired	100	600	700	70
Total N	250	750	1000	100
%	25	75	100	

Let us also assume that a reinterview rate of 50% is achieved, with reinterview rates varying with past and current impairment. Suppose the following rates apply:

Impairment	Reinterview Rate
Both times	10%
Second time only	30%
First time only	55%
Neither time	64%

If we apply these rates to the preceding table, we get precisely the rate of 12% impaired reported by Srole, as shown in the following:

	Time 1			
Time 2	Impaired	Not Impaired	Total	
Impaired	150 × .10 = 15	150 × .30 = 45	60	12%
Not Impaired	100 × .55 = 55	600 × .64 = 385	440	88%
			500	100%

This argument assumes that the ill are disproportionately lost to follow-up. This assumption seems reasonable, because a number of studies have shown psychiatric illness and drug use to be related to loss to follow-up (Cox, Rutter, Yule & Quinton, 1977; Josephson & Rosen, 1978). Whereas we doubt that the bias towards loss of the psychiatrically disabled was actually as great as in the example we concocted, the trend is probably in that direction. As noted, the chapter states that many differences between the target sample of 1394 and the 858 located were examined and found to be trivial, and that loss to interview by refusal of 19% of these located did not cause any important changes in the composition of the samples. However, there is no indication that the differences examined included the overall level of psychiatric disorder, the variable most relevant to sustaining the argument that loss did not bias results with respect to impairment rates. Certainly the considerable difference in Time 1 impairment rates between the original and the reinterviewed samples strongly suggest either that recovery rates were biased against the impaired or that the computer method of assessing impairment identified fewer cases than psychiatrists had. Because one or both of these factors or a change in the type of interviewer *might* have explained the results, we should be cautious in accepting them. It might be thought that the fact that the findings are specific to women argues against these doubts, but that may only mean that these sources of bias affected more women than men. Of course, the fact that certain artifacts *might* have accounted for the finding is no proof that this actually occurred. But because the finding itself, as well as its interpretation, remains dubious, we must respond to this fascinating idea with a cautious "interesting if true".

REFERENCES

Astrup, C. (1966). The prognostic importance of genetic factors in functional psychoses. *British Journal of Psychiatry, 112,* 1293–1297.

Cox, A., Rutter, M., Yule, B., & Quinton, D. (1977). Bias resulting from missing information: Some epidemiological findings. *British Journal Preventive and Social Medicine, 31,* 131–136.

Erlenmeyer–Kimling, L., Wunsch–Hitzig, R., & Deutsch, S. (1980). Family formation by schizophrenics. In L. N. Robins, P. Clayton, & J. Wing (Eds.), *The social consequences of psychiatric illness.* New York: Brunner/Mazel.

Hankin, J. R., & Shapiro, S. (1980). The demand for medical service by persons under psychiatric care. In L. N. Robins, P. Clayton, & J. Wing (Eds.), *The social consequences of psychiatric illness*. New York: Brunner/Mazel.

Josephson, E., & Rosen, M. A. (1978). Panel loss in a high school drug study. In D. B. Kandel (Ed.), *Longitudinal research on drug use: Empirical findings and methodological issues*. Washington, DC: Hemisphere.

Rosenthal, D. (1975). Discussion: The concept of subschizophrenic disorders. In R. R. Fieve, D. Rosenthal, & H. Brill (Eds.), *Genetic research in psychiatry*. Baltimore: The Johns Hopkins University Press.

Schaie, K. W. (1970). A reinterpretation of age related changes in cognitive structure and functioning. In L. R. Goulet & P. B. Baltes (Eds.), Life-span developmental psychology. New York: Academic.

Srole, L., Langner, T. S., Michael, S. T., Opler, M. K., & Rennie, T. A. C. (1962). *Mental health in the metropolis, The Midtown Manhattan Study* (Vol. I). New York: McGraw–Hill.

Vaillant, G. E. (1962). The prediction of recovery in schizophrenia. *Journal of Nervous and Mental Disease, 135*, 534–543.

17

Life History Research in Psychopathology is Like a Dog Walking on Its Hind Legs or Discussion of Chapters 12–15

George E. Vaillant

At present long-term follow-up studies of psychopathology are analogous to two-legged walking by dogs. As Samuel Johnson suggested, "What is astonishing is not that it is done well, but that it is done at all." All the previous four chapters make valuable contribution to the longitudinal study of psychopathology and each demonstrates methodological flaws. Underscoring these shortcomings is more for heuristic purposes than to cast aspersions on the studies themselves— each of which reflects the current state of the art.

On the positive side, Dr. Srole's chapter underlines what Paul Baltes has been telling us for years. If we are to appreciate the effect of age on adult develop-ment, the effects of the subject's historical cohort must be teased out from the effects of aging per se. By studying the women in the Midtown Manhattan study at two points in time, the authors found that the seeming age-dependent increase in psychological problems in women appears to be an artifact of birth cohort. Thus, two groups of same-aged women revealed different degrees of psycho-pathology at two very different periods in history. Changes in popular attitude toward the role of women in society appears to offer a possible explanation.

On the negative side, longitudinal studies are believable only to the degree that selective attrition is avoided. Dr. Srole's attrition, especially for the women, is much higher than the 5 to 10% that seems acceptable for studies of that duration. It is true that in a chronically mentally ill population (where follow-up depends on clinic and institutional records) lost subjects may often represent relatively good outcomes. However, in a community study like Dr. Srole's, the women who are lost are most likely to be those who are: (1) highly geograph-ically mobile, (2) uncooperative or suspicious, (3) out of touch with their fami-lies of origin, (4) divorced, (5) either without a telephone or with an unlisted

247

number, or (6) dead. Each of the preceding variables statistically correlates with psychopathology. Thus, before we can accept Dr. Srole's finding, selective attrition must be ruled out. This he has not done.

The chapter by Wilder et al. illustrates the power and the limitation of longitudinal study to unravel "horse and cart" problems. It is well known that the elderly are often both demoralized and physically disabled, but in cross-sectional studies it is impossible to unravel the causal relationship between these two sources of affliction.

In a 4-year follow-up, Wilder et al. show that chronic demoralization often occurs independently of chronic physical disability and thus is not necessarily caused by chronic physical disability. However, demoralization of recent onset seems closely associated with *prior* onset of physical disability and enjoys a relatively good prognosis.

On the negative side, a study like that of Wilder et al. demonstrates that only 4 years and only two points in time are inadequate to produce a definitive cause-and-effect-study for the problems that they examine. To unravel the interrelation between both chronic and recent demoralization and physical disability in the elderly would appear to demand a minimum of three points of observation and a longer period of follow-up. I hope that they will continue their valuable study.

Dr. Clausen's study reveals the excitement and surprise that accrue from continuing to follow decades-later studies that were originally intended to be cross sectional. One of the important lessons that Dr. Clausen's study provides for our understanding of psychopathology is that the long-term course of true *first* admissions in a chronic illness is very different than the prognosis for admissions *per se*. In any chronic illness, the poor prognosis patients, especially those with complications and secondary social problems, produce a disproportionate number of clinic exposures and admission to any given institution. Follow-up of chronic patients who may be counted as "first admissions" by a new clinic tends to produce the artificially dismal picture that we now have of schizophrenia. This is a gloom that longitudinal studies like those of Clausen and Manfred Bleuler are doing much to dispel.

The biggest flaw that I perceive in Clausen's report lies in his small numbers. One of the inevitable hazards of longitudinal follow-up is that numbers of subjects are often very small. On the one hand, it is hard to follow large numbers of subjects for long periods of time; and, on the other hand, the power and excitement of uncovering even a single life story tempts authors to overgeneralize. Thus, most of the comparisons that Clausen makes may well be due to chance differences. Just as longitudinal studies must demand rigor in reducing attrition, so they must strive for samples large enough to allow tests for statistical significance.

Dr. Tsuang's chapter avoids the small "N," the short follow-up, and the attrition that limited the previous studies. In many ways, the follow-up studies by him and his colleagues on the "Iowa 500" represent as fruitful and as well-designed a model as we have of the follow-back strategy in longitudinal studies. The Iowa 500 represents an unusually well-studied clinical cohort from the distant past that has been conscientiously followed up by either personal interview or by death certificates and thereby makes a unique contribution to our understanding of the natural history of psychopathology. To design a truly prospective study of the magnitude and duration of the Iowa 500 would pose virtually insurmountable difficulties in expense, in continuity of funding, in competent research leadership, and in waning patience by the expectant scientific community.

However, Tsuang himself points out the most serious limitation of this design. Follow-back studies try to graph a lifetime with only two points on the graph. Because outcome of chronic illness may vary enormously at different times in the life cycle and because a generally good-outcome patient may be in relapse at the time of the follow-up, we will never fully understand prognosis until we examine the effect of predictors at different points in time. This, Tsuang's study does not do.

18 Depressive Symptoms as a Risk Factor for Mortality and for Major Depression

Myrna M. Weissman
Jerome K. Myers
W. Douglas Thompson
Arthur Belanger

Clinical depression is the most prevalent psychiatric disorder in the community, with an estimated current prevalence rate of about 3–4% (Weissman & Myers, 1978a). The rates of mild to moderate depressive symptoms, independent of specific disorder, are even higher and are estimated in several independent studies as being in the range of about 15% current prevalence (Weissman & Myers, 1978b).

The clinical course and importance of depressive symptoms are unclear. For example, it is unclear whether depressive symptoms are a risk factor for a later clinical depression or whether they predict physical health problems and mortality. Such information could have potential value for early case finding, for understanding psychopathology, and for assessing the importance of depressed mood as a public health problem.

The concept of a risk factor is an epidemiologic one that has been widely used in chronic disease epidemiology but less so in psychiatric epidemiology. Risk factors are characteristics that are observable prior to the onset of a clinical disorder and that increase the likelihood that the individual or group will subsequently manifest the clinical disorder. Examples of well-established risk factors in epidemiology are smoking as a risk factor for lung cancer and increased cholesterol level as a risk factor for heart disease. In the case of depression, possible risk factors that have been studied include female sex, life stress, family history of depression, and lack of an intimate confiding partner. In turn, major psychiatric disorders have been established as risk factors for subsequent mortality although the impact of more minor psychiatric disorder on mortality remains unclear. Once a risk factor is established by careful research, it can be a powerful clue as to the etiology and pathogenesis of the clinical disorder.

In this report, we look at depressive symptoms as a risk factor for a subsequent first episode of major depression and for mortality.

METHODS

In 1967, a longitudinal survey of the population of a community mental health center catchment area in New Haven, Connecticut (Myers, Lindenthal, & Pepper, 1975). The catchment area has a population of approximately 72,000, which includes a changing innercity section of 22,000 and a more stable industrial town of 50,000. It represents a cross section of the community's population and includes all ethnic, racial, and socioeconomic groups.

Sampling

A systematic sample of 1095 households was selected; one adult (18 years of age or over) was chosen at random from each for inclusion in the sample. An inperson interview was conducted with each respondent in 1967. Of the 1095 individuals contacted, 12% refused to be interviewed, 2% could not be reached at home to be interviewed, and 86% ($N = 938$) were interviewed.

Two years later, in 1969, the same population was reinterviewed. Of the original 938 interviewees, 4% had died, 8% refused to be reinterviewed, 11% could not be located, and 77% ($N = 720$) were reinterviewed. With one exception, the reinterviewed sample did not differ significantly ($p < .05$) from the original cohort within any of the major categories of the following variables: social class, race, sex, religion, marital status, mental status, and age. The exception just cited was the under-30 age group, which dropped from 25% in 1967 to 19% in 1969.

In 1975–1976, the 720 subjects interviewed in 1969 were again followed up. Of the 720 subjects, 72% ($N = 515$) were interviewed, 9% had died, 8% could not be located, and 11% refused to cooperate. The rates in this report are based on 511 subjects, as diagnostic data were missing on four subjects.

The reinterviewed sample did not differ significantly ($p < .05$) from the original cohort within the major sociodemographic categories with the exception of race and class—there were fewer nonwhites and fewer lower social class individuals. However, when we examined the symptom status in 1967 and in 1969 between the subjects interviewed and not interviewed in 1975, we found no significant ($p < .05$) differences. It is also possible that some of the subjects who could not be located had died and every effort was made to determine this.

Diagnostic Assessment of Major/Minor Depression

Information for making diagnostic judgments including depression was collected on the Schedule for Affective Disorders and Schizophrenia (SADS) in the 1975–76 sample only, as this is when the instrument became available. The SADS is a structured interview guide with an accompanying inventory of rating scales and specific items (Endicott & Spitzer, 1978). It records information on the subject's functioning and symptomatology. Although the name of the instrument suggests that it only includes information on affective disorders and schizophrenia, in fact it is an overall mental status inventory and contains the information necessary for making diagnostic judgments for most major psychotic, neurotic, and personality disorders.

Based on the information collected on the SADS, the subjects were classified on the Research Diagnostic Criteria (RDC). The RDC are a set of operational diagnostic definitions with specific inclusion and exclusion criteria for a variety of nosologic groups (Spitzer, Endicott, & Robins, 1978).

Diagnoses on the RDC for major depression are made both for the current time period and for one's lifetime. The age at first onset is also obtained for those persons who meet the criteria for a particular diagnosis.

Interviewers' Training and Reliability

There were two raters, one with a college education and one with a graduate-level education. Both had previous clinical experience in psychiatry and interviewing. Both underwent a 3-month period of training on the SADS and RDC under the supervision of doctoral-level persons, with the consultation of psychiatrists. After the training period, interrater reliability was tested between interviewers and supervising staff and found to be excellent.

The RDC diagnoses were also checked against psychiatric treatment records when available and when the subject's permission had been received. In 33 of the 35 cases checked, there was agreement between the psychiatrist's diagnosis or description of symptoms and the RDC diagnosis.

A search of mental health center records for all subjects in the catchment area disclosed that cases reported as not ill had not had psychiatric treatment. However, cases that were treated outside the catchment area or treated before the services became available in 1966 could have been missed. In addition, all cases presenting diagnostic problems were reviewed weekly by the supervising staff. If consensus could not be reached, the subject was reinterviewed by a different interviewer who was blind to the initial findings.

Assessment of Depressive Symptoms

In the original New Haven Community Survey the primary interest was in the overall severity of psychiatric symptoms rather than in depression or other clinical syndromes. Therefore, the major measure of psychopathology was the Index of Mental Status developed by Gurin and associates (Gurin, Veroff, & Feld, 1960). Most of the items were taken from the Stirling (Macmillan, 1957) and Midtown (Rennie, 1952) community studies. The Index of Mental Status utilizes a list of 20 psychiatric symptoms that are scored and combined into an index of mental status. An example of a question is, "Do you ever have trouble in getting to sleep or staying asleep?" A response of "often" is scored 1; "sometimes," 2; "hardly ever," 3; "never," 4. Scale scores range from 20 (maximum impairment) to 80 (total absence of symptoms).

In addition to this overall impairment scale, some items were included in 1967 and 1969 to measure various dimensions of mental illness. Three such depression items plus five Gurin scale items that measure depressive symptoms were selected, and these items are listed in Table 18.1. Scores on a composite 8-item depression index were available for each of the three interviews. The items selected covered the areas of dysophoric mood, pessimism, anergia, sleep disturbance, and appetite disturbance. Responses were scored from 1 (often) to 4 (never). Total scores ranged from 8 (maximum depressive symptomatology) to 32 (total absence of symptoms). Scores of 25 or below were considered to represent moderate to severe depressive symptomatology.

In order to determine the sensitivity of the 8-item index to clinical depression, the scale was administered to a separate sample of 10 acutely depressed patients who were receiving antidepressant treatment as part of a clinical trial and were considered to be at least moderately depressed. The severity of symptoms was based on the Raskin Three Area Depression Scale, which assesses verbal report, behavior, and secondary symptoms of depression (Raskin, Schulterbrandt, Re-

TABLE 18.1
Assessing Depression by the 8 Item
Depression Index

Area Covered	Item
Dysphoric Mood:	"Do you feel in poor spirits?"
Pessimism:	"Do you sometimes wonder if anything is worthwhile anymore?"
Anergia:	"Are there times when you can't take care of things because you can't get going?"
Sleep disturbance:	"Do you ever have any trouble getting to sleep or staying asleep?"
	"Do you ever tend to feel tired in the morning?"
Appetite disturbance:	"Do you ever have loss of appetite?"
	"Do you ever tend to lose weight when you have something important bothering you?"
Somatic complaints:	"Do you ever feel that you are bothered by all sorts of pains or ailments in different parts of your body?"

atig, & McKeon, 1969). The mean Raskin score for the depressed sample was 9 (scale range 3–15), and a score of at least 7 was required to be eligible for treatment. The 8-item derived depression index was administered by a research assistant who was not informed of its intent but was instructed to read the items to the patients. All the depressed patients received scores of 25 or below on the 8-item index, which put them in the moderately or severely depressed category as defined for this study.

Determination of Incidence of Major Depression Between 1969 and 1975

Using the data on lifetime occurrence and age of onset for major depression, we obtained estimates of incidence rates for major depression between 1969 and 1975. The denominator for these rates included only those individuals who, as of 1969, were at risk for developing the particular disorder, that is, only those who had not developed the disorder as of 1969.

Determination of Relative Risk

Relative risk is the ratio of the risk of the disorder (in this case incidence of major depression between 1969 and 1975) among those exposed to the risk factor (high depressive symptoms in 1967 and 1969) to the risk among those not exposed. Therefore, the relative risk is the incidence rate among exposed (high symptoms) individuals divided by the incidence rate among nonexposed (low symptoms) individuals. For these analyses, we were interested in the relative risk for high versus low depressive symptoms in 1967 and/or 1969 in terms of the development of a first episode of major depression or of mortality between 1969 and 1975.

RESULTS

Depressive Symptoms as a Risk Factor

Table 18.2 shows the risk for developing a first episode of major depression between 1969 and 1975 according to symptom status in 1969. As can be seen, the absolute risk of a major depression for persons with high depressive symptoms in 1969 was 25% as compared to 6.3% for those with low depressive symptoms in 1969. Therefore, the relative risk is the 25% incidence rate among those exposed to the risk factor (high symptoms) divided by the 6.3% incidence rate among those not exposed (low symptoms), yielding a relative risk of 4.0%.

Table 18.3 shows a similar analysis but examines depressive symptoms in 1967 and/or 1969 as risk factors for subsequent depressive disorder. The risk for

TABLE 18.2
Incidence of Major Depression Between 1969 and 1975 by
Depressive Symptoms in 1969

| Depressive Symptoms in 1969 | Absolute Risk | Relative Risk |
	Percentage With First Onset Major Depression Between 1969 and 1975	Comparison With Risk Group Having Low Symptoms in 1969
High (N = 48)	25%	3.4
Low (N = 397)	6.3%	—

persons who have high depressive symptoms in both 1967 and 1969 is similar to the risk for persons who have high depressive symptoms only in 1969. When compared with persons who have high symptoms in neither 1967 nor 1969, the relative risk for these two groups were 3.1 and 4.6, respectively. For the group that had high depressive symptoms in 1967 but not in 1969, the risk for developing a first episode of major depression was similar to the risk for those who had high symptoms in neither 1967 nor 1969 (relative risk of 1.3).

Degree of Depressive Symptoms as a Risk Factor

Table 18.4 shows the relationship between degree of depressive symptoms in 1969 and a new episode of major depression between 1969 and 1975. High symptoms were defined as a score of 25 or less, mild symptoms as a score of 26–30, and no symptoms as a score of 31–32. The division between the mild and asymptomatic groups was made by dividing at the median among the subjects who scored over 25. As can be seen, there is a relationship between degree of symptoms in 1969 and the first onset of a major depression between 1969 and

TABLE 18.3
Incidence of Major Depression Between 1969 and 1975 by
Depressive Symptoms in 1967 and 1969

| Depressive Symptoms | | Absolute Risk | Relative Risk |
		Percentage With First Onset Major Depression Between 1969 and 1975	Comparison With Risk Group Having Low Symptoms In 1967 and 1969
High in 1967 Only	(N = 52)	7.7%	1.3
High in 1969 Only	(N = 32)	28.1%	4.6
High in 1967 and 1969	(N = 16)	18.8%	3.1
Low in 1967 and 1969	(N = 345)	6.1%	—

TABLE 18.4
Dose-Response Relationship Between Depressive Symptoms in 1969
and Onset of Major Depression Between 1969 and 1975

| | Major Depression | |
Depressive Symptoms in 1969	Absolute Risk (Percentage With First Onset Between 1969 and 1975)	Relative Risk (Comparison With Risk for Group Having No Symptoms in 1969)
High (N = 48)	25.0%	4.9
Mild (N = 181)	7.7%	1.5
None (N = 216)	5.1%	—

1975. The risk is by far greatest for the persons in the highest symptom group. The relative risk for each symptom level as compared to the asymptomatic group is given. The relative risk for major depression in the high and mild symptom groups is 4.9 and 1.5, respectively.

Depressive Symptoms as a Risk Factor for Mortality

The mortality rate between 1969 and 1975 for the 515 subjects was 9% ($N = 46$). The depressive symptoms in 1967 and in 1969 of those 46 subjects who had subsequently died by 1975 were examined. The relative risk between high depressive symptoms in 1967 and in 1969 and subsequent mortality was quite low, 1.2 and 1.4, respectively. These findings suggest that high depressive symptoms did not predict subsequent mortality.

DISCUSSION

The data show that:

1. Depressive symptoms increase the risk of a future major depression three-fold.

2. The risk for depression between 1969 and 1975 is not elevated if the subject has high depressive symptoms in 1967 and not in 1969. If the subject has low symptoms in 1967 and high symptoms in 1969, then the risk is similar to that of those who have high symptoms in both 1967 and 1969. Having had depressive symptoms does not put one at increased risk for a future depression provided that one has subsequently returned to a low symptom level without an episode of major depression.

3. There is a dose-response relationship in that people with a high level of depressive symptoms in 1969 have a higher risk for a major depression than do

people with a mild symptom level; in turn, people with a mild symptom level have a higher risk than do people with no symptoms. However, the risk is by far greatest for the subjects in the higher symptom group.

4. Depressive symptoms in 1967 or in 1969 do not substantially increase the risk of mortality up to 1975.

Limitations in the Study

The limitations of this study must be acknowledged and the data must be viewed in light of these limitations. The data on depressive diagnosis and age of onset were obtained retrospectively and are subject to problems of recall and difficulty in ascertaining onset for any chronic disease. Because we do not have data on diagnosis in 1967 and 1969, it is not possible to determine whether the subjects with high depressive symptom scores were, in fact, depressed in 1967–69 even though they did not report it in retrospect. Longitudinal studies are required to determine incidence data more accurately.

Implications

These findings have potential clinical and theoretical implications. Clinically, they suggest that there is value in routine assessment of depressive symptoms using relatively simple self-report measures. The clinical impression that persons with many symptoms but no definable disorder are at increased risk for developing a clinical disorder is partially supported by these data. These persons are troubled but often not impaired. Although their distress may not meet the criteria of a definable disorder, they are hurting and many seek help in the health care system. These persons may be detected by routine screening.

Clinicians have also advocated intervention, particularly individual psychotherapy, for persons who are distressed and unhappy. In fact, many such persons do currently seek help from the health care system where they receive treatments as diverse as Valium, vitamin B-12, and psychoanalysis. It is premature to say that early intervention would prevent the full-blown disorder or to say what specific type of intervention might be effective. The efficacy of early preventive intervention for persons with symptoms needs to be established through controlled and randomized clinical trials. There is evidence from these data that reduction of symptoms or recovery from them reduces the risk of subsequent depression. This finding suggests the potential value of symptom reduction in the prevention of future depressive disorders.

Of particular interest is the fact that depressive symptoms seemed to be specific predictors of subsequent clinical depression and do not predict increased mortality. Previous research has shown increased mortality in persons with diagnosed psychiatric disorders such as depression, schizophrenia, etc. (Babigian &

Odoroff, 1969; Tsuang & Woolson, 1977; Winokur, Clayton, & Reich, 1969). The fact that depressive symptoms, unlike psychiatric disorders, did not predict mortality suggests that such symptoms are preclinical states.

The interpretation of the data is less clear with respect to theoretical implications. There are at least two alternative explanations: the prodromal endogenous disorder versus cumulative stress. According to the first, symptoms would be regarded as the prodromal manifestation of an underlying disorder and would be enduring, leading ultimately to clinical depression. According to the second explanation, the depressive symptoms would be regarded as response to intermittent stress. If the stresses are repeated and the individual is unable to cope, the cumulative impact will result in a full-blown clinical disorder such as depression.

The data support the second hypothesis in that subjects who had high depressive symptoms in 1967 but who recovered from them in 1969 were not at increased risk for a subsequent clinical depression. However, these data would need to be examined further in light of intervening life events.

This study, of course, requires replication using a longitudinal design before definitive conclusions can be drawn. Such research is currently underway in New Haven, Connecticut, and elsewhere from the NIMH Epidemiologic Catchment Area Study (Myers, Weissman, Tischler, Holzer, Leaf, Orvaschel, Anthony, Boyd, Burke, Kramer, & Stoltzman, 1984; Regier, Myers, Kramer, Robins, Blazer, Hough, Eaton, & Locke, 1984; Robins, Helzer, Weissman, Orvaschel, Gruenberg, Burke, & Regier, 1984).

ACKNOWLEDGMENTS

This work is supported by US PHS research grant #1 R01 MH25712, from the Center for Epidemiologic Studies, National Institute of Mental Health; Alcohol, Drug Abuse, and Mental Health Administration (ADAMHA), Rockville, Maryland. W. Douglas Thompson was supported by Training Grant #1 T01 MH14235 also from the Center for Epidemiologic Studies.

REFERENCES

Babigian, H. T., & Odoroff, C. (1969). The mortality experience of a population with psychiatric illness. *American Journal of Psychiatry, 126,* 470–480.

Endicott, J., & Spitzer, R. L. (1978). A diagnostic interview: The schedule for affective disorders and schizophrenia. *Archives of General Psychiatry, 35,* 837–844.

Gurin, G., Veroff, J., & Feld, S. (1960). *Americans view their mental health: A nationwide interview study.* New York: Basic Books.

MacMillan, A. M. (1957). The Health Opinion Survey: Techniques for estimating prevalence of psychoneurotic and related types of disorder in communities. *Psychology Reports, 3,* 325–339.

Myers, J. K., Lindenthal, J. J., & Pepper, M. P. (1975). Life events, social integration and psychiatric symptomatology. *Journal of Health and Social Behavior, 16,* 421–427.

Myers, J. K., Weissman, M., Tischler, G. L., Holzer, C. E., Leaf, P. J., Orvaschel, H., Anthony, J., Boyd, J. H., Burke, J. D., Kramer, M., & Stoltzman, R. (1984). *The prevalence of psychiatric disorders in three communities: 1980–1982.* Archives of General Psychiatry, *41*, 959–967.

Raskin, A., Schulterbrandt, J., Reatig, N., & McKeon, J. (1969). Replication of factors of psychopathology in interview, ward behavior and self-report ratings of hospitalized depressives. *The Journal of Nervous and Mental Disease, 148,* 87–98.

Regier, D. A., Myers, J. K., Kramer, M., Robins, L. N., Blazer, D. G., Hough, R. L., Eaton, W. W., & Locke, B. Z. (1984). *The NIMH Epidemiologic Catchment Area (ECA) Program: Historical context, major objectives, and study population characteristics.* Archives of General Psychiatry, *41*, 934–941.

Rennie, T. A. C. (1952). *The Yorkville Community Mental Health Research Study. Interrelations between the Social Environment and Psychiatric Disorders.* Milbank Memorial Fund, Twenty-Ninth Annual Conference.

Robins, L. N., Helzer, J. E., Weissman, M., Orvaschel, H., Gruenberg, E., Burke, J. D., & Regier, D. A. (1984). *Lifetime prevalence of specific psychiatric disorders in three sites.* Archives of General Psychiatry, *41*, 949–958.

Spitzer, R. L., Endicott, J., & Robins, E. (1978). Research diagnostic criteria: Rationale and reliability. *Archives of General Psychiatry, 35,* 773–782.

Tsuang, M., & Woolson, R. F. (1977). Mortality in patients with schizophrenia, mania, depression and surgical conditions. *British Journal of Psychiatry, 130,* 162–166.

Weissman, M. M., & Myers, J. K. (1978a). Affective disorders in a United States community: The use of research diagnostic criteria in an epidemiological survey. *Archives of General Psychiatry, 35,* 1304–1311.

Weissman, M. M., & Myers, J. K. (1978b). Rates and risks of depressive symptoms in a United States urban community. *Acta Psychiatrica Scandinavica, 57,* 219–231.

Winokur, G., Clayton, P., & Reich, T. (1969). *Manic–depressive illness.* St. Louis: Mosby.

19 Toward the Prediction of Dementias Arising in the Senium

Asenath La Rue
Lissy F. Jarvik

Dementia is a costly and debilitating disease that affects a substantial number of the 24 million older adults in the United States today. The best estimate, based on summaries of reports in the literature (Katzman, 1976; Terry, 1976; Terry & Davies, 1980) is a prevalence rate of approximately 15% for all organic brain syndromes in the population over 65 years of age, with an increase to more than 20% after age 80. Moderate to severe dementia, in which the ability to perform activities of daily living is impaired, is estimated to affect 4 to 5% of those over 65, with an additional 10 to 11% being reported as having mild dementia (Katzman, 1976; Terry, 1976). Approximately 80% of organic brain syndromes are believed due to primary degenerative (Alzheimer type) dementia, cerebrovascular (multi-infarct) dementia, or a mixture of both types of lesions. There is evidence that both conditions represent pathologic rather than physiological aging, but at the moment, no effective treatment to halt or reverse the pathologic processes is available. Alzheimer-type dementia (also called senile dementia when onset is after age 65) is the more common of the two diseases, accounting for at least half of all cases of severe intellectual impairment in the elderly (Katzman, 1978; Marsden & Harrison, 1972; Tomlinson, Blessed, & Roth, 1970; Wells, 1978). Clinically, the disease is characterized by a gradually progressive loss of cognitive ability over a period of 5 to 10 years; in the early stages, deficits are most noticeable on tests of recent memory, but, eventually, other aspects of cognition are impaired, including judgment, abstract reasoning, visuospatial processing, and remote recall. On autopsy, characteristic signs of Alzheimer-type dementia include neurofibrillary tangles in the neurons and degenerative neuritic plaques. Multi-infarct dementia also eventually results in global intellectual impairment, but the losses tend to occur in a patchy, stepwise

261

fashion. This disease results from multiple occlusions of small cerebral arteries and is most likely to develop among individuals with hypertension or other signs of generalized atherosclerotic disease.

It is not as yet possible to differentiate prospectively those individuals who will develop dementia from those who will live to comparable ages without substantial intellectual impairment. This chapter focuses, therefore, on two lines of research that we expect to prove fruitful in the eventual early identification of vulnerable individuals. First, evidence for genetic factors in the development of dementia is reviewed, because studies have consistently shown an increased risk for first-degree relatives of aged patients with Alzheimer-type dementia. Second, because the diagnosis of dementia is based on behavioral criteria, most notably the cognitive markers of memory loss and general intellectual deterioration, the possibility of identifying a behavioral phenotype for dementia-prone individuals is explored, using data from a 20-year longitudinal study. The final section (Summary and Conclusions) discusses ways in which genetic and psychometric methodologies might be combined in future investigations.

Genetic Factors in the Development of Dementia

Family Studies.   Family studies (Akesson, 1969; Constantinides, Garrone, & de Ajuriaguerra, 1962; Heston, 1976; Heston & Mastri, 1977; Larsson, Sjögren, & Jacobson, 1963) and the sole United States geriatric twin study (Kallmann, 1953) provide strong evidence for genetic factors in the etiology of dementia of the Alzheimer type. Such studies date back over 50 years to Meggendorfer's (1925) report of 19 secondary cases in the 16 families of 60 histopathologically verified cases of senile dementia (i.e., Alzheimer-type dementia with senile onset) and Weinberger's (1926) finding of 12 secondary cases among the families of 51 probands. Cresseri (1948) and Constantinides et al. (1962) also observed an increased familial risk for this disease. Despite the small sample sizes, these studies are consistent with the contention that there are specific hereditary factors in the etiology of senile dementia, a contention receiving further support from Kallmann's (1953) twin study. Kallmann's (1953) data show concordance rates for dementia of 8% for dizygotic twins and 42.8% for monozygotic twins with morbidity risks of 6.5% for siblings and 3% for parents of affected probands. A high concordance rate for monozygotic twins was also reported by Jarvik, Ruth, and Matsuyama (1980) in a 25-year follow-up of a sample of normal aging twins (Jarvik, Yen, Fu, Matsuyama, 1976; Kallmann & Sander, 1949). Of the 20 intact twin pairs in this study, there were seven (six monozygotic and one dizygotic) in which at least one member developed Alzheimer-type dementia. Three of the monozygotic pairs were concordant and three disconcordant for dementia; the single dizygotic pair was disconcordant.

In the most extensive clinical genetic study to date (Larsson et al., 1963), the risk of senile dementia was four times greater for first-order relatives of probands with senile dementia than for age-matched controls. The data derive from the screening of records from two large mental hospitals in Stockholm for those diagnosed as having senile dementia over a period of 15 years. The case records were carefully analyzed and those meeting diagnostic criteria for dementia (cf. Roth, 1955) were included in the study. In this way, 377 index cases were identified, with 3426 relatives. Field investigations were carried out on a total of 2675 family members, and 55 cases of senile dementia were identified among these family members. Further, the cases identified among the relatives did not deviate from the probands with regard to onset, symptoms, or course of the disease. Not a single case of presenile dementia was said to have been discovered among the relatives, suggesting that Alzheimer presenile dementia and senile dementia of the Alzheimer type represent different disease entities. Actually, based on general population figures and the small sample size, none would be expected, and other investigators have reported both Alzheimer disease and senile dementia within the same family (Constantinides et al., 1962; Heston & Mastri, 1977). No evidence for sex linkage was found in the Larsson et al. study, and sociomedical factors did not appear to influence the morbidity risk for dementia. More recently, in another study emanating from Sweden, Akesson (1969) also observed a markedly elevated risk for senile dementia in parents and siblings of 47 patients with the diagnosis of senile psychosis. The frequency of senile psychosis increased with age, the rate for siblings between 60 and 70 years was 7.1%, and it rose to 30.8% for relatives over 80 years old.

Various modes of genetic transmission have been proposed (for reviews, see Jarvik, 1978; Matsuyama & Jarvik, 1980). In particular, for senile dementia, autosomal dominance with partial penetrance has been suggested (Constantinides et al., 1962; Larsson et al., 1963), meaning that expression of the disease is assumed to be under the partial control of a single dominant gene. Both a polygenic (i.e., controlled by many genes) and an autosomal dominant model have been suggested for the presenile form (Constantinides et al., 1962; Sjögren, Sjögren, & Lindgren, 1952). Heston (Heston, 1976; Heston & Mastri, 1977) noted a 10% morbidity risk for siblings and 23% for parents of individuals affected with presenile dementia, and discovered, in addition, a relationship among Alzheimer disease, Down's syndrome, and myeloproliferative disorders. Because all three disorders were found more often in close relatives of dementia patients than in the general population, Heston and his colleagues hypothesized that there may be a common pathological mechanism: specifically, a defect in the spatial organization of microtubules. The microtubules are involved in the formation of spindle fibers, and it is known that a defect in these fibers may lead to nondisjunction and to the extra G-group chromosome responsible for Down's syndrome. It has also been established that individuals with Down's syndrome have a markedly increased risk of leukemia (Ager, Schuman, Wallace, Rosenfeld, & Gullen, 1965). Aside from the statistical association between Down's syndrome and leukemia, there is the fact that nearly all patients with Down's syndrome show premature signs of aging, including the development of dementia in their 30s and 40s with characteristic Alzheimer-type brain changes (Jervis,

1970; Olson & Shaw, 1969). By contrast, only 14% of persons whose mental retardation had causes other than Down's syndrome show such brain pathology (Malamud, 1972). Heston's hypothesis is the most specific to date with regard to a genetic etiology of dementia. However, a recent analysis (Heston, Mastri, Anderson, & White, 1981) suggests that associations among dementia, Down's syndrome, and leukemia may exist only within families of patients with early-onset dementia, as opposed to the more common senile-onset form. It is not clear, therefore, how the hypothesis of microtubular dysfunction applies to Alzheimer-type dementia as manifested in later life.

Considered together, the reports of Larsson, Heston, and earlier investigators are quite consistent in indicating familial aggregation of Alzheimer-type dementias. Nonetheless, the specificity of this tendency toward aggregation is in need of further investigation. It is possible, for example, that the risk of developing Alzheimer-type dementia is no greater among relatives of identified Alzheimer patients than it is among those related to patients with multi-infarct dementia. Genetic studies of multi-infarct dementia as a clinically distinct entity have been practically nonexistent, owing in part to the difficulties inherent in establishing this diagnosis ante mortem. In a study of 31 patients with arteriosclerotic psychosis (presumably multi-infarct dementia), Akesson (1969) found morbidity risk rates for both siblings and parents of index patients in excess of the risk of 0.21% for the population at large. The risk rates for siblings at ages 60–70, 70–80, and 80 years and older were 2.3, 6.1, and 14.3%, respectively, whereas the corresponding rates for parents were 7.1, 16.7, and 5.0%. The familial risk of this type of dementia appeared to be somewhat lower than, and relatively independent of, familial risk rates for senile (Alzheimer type) dementia; however, Akesson cautioned that, for both types of dementia, the figures were uncertain and noted that the distinction between arteriosclerotic and senile psychosis was an "operational" one based on rather general clinical criteria.

Additional family studies will also be needed before the dementias of the senium can be viewed as disease entities that are genetically distinct from other mental disorders prevalent among the aged, most notably, depression. A number of studies implicate genetic factors in the common clinical observation of strong familial aggregation in unipolar depressive illness and other major affective disorders (e.g., Baker, Dorzab, Winokur, & Cadoret, 1972; Dorzab, Baker, Cadoret, & Winokur, 1971; Marten, Cadoret, Winokur, & Ora, 1972; Winokur & Clayton, 1967), but data are lacking on the co-occurrence of dementing and depressive illness within the same family lines. This is an important issue to address in view of the fact that a high proportion of dementia cases are initially diagnosed as affective disorders (Liston, 1977).

Chromosomal Findings. Cytogenetic studies have provided an additional method for investigating genetic determinants in senile dementia. Jarvik, Altshuler, Kato, & Blumner (1971) and Nielsen (1970) reported that women with senile dementia, but not with arteriosclerotic (multi-infarct) dementia, show a significant increase in chromosome loss (hypodiploidy) when compared to normal women of comparable age. These findings were not present in men, but the data base for men was small, and further studies of this possible sex difference are warranted.

The chromosome findings of an increased frequency of hypodiploidy in persons with senile mental disorders led to a biobehavioral hypothesis wherein it is postulated that different degrees of hypodiploidy are associated with individual differences in degree of senile mental decline (Jarvik et al., 1971); that is, by analogy to the gross physical defects and/or mental retardation that are characteristic consequences of chromosome abnormalities in young organisms, dementia may be one of the consequences of chromosome abnormalities in the aging individual.

In a recent study of patients with familial Alzheimer disease and their descendants, higher percentage of aneuploid cells (i.e., cells with greater or less than the normal 46 chromosomes) was found in all affected members than among controls matched for age and sex (Cook, Ward, & Austin, 1979). Six asymptomatic family members were also studied, and two were found to have high aneuploidy frequencies. The investigators hypothesized that increased aneuploidy will prove to be a predictor of Alzheimer disease and that the two asymptomatic individuals with high aneuploidy frequencies would be expected to develop the condition. Cook et al. maintained, however, that prediction based on aneuploidy is likely to hold true only within family lines for which there is evidence of familial Alzheimer disease, as not all the cases of sporadic Alzheimer disease that they studied showed increased aneuploidy.

The combination of family-study and cytogenetic methodologies, such as in the Cook et al. (1979) study, would appear to be a promising direction for future investigations addressing the issue of prediction, as would more extensive biobehavioral investigations. It would be of interest, for example, to examine a wide range of behavioral capacities among currently asymptomatic family members in Cook et al.'s sample, contrasting such capacities for individuals with and without an increased frequency of aneuploidy. As the following data suggest, assessment of premorbid cognitive abilities might prove to be particularly useful.

Cognitive Predictors of Dementia: An Exploratory Analysis

Because substantial and progressive cognitive loss is the key diagnostic feature in the dementias of old age, it is surprising that the premorbid cognitive characteristics of persons developing dementia have not been systematically investigated. However, longitudinal data that include both psychometric and psychiatric measures are needed for such an investigation, and there are but few relevant studies. Research by Schaie and colleagues (e.g., Schaie, Labouvie, & Beuch,

1973) on community-resident aged persons includes the requisite repeated assessments of cognitive functioning but lacks the psychiatric data. The Duke Longitudinal Study (e.g., Eisdorfer & Wilkie, 1973; Palmore, 1974; Wilkie & Eisdorfer, 1974), the Bath VA studies (Berkowitz & Green, 1963, 1965), the NIMH investigation of healthy aged men (Birren, Butler, Greenhouse, Sokoloff, & Yarrow, 1963), and the studies conducted by Savage and colleagues in the United Kingdom (Hall, Savage, Bolton, Pidwell, & Blessed, 1972; Savage, Britton, Bolton, & Hall, 1973) include both psychiatric and psychometric data, but relationships between premorbid psychological performance and subsequent development of dementia have not been included in the published results.

Based on data collected in the course of a 20-year longitudinal follow-up of a sample of aged twins, we have conducted some analyses bearing on the issue of premorbid cognitive predictors (La Rue & Jarvik, 1980).

METHODS

Subjects. The subjects were survivors of a group of 268 twins who had entered the New York State Psychiatric Institute Study of Aging Twins between 1947 and 1949 (Blum, Clark, & Jarvik, 1973; Jarvik & Blum, 1971; Jarvik, Kallmann, & Falek, 1962; Kallmann & Sander, 1949). All had been over the age of 60 years (mean = 70 years; range = 60–89 years) at the time of initial assessment and all were members of same-sexed Caucasian, English-speaking pairs. With regard to education, the initial sample closely resembled the total white population of New York State at that time, but in terms of occupation, farmers and their wives were overrepresented, whereas factory and clerical workers were underrepresented.

The sample of interest within the context of the present discussion consisted of 65 individuals who were assessed psychiatrically in 1967. There were 24 men and 41 women, ranging in age from 78 to 94 years, with a mean age of 84.27 years. Twenty-six had attended or completed grade school, and 36 had gone beyond the grade school level, usually to 1 or 2 years of high school. The educational status of the remaining three subjects could not be classified, because their interviews contained such statements as "left school at age 14," which could imply either completion of grade school only or preliminary attendance at a secondary school. Thirty-six of the 65 subjects were judged to be free of dementia on the basis of a careful mental status examination (see later), and 29 were diagnosed as showing dementia of mild to severe degree.

Procedures. The initial assessment (referred to hereafter as the "1947" testing) consisted of personal and family history interviews and psychometric testing (the Similarities, Digits Forward and Backward, Digit Symbol, and Block Design subtests from the Wechsler–Bellevue Intelligence Scales, Vocabulary List I from the Stanford–Binet Intelligence Scale, and a tapping test of psychomotor speed). The latter were repeated for subsamples of survivors in a series of follow-up assessments (1948, 1949, 1955, 1957). Between 1966 and 1968 (from now on referred to as the "1967" testing), medical and psychiatric examinations were carried out in addition to the psychometric testing and life-history interviews obtained in prior years.

The psychiatric examinations, conducted by staff from the New York State Psychiatric Institute, included a series of questions assessing orientation, recent memory, calculation, and fund of stored information. Diagnoses of dementia were based on responses to these questions, using criteria adapted from Goldfarb's (1964) guidelines for the diagnosis of organic brain syndrome. Specifically, mild dementia was said to exist if a subject's memory and orientation were intact but some intellectual difficulties were present, e.g., errors on two or less of the 12 general information items and/or errors in calculation; moderate dementia was considered to be present if orientation was intact but some impairment of memory was evident in addition to some deficiencies in calculation and in general information (i.e., errors on three to eight items); and, severe dementia was diagnosed if memory, orientation, and cognitive function were all impaired. Although psychological assessment was also conducted in 1967, the psychiatric judgments as to presence and severity of dementia were made without knowledge of the psychological test scores.

RESULTS

Analyses of covariance were performed for each of the 1947 psychometric measures with dementia status (present vs. absent) in 1967 as the independent variable, and age and education (grade school vs. some high school) as covariates. With variance due to age and education removed, the effect of dementia status was significant for Vocabulary ($F(1,59) = 12.51$, $p < .01$), Similarities ($F(1,58) = 14.22$, $p < .01$), and Digit Symbol ($F(1,56) = 5.68$, $p < .05$); that is, as a group, individuals who later developed symptoms resulting in a psychiatric diagnosis of dementia, had significantly lower scores on these three tests of cognition as long as 20 years before the diagnosis of dementia was made. Moreover, examination of Table 19.1 indicates that there was a tendency for subjects in the dementia group to score lower on all the initial psychometric tests, although this effect was not statistically significant for Digits Forward and Backward, Block Design, or the Tapping test of psychomotor speed.

This pattern of findings suggests that it may be possible to distinguish elderly persons who develop dementia from age peers without dementia on the basis of earlier performance on standardized cognitive tests. To apply results such as the present ones predictively, however, cutoff points would need to be established for the various psychometric tests, to delineate ranges of scores indicative of increased risk for developing dementia. As a first step toward cutoffs, distributions of raw scores from the first test round for the Vocabulary, Similarities, and

TABLE 19.1
Mean Scores on 1947 Psychometric Tests for Subjects With and Without
Dementia in 1967

Psychometric Test	Psychiatric Status					
	No Dementia			Dementia[b]		
	n[a]	M	SD	n	M	SD
Vocabulary	36	31.17	4.16[d]	29	27.07	6.10
Similarities	36	12.78	3.96[d]	28	8.79	4.53
Digit symbol	35	35.11	9.94[c]	27	28.22	9.29
Digits forward	36	6.08	0.97	29	5.97	1.02
Digits backward	35	4.63	1.17	29	4.38	1.40
Block design	31	16.45	6.75	23	13.43	6.08
Tapping	34	73.29	13.61	27	66.04	14.82

[a]The numbers of scores differ from subtest to subtest because subjects were occasionally unable or unwilling to complete a particular task.
[b]Includes cases of mild, moderate, and severe dementia.
[c]$p < .05$
[d]$p < .01$

Digit Symbol Substitution subtests were divided into quartiles, and the performance of individuals relative to these quartiles was used to predict their subsequent membership in the dementia versus no-dementia groups. Specifically, subjects who scored in the highest quartile on any of the subtests were predicted to fall in the no-dementia category, and those with scores in the lowest quartile were expected to be part of the dementia group. On Vocabulary, 10 out of the 13 (76.9%) in the highest quartile were correctly classified as belonging to the no-dementia subgroup in 1967, as were 9 out of 12 (75.0%) in the lowest quartile who later developed dementia. On Similarities, 10 out of 12 (83.3%) in the upper quartile were later rated as being free of dementia, whereas 11 out of 13 (84.6%) in the lowest quartile were judged to be demented in 1967. On Digit Symbol, the corresponding figures were 9 out of 11 (81.8%) in the upper quartile correctly predicted to be free of dementia, and 8 out of 12 (66.7%) in the lowest quartile with subsequent ratings of dementia. The pooled "hit" rates for the highest and lowest quartiles were 76, 84, and 74% for Vocabulary, Similarities, and Digit Symbol, respectively.

DISCUSSION

Our findings could be interpreted in a number of ways. For example, it is clear that the 1947 test round identified a subgroup of individuals, who for biological and/or sociocultural reasons, fell into the lower ranges of normal distributions on certain cognitive tests; it may simply be the case that as such individuals underwent further aging changes—possibly at a rate quite similar to their initially more able peers—the likelihood of their falling into the dementia category was disproportionately high. Gurland (1978) cites a number of studies indicating that the rate at which diagnoses of dementia are made varies with the educational level of the persons assessed, with less well-educated individuals being labeled as demented more often than highly educated ones. In our study, covariance procedures were used to control for differences in initial education, but it is possible that other factors (e.g., occupational status) may have distinguished the dementia and no-dementia groups. We have compared the two groups on measures of physical health and involvement in social, physical, household, and creative activities and have found no significant differences. As to the similarity or difference in rates of intellectual changes over time, subsequent analyses have indicated that subjects who developed dementia declined more rapidly between 1947 and 1967 than those who did not on both the Vocabulary and Digit Symbol subtests (see Table 19.2). Thus, not only did dementia-prone subjects score lower on cognitive tests when initially examined at a mean age of 67 years; they also experienced further losses of function at a rate more pronounced than comparably aged persons remaining free of dementia.

An alternative interpretation of the data is that the development of dementia is an even more insidious process than had heretofore been assumed, and that those individuals whose initial scores were low had already suffered a degree of brain damage, even though they were not as yet clinically demented. Thus, current notions about the time course of dementia may need to be reexamined. This latter hypothesis is consistent with recent reports that, even after a diagnosis of dementia has been made, survival durations average around 6 years for Alzheimer-type dementias (Wang, 1978), and some data even suggest that the survival curve for dementia patients is beginning to approximate that of the general population (Gruenberg, 1978).

TABLE 19.2
Mean Difference Scores on Psychometric Tests (1947–1967) for
Subjects With and Without Dementia in 1967

	Psychiatric Status							
	No Dementia			Dementia				
Psychometric Test	n^a	M	SD	n	M	SD	F value[a]	p value
Vocabulary	34	−0.15	2.43	28	2.32	4.04	8.01	.006
Similarities	34	1.97	3.39	27	1.67	3.45	2.13	.150
Digit symbol	31	10.71	7.67	22	12.64	7.87	5.19	.027

[a]The F-values correspond to the main effect of psychiatric status, with age, education, and initial (i.e., 1947) level of performance covaried.

More extensive investigations than the present one would be required in order to determine whether or not there is a specific configuration of subtests that is particularly useful in differentiating dementia-prone and cognitively stable individuals. It is intriguing that the measures that were observed to vary significantly with dementia status (i.e., Vocabulary, Similarities, and Digit Symbol) are the same ones previously labeled as "critical loss" tests, because specified declines on these measures have been found to relate to nearness to death (Blum et al., 1973; Jarvik & Blum, 1971; Jarvik et al., 1962). However, from a neuropsychological perspective Vocabulary, Similarities, and Digit Symbol Substitution would be expected to tap quite dissimilar areas of neurobehavioral function (Kramer & Jarvik, 1979; La Rue & Jarvik, 1980; Lezak, 1976; McFie, 1975).

Our findings clearly cannot be viewed as final in light of the small and very select sample on which they are based, but we hope that they may serve to stimulate attempts at replication. At best, our results suggest that the cognitive performance of "young–old" subjects (cf. Neugarten, 1975) may become useful in identifying individuals prone to develop cognitive deficits as they survive to an "old–old" age. If we can use such prognostic indices in an appropriate manner, avoiding the negative labeling that so often characterizes applications of standardized cognitive tests at younger ages, such findings may contribute to the maintenance of intellectual skills in individual older persons, as well as extending general knowledge about the correlates and causes of dementia in old age.

SUMMARY AND CONCLUSIONS

After reviewing the literature on genetic factors in dementia and considering the possibility of identifying premorbid behavioral clues to this disorder, we continue to be impressed with the lack of knowledge in this area. As noted in the introduction, it is not as yet possible to differentiate predictively those elderly individuals who will develop dementia from those who will not. Nonetheless, the need to develop such knowledge is great, because prediction could eventually lead to rational therapy and prophylaxis. Some three million elderly Americans are afflicted with dementia today, and as the aged are the fastest growing segment of our population, increasing numbers of persons are likely to be affected.

The current clinical consensus that dementia strikes indiscriminately relative to premorbid capacities and characteristics merely underscores our ignorance about this disease. As our review indicates, there have been very few studies that have even attempted to identify predictors, and most of these have examined only a single variable. Integrated psychobiological investigations of dementia are needed to address the issue of prediction, especially those using a family study methodology. Relatives of dementia patients constitute the most readily identifiable source of persons at increased risk of developing dementia, and it is to be hoped that, through the combined investigation of cytogenetic, psychometric, biologic (e.g., immunologic), and social characteristics of family members, we may begin to identify profiles to assist in predicting and preventing the late-life dementing disorders. Prospective longitudinal follow-ups of asymptomatic family members are particularly needed, although it is difficult in our current state of knowledge to know which variables to monitor over time. Our review of the existing literature suggests that any such study should include chromosome analyses, as aneuploidy frequencies generally differ for groups of demented and nondemented subjects and high rates of aneuploidy have been noted in a subset of relatives of dementia patients (Cook et al., 1979). Psychometric assessment should also be routinely included in follow-ups of family members, as our data for aging twins suggest that scores on these tests may be more sensitive to early dementia than heretofore thought.

ACKNOWLEDGMENTS

We wish to thank: Our twin subjects, their relatives, friends, and physicians; Drs. F. C. Bowden, S. Goldstein, R. Manheimer, and P. Yarden for assistance with psychiatric and medical examinations; Dr. J. Steuer and L. Bank for their helpful comments on various revisions of this chapter; and C. Neves and A. Waldbaum for secretarial assistance. Special appreciation is expressed to Dr. S. Matsuyama for his assistance in writing and review of the section on genetic investigations. The twin study analyses were supported in part by research grant HD01615 from the National Institute of Child Health and Human Development and by the Medical Research Service of the Veterans Administration.

REFERENCES

Ager, E. A., Schuman, L. M., Wallace, H. M., Rosenfeld, A. B., & Gullen, W. H. (1965). An epidemiological study of childhood leukemia. *Journal of Chronic Diseases, 18,* 113–132.

Akesson, H. W. (1969). A population study of senile and arteriosclerotic psychoses. *Human Heredity, 19,* 546–566.

Baker, M., Dorzab, J., Winokur, G., & Cadoret, R. (1972). Depressive disease. Evidence favoring polygenic inheritance based on an analysis of ancestral cases. *Archives of General Psychiatry, 27,* 320–327.

Berkowitz, B., & Green, R. F. (1963). Changes in intellect with age: Longitudinal study of Wechsler–Bellevue scores. *Journal of Genetic Psychology, 103,* 3–21.

Berkowitz, B., & Green, R. F. (1965). Changes in intellect with age: V. Differential changes as functions of time interval and original score. *Journal of Gerontology, 107,* 179–192.

Birren, J. E., Butler, R. N., Greenhouse, S. W., Sokoloff, L., & Yarrow, M. R. (1963). *Human Aging.* Washington, DC: Public Health Service Publication (No. 986).

Blum, J. E., Clark, E. T., & Jarvik, L. F. (1973). The New York State Psychiatric Institute study of aging twins. In L. F. Jarvik, C. Eisdorfer, & J. E. Blum (Eds.), *Intellectual Functioning in Adults.* New York: Springer.

Constantinides, J., Garrone, G., & de Ajuriaguerra J. (1962). L'hérédité des démences de l'age avancé. *Encéphale, 51,* 301–344.

Cook, R. H., Ward, B. E., & Austin, J. H. (1979). Studies in aging of the brain. IV. Familial Alzheimer disease: Relation to transmissible dementia, aneuploidy, and microtubular defects. *Neurology, 29,* 1402–1412.

Cresseri, A. (1948). l'Ereditarietà della Demenza Senile. *Bollettino-Societa Italiana Biologia Sperimentale* (Napoli), *24,* 200–201.

Dorzab, J., Baker, M., Cadoret, R. J., & Winokur, G. (1971). Depressive disease: Familial psychiatric illness. *American Journal of Psychiatry, 127,* 1128–1133.

Eisdorfer, C., & Wilkie, F. (1973). Intellectual changes with advancing age. In L. F. Jarvik, C. Eisdorfer, & J. E. Blum (Eds.), *Intellectual functioning in adults.* New Yorker: Springer.

Goldfarb, A. (1964). The evaluation of geriatric patients following treatment. In P. H. Hoch & J. Zubin (Eds.), *The evaluation of psychiatric treatment.* New York: Grune & Stratton.

Gruenberg, E. (1978). Epidemiology. In R. Katzman, R. D. Terry, & K. L. Bick (Eds.), *Alzheimer's disease: Senile Dementia and related disorders.* New York: Raven Press.

Gurland, B. (1978). *The borderlands of dementia: The influence of socio-cultural characteristics on rates of dementia occurring in the senium.* Paper presented at the Conference on the Clinical Aspects of Alzheimer's Disease and Senile Dementia, sponsored by the National Institute of Mental Health, and The National Institute of Neurological and Communicative Disorders and Stroke, Washington, DC.

Hall, E. H., Savage, H. D., Bolton, N., Pidwell, D. M., & Blessed, G. (1972). Intellect, mental illness, and survival in the aged: A longitudinal investigation. *Journal of Gerontology, 27,* 237–244.

Heston, L. L. (1976). Alzheimer's disease, trisomy 21, and myeloproliferative disorders: Associations suggesting a genetic diathesis. *Science, 196,* 322–323.

Heston, L. L., & Mastri, A. R. (1977). The genetics of Alzheimer's disease: Associations with hematologic malignancy and Down's syndrome. *Archives of General Psychiatry, 34,* 976–981.

Heston, L. L., Mastri, A. R., Anderson, V. E., & White, J. (1981). Dementia of the Alzheimer type: Clinical genetics, natural history, and associated conditions. *Archives of General Psychiatry, 38,* 1085–1090.

Jarvik, L. F. (1978). Genetic factors and chromosomal abberrations in Alzheimer's disease, senile dementia, and related disorders. In R. Katzman, R. D. Terry, & K. L. Bick (Eds.), *Alzheimer's disease: Senile Dementia and related disorders* (Vol. 7). New York: Raven Press.

Jarvik, L. F., Altshuler, K. Z., Kato, T., & Blumner, B. (1971). Organic brain syndrome and chromosome loss in aged twins. *Diseases of the Nervous System, 32,* 159–170.

Jarvik, L. F., & Blum, J. E. (1971). Cognitive declines as predictors of mortality in twin pairs: A twenty-year longitudinal study of aging. In E. Palmore & F. C. Jeffers (Eds.), *Prediction of life span.* Lexington, MA: Heath.

Jarvik, L. F., Kallmann, F. J., & Falek, A. (1962). Intellectual changes in aged twins. *Journal of Gerontology, 17,* 289–294.

Jarvik, L. F., Ruth, V., & Matsuyama, S. S. (1980). Organic brain syndrome and aging: A six-year follow-up of surviving twins. *Archives of General Psychiatry, 37,* 280–286.

Jarvik, L. F., Yen, F. S., Fu, T. K., & Matsuyama, S. S. (1976). Chromosomes in old age: A six-year longitudinal study. *Human Genetics, 33,* 17–22.

Jervis, G. A. (1970). Premature senility in Down's syndrome. *Annals of the New York Academy of Sciences, 171,* 559–561.

Kallmann, F. J. (1953). *Heredity in health and mental disorder.* New York: W. W. Norton.

Kallmann, F. J., & Sander, G. (1949). Twin studies on senescence. *American Journal of Psychiatry, 106,* 29–36.

Katzman, R. (1976). The prevalence and malignancy of Alzheimer disease. *Archives of Neurology,* *33,* 217–218.

Katzman, R. (1978). Normal pressure hydrocephalus. In R. Katzman, R. D. Terry, & K. L. Bick (Eds.), *Alzheimer's disease: Senile Dementia and related disorders* (Vol. 7). New York: Raven Press.

Kramer, N. A., & Jarvik, L. F. (1979). Assessment of intellectual changes in the elderly. In A. Raskin & L. F. Jarvik (Eds.), *Psychiatric symptoms and cognitive loss in the elderly.* Washington, DC: Hemisphere.

Larsson, T., Sjögren, T., & Jacobson, G. (1963). Senile dementia: A clinical sociomedical and genetic study. *Acta Psychiatrica Scandinavica* (supplement 1967), *39,* 1–259.

La Rue, A., & Jarvik, L. F. (1980). Reflections of biological changes in the psychological performance of the aged. *Age, 3,* 29–32.

Lezak, M. D. (1976). *Neuropsychological assessment.* New York: Oxford Press.

Liston, E. H. (1977). Occult presenile dementia. *Journal of Nervous and Mental Diseases, 164,* 263–267.

Malamud, N. (1972). Neuropathology of organic brain syndrome. In C. M. Gaitz (Ed.), *Aging and the brain.* New York: Plenum Press.

Marsden, C. D., & Harrison, M. J. G. (1972). Outcome of investigation of patients with presenile dementia. *British Medical Journal, 2,* 249–252.

Marten, S. A., Cadoret, R. J., Winokur, G., & Ora, E. (1972). Unipolar depression: A family history study. *Biological Psychiatry, 4,* 205–213.

Matsuyama, S. S., & Jarvik, L. F. (1980). Genetics and mental functioning in senescence. In J. E. Birren & B. Sloane (Eds.), *Handbook of mental health and aging.* Englewood Cliffs, NJ: Prentice-Hall.

McFie, J. (1975). *Assessment of organic intellectual impairment.* New York: Academic Press.

Meggendorfer, F. (1925). Über familiengeschichtliche Untersuchungen bei arterioskerotischer und seniler Demenz. *Zentralblatt fur die Gesamte Neurologie und Psychiatrie, 40,* 359.

Neugarten, B. (1975). The future of the young–old. *The Gerontologist, 15,* 4–9.

Nielsen, J. (1970). Chromosomes in senile, presenile and arteriosclerotic dementia. *Journal of Gerontology, 25,* 312–315.

Olson, M. I., & Shaw, C. M. (1969). Presenile dementia and Alzheimer's disease in mongolism. *Brain, 92,* 147–156.

Palmore, E. (1974). *Normal aging II.* Durham, NC: Duke University Press.

Roth, M. (1955). The natural history of mental disorders in old age. *Journal of Mental Science, 101,* 281–301.

Savage, R. D., Britton, P. C., Bolton, N., & Hall, E. H. (1973). *Intellectual functioning in the aged.* London: Methuen.

Schaie, K. W., Labouvie, O. U., & Beuch, V. U. (1973). Generation and cohort-specific differences in adult cognitive functioning: A fourteen-year study of independent samples. *Developmental Psychology, 9,* 151–166.

Sjögren, T., Sjögren, H., & Lindgrew, A. G. H. (1952). Morbus Alzheimer & Morbus Pick *Acta Psychiatrica et Neurologica Scandinavica.*

Terry, R. (1976). Dementia: A brief and selective review. *Archives of Neurology, 33,* 1–4.

Terry, R. D., & Davies, P. (1980). Dementia of the Alzheimer type. *Annual Review of Neurosciences, 3,* 77–95.

Tomlinson, B. E., Blessed, G., & Roth, M. (1970). Observations on the brains of demented old people. *Journal of the Neurological Sciences, 11,* 205–242.

Wang, H. S. (1978). Prognosis in dementia and related disorders in the aged. In B. Katzman, R. D. Terry, K. L. Bick (Eds.), *Alzheimer's disease: Senile Dementia and related disorders.* New York: Raven Press.

Weinberger, H. L. (1926). Über die hereditaren Beziehungen der senilen Demenz. *Zentralblatt fur die Gesamte Neurologie und Psychiatrie, 106,* 666–701.

Wells, C. E. (1978). Chronic brain disease: An overview. *American Journal of Psychiatry, 135,* 1–12.

Wilkie, F., & Eisdorfer, C. (1974). Terminal changes in intelligence. In E. Palmore (Ed.), *Normal aging II.* Durham, NC: Duke University Press.

Winokur, G., & Clayton, P. (1967). Family history studies. II. Sex differences and alcoholism in primary affective illness. *British Journal of Psychiatry, 113,* 973–979.

20 Prediction in the Onset and Detection of Huntington's Disease

Arthur Falek
Richard H. Myers
Ray Craddick

Huntington's Disease (HD) is an inherited neuropsychiatric disorder with a late age of onset. Carriers of the gene for HD generally exhibit no clinical symptoms of the disease until middle age. Onset is insidious and leads invariably to death within 15 to 20 years. As this is a dominantly inherited disorder, each child of an affected parent has a 50% chance of developing it. Therefore, many high-risk family members identify with the affected relative and his or her pattern of illness. This devastating illness, in addition, confronts younger family members with the realization of their own mortality.

AGE OF ONSET STUDIES

The average age at which the first signs of HD appear is about 41 years (Husquinet, Mackenzie–van der Noordaa, Myrianthopolous, Petit, Volkers, & Went, 1973) but ranges from 4 years through 70 years of age. Several familial factors relating to the age of onset of HD have been investigated in our laboratory. For the past 12 years, detailed family histories have been collected from HD families in the Southeastern United States, and pedigrees for 98 extended families have been recorded. In every instance at least one family member at risk for HD or the spouse of a diagnosed HD patient was interviewed. Whenever possible, this information was supplemented by medical records and by written correspondence with additional family members. Information regarding the sex, year of birth, year of death, cause of death, place of birth, place of death, and the number and year of birth of all children was collected for as many family members as possible. In addition, data were also collected for affected individuals on age of onset, initial symptoms, age at diagnosis, diagnosing physician, and information on treatment and institutionalizations. Special efforts were devoted to determining the age of onset of symptoms as patients often were not diagnosed until many years after the initial symptoms. The family history collection procedure has remained unchanged for the duration of the study.

The average age of onset for the 63 male gene carriers was 39.54 years and for the 53 female carriers it was 38.43 years. The difference between the sexes is not significant and these data have been pooled in Fig. 20.1. Although there is some ambiguity and inconsistency in the estimation of age of onset, it was also found that the estimated age of onset correlated highly with the age of death (Myers, Madden, Teague, & Falek, 1981). This relationship between estimated age of onset and age at death gives further credence for the use of age of onset in these analyses and suggests that the latter is related to the manifestation and clinical progression of the disorder. This finding is in agreement with the observations of Husquinet et al. (1973) concerning the lack of variation of age of onset among sibships within kindreds, whereas between-kindred comparisons are so different as to suggest genetic heterogeneity of HD.

The pedigree data were analyzed with regard to four different factors relating to age of onset. These were: (1) the consistency in age of onset within families, (2) the influence of the sex of the transmitting parent, (3) the progressively earlier age of onset in successive generations (anticipation), and (4) the effect of the interval between the birth of a subsequently affected offspring and the onset of HD in the parent on the age of onset in the offspring (Brackenridge & Teltscher, 1975). In other words, does the circumstance of a parent being very close to his or her own onset at the time of parenting an offspring who inherits the HD gene influence the age of onset in that offspring? We call this last factor the Parent-Onset Interval.

The analysis of consistency of age of onset within families revealed a significant correlation of parent and offspring onset ages ($r = 0.78$, $t_{49} = 8.7$, $p < 0.001$). The consistency of onset age within a family suggests that the onset of HD may be influenced by either common environmental factors or by other shared genetic factors. The finding of within-family consistency has particular relevancy for studies in aging. Within-family analyses of aspects of aging may reveal patterns that are not apparent in random samples (Kallmann, Aschner, & Falek, 1956; Pearl & Pearl, 1934).

The second factor relating to age of onset of HD was the sex of the parent. Within our sample of HD patients, 9 persons exhibited symptoms before the age of 21. Of these 9 "juvenile onset" HD patients, 7 had inherited the HD gene from an affected father. The preponderance of paternal transmission in cases of juvenile HD has been reported by HD researchers around the world (Bird, Caro, & Pilling, 1974; Brackenridge, 1971; Bruyn, 1969; Hayden, MacGregor, Saffer, & Beighton, 1982; Conneally, Rahman, & Drew, 1969; Newcombe, Walker, & Harper, 1981; Oepen, 1965). In addition, as first suggested by Merritt (Merritt et

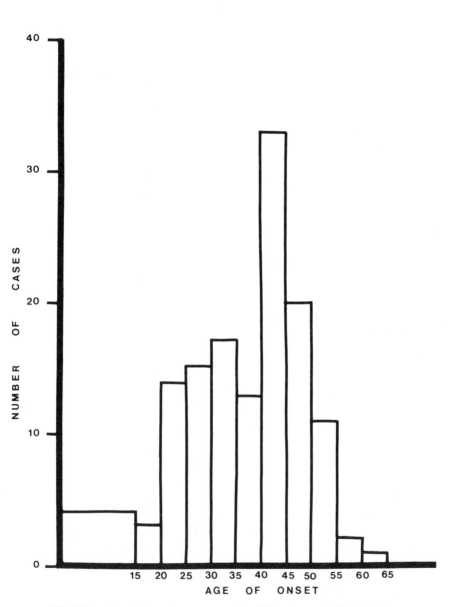

FIG. 20.1. Distribution of age at onset for 116 patients with Huntington's Disease.

al., 1969), we noted a trend toward earlier onset for all offspring with paternal inheritance of HD.

The basis for this difference is unknown. Do paternal carriers transmit in addition to the HD gene a factor that hastens the onset of the disorder in offspring, or do maternal carriers transmit a factor that delays onset in their children? If such a regulator does exist is it located on a chromosome, or if it is under maternal control is it a mitochondrial gene located in the cytoplasm of the cell? There are, in fact, recent reports in the literature with models of mitochondrial transmission in Huntington's Disease (Boehnke, Conneally, & Lange, 1983; Myers, Goldman, Bird, Sax, Merril, Schoenfeld, & Wolf, 1983).

Evidence of a trend toward an earlier age of onset in successive generations was found in our data, although the difference does not reach statistical significance. The average age of onset for the 51 offspring was 38.33 years compared to 41.54 years for the 28 parents. Moreover, within the sample of parents, the youngest age of onset was 24 years, whereas 7 of the offspring exhibited symptoms before the age of 24. Of these 7, 5 remained childless. It may be that persons exhibiting symptoms of HD very early in life are nonreproductive and would, therefore, not be included as parents in comparisons of successive generations.

The analysis of the Parent-Onset Interval revealed that fathers average 31 years of age and mothers 26 years of age at the time of birth of a gene-inheriting child ($F_{47} = 8.02$ $p < 0.01$), whereas the average age of onset for both sexes was in the late 30s. Thus, compared to mothers, fathers are closer to their own onset at the time that they become parents. Unfortunately, our sample did not contain enough large sibships to evaluate a possible birth-order effect that would be predicted by this hypothesis.

EARLY DETECTION STUDIES

As an autosomal dominantly inherited disorder, HD is expected to occur in half the sons and daughters of affected individuals. There is currently no means for detection of carriers prior to the onset of HD symptoms usually in middle age. Studies aimed at the early diagnosis of HD in the offspring of affected individuals include investigations of ocular movements (Petit & Milbled, 1973), psychomotor tests (Baroff, Falek, & Haberlandt, 1958), psychological tests (Goodman, Hall, Terango, Perrine, & Roberts, 1969; Hansotia, Cleveland, & Chun, 1968; Palm, 1973; Pearson, Peterson, Lazarte, Blodgett, & Kley, 1955), EEG (Patterson, Bagchi, & Test, 1948), and L-dopa loading tests (Klawans, Paulson, Ringel, & Barbeau, 1973). In many instances these studies have divided the offspring into two groups: those who respond in a similar fashion to normal controls and those who produce altered results. Follow-up studies of two of these investigations have been completed. Chandler (1969) has reported that the EEG (Patterson et al., 1948) was not useful in predicting gene carriers. Lyle and Gottesman (1977) have found that, as a group, those persons who had manifested HD on a 15- to 20-year follow-up of the Pearson et al. (1955) sample originally had significantly lower scores on the Wechsler IQ test. Lyle and Gottsman have thus concluded that intellectual abilities of gene carriers are diminished long before choreic movements become apparent.

We have reported a procedure for early detection (Falek, 1969; Falek & Britton, 1976; Myers & Falek, 1979) that uses a piezoresistive accelerometer in the measurement of minute levels of muscle tremor for the early detection of HD gene carriers. In this series of studies, 52 at-risk persons have been tested, and tremor scores similar to those of HD patients have been noted for 15 of the subjects. This number is less than the expected 50% (26 subjects). Similarly, other studies have also detected aberrant test results for fewer than 50% of the persons at risk for HD who were tested. Klawans et al. (1973) reported deviant tests in only 10 of 30 at-risk subjects using L-dopa loadings, and Lyle and Gottesman (1977) reported deviance in 29 of 85 at-risk subjects using psychometric testing. It may be that these different tests are not sufficiently sensitive to detect all gene carriers. Perhaps HD represents disorders with more than one etiological basis and although a particular test is able to recognize carriers of one type, it is not able to do so for the others. Alternatively, the gene for HD may become active only in mid-life with tests prior to that time failing to detect some of the individuals who will later become ill. Temporal genes regulating the expression of the structural genes for enzymes at different stages of ontogenetic development have been demonstrated in mammalian tissues (Paigen, 1979). Paigen has suggested that temporal gene mutants may either turn on or turn off an otherwise intact structural gene in HD (Paigen, 1980). Whereas it would be of interest to determine whether or not the three tests (i.e., L-dopa loadings, psychometric tests, and tremor measures) are identifying the same individuals, no study has as yet examined more than one of the types or measures.

A second important finding of the HD accelerometer studies is the relationship of altered tremor physiology to the progression of the disorder (Myers & Falek, 1979). Persons who have exhibited symptoms for longer periods of time show an increasing modification of tremor. HD is characterized by a slowing of tremor to the 6 or 7 Hz range from the 9 Hz frequency in controls as well as a disruption in regularity of tremor by short bursts of high frequencies between 15 Hz and 20 Hz. In addition, tremor scores reflect the ameliorative effects of some medications (Myers & Falek, 1979). The use of accelerometer measurements of muscle tremor may, therefore, prove to be useful in evaluating new medications for individuals affected with HD. In the event that an effective method of treatment is developed, early recognition of HD gene carriers by accelerometer tremor measurement could result in control of the disorder prior to substantial neurological damage.

COPING STUDIES

Changes in personal as well as professional and business commitments are often initiated with the first signs of HD. The affected individual experiences progressive deterioration of both motor movement and psychological controls. Attempts to adapt to such changes in order to achieve some aspects of normality become paramount for the patient and family. Over time the ever increasing inability of the patient to care for his own basic needs produces frequent displays of frustrations, which lead to the discarding of outside interests by both the family and the patient. Eventually, attention is focused on required nursing care. The inability to slow or divert the course of this disorder has led to its consideration as a terminal illness lasting one to two decades (Falek, 1969).

HD is a useful model to increase our knowledge in evaluating the process of coping with serious, chronic, long-term debilitating disorders and affords an opportunity to evaluate on a longitudinal basis persons aware of and exposed to their own mortality. Initial data in this area are based on the Craddick Lifeline Test (Craddick, 1970).

The Lifeline Test is designed to measure both an objective and subjective (projective) view of one's life-span. The Lifeline Test, as presented in Fig. 20.2, is a simple device for measuring the subjective concept of time in terms of unidimensional (line) life space. This dimension consists of a line of fixed length (136 mm) in a horizontal position placed on white bond paper with the instructions as shown. The test was first employed to discriminate between persons who have attempted suicide and nonsuicidal patients admitted to the emergency service at Grady Hospital in Atlanta (Carter, 1971). In that study, the test offered an objective measure of time perspective pertaining to global life events. The test was recently employed to assess whether a subject at risk of inheriting HD has integrated the knowledge that this disorder may shorten her or his life (Myers, 1979).

Results of two of the scores obtained in this study (Myers, 1979) are reported here: (1) the placement of the "X" as measured in millimeters from the left end of the lifeline (the placement of a 1, important past event, and a 2, important future event, indicate whether the left or the right end of the line is used as birth point; every subject in this study began on the left end); (2) the estimated total length of life in years.

Group differences were revealed by the Craddick Lifeline Test in Myers' study in which 25 persons at risk for HD, 17 spouses of at-risk persons, and 26 unstressed, not at-risk control subjects with no family history of neurological disorder were evaluated. With regard to the estimated total life-span, controls predicted that they would live 80.64 years; subjects at risk for HD 67.08 years; and spouses of these at-risk subjects 78.56 years ($F_{2.63} = 9.05$, $p < 0.001$). Thus, group comparisons revealed that at-risk persons stated that their life-spans would be years shorter than controls or spouses. The average age of death for our

NAME _____ DATE _____

SEX _____ AGE _____

HANDEDNESS (Left or Right) _____

Consider the line below as a form of "lifeline". Mark with an "X" where you consider yourself to be at this time on this lifeline. Mark with a "1" the point on the lifeline you consider as the most important event to have happened to you *in the past*. Now mark with a "2" the point at which you feel the most important event will happen to you *at some future time*.

In the space indicated below the line and noted (1) and (2) please write the event that took place and the event that will take place that you indicated as "1" and "2" on the lifeline.

_____

The event marked "1" was ....

Approximate year of "1" ....

The event marked "2" will be ....

Approximate year of "2" ....

Now estimate in years what you believe the total length of your life

will be ....

Ray A. Craddick
Georgia State University
1970

FIG. 20.2   Craddick Lifeline Test

Southeastern HD population was 55 years. Thus the estimate of 67.08 years of life is almost exactly halfway between the estimate of 80.64 years of the not at-risk controls and average age of death of HD patients. Because the risk of inheriting HD is 50%, the stated life-span scores of persons at risk are in remarkable agreement with expectation.

In marking that point on the lifeline that those at risk perceive as their present age, however, they place the X no differently than do their spouses and the controls. These data indicate that, whereas on a verbal level the at-risk person is cognizant of the threat of a shortened life, on the nonverbal level he or she may not be using this information in a decision-making process. One cause of this discrepancy may be denial. The person who is at risk of inheriting HD does not, perhaps, believe that he or she really could be a carrier of the gene, and the threat of shortened life is not incorporated into his or her concept of self. This is assuredly an important means of coping with the threat of a life-shortening illness. Therefore, providing such a client with additional information related to his or her own limited mortality may result in a verbal acceptance but not necessarily a change in behavior. The degree to which information is assimilated by the counselee needs to be evaluated in other chronic illnesses that affect individuals at any age. Equally important is the need for an understanding of the way that the life-span is viewed in those who are aged without evidence of life-threatening illness but who are inherently closer to death. Although much has been written on the process of coping with life-threatening illness and dying (Falek, 1979; Falek & Britten, 1974; Kubler–Ross, 1969), little empirical work has been done in this area.

CONCLUSIONS

Huntington's Disease is a genetic disorder transmitted as an autosomal dominant. The remarkable manner in which this illness is manifest provides a unique opportunity to gain understanding in the aging process, the interaction of environmental and genetic variables, the mechanism of gene expression, and the psychological impact of a life-threatening illness.

The HD gene carrier lives an ostensibly normal life for approximately 40 years. Among the individuals studied in our sample were professors of economics and biology and a physician, as well as a policeman, a lab technician, and a minister. Neurological disability is not apparent prior to the onset of clinical symptoms. Despite the clear genetic etiology, the age of onset of symptoms and the age of death is highly variable. By ascertaining those familial factors that are related to the age of onset, it may become possible to identify environmental variables that influence onset and the disease process. The substantial differences that are noted in the expression of an established inherited illness have relevances for other diseases of unknown etiology. In HD a wide spectrum of symptoms in different individuals may have a common underlying cause.

A major finding reported in November, 1983 was the detection of a polymorphic DNA marker on chromosome 4 genetically linked to Huntington's disease (Gusella, Wexler, Conneally, Naylor, Anderson, Tanzi, Watkins, Ottina, Wallace, Sakaguchi, Young, Shoulson, Bonilla, and Martin, 1983) that is now being tested to insure consistent recognition of gene carriers in various at-risk populations. It is conceivable, however, that although the gene carrier is identifiable at the DNA level, there is no detectable clinical deficit prior to the onset of symptoms in midlife. Certainly, biological milestones in mid-life are part of normal human development and aging. HD and other mid-life onset disorders such as Alzheimer's disease and Parkinson's disease would appear to be related to mid-life metabolic changes. For example, the inability of a population of cells to continue the production of prior levels of a gene product may mark the initiation of a disease process. It may be that only when the gene for Huntington's disease and its function(s) are determined will we understand the initiating defect that results in the pleiotropic consequences in Huntington's disease.

Once the reliability and validity of a preclinical detection probe is established, those not so identified will be assured that they and their children will no longer have to fear the onset of this disorder. However, for the 50% of immediate relatives identified as gene carriers, while there is no knowledge of treatment to control the progress of this disease in already affected individuals or prevent its onset in gene carriers, attention needs to be directed to an expected, significant increase in reality-based depression and suicide.

At the level of social interaction, the impact of a threat such as HD to established life patterns is profound. Furthermore, the manner by which different people learn to deal with this threat is quite diverse. Although patterns of behavior are recognizable and some may be regarded as resulting in more or less "productive" or "fruitful" lifestyles and careers, no single pattern would be appropriate for everyone. The study of these coping styles lends insight into the manner by which each of us deals with the temporary nature of our existence as we know it.

REFERENCES

Baroff, G. S., Falek, A., & Haberlandt, W. (1958). Impairment of psychomotor function in the early diagnosis of Huntington's chorea. In H. Hoff and R. Reisner, (Eds.), *Wiener-Zertschrift Fur Nervenheilkunde und Deren Grenzgebiete*. Wien: Springer Verlag.

Bird, E. D., Caro, A. J., & Pilling, J. B. (1974). A sex-related factor in the inheritance of Huntington's chorea. *Annals of Human Genetics (London), 37*, 255–260.

Boehnke, M., Conneally, P. M., & Lange, K. (1983). Two models for a maternal factor in the inheritance of Huntington's disease. *American Journal of Human Genetics, 35*, 845–860.

Brackenridge, C. J. (1971). The relation of type of initial symptoms and line of descent in Huntington's disease. *Clinical Genetics, 2*, 287–297.

Brackenridge, C. J., & Teltscher, B. (1975). Estimation of the age at onset of Huntington's disease from factors associated with the affected parent. *Journal of Medical Genetics, 12*, 64–69.

Bruyn, G. W. (1969). The Westphal variant and juvenile type of Huntington's chorea. In A. Barbeau & J. R. Brunette (Eds.), *Progress in neuro-genetics*. Amsterdam: Excerpta Medica Foundation.

Carter, D. L. (1971). *Personality, life style, and time perspective comparisons of suicidal and nonsuicidal females*. Master's thesis, Georgia State University.

Chandler, J. H. (1969). EEG in the prediction of Huntington's chorea. In A. Barbeau & J. R. Brunette (Eds.), *Progress in neuro-genetics*. Amsterdam: Excerpta Medica Foundation.

Craddick, R. A. (1970). *Lifeline test*. Unpublished manuscript, Georgia State University.

Falek, A. (1969). Preclinical detection in Huntington's chorea. Preliminary report. In A. Barbeau & J. R. Brunette (Eds.), *Progress in neuro-genetics*. Amsterdam: Excerpta Medica Foundation.

Falek, A. (1979). Observations on patient and family coping with Huntington's disease. *Omega,* *10,* 35–42.

Falek, A., & Britton, S. (1974). Phases in coping: The hypothesis and its implications. *Social* *Biology, 21,* 1–7.

Falek, A., & Britton, S. (1976). *Ongoing studies in early detection of Huntington's disease.* Paper presented at World Federation of Neurology, Small Committee on Huntington's disease, Jerusalem.

Goodman, R. M., Hall, C. L., Jr., Terango, L., Perrine, G. A., Jr., & Roberts, P. L. (1969). A clinical approach to early recognition of Huntington's chorea. In A. Barbeau & J. R. Brunette (Eds.), *Progress in neuro-genetics.* Excerpta Medica Foundation.

Gusella, J. F., Wexler, N. S., Conneally, M., Naylor, S. L., Anderson, M. A., Tanzi, R. E., Watkins, P. C., Ottina, K., Wallace, M. R., Sakaguchi, A. Y., Young, A. B., Shoulson, I., Bonilla, E., & Martin, J. B. (1983). A polymorphic DNA marker genetically linked to Huntington's disease. *Nature, 306,* 234–238.

Hansotia, P., Cleveland, C. S., & Chun, R. W. M. (1968). Juvenile Huntington's chorea. *Neurology, 18,* 217.

Hayden, M. R. (1981). *Huntington's chorea.* Berlin: Springer–Verlag.

Hayden, M. R., MacGregor, J. M., Saffer, D. S., & Beighton, P. H. (1982). The high frequency of Huntington's chorea. *Journal of Medical Genetics, 19,* 94–97.

Husquinet, H., Mackenzie–van der Noordaa, M. C., Myrianthopoulos, N. C., Petit, H., Volkers, W., Went, L. N. (1973). Analysis of Huntington's chorea in Northwestern Europe. *Advances in* *Neurology, 1,* 161–170.

Kallmann, F. J., Aschner, B., & Falek, A. (1956). Comparative data on longevity adjustment to aging, and causes of death in a senescent twin population. In L. Gedda (Ed.), *Novant'anni delle* *Leggi Mendeliane.* Rome: Instituto Gregoria Mendel.

Klawans, H. L., Paulson, G. W., Ringel, S. P., & Barbeau, A. (1973). The use of L-Dopa in the presymptomatic detection of Huntington's chorea. *Advances in Neurology, 1,* 295–300.

Kubler–Ross, E. (1969). *On death and dying.* New York: MacMillan.

Lyle, O. E., & Gottesman, I. I. (1977). Premorbid psychometric indications of the gene for Huntington's disease. *Journal of Consulting and Clinical Psychology, 45,* 1011–1022.

Merritt, A. D., Conneally, P. M., Rahman, N. F., & Drew, A. L. (1969). Juvenile Huntington's chorea. In A. Barbeau & J. R. Brunette (Eds.), *Progress in neuro-genetics.* Excerpta Medica Foundation.

Myers, R. H. (1979). *Psychological stress in an early detection study for Huntington's disease.* Doctoral dissertation, Georgia State University.

Myers, R. H., & Falek, A. (1979). Quantification of muscle tremor of Huntington's disease patients and their offsprings in an early detection study. *Biological Psychiatry, 14,* 777–789.

Myers, R. H., Goldman, D., Bird, E. D., Sax, D. S., Merril, C. R., Schoenfeld, M., & Wolf, P. A. (1983). Maternal transmission in Huntington's Disease. *The Lancet II,* 208–210.

Myers, R. H., Madden, J. J., Teague, J. L., & Falek, A. (1981). Factors influencing age of onset of Huntington's disease. *American Journal of Human Genetics, 34,* 481–488.

Newcombe, R. G., Walker, D. A., & Harper, P. S. (1981). Factors influencing age at onset and duration of survival in Huntington's chorea. *Annals of Human Genetics, 45,* 387–396.

Oepen, H. (1965). Geschlechtsabhangige Modifijen der Geburtenrate, des Erkrankungsund des Sterbealters bei Huntingtonscher Chorea. *Hormone and Metabolic Research Supplement, 9,* 296.

Paigen, K. (1979). Acid hydrolases as models of genetic control. *Annual Review of Genetics, 13,* 417–466.

Paigen, K. (1980). Temporal-genes and other developmental regulators in mammals. In W. Loomis & T. Leighton (Eds.), *The molecular genetics of development.* New York: Academic Press.

Palm, J. D. (1973). Longitudinal study of a preclinical test program for Huntington's chorea. *Advances in Neurology, 1,* 311–324.

Patterson, R. M., Bagchi, B. K., & Test, A. (1948). The prediction of Huntington's chorea: An electroencephalographic and genetic study. *American Journal of Psychiatry, 104,* 786–797.

Pearl, R., & Pearl, R. W. (1934). *The ancestry of the long lived.* Baltimore: Johns Hopkins University Press.

Pearson, J. S., Peterson, M. C., Lazarte, J. A., Blodgett, H. E., & Kley, I. B. (1955). An educational approach to the social problem of Huntington's chorea. *Proceedings of the Mayo Clinic, 30,* 349–357.

Petit, H., & Milbled, G. (1973). Anomalies of conjugate ocular movements in Huntington's chorea: Application to early detection. *Advances in Neurology, 1,* 287–294.

21

Discussion: Two Views of Time

Ernest M. Gruenberg

Space is too short to comment on all the good things contained in this section with which I agree, and it is certainly insufficient to comment on all the statements with which I disagree. Instead, I try to point out some specific ways of looking at the time dimension in longitudinal studies. I use data from a particular longitudinal study to illustrate my remarks, but these remarks apply to all longitudinal studies.

I discuss some data reported in 1976 but still unpublished from the Lundby study (Gruenberg & Hagnell, in press). The study began with a cross-sectional survey in 1947 by Professor Essen–Möller (1956) and some colleagues who carried out a 100% survey by means of extremely detailed face-to-face interviews of the 2000 registered residents of two adjacent parishes over the age of 10. Subsequently, Olle Hagnell (1966) did his M.D. thesis on the 10-year interval between 1947 and 1957. Hagnell recontacted very nearly all (over 95%) the people in the first study, including those who had moved out of the area. In addition to reexamining the subjects of the original 1947 study, Hagnell obtained their medical and psychiatric records and a history of all episodes of mental disorders occurring during the decade.

I met Hagnell just when he was starting off on the 1957 follow-up and I was very impressed by the meticulousness with which he had set up his standards of diagnosis and data gathering and by the intimacy of the relationship between the investigator and the subjects. Everyone in town was a member of the study and was proud of it. The code name given to the town was Lundby, but everybody knew that "Lundby" was their town and they all felt they were an important part of the study. They told the investigator about each other as well as about themselves.

Although the Lundby sample is small, it has the advantage of having been very well followed. The material I am going to discuss represents 25 years of prospectively gathered data (Hagnell & Öjesjö, 1975). By "prospectively gathered," I mean that the study started with face-to-face data gathering in 1947 and, whereas information on the next decade was gathered retrospectively, there was another cross-sectional picture in 1957. A further time interval went by when volunteered information was recorded but not systematically pulled together, and then in 1972, another point prevalence study began and all intervening data were systematically gathered and evaluated.

One way of looking at time in this data base is by birth cohort. The subjects were followed for 25 years starting from a natural standing age distribution in 1947. Each 1947 age group came from a different birth cohort so that the circumstances under which each age group was born differed from those of the other age groups. For example, some years had serious epidemics when many newborns were killed, so that there were fewer subjects in those age cohorts. There were probably many other historical factors, in terms of health and past migrations, that affected the way that the population was composed in Lundby in 1947.

Annual Incidence of Senile Dementia
Over a 25 Year Period

A second fruitful and easy thing to do with longitudinal data makes no use of the developmental data. It treats all the data for all the birth cohorts and for every year of observation according to the *age* of each subject when an event occurred.

Figure 21.1 is the annual incidence of Senile Dementia (Alzheimer's Type, SDAT), by age in men and women (Hagnell, 1978). As can be seen, the annual incidence rises rapidly with age from around 1% per year at about 65 years of age to over 5% per year at about age 85–90. Since death is a strong competitor in these age groups, some of the data referred to in the chapter by Jarvik and La Rue perhaps require more cautious interpretations. By that I mean that one never can be certain that the people who had *not* developed the condition before they died *would not* have developed it had their lives been extended a few more years. Perhaps Life-Table types of analyses would make the studies of familial aggregation, referred to by Jarvik, more useful (see Sluss et al., 1981).

These incidence data are on 25 years of observation. The denominator for each point is the number of person-years lived through that age, 60–61, 62–63, 70–71, 72–73 to 90–91. The denominator diminishes as age increases because it started off with a standing population, so that the last points are less reliable. Some points are based on only two or three person-years of exposure. Nonetheless, there is a coherence to the data, and it can be seen that men and women do not differ in the age-specific annual incidence rate of SDAT.

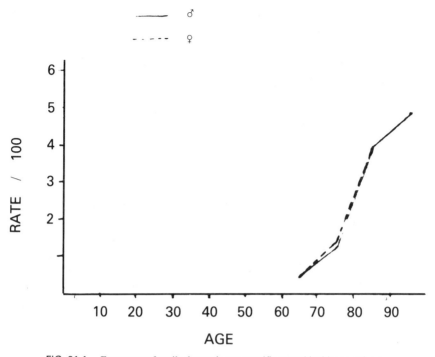

FIG. 21.1.   Frequency of senile dementia age-specific annual incidence estimate.
A preliminary estimate attained by subtracting "dementia arteriosclerotica" rates
on cohort ($N = 1,877$) from "brain syndrome" annual incidence rates. Source:
Hagnell, O. Mental Disorders of Older People: Findings from a Longitudinal
Survey. October 18, 1978, MS. Personal communication.

This analysis not only collapses 25 years but it also collapses all the birth
cohorts. Although the data were gathered longitudinally, the analysis is not
longitudinal. Nor is it really a cross-sectional analysis, because it allows 1 year
of time to elapse; one could not get these data from a point prevalence survey.
The analysis makes use of time, but it doesn't use time in a longitudinal sense,
and it doesn't display sequence. Although the analysis throws away a lot of the
advantages of longitudinal data, it is nevertheless a very valuable type of outcome from longitudinal data gathering. One of the things that people find hard to
conceptualize sometimes is that longitudinal studies provide a lot of data that can
be summarized in other ways and that we shouldn't ignore these other uses of
longitudinally gathered data. This analysis is an example of another way of using
such data. The analysis summarizes 25 years of longitudinal data as though every
calendar year were equivalent to every other year. If one were planning a study to
produce such findings, one would locate a sample population 25 times as large as

the Lundby population stratified by age and follow it for 1 year to locate each new case of SDAT. I know of no such study. Such a study would require several years of follow-up on some subjects to reproduce the case ascertainment advantages of a longitudinal study. This is due to the fact that dementia is a permanent change in cognition that sometimes requires prospective data for identification.

Point Prevalence of Senile Dementia Over 25 Years

Each case of dementia had an onset in one of the 25 calendar years and, of course, during those 25 years the world was changing. One question that can be asked is, "Did the condition under study, SDAT, itself undergo a change in this population during those years?"

There were more than 400 people over age 60 in the study population on July 1, 1957, and somewhat fewer on July 1, 1947. What was the point prevalence rate of dementia at those two times a decade apart? Among approximately 400 people of age 60 on July 1, 1947, there were 13 cases of progressive dementia. In the very slightly larger population in that age group on the same date in 1957, there prevailed about *twice* as many cases. Why had the point prevalence rate of dementia doubled in a decade? It is important to know that this was an unexpected observation.

Hagnell first approached me for help in understanding why his 1957 point prevalence rates were higher than those observed in 1947. Only after a number of false starts did we have the wit to multiply the 1947 age and sex-specific prevalence rates by the 1957 population and thus reveal that the excess of 1957 cases were heavily concentrated in people who had passed their 60th birthdays. We then focused on senile dementia cases.

Among the hypotheses that were advanced was the possibility that diagnostic standards had shifted toward the identification of milder cases. Psychotropic medications had been discovered in 1954 with chlorpromazine, which received a good deal of publicity (cf. International Symposium on Chlorpromazine, 1956). The result was that more people began to think of mental symptoms as organic, and, perhaps, therefore, people felt less embarrassed about such symptoms and freer to talk about them than they had in earlier years. Moreover, Hagnell, the interviewer in 1957, may have been more psychologically oriented than his mentors (Essen–Möller and colleagues), who had conducted the earlier interview, so that it was possible that more symptoms were elicited in the 1957 interviews on this ground. Further, the study had been ongoing for a decade, and rapport with the community was good; thus, the investigators may have had more opportunity to learn about milder cases in 1957. Cross-checks within the data gave no support to such theories, so we began to think of substantive rather than methodological explanations. In particular, if individuals with dementia had longer life expectations by the later period under study, the increased prevalence rate between 1947 and 1957 could be explained. Within the limitations of the data available, how could we test that hypothesis?

To answer that question, the data must be organized differently, as shown in Fig. 21.2. The problem being studied can be seen on the left-hand vertical line labeled 0 in the figure.

This is another aspect of analyses that can be carried out in longitudinal studies. We had a large pool of data, a tremendous data base gathered over a quarter of a century. We observed an increase in prevalence rates of dementia over a period of a decade, we set up a hypothesis to account for the increase, and we turned to the available data to test the hypothesis. One possibility would have been to look at the accumulation of dementia cases before the prevalence dates, that is, how long each case had been in existence prior to the prevalence data. Unfortunately, that information was not available because the investigators in 1947 had not thought of finding out about dates of onset.

Data on survivorship after the prevalence dates were available, however, and were applicable to testing the hypothesis of increased life expectancy. So, we asked, "What was the mortality rate during the period after each prevalence count?" The two upper pairs of lines in Fig. 21.2 represent the survivorship curves of the two populations in 1947–1957 and 1957–1967, respectively. The curves are straight lines on this logarithmic scale, but they are not quite parallel. Survival in the 10-year period following the 1957 interview was slightly better than in the decade after the 1947 interview.

Note, however, the survivorship experience of the demented cases who were present in these same two populations. The top curve in Fig. 21.2 shows the survivorship for the 1957 group of cases and the bottom curve is for the earlier group of cases. With the direct graphing of each point, one can see when each of the cases died. All 13 cases of dementia from the 1947 population were dead within 6 years, and, hence, none survived to be counted again in the 1957 prevailing cases. However, the second group of cases had not all died by the end of the decade following the 1957 interview, so that some are left to be counted in 1967. (These analyses were made when we had obtained death certificates through 1967. Another 10 years, to 1977, can be added to subsequent analyses.)

It is the smaller *difference* in the slopes of the survivorship curves between the general population and the cases of dementia in the later, compared to the earlier, period that accounts for the doubling of the prevalence rate. The differential mortality rate has become smaller, because, whereas persons in the general population are living a little longer than they used to, individuals with dementia are living a lot longer than before.

We are stretching out the duration of senile dementia. Presumably, this is a consequence of medical progress (Gruenberg, 1977). For example, most deaths in senile dementia occur as a result of pneumonia—which used to be called the "old man's friend." Since the widespread use of antibacterials such as penicillin

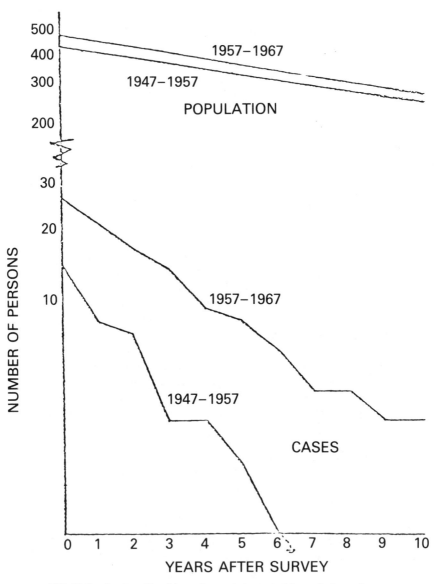

FIG. 21.2. Survivorship of the study population and of the senile dementia cases during 10 years following prevalence surveys in 1947 and 1957. (From: The Lundby Studies). Source: Gruenberg, E. M., and Hagnell, O. The Rising Prevalence of Chronic Brain Syndrome in the Elderly. MS

following the Second World War, death from pneumonia has tended to be postponed until later attacks by a drug-resistant organism.

I end my discussion with a quotation from King Lear. He is blind, bleeding to death, and his favorite daughter has died. His best friend says to the servants who go to help him: "Vex not his ghost. Oh, let him pass! he hates him / That would upon the rack of this tough world / Stretch him out longer."

REFERENCES

Essen–Möller, E. (1956). Individual traits and morbidity in a Swedish rural population. *Acta Psychiatrica Scandinavica Supplement, 100.*

Gruenberg, E. M. (1977). The failures of success. *Milbank Mem. Fund Q., 55* (1), 3–24.

Gruenberg, E. M., & Hagnell, O. (in press). The rising prevalence of chronic brain syndrome in the elderly. In L. Levi & A. Kagan (Eds.), *Society, stress and disease: Aging and old age.* New York: Oxford University Press.

Hagnell, O. (1966). *A prospective study of the incidence of mental disorders in a Swedish population together with an evaluation of the aetiological significance of medical, social, and personality factors.* Stockholm: University Books.

Hagnell, O. (1978, October 18) *Mental disorders of older people: Findings from a longitudinal survey.* Lapouse Memorial Lecture. Paper presented at the American Public Health Association Annual Meeting, Los Angeles.

Hagnell, O., & Öjesjö, L. (1975). A prospective study concerning mental disorders of a total population investigated in 1947, 1957 and 1972. *Acta Psychiatrica Scandinavica Supplement, 263.*

International Symposium on Chlorpromazine and Neuroleptic Drugs. (1955). Paris, Encaphale, 1956. (special issue)

Shakespeare, W. *King Lear,* Act V, Scene iii, lines 314–316. In H. F. Furness, A New Variorum Edition of Shakespeare King Lear J. B. Lippincott & Co., 1880. Reprinted by Dover Publications, Inc., New York, 1963. P.348n has detailed discussion of whether it should be a "rough" or a "tough world".

Sluss, T. K., Gruenberg, E. M., Kramer, M. (1981). The use of longitudinal studies in the investigation of risk factors for senile dementia—Alzheimer type. Chapter 8. In J. A. Mortimer & L. M. Shuman (Eds.), *The Epidemiology of Dementia.* New York: Oxford University Press.

Author Index

Subject Index